Women and Leadership

Karin Klenke, PhD, is Associate Professor of leadership studies at the University of Richmond, VA. She received her BS and MS degrees in psychology from Old Dominion University, VA, and her PhD in organizational psychology also from Old Dominion University. Her fields of research include leadership in information intensive organizations, the relationships between information technologies and leadership styles, leadership in emergent organizational forms, dispersed leadership in high performance teams, innovative methodologies in the study of leadership, women and leadership, and cross-cultural studies of leadership practices. Her work has been published in four books, numerous professional journals, book chapters, and proceedings of professional conferences. In addition to her work as a leadership educator, scholar, and consultant, Dr. Klenke is the founder and Editor-in-Chief of the *Journal of Management Systems*, a multidisciplinary organizational behavior journal. Finally, Dr. Klenke heads the Leadership Development Institute (LDI) International, a leadership consulting firm that offers a variety of leadership education and development programs to private and public sector organizations.

Women and Leadership

A Contextual Perspective

Karin Klenke, PhD

SPRINGER PUBLISHING COMPANY

Springer Publishing Company, Inc.
536 Broadway
New York, NY 10012-3955

Cover design by Tom Yabut
Production Editor: Joyce Noulas

Third Printing

99 00 01 02 / 6 5 4 3

Library of Congress Cataloging-in-Publication Data

Klenke, Karin.
    Women and leadership : a contextual perspective / Karin Klenke.
      p.   cm.
    Includes bibliographical references and index.
    ISBN 0-8261-9220-3
    1. Leadership. 2. Women—Social conditions. 3 Women civic leaders.
    4. Sex role. I. Title.
    HM141.H3345 1996
    303.3′4—dc20   95-40436
                                                    CIP

*For my husband, Will, my children, Katja and Max,
and my friend, Alison—leaders of a different kind*

*and for my Leadership Studies students
who provided ideas and inspiration
during the development of this book*

CONTENTS

FOREWORD

Women and Leadership: A Contextual Perspective is an essential book for all leaders. Dr. Klenke has examined leadership through a new set of lenses allowing us to see more clearly and precisely where limits have existed and where they continue to exist today.

Over half of our population has been shut out of leadership historically. Which half am I speaking of? The half that is female.

Prejudices, beliefs, and habits have made it virtually impossible for women to hold leadership positions. But a few women have broken through. Who are these remarkable women and how did they find their way?

Dr. Karin Klenke has combed the existing literature, providing a comprehensive view of women in leadership, revealing their stories and highlighting their contributions to politics, religion, business, and medicine. This book provides a detailed historical overview, presenting a multidisciplinary perspective on culture and context.

In a time when planetary change can be initiated from any terminal anywhere in the world, in a time when the rate of change is continuing to accelerate, we must plumb the depth of our leadership pool. *Women and Leadership* reveals areas we can grow in, pinpointing the limitations still in place, the hows and whys of the glass ceiling so many women find themselves bumping up against. Recognizing and surpassing these limits will enable both men and women to put aside old considerations so that we can call on the full extent of our leadership potential, so that we can move beyond the traditional limits to solve problems that confront us, so that we can call upon that other half of our population to support us in creating the world we all want.

As a leadership researcher, I am enthralled by what is presented here. As a woman who spent a lifetime developing her own leadership skills, I feel that Dr. Klenke has initiated me into a far larger society than I have ever known—the society of women who lead the world to new heights. I am now privy to their stories and circumstances. It is inspiring to read about women in leadership, to hear their unique stories, to recognize the profound changes that women have made in religion, politics, business, and arts and sciences.

Susan Collins
Consultant to corporations, schools and governments
Author of *Our Children Are Watching:*
Ten Skills for Leading the Next Generation to Success

PREFACE

> The leader is the evangelist for the dream.
> *Dave Patton, Apple Computers*

The study of leadership usually starts with the idea that leaders are necessary for the functioning of organization, ranging from families to nations. *Women and Leadership: A Contextual Perspective* is intended to stimulate creative thinking about women and leadership and encourage a re-examination of the worn belief that women are unfit for leadership. Moreover, the book suggests that gender is a significant cultural rather than an individual difference or demographic variable which has important implications for individuals and organizations. As transmitters of culture, women leaders are helping us to rethink and restructure our assumptions about leadership and leaders in virtually every field.

My purposes in writing this book included: (1) to analyze the existing literature on women and leadership, taking stock of what we know about the topic to develop prescriptions and descriptions for the future; (2) to examine the pervasive role of gender as a contextual and cultural variable; (3) to demonstrate the importance of context in which leadership is played out and the consequences of context for the study and practice of leadership; (4) to analyze the tensions and contradictions that exist between popular literature on women leaders and leadership and scientific research on this topic, and finally; (5) to provide a treatise on women and leadership that transcends the prevailing interview and small sample approach to arrive at a critical analysis that balances the contributions of particular approaches to the study of leadership with the morass of equivocality that pervades the literature.

I chose the title *Women and Leadership: A Contextual Perspective* as opposed to other possible titles such as *Women Leaders Past and Present* to avoid the connotations associated with "women leaders," which implies that women in leadership roles are women first and leaders second. The "women leader" combination still represents an exception that is distinguished from leaders in general. Nevertheless, the term "woman leader" occurs frequently throughout the book. Unlike popular books about women and leadership that are based on interviews with a few selected women in a homogeneous environment, I took a broad brush to paint a multi-faceted approach including gender, context, and culture of women leaders in diverse environments.

As a social scientist, I believe that knowledge about leadership accumulates in a systematic manner. Furthermore, I argue that one indicator of maturity in a discipline, as in the case of leadership studies, is the amount of attention directed to model testing and theory development and the methodological issues associated with these activities. Mapping the intellectual structure of leadership studies as an academic discipline was beyond the scope of this book. But such an effort would reveal multiple roots stemming from many disciplines including psychology, religion, sociology, anthropology, politics, history, and literature, which made contributions to the art and science of leadership. In short, leadership is an ageless phenomenon that has intrigued people since the beginning of recorded history.

This book was written for a variety of audiences: students of leadership of all ages, leadership educators and scholars, women and other minorities exercising leadership in families, churches, organizations, and nations. It was written for the emerging novice, as well as the seasoned leader. It is based on the premise that there is a leader in all of us, and, with the motivation to lead, all of us can develop our leadership potential. Finally, I believe that we need to look at self-development and leadership development as a lifelong commitment to learn how to be learner and leader throughout the life cycle.

Chapter 1 is an introduction to the central themes of this book. It starts with a discussion of the turbulent history of the study of leadership and the roles women have played in changing conceptions of leadership over time. It also describes contextual forces such as the women's movement and civil rights legislation and shows how these factors have facilitated or impeded women's access to leadership. In addition, I introduce a variety of definitions of leadership and argue that a widely agreed upon definition of leadership is unlikely to emerge because leadership is a dynamic, constantly changing, process. The core of Chapter 1 is the introduction of a model that uses a series of overlapping prisms or lenses as the focal metaphor outlining the interactions of leadership, gender, context, and culture.

Chapter 2 takes the reader on a historical journey by offering portraits of women leaders. Women leaders in the context of religion, politics, and social movements are discussed to provide evidence supporting my basic position that leadership is largely shaped by context. A woman leader in the context of religion is confronted with different challenges, problems, and constituencies than her counterpart in politics.

Chapter 3 provides a review of the major contemporary schools of leadership thought and the roles theory and measurement play in the practice of leadership involving the various aspects of leadership style, leader behaviors, and traits. While Chapter 3 is intended to help the reader to understand the conceptual foundations of leadership, it also alerts the reader to both the multitude of theoretical models and the inconsistencies of the research that is designed to validate the various theories introduced in this chapter. In addition, for each theory presented, I describe an application to show how the theory might work in practice. These applications are designed to show that theories vary in the extent to which they are useful to the practicing leader.

Chapter 4 explains the differences between leadership and management and describes leadership in terms of people, not as a system of processes. I introduce vignettes of women leaders and women managers and point out that management and leadership are complementary modes of action. Elevating one, usually leadership, at the expense of the other, usually management, contributes little to our understanding of both processes.

Chapter 5 begins with a discussion of how the media provide yet another unique context in which we can study leadership. My analysis of the portrayal of women leaders in newspapers and television indicates that although things are changing, women leaders are shortchanged. Sex role stereotypes and worn-out assumptions and beliefs about women's ability to lead continue to permeate the presentation of women leaders in the mass media. The popular literature, on the other hand, glorifies and romanticizes women leaders, drawing attention to the importance that unique feminine qualities bring to leadership.

In contrast, Chapter 6 basically indicates that while we stress the importance of the differences that exist between women and men in terms of education, work experience, and access to leadership opportunities, few significant differences actually exist in the way women and men lead. I identify a number of conditions that are likely to produce gender differences in scientific research, which include biases inherent in the ways leadership has been measured in scientific research, situational factors, and the role power plays in research on gender differences in leadership.

In the next two chapters I argue again that context, rather than gender, is the raw material that provides the basis for which men and women structure their leadership models. Chapter 7 offers a discussion of the unique barriers, challenges, and opportunities women have to confront when aspiring to leadership roles. Among the barriers, we find again that negative gender stereotypes continue to block women's access to leadership. In addition, the widely discussed glass ceiling and the treatment of women leaders as token minorities have adverse affects on women. Finally, the exclusion of women from informal organizational activities often prevents women from gaining access to critical information that may be valuable in planning women's career paths to include increasing leadership responsibilities. On the positive side, opportunities now exist for women to become more comparable in terms of education and organizational experiences.

Chapter 8 presents a discussion of contemporary women leaders and may be viewed as an extension of Chapter 2 which introduced historical women leaders. I discuss sports and politics as contexts in which the number of women leaders has yet to reach a critical mass. Each context is analyzed for contextual characteristics and features which set the parameters and establish the boundaries that allow women to demonstrate their effectiveness as leaders. Also examined are the consequences of deviating from female gender stereotypes. Women leaders in politics and sports continue to challenge the ''masculine'' worlds of these two contexts.

Chapter 9 moves the reader to the international scene. Given the steadily increasing trend toward internationalization, the realities of the global village, and the information highway, I introduce the reader to the importance of cultural competence and cultural adaption as key leadership competencies and gateways to leadership effectiveness in the international community. I review various cross-cultural models and empirical studies of leadership and present profiles of women leaders in Europe, Asia, and Latin America.

Chapter 10 addresses the topic of leadership education and development as well as the leadership requirements for the 21st century that should be essential to the development of new programs. We cannot afford to teach leadership students, whether undergraduates or senior executives, yesterday's leadership models and skills. This chapter presents a review of a variety of approaches to leadership education ranging from personal growth programs to formal academic and commercial programs. The chapter also addresses the question of whether or not women need special programs to develop leadership competencies.

Finally, the concluding chapter summarizes the issues discussed and projects into the future. The chapter describes some of the leadership requirements for the 21st century and the roles of women leaders in the constantly changing landscape of our times. New organizational forms that are vertical rather than horizontal demand different approaches to leadership—approaches that value the contributions of *both* women and men.

ACKNOWLEDGEMENTS

This book would not have materialized without the contributions of many people. I want to acknowledge those individuals who helped me create this book. I give my thanks to Dr. Ursula Springer, Mary Grace Luke, and Bill Tucker of Springer Publishing Company for their valuable feedback in editing the manuscript and for their professional leadership in seeing this book to fruition. Alison Hettrick not only produced all the graphs, charts, and tables found in the book, but also read the entire manuscript. I am thankful for her contributions to this project. I want to thank Susan Collins who shared the journey into the mysteries of leadership for her critical feedback and helpful suggestions.

At the University of Richmond, my students, Leadership Studies majors at the Jepson School of Leadership Studies, included the classes of '94, '95, and '96. They were a daily source of inspiration and supported me in the completion of this project with their enthusiasm, ideas, and critical questions. I want to thank my colleague, Dr. William Howe, who was always willing to find time to discuss specific leadership concepts and ideas that were important to me during the various stages of this project. Finally, Lit Maxwell of the university library provided valuable assistance with literature and database searches.

As a consultant, I am indebted to my client organizations including several female-led companies because they allowed me to observe leadership in action and apply leadership theories to real life organizational systems.

1 Changing Conceptions of Leadership

> There is nothing more difficult to take in hand, more perilous to conduct, or more uncertain in its success, than to take the lead in the introduction of a new order of things.
>
> *Niccolo Machiavelli*

INTRODUCTION

The study of leadership and leaders has a long and multifaceted history rich in rituals, metaphors, symbols, and stories. As a field of scientific inquiry, leadership has intrigued scholars and practitioners from many disciplines, as diverse as religion and political science, psychology and economics. In our everyday conversation, we talk about the lack of sound leadership, and the need for more effective leadership in the family, our organizations, communities, and nations. On the other hand, some of our greatest cultural, social, political, and artistic accomplishments are attributed to leadership, as have many political catastrophes and social ills. Leadership has been and is a cause and effect of greatness and success as well as insignificance and failure. Since recorded history, ideas of leadership have been found in every culture and the literature of the oldest civilizations around the world. They are embedded in mythology, legends, sagas, religions, and the social life of early and contemporary societies. In the past as well as in the present, leadership has been vital in every historical period and in every culture.

WOMEN AND LEADERSHIP: PAST AND PRESENT

Historically, leadership has been conceptualized as the "man on the white horse," that is, the study of leadership has been seen as the study of "great men." Moreover, it has been primarily the study of political leadership exercised by a privileged group of "great men" who defined power, authority, and knowledge.

1

While most of us are familiar with famous political leaders from Alexander the Great to Franklin D. Roosevelt, it is worthwhile noting that even great men who did not serve in political leadership roles as kings, rulers, or monarchs were often treated from a political perspective. Moreover, this emphasis on political leadership implied that there are no legitimate leadership positions, roles or functions in other contexts such as social movements, family, or community and volunteer organizations, contexts in which women have historically exercised leadership.

Although history has produced some great women (see Chapter 2), from the life-giving goddesses of the paleolithic and neolithic periods to contemporary women leaders such as Mary Robinson, current President of Ireland, or Mother Teresa, they are greatly outnumbered by the many great men. It is through the lenses of the lives, prestige, courage, and grandeur of those men that much history and leadership is viewed. Even the portrayals of historical women leaders like Joan of Arc, Elizabeth I, or Catherine the Great of Russia leave us with the impression that women really cannot be effective leaders unless they are exceptional by men's standards. In more recent history, particularly during the early 20th century, women such as Eleanor Roosevelt, Jane Addams, or Rosa Luxemburg, while not occupying formal leadership positions, in many ways played important leadership roles. However, it was not until the 1980s that the number of women leaders reached critical mass and began to gain visibility. Thus, despite the many great women in history and the even greater number of women who exercised leadership in informal roles, from mothers and heads of extended families to warrior queens, whose leadership has not been formally recognized, female leadership has only recently moved into the limelight of public interest.

Among the factors that were instrumental in casting a more diverse net of leaders was the liberal atmosphere created by the Kennedy administration, which made the passage of landmark civil rights legislation, Title VII, possible. This legislation banned sex discrimination in the workplace and led to the establishment of the Equal Employment Opportunity Commission (EEOC) charged with the responsibility of enforcing Title VII of the 1964 Civil Rights Act. Although the new laws on equal employment opportunities did create opportunities, they did not result in equity for women.

In the 1960s two other events, combined with the passage of Title VII, had significant impact on women, their rights in the workplace, their status in society in general, and their opportunities to assume leadership roles. One of these events was the publication of Betty Friedan's (1975) feminist classic, *The Feminine Mystique*. The title of the book refers to a belief system that most women of the time bought into. Women growing up in the 1940s and 1950s were socialized to believe that they could only find happiness by marrying a domineering man and by carrying his children. Friedan debunked the myth that women's nature and needs are dictated by biology, and denied that differences between men and women were as great as the "mystique" made them out to be. The book was both controversial and empowering; it opened windows of opportunities for women by condoning and justifying lifestyles other than those focused on marriage and the family.

The second and related event occurred in 1966, the foundation of the National Organization of Women (NOW) by Betty Friedan, at a time when feminists were angry and frustrated with the EEOC because of the agency's intransigence. The formation of NOW is one of the many examples of crisis-induced leadership which often produces charismatic leaders. However, despite the emergence of these few leaders, the women's movement suffered from a lack of leadership, especially political leadership, as well as the lack of a political theory which may explain feminist leadership (Evans, 1977). As Davis (1991) stated, "women's liberation groups tried to create radical equality within the group by operating without formal leadership" (p. 484).

The women's movement, as a prototype of a social movement, was characterized by a puzzling contradiction in the early days: the urgent need for leadership and direction on the one hand, and a profound aversion for hierarchical organizational structures and dominating leader figures on the other. The power male leaders exercised and the elite they represented were seen as hopelessly obsolete and dysfunctional masculine structures. Women gathered in small consciousness-raising groups which marked the embryonic period of both the women's liberation movement and NOW. These groups, without a political agenda, essentially were anti-structure. Even when the movement was building political momentum and the need for assigning responsibility to individuals for accomplishing the mission, allocating positions, and formulating policy became apparent, there was a strong desire for structurelessness and anarchy.

However, despite the informal leadership embraced by women in the early days of the movement, this way of organizing poorly masked the ongoing struggles over formally recognized leadership roles. According to Bunch and Fisher (1976), there was much hidden leadership even in the early days. This was bad for both leaders and followers, it was subtle and manipulative, since the leaders were neither recognized nor held accountable. As a result of the desire to eliminate bureaucratic structures and elitist leadership, the early women's movement fell into a state of immobilization with no defined tasks and responsibilities, thereby making it difficult to carry out the mission. Bunch and Fisher (1976), reflecting on the beginnings of the movement, stated that the irony lay in the fact that the lack of structure had the opposite effect of what was desired. Women in the movement actively sought no structure and no leadership in order to have participatory decisionmaking and shared responsibility. However, by deciding against formal leadership, it became more difficult for group members to participate in the accomplishment of the goals of the organization, knowing whom to call to increase membership, and the way to get the message out. However, despite the efforts to suppress leadership, it happened anyway. Although no single woman stood out as the leader who spoke for the entire movement, there were recognized opinion leaders who interpreted the ideology of the movement in public speeches. The women who emerged as leaders were those who had the information, attended the meetings, and led the discussions. As a result, the movement transformed itself from an amorphous, apolitical consciousness-raising group of women defining themselves largely in personal terms, to the politically charged NOW with its hierarchical leadership.

The events of the 1960s set the stage for the developments of the next two decades, which witnessed more legislation including the Women's Educational Equity Act; the Comprehensive Child Act; and a series of activist movements such as the women's health movement, lesbian feminism, and the gay rights movement. After the defeat of the ERA in 1982, other social movements promoted female leadership. Ecofeminism, for example, a blend of feminist and environmental concerns, developed partially in response to the disaster at the Three Mile Island nuclear plant in 1980. It led to the formation of grass-roots organizations headed by women like Starhawk, the California activist who founded the Woman-Earth Institute, the first national ecofeminist organization. By the late 1980s, some mainstream environmental groups had feminists in leadership positions (Davis, 1991).

Over the last three decades women have entered many traditionally male domains of leadership, including politics and business, in increasing numbers. Women have served as prime ministers of England (Margaret Thatcher), India (Indira Gandhi), Pakistan (Benazir Bhutto), Israel (Golda Meir), and the Philippines (Corazon Aquino). In 1990 Mary Robinson was elected Ireland's first woman president (see Chapter 9). Although her office is largely ceremonial, Mary Robinson is one of Ireland's foremost international lawyers and has become the symbol of change and renewal of a country haunted by the division between North and South and besieged by the persistence of terrorism. Not only is Ireland run by a woman, but so is Norway. In addition, women lead all three Norwegian political parties. Thus, in Northern Europe women are setting the pace as presidents and prime ministers.

In the United States, Geraldine Ferraro ran for the office of vice president in 1973 and served as the Democratic party vice-presidential nominee in 1984. When her candidacy was announced at the Democratic convention on July 10, 1984, every woman activist from coast to coast was present: Gloria Steinem, founder and editor of *Ms.* Magazine; Senator Diane Watson of California; Madeleine Kunin, soon to be elected governor of Vermont; Betty Friedan, founder of NOW; Dorothy Height, president of the National Council of Negro Women; former Congresswoman Bella Abzug; and virtually all the Democratic women in Congress. Told by Mondale's advisors not to focus on women's issues, Ferraro said she wanted the people to vote for her not because she is a woman, but because they thought she would make the best Vice President (Ferraro, 1985). At the time, it seemed that everybody forgot that the campaign issues were related to gender issues. According to Ferraro (1985), the gender gap showdown had picked up momentum in 1982, when exit polls showed that more women voted for Democratic candidates than Republicans by a 17-point margin, and that more women had voted for a Democrat than had men in 33 of 44 U.S. senate and gubernatorial races. Not only were women emerging as a potential voting force, they were also running for office themselves. However, after the election, once the Mondale team had nominated a woman, they seemed to develop cold feet worrying about male backlash.

Nevertheless, after Ferraro's nomination, thousands of American women began to show an avid interest in American politics. This interest seemed to culminate in 1992, yet another election year. In this year, declared as the "year of women in politics," 16 female Democrats and 2 women Republicans served in the U.S. Senate. In the House, 97 women Democrats and 57 women Republicans were represented. In addition, six women served as governors and three as lieutenant governors, while others occupied leadership positions as U.N. Ambassador (Jeanne Kirkpatrick), Mayor (Pratt, former Mayor of Washington, DC), Attorney General (Janet Reno), Surgeon General (former Surgeon General Jocelyn Elders), and Supreme Court Justices (Sandra Day O'Connor, Ruth Bader Ginsberg). Aburdene and Naisbitt (1992) predict that the first woman president of the United States will come on the national scene early in the 21st century.

In addition to women in politics, countless lesser-known women occupy leadership positions in education, health care, industry, and family-owned businesses. For example, there has been a significant growth in female entrepreneurs, and the increase in numbers of women business owners is having an apparent effect on the U.S. economy. The United States Small Business Administration (SBA) collected data showing that the percentage of businesses owned by women has increased from 2.6 million to 4.1 million, an increase of about 58%. This rate of growth is more than 4 times the rate for all businesses (SBA, 1991, p. v). Likewise, Carey and Bryant (1995) reported that for the 1991–1994 period women-owned business are expanding into industries dominated by men. More specifically, in manufacturing woman-owned businesses grew by 13%, in transport/communications by 18%, in construction by 19%, and in finance/real estate by 21%. While Fortune 500 companies continue to shed employees, woman-owned firms continue to grow. Economists predict that by the end of 1995, woman-owned businesses will employ significantly more people than all Fortune 500 corporations combined. Today, woman-owned businesses represent one of the fastest-growing segments of the U.S. economy.

DEFINING LEADERSHIP

The ways in which we define a phenomenon such as leadership have a great deal to do with how we study it, how we measure it, what kinds of metaphors and symbols we apply to it, and how we use it in practice. It also determines how we try to make sense of leadership situations, many of which are characterized by complexity and ambiguity. Moreover, "leadership" means different things to different people. Though the call for leadership may be universal, individuals, groups, organizations, and nations agree that there is little clarity concerning what the term means. According to Bolman and Deal (1991a), for many Americans leadership is a word that has risen above normal workday usage as a conveyor of meaning, and has become a kind of incantation. Moreover, these authors point out, many definitions imply an unquestioned, widely shared canon of common sense that holds leadership is a good thing and that we need more of it, at least more of the right kind. Leadership, rather than being defined neutrally, is a value-laden term that engenders passion, love, fear, disappointment, and a host of other emotions.

The word "leadership" is found in every language. It can be traced back at least as far as ancient Egypt. In Egyptian hieroglyph, we find the words for leadership, leaders, and followers. In early Greek and Latin, the word leadership is derived from the verb to act. Two Greek verbs, *archein* (to begin to lead, to rule) and *prattein* (to pass through, achieve) correspond to the Latin verb *agere* (to set into motion, to lead) (Jennings, 1960). In English, the word "leader" is more than 1000 years old, and little has changed from its Anglo-Saxon root *laedere*, meaning "people on a journey" (Bolman & Deal, 1991a). In modern languages, the terms used for leader are not always equivalent. For example, the meaning of the German word *Führer* is different than that of the French *le meneur*.

As a leadership educator, I usually ask students in a foundations of leadership course to define leadership and draw a picture of a leader. In most of the classes, there is a gender balance, as far as the enrollment of female and male students is concerned. Of particular interest to me, of course, is the question whether young men and women who are self-selected into a comprehensive leadership studies program, many of whom are aspiring leaders, define leadership differently. As it turns out, I am always surprised to find that the definitions of these young people not only reflect many traditional concepts of leadership embedded in formal definitions but also show no differences along gender lines. For example, a female student defined leadership as "the process where one individual (or in some few cases a few individuals) takes control of the situation and motivates others to complete a specific task," while one of her male counterparts stated that leadership is a process of influencing others by providing direction, purpose, and motivation. For many students of leadership, definitions imply power, control, goal achievement, motivation, and vision but reflect little awareness that tradition-ally most definitions have excluded the female half of the population.

Leadership has been formally defined in terms of traits, behaviors, influence processes, power, politics, authority, change, goal achievement, management, and transformation among other concepts. It also has been defined as drama and an art. Some of the formal definitions of leadership found in the scholarly literature which reflect these concepts include:

1) Leadership is "both a personality phenomenon and a group phenomenon; it is also a social process involving a number of persons in mental contact in which one person assumes dominance over the others. It is the process in which the activities of the many are organized to move in a specific direction by the one. It is the process in which the attitudes and values of the many may be changed by the one. It is the process in which at every stage the followers exert an influence, often a changing counter-influence, upon the leaders" (Bogardus, 1934, p. 5).

2) Leadership is "the influential increment over and above mechanical compliance with the routine directives of the organization" (Katz & Kahn, 1978, p. 528).

3) Leadership is "a particular type of power relationship characterized by a group member's perception that another group member has the right to prescribe behavior patterns for the former regarding his activity as a group member" (Janda, 1960, p. 358).

4) Leadership is "the performance of the sponsor, or managerial function where the person who exercises it emerges from a more or less undifferentiated group or is placed in that position by formal appointment" (Kuhn & Beam, 1982, p. 381).

5) Leadership is "an influence relationship among leaders and followers who intend real changes that reflect their mutual purposes" (Rost, 1991, p. 102). This is one of the more recent definitions which takes the role of followers in the leadership situation into account.

6) Leadership, according to U.S. Senator Barbara Mikulski, is "creating a state of mind in others. President Kennedy's legislative accomplishments were skimpy but he created a state of mind in this country that endures long after his death. Churchill created a state of mind that enabled Great Britain to endure the blitz and marshal resources to help turn the tide of World War II. Martin Luther King, Jr. created a state of mind. Florence Nightingale created a state of mind in people about what nursing should be, that it shouldn't be those who were derelicts and ladies of the night, that it was a profession" (quoted in Cantor & Bernay, 1992, p. 59).

Still others (e.g., Meindl, Ehrlich, & Dukerich, 1985) have romanticized leadership, suggesting that leaders do and should have the ability to control and influence the fates of the organizations in their charge. The authors argued that the romance and mystery surrounding leadership are critical for sustained followership. Feminists, on the other hand (e.g., Carroll, 1984) often equate leadership with empowerment. Hagberg (1984), for example, writing from a feminist perspective, adopted Burns' (1978) transforming model, but viewed leadership as a form of power.

Additionally, several definitions equate leadership with an effective leader (i.e., equating process and person), a conceptual inconsistency found in numerous definitions of leadership. Still others (e.g., Kotter, 1992) include educational functions in their definitions of leadership. Because leaders often have in-depth, hands-on experience, they are expected to communicate to their followers the knowledge they have acquired through this experience. Bolman and Deal (1995) describe the ties between spirituality and leadership. The authors note that

> two images dominate in concepts of leadership: one of the heroic champion with extraordinary stature and vision, the other of the policy wonk, the skilled analyst who solves pressing problems with information, programs, and policies. Both images miss the essence of leadership. Both emphasize the hands and heads of leaders, neglecting deeper and more enduring elements of courage, spirit and hope. (p. 5)

Leadership not only means different things to different people, to scholars as well as laypersons, but probably has as many definitions as there are persons defining the concept. For some, leaders are heroes and heroines, supermen and superwomen; for others they are villains, exploiters, demagogues, or powermongers. Leaders are spellbinders and dreamers, pathfinders and trailblazers: they are champions such as Isabella of Spain and Napoleon, saviors such as Florence Nightingale and Moses, servants such as Mother Teresa and Mahatma Gandhi, visionaries such as Joan of Arc and Martin Luther King, and revolutionaries such as Rosa Luxemburg and Fidel Castro who are imbued with superhuman qualities. For still others (i.e., Collins, 1995) we are all leaders now—the parents, the managers, the one governing, all of whom together face an historic dilemma. Collins argues that in the information age the success of our children depends on each of us taking on leadership roles to insure that the next generation will fulfill its promise—inventing new products, developing systems, and designing ways of living that we cannot imagine today. Yet virtually everyone who has studied leaders and leadership knows that there is a widespread disagreement about the meaning of leadership.

Rost (1991), after analyzing 221 definitions of leadership found in books, book chapters, and journal articles written between 1900 and 1990, concluded that the leadership definitions he reviewed assumed that leadership is rational, management-oriented, male, technocratic, quantitative, cost-driven, hierarchical, short-term, pragmatic, and materialistic. The author asserted that:

At the beginning of the 1990s we clearly have old wine in new bottles:

great man/woman, trait, group, organization, and management definitions and theories of leadership that look new because they bespeak
excellence, charisma, culture, quality, vision, values, peak performance,
and empowerment. (p. 91)

Furthermore, the confusion of leadership with management, and the equation of
leaders with leadership, causes problems not only for scholars, but also practitioners, the presumed consumers of scholarly work on leadership. These problems are difficult to resolve.

The difficulty is not that we lack definitions, but that the definitions we use
are often ambiguous and even contradictory. Moreover, some have argued that
leadership as a concept is so general that we do not know what it refers to; still
others claim that the term is too specific to cover the full range of complexities
and possibilities that characterize leadership. Bennis (1959) concluded:

Always, it seems, the concept of leadership eludes us or turns into
another form to taunt us again with its slipperiness and complexity. So
we have invented an endless proliferation of terms to deal with it . . .,
and still the concept is not sufficiently defined. (p. 259)

Formal definitions of leadership, as Borman (1990) noted, have often fallen prey
to the philosophical disease of starting with a stipulated definition and then
discovering new meaning in the definition until a factual argument emerges
which is based purely on assumptions hidden in the definition. For the most part,
for instance, definitions of leadership are presented as if leadership were gender-
neutral. Yet traditionally women were believed to lack the traits and behaviors
considered prerequisites for effective leadership, traits such as aggression, competitiveness, dominance, Machiavellianism, ambition, and decisiveness. Similarly, high levels of energy, tallness, a commanding voice, persistence, and
assertiveness were presumably requisites to lead effectively; but they are also
qualities which typically have been missing from descriptions of women.

Instead of lacking the requisite skills for leadership, women are more likely
to lack opportunities for exercising leadership and role models they admire and
wish to emulate. According to Polster (1992):

It seems clear that young men have a popular gallery of heroes stretching
back for centuries and continuing into the present. Our contemporary
myths are often modern versions of the ancient hero tale dressed up in
new clothes. Moses, Joshua, Achilles, and Odysseus turn up again as
Luke Skywalker, Rambo, Superman, and the Terminator. But to whom
can a young woman look up to for inspiration? Her classic models are
Penelope, the devoted stay-at-home wife, Cassandra, unheeded prophet
and sexual prize of war, Guinevere, Arthur's faithless queen, and Helen
of Troy, the beautiful troublemaker. (p. 49)

Definitions must take into account that leadership involves change; change that may be dramatic or radical, subtle or incremental, continuous or discontinuous. Women and other minorities are important contributors to the change process. As leaders, women are in a state of transition trying to overcome their minority status and marginality. The ambivalent situations women find themselves in as leaders have their origins in conflicting and often mutually exclusive social norms: those contained in the gender stereotype, and those of social representations of leadership which have been predominantly male (Moscovici, 1986) (see Chapter 6).

Rather than adding yet another formal definition of leadership, I prefer to think about critical features of leadership which may combine in an infinite number of ways. These essential elements include integrity, veracity, trust, commitment, morality, shared experiences, and dynamic networks as opposed to static, patterned interactions between leaders and followers. They exalt values like teamwork, collaboration, and the interdependence and unity of leadership and followership. Leaders embracing these values exhibit self-determination and risk-taking, courage, decisiveness, and a strong sense of ethics. They believe in the importance of thinking systemically (that is, seeing connections between people, issues, and outcomes), metaphorically, globally, and futuristically. Above all, leadership is not a position or the outcome of election or appointment. In fact, definitions which combine these elements see political leadership as an oxymoron, since politicians are elected or appointed to their leadership positions. This is not to say that elected or appointed officials are not leaders; it simply means that elections and/or appointments do not make a person a leader.

These elements, as the leadership diamond depicted in Figure 1.1 suggests, arrange themselves in varying constellations around leadership/followership interdependencies, gender, culture, and context to produce varying definitions of leadership.

There are a number of reasons why I do not want to commit myself to yet another definition of leadership. First, while many scholars (e.g., Rost, 1991) have deplored the absence of a universal definition of leadership, I disagree that a single definition of leadership is necessary to achieve a complete understanding of leadership. Since the fundamental premise of this book is that leadership is shaped by culture, a second premise follows: that definitions change from one context to next. For example, in traditional, hierarchical organizational structures, leadership is defined on the basis of position power of the Chief Executive Officer Leadership Diamond (CEO), top-down communications, and status differentiation between the CEO and the rest of the employees. In the flat, networked organizations which are beginning to replace the bureaucratic pyramid in many industries,

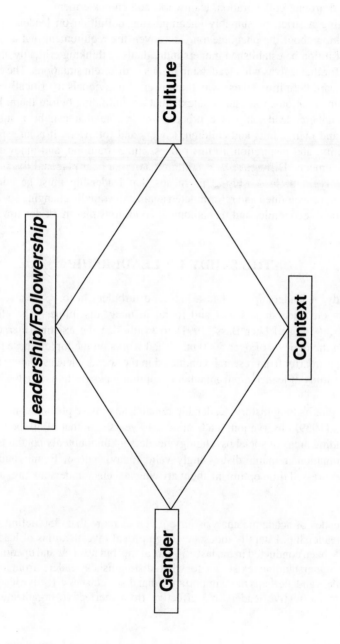

Figure 1.1 Leadership Diamond

leadership may be defined on the basis of leader-follower relations, which are structured around collaboration, teamwork, and empowerment.

Putting a strict, presumably encompassing definition on leadership limits our thinking about the phenomenon. Moreover, the requirement that an agreed-upon definition be established hinders individuals in thinking critically and deciphering for themselves what leadership means in different situations. The creation of a standard definition takes away the power of individuals to critically analyze leadership situations, roles and contexts that are unfolding before them. Instead, as treated here, leadership is a process and a role that can be assumed by women and men, adults and children, leaders and followers; it is an aspiration, opportunity, and inspiration. In this process, time, tradition, and innovation are critical elements. Different times, both in history and our personal lives, call for different types of leadership. This means that leadership must be constantly examined, re-examined and reformulated against the rapidly changing sociocultural, political, economic, and technological conditions that mark our times.

THE STUDY OF LEADERSHIP

The study of leadership has had a long and turbulent history. As a result, the literature on leadership is vast and found in many disciplines. The efforts of Stogdill (1974) and later Bass (1991) to synthesize the existing literature are based on the reviews of over 5000 published works on the topic. These reviews, drawing primarily from research conducted in the social sciences, barely touched upon the study of leadership from other disciplinary perspectives like the humanities.

Despite its long history, leadership remains an elusive phenomenon. Warren Bennis's (1959) observation, made almost 40 years ago, that of all the hazy and confounding areas of social psychology, leadership undoubtedly contends for the top nomination, remains distressingly valid today. Indeed, Bennis and Nanus (1985) expressed little optimism about arriving at a clear understanding of leadership:

> Decades of academic analysis have given us more than 350 definitions of leadership. Literally thousands of empirical investigations of leaders have been conducted in the last 75 years alone, but no clear and unequivocal understanding exists as to what distinguishes leaders from non-leaders and, perhaps more important, what distinguishes effective leaders from ineffective leaders and effective from ineffective organizations. (p. 4)

Despite 100 years of analysis and research which produced mountains of work ranging from poetry to mathematical models, leadership remains a slippery concept. Invariably, in our attempts to define leadership, we become bogged down in such indeterminable questions of whether leadership is innate or learned, personality or fate, or whether sports idols or committee chairs are leaders. Ultimately, as the Greek philosopher Xenophanes said some 2500 years ago, when applied to leadership, our knowledge about this ageless phenomenon is hypothetical; it is not certain knowledge, but conjectural knowledge (Popper, 1989).

WOMEN AND LEADERSHIP: THE PRISM METAPHOR

Examining, re-examining, and reformulating leadership vis-à-vis the dynamics of the outgoing 20th century means developing new conceptions of leadership and searching for new paradigms. One way of breaking with established ways of conceptualizing leadership is by drawing on symbolic constructs or metaphors. Metaphors are commonly used vehicles for understanding or ways of experiencing one phenomenon in terms of another. They create images that serve as windows on some facet of leadership, and therefore provide a set of filters for the study and practice of leadership.

The process of metaphorical conception, according to Morgan (1980),

is a basic mode of symbolism central to the way in which we forge our experience and knowledge of the world in which we live. More fundamentally, it is a creative form which produces its effects through a crossing of images. The creative potential of the metaphor depends on the degree of difference between the subjects involved in the metaphorical process. (p. 611)

Through language, metaphors are an essential medium which helps us form new social realities. Moreover, as Wilson (1992) suggested, metaphors are functional in bringing about a new order and change. They help to control change by capturing insights that elude a more scientific approach.

Metaphors proceed through the assertion that subject A (that is, leadership) is, or is like, subject B (that is, an amoeba, or whitewater rafting). They involve the transfer of meaning from one domain to another and build bridges between the familiar and the unknown. Through processes of comparison, substitution, and interactions between the images of A and B, metaphors act as generators of new meaning (Black, 1962). Metaphors generate new meaning and insights because they force us to discard old concepts and words. According to Brown (1976) metaphoric thinking maintains "double vision" because it encourages us to hold a concept such as leadership simultaneously in two or more points of view. By doing so, we enrich our concepts and understanding of leadership. According to Pondy, Frost, Morgan, and Dandridge (1983), metaphors have a dual purpose: that of facilitating change while maintaining stability; "the use of metaphor simultaneously facilitates change and reinforces traditional values . . . metaphor can fulfill the dual function of enabling change and preserving continuity" (p. 164).

Thinking metaphorically is not new. Philosophers like Aristotle were intrigued by the use of metaphors. More recently, organizational theorists (e.g., Pfeffer & Salancik, 1978) have created metaphors of organizations to transcend their conceptualization as rational, goal-oriented entities. Gareth Morgan (1980, 1986) in particular analyzed organizations using metaphors such as machines, organisms, psychic prisons, theaters, and instruments of domination, suggesting that the logic of metaphor also has implications for leadership. Just as no one metaphor can capture the total nature of organizational life, a single metaphor also cannot describe the essence of leadership. Instead, "different metaphors constitute and capture the nature of leadership in different ways, each generating powerful, distinctive, but essentially incomplete kinds of insight" (Morgan, 1980, p. 612). Although lacking in completeness, the power of metaphorical analysis allows us to better understand and communicate the leadership process. However, users of metaphors must be aware of the fact that metaphors may produce inappropriate and unintended meanings.

One way of thinking metaphorically about women and leadership is as a series of interconnected prisms created by the juxtaposition of gender (see Figure 1.2), different contexts, and the different cultures which develop from gender. Prisms are found in geometry and optics. They are defined as figures of certain shapes, crystalline or transparent bodies, or more generally, anything that refracts light. Light, of course, is a frequently used metaphor of knowledge. Similarly, the hologram, a three-dimensional image created by interacting lights, is frequently used as a metaphor of a vision shared by leaders and followers.

To be useful, we must learn something new from metaphors. What, then, is gained by thinking about women and leadership as a series of prisms? A look at the leadership prisms presented here holds some answers which, like the light that prisms refract, take on different colors for each of us. The colors may be dazzling or dull depending on our personal roles as leaders and followers, and on the contexts and cultures in which we perform these roles.

Leadership and Gender

When examining, analyzing, and evaluating female and male leaders, gender operates as the first of a series of prisms. "Gender" refers to the historical, social, and cultural construction of biological sex, and is usually defined "by default,'' since what we attribute to one gender is typically denied to the other. It is a powerful symbol because the very word "gender" encapsulates all the signs that a culture elaborates to account for biological differences between women and men (Gherardi, 1994). We are gendered as human beings from the day we are born when baby girls are dressed in pink outfits and baby boys in blue. However, gender should not be conceived as a fixed property of individuals, but as part of an ongoing process by which women and men are constituted, often in paradoxical ways (Van Zoonen, 1994). For example, the adolescent girl who initially conforms to cultural stereotypes of femininity may adopt a masculine leadership style as an executive in a male-dominated industry.

Connell (1987) used the concept of *gender order* to overcome dichotomized conceptualizations of gender. "Gender order" begins with the assumption that gender is better thought of as a process rather than a "thing" that people have. The author suggested that gender order is a dynamic process that is constantly in a state of change. It is a historically constructed pattern of power relations between men and women, relations that unfold within changing structural contexts. Viewed in this fashion, gender and leadership are equally dynamic, evolving, ambiguous, and paradoxical.

In the study of leadership, gender has been employed in ways other than a strictly categorical variable distinguishing women leaders from their male counterparts. In many cases, it has been used as an explanatory factor to account for the underrepresentation of women in leadership. In many disciplines engaged in the study of leadership, women have been excluded; they have been ignored as research participants in empirical studies, and their contributions to society and to our understanding of leadership have been belittled, ridiculed, and distorted. The topic of women and leadership has until fairly recently been rarely approached in empirical research. Most leadership research prior to the 1980s was carried out by men and dealt almost exclusively with male leaders, variously defined as supervisors, managers, administrators, or commanders. Similarly, virtually all theories of leadership, past and present, have been developed by men, and only recently have feminist scholars begun to respond to the androcentrism which permeates study in this field. Because women have been largely absent in the study of leadership, much of our knowledge of leadership has been derived from the description and analysis of male leaders reported by male researchers.

In fact, for many people, scientists, historians, politicians, and managers alike, leadership has been synonymous with masculinity, and we have only begun to get beyond that synonymy. In terms of conventional reference, as Eisler (1991) observed, the term "women leader" is itself an anomaly. We might smile today at Schopenhauer's (1994) statement that the idea of seeing a woman governing in the place of men makes one burst out into laughter, but for many women leaders this statement still has a familiar ring. Women in leadership roles today hardly are allowed to forget that they are *women leaders*, no more than blacks

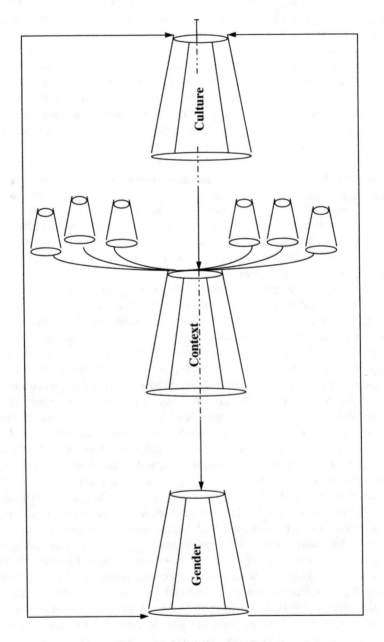

Figure 1.2 Leadership Prisms

in a white nation or Catholics in a Protestant state can forget their minority status. Gender is always in the way when female leaders are evaluated and acts as a filter for assessing women's leadership skills and effectiveness. Women leaders do not lack confidence in their leadership abilities nor the competence to function effectively as leaders, but they experience a sense of tokenism, vulnerability, and precariousness. These sentiments are present elements of the social ecology in which women practice leadership on a daily basis (Apfelbaum & Hadley, 1986). As a result, women are still at a disadvantage when called upon as leaders.

The rise of women to highest elective office, the unprecedented number of women seeking public office, holding state and congressional office, and serving in leadership capacities in medicine, health care, sports, and business, as well as the rise of women leaders in developing countries as diverse as Poland and Panama, is seriously challenging the myth that women are unfit for leadership. However, despite the inroads women have made as leaders in politics, private and public sector industry, the arts, and the sciences, these prominent women are but a small percentage of all women in the population of leaders compared to men. The minority status of female leaders was glaringly evident during the Anita Hill–Clarence Thomas hearings in 1992 (see Chapter 5) when an unflinching camera repeatedly focused on the few women in Congress (2 out of 100 in the Senate; 28 out of 435 in the House). A closer look at what some called record gains in women's political strength reveals that these gains are not as dramatic as portrayed. For example, according to Witt, Paget, and Matthews (1994), between 1975 and 1991 the representation of women in Congress rose from 4% to 6%. If change continued at the present rate, it would take more than 300 years before men and women would be represented equally in Congress (see Chapter 8).

The minority status of women leaders in politics is mirrored at the senior executive level in both private and public sector organizations. Although women today fill nearly a third of all management positions (up from 19% in 1972), the majority of them occupy jobs with relatively little authority or power. Only one of 15 highest ranking managers is a woman. The lack of female representation at the top of corporations is known as the "glass ceiling," an invisible, yet impenetrable barrier of discrimination that keeps women from senior leadership positions. In the public sector, the United States government reported only 8% of women in the Senior Executive Service (SES) levels (United States Office of Personnel Management, 1989). When it comes to pay, no matter how hard women work, experience and education do not offset the pay differential that continues to exist in the salaries of working women and men. A recent survey of 194 mid- to upper-level managers at major companies across the country conducted by economics professor Peter Hammerschmidt (1992, p. 21) revealed that the men earned a mean annual salary of $80,722, compared to $65,258 for the women (p. 21). After breaking down the executives' compensation and assigning a dollar value to each of seven major factors—age, firm size, education, degree, sex, type of organization, and management level—Hammerschmidt determined that just $3,740 of the salary discrepancy could be deemed legitimate. The remaining shortfall could only be attributed to one thing: the executives' chromosomes.

Leadership and Context

The gender prism may be seen as the first of a series of lenses through which leadership operates. The next set of lenses is represented by contexts. Context, in the most general sense of the word, refers to the setting in which leadership emerges and is exercised. Context may be historical or situational. Contextual aspects of organizations include their existing social structure, personnel and compensation practices, and industry type. Just as different times call for different leaders and different types of leadership, so do different contexts (see Figure 1.3).

Context influences what leaders must do and what they can do. A leader's mission and purpose—her reason for serving as a leader in their family, church, organization, community, or nation—is partly answered by context. At all levels, individual, group, organizational, and societal, leadership is tied to context. It is the context that shapes the process of leadership. Therefore, examining women and leadership from this perspective means analyzing different contexts such as history, business, politics, technology, sports, economics, the media, and the global village.

Contextual factors set the boundaries within which leaders and followers interact and determine the constraints and demands that are put on leaders. Therefore requirements and demands for leadership differ depending on these boundaries. For example, exercising leadership in the context of political systems in which leaders are appointed or elected is different from practicing leadership in social movements where leaders emerge as a result of a crisis or shared ideology. Evaluating a leading artist calls for different criteria than evaluating a leading scientist. Religion, science, the arts, and formal and informal organizations are complex networks of relationships, each with its own contextual parameters. The context of leadership may be private or public, or a small or large organization, an affluent or poor community, or a developed or underdeveloped nation. Because many leaders function in more than one context, no single formula is possible or advisable for the range of potential settings leaders encounter (Bolman & Deal, 1991b). Similarly, prototypes of effective leaders (i.e., George Patton in the context of the military, or Susan B. Anthony of the women's suffrage movement) vary from setting to setting.

Historically, however, leadership has been narrowly studied and interpreted through the lenses of great men cast as political actors. From Plato's vision of training leaders for the ideal political state as described in *The Republic*, to Hitler's ideas of transforming Germany set forth in *Mein Kampf*, political

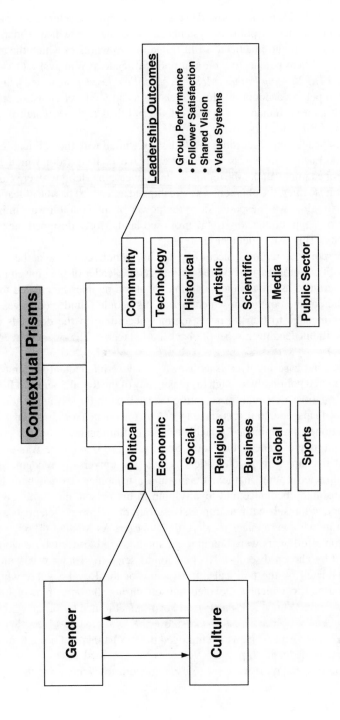

Figure 1.3 Diversity of Contexts

doctrines and ideologies have provided the primary frame of reference for leadership. The prevalence of political systems as the context in which leadership is most often studied and practiced is illustrated in two works in which the authors imposed a political perspective on non-political leaders. Wildavsky (1984), for example, in *The Nursing Father: Moses as a Political Leader* presented a fascinating and compelling account of Moses seen not as a moral, religious, or spiritual leader, but as a politician and creator of the political regimes which provided the context for his leadership.

Moses' leadership, according to Wildavsky, varied with the political regimes he created. Each regime was congruent with the context from which it was derived. For example, under the regime called slavery, the Hebrews were enslaved in Egypt whose ruler, the pharaoh, was worshipped as a god. The rule of leadership during this regime was despotic, since the power of the pharaoh was unlimited. Later, out of Egypt on the way to the promised land, Moses designed the regime of hierarchy. This was a democratic regime.

These political regimes, according to the author, constituted the map of Moses' political progression and regression. As the leader of the chosen people, Moses functioned as the architect and master of the regimes he created to meet the demands of the context in which he and his people found themselves. How did Moses manage to transform his regimes according to the demands of the situation without leading his people back into slavery? The answer, according to Wildavsky, is that Moses was a consummate politician.

The second case involves Isaac Newton, whose intellectual leadership has been interpreted politically through his presidency of the Royal Society in London. While the qualities essential for scientific leadership are far less understood than those of political leadership, it is agreed that Newton created for himself a position of unquestioned preeminence which became institutionalized by his political appointment as president of the Royal Society in 1703, when he was 60 years of age. At that time, his mathematical genius was universally recognized, and Newton attracted young mathematicians and astronomers from whom he demanded absolute obedience and loyalty both to his person and to his doctrine. He surrounded himself with an impressive group of followers, scientists as well as aristocrats who were eager to serve their master. As Manuel (1968) pointed out, Newton's followers were bound to an apotheosized leader whose word was propagated by chosen disciples. His position as scientific leader was reinforced and consolidated by the political infrastructure of the Royal Society which he had created and to which he devoted himself during the latter part of his life. The Royal Society, in which science and government joined to form an exclusive club, provided the political context that allowed Newton to consolidate his scientific empire. Like Moses, Newton employed the mechanisms of a political ideology to sustain his leadership.

By contrast, today, if we were to use one word to characterize the study of leadership, that word is diversity; diversity of theories and paradigms; diversity of ethnicity and gender; and diversity of contexts. A brief comparison of the characteristics of two contexts in which women have emerged as leaders are technology and community organizations. This comparison illustrates the characteristics and boundaries set by specific leadership contexts.

Technologies involve products and processes that facilitate the flow of activities, whether at work or at home. They are designed and implemented to expedite the flow and exchange of human, material, financial, and information resources between individuals and work units. Like leadership, technologies have people, structural, political, and symbolic domains. Technologies also create enabling structures, such as user groups formed around the application of a new information system that encourage change and learning. Furthermore, technologies create new leadership tasks which include what Senge (1990a, 1990b) called building learning organizations, defined by one writer as "consummately adaptive enterprises" (Domain, 1989). In the learning organization,

> Leaders' roles differ dramatically from that of the charismatic decision maker. Leaders are designers, teachers, and stewards. These roles require new skills: the ability to build a shared vision . . . and foster systemic patterns of thinking. (Senge, 1990b, p. 442)

Leading in high technology, information- and knowledge-intensive organizations requires flexibility, technical competence, the capacity to adapt on the spot, commitment to high quality innovation, and the ability to build collaborate cultures. High-performing firms in technology driven organizations and their leaders value personal responsibility, intrinsic motivation, and autonomy, as well as high levels of follower (i.e., users of information systems) involvement. They value performance orientation and reward it with performance-oriented incentives such as profit sharing. Finally, high-performing, technology-intensive companies are socially responsible organizations which contribute to the welfare of the larger community.

Women leaders in this context include Grace Hopper and Sandra Kurtzig. Grace Hopper earned her Ph.D. in 1934, served in the U.S. Naval Reserve, was called to active duty, and eventually earned the grade of rear Admiral. While at Harvard University, she learned computer programming. For more than three decades she was an innovator and major contributor to the development of programming languages and inspired major developments in computer programming. One of the characteristics that made Hopper a pioneer was her technical vision. She foresaw many applications for computing, including artificial intelligence. Hopper was admired and respected not only for her technological achievements, but also for her energy, enthusiasm, and willingness to serve as a mentor (Billings, 1989). Her insight and leadership have helped to create some of the industry's most important landmark work (Gautereaux, 1990).

Sandra Kurtzig founded ASK Computer Systems in 1971, building the company from a $2,000 personal savings investment to one of the nation's largest software firms and the largest public company founded and run by a woman. By 1982, ASK was the fastest-growing software company in the United States, with revenues over $400 million, and Kurtzig was the first woman to take a high-tech company public. When people heard she was "in software," Kurtzig (1991) said, they thought she was making lingerie.

Both high-technology firms and community organizations represent gendered leadership contexts, male and female leadership domains, respectively. Like leadership, technologies are shrouded in the myth of neutrality; like leadership, they are largely socially constructed. Limitations on the use of technologies are imposed by social norms rather than technological constraints. Instead of being neutral, information technologies propagate gender politics built on women's presumed negative attitudes toward computers or even aversion to technology known as techno- or cyberphobia. As a context, information technology is largely a male world, in which women are perceived as inexperienced, unprepared, alien, or unwilling participants (Edwards, 1990). As technology becomes more and more of an imperative in our personal and professional lives, the relation of technology to gender, and the way technology differentially affects women's and men's lives, has important implications for gendered utilization of information technology.

Presently, technology as a context for leadership favors men, and community organizations, as a context, are more open to women leaders. In this latter context, so-called feminine qualities and behaviors such as caring, nurturing, and empowering are held in high esteem. Often, community organizations do not have an elected or appointed leader, but are characterized by wide participation by community members participating in the leadership process. In contrast to high-technology organizations, where profitability and indices of financial performance such as return on investment are important indicators of success, many community organizations are not operated for profit and are staffed by volunteers. Since volunteers have no contractual relationship with the nonprofit organization they serve, leaders must be able to depend on intrinsically motivated followers. Furthermore, community organizations are frequently anti-hierarchical, and their structures are likely to be fluid. Leadership in these organizations is more likely to be determined by commitment to purpose than by position on the organizational chart.

The Girl Scouts community and its former leader, Frances Hesselbein, exemplify leadership in the context of non-profit community organizations. Frances Hesselbein served as National Executive Director of the Girl Scouts of the United States of America, the world's largest women's organization, from 1976 to 1990, and is now President of the Drucker Foundation of Non-Profit Management. She started as the temporary leader of a Girl Scout troop. She assumed leadership of the organization at a time when the Girl Scouts were re-examining their mission in view of demographic changes in the population it served; i.e., the increasing number of working women had reduced the number of women who had the time to serve as troop leaders, the career aspirations of young girls were changing. After restructuring the organization based on the new market, implementing new programs such as the Girl Scouts Environmental Scanning Systems and continuous training for volunteers and professional staff, and designing a new planning and management system, Hesselbein led an organization which Drucker (1990) described as "the best-managed organization around" (p. 122).

Leadership and Culture: Gender as Culture

Many successful organizations have a distinctive personality that is shaped by gender. When a corporation has many more men than women (or vice versa) in influential positions, the culture tends to adopt attributes that favor the dominant gender. Such corporations are known as gendered organizations.

Gendered organizations have strong cultures in which gender, contextual factors, and cultural stereotypes interact. Creators, transmitters, and preservers of technological cultures (i.e., men), for example, develop and design computer applications that reinforce the male value system. Likewise, women build community cultures that perpetuate a system believed to be congruent with female values. Gender is treated as culture here because gender-centered perspectives on leadership predominate. As defined here, gender is an intrinsic part of culture. Culture concerns the conditions and the forms in which meaning and value are structured and articulated within a society. Since culture concerns the daily interactions between men and women within and between subcultures and other collectivities, invariably gender is a crucial, if not the *most* crucial, component of culture (Corner, 1991). The author goes on to say that culture concerns "the conditions and forms in which meaning and values are structured and articulated within a society" (p. 131). According to Hofstede (1980) culture is to human collectivity, that is, the population of women and men, what personality is to an individual. Additionally, this writer suggests that cultural differences between organizational structures, and hence leadership, reflect differences in value systems.

Gender gives collective meanings to perceptions of leadership which, in turn, abound with gender and cultural biases. Rather than treating gender as an individual characteristic, it is considered here as a matter of social relations and culture. Culture determines the identity of a human group in the same way as personality determines the identity of an individual. Gender is one, but not the sole, basis of culture. However, like language, it is one of the most recognizable aspects of culture. Examples of the treatment of gender as culture in the popular literature are found in the books *Beauty Myth* (Wolf, 1990), which is concerned with the onerous cultural messages about women's appearances; *Backlash* (Faludi, 1990), which calls for a return of conservativism and antifeminism in American media; and *Sexual Persona* (Paglia, 1990), which portrays the cultural struggles of femininity, masculinity, and feminism.

CONCLUSIONS

This chapter laid the foundation for contextualizing leadership and framing it metaphorically as a series of prisms. The approach presented here suggests that the setting in which leaders and followers interact influences leadership outcomes. Seen prismatically, leadership is viewed as a series of juxtaposed lenses. Each prism, gender, context, and culture, contributes to our understanding of leadership in a unique way. Each leadership prism refracts knowledge and different insights into the process of leadership and the roles women and men play in this process.

We cannot speak dispassionately of leadership during this decade, *le fin de siecle* which has witnessed many changes. The fall of the Berlin Wall and the collapse of the former Soviet Union, unprecedented technological transformations, and ever tougher international competition are among the multitude of factors that have sparked an animated discourse about leadership which takes place in academic circles as well as on the shop floor. As we are preparing to enter the 21st century, we will increasingly hear cries for new leadership paradigms, more effective leaders, better leadership education, and more diversity in the practice of leadership. Gone are the 1-minute manager, the secrets of Attila the Hun, and the one-best approach. Millennium expectations as to what constitutes effective 21st-century leadership are complex and multifaceted. They have also turned leadership training and development into a flourishing industry (see Chapter 10).

The perspective on women and leadership offered here is a contextual approach. It is derived from the frequently heard criticism that the contemporary study of leadership lacks adequate concern for context, either historical or situational (Heilbrunn, 1994). Heilbrunn asserted:

> Besides scanting the historical dimension, leadership studies neglect the variety of arenas in which different kinds of leaders operate. Successful captaining in business, government, or the military does not necessarily transfer to other fields—or even among those three. Moreover, thanks to academic neglect, we are largely clueless as to what makes a strong religious leader, culture leader, reform leader, intellectual leader, culture leader. (p. 70)

To deal with the demands for a new leadership, we must recognize the critical importance of context. In each context—political, intellectual, artistic, religious, scientific, social, cultural, and international—leadership manifests itself differently. The changing sociopolitical landscape of Europe, the collapse of Communism, the rise of underdeveloped countries such as Thailand and Korea, and the aging of developed countries such as United States, Europe, and Japan are setting the stage for a new social order. The shared values of this new order, according to Aburdene and Naisbitt (1992), include worldwide multiparty democracies, freedom of choice, free trade and privatization of industry, and global recognition and protection of human rights. These trends and expectations create yet another context of leadership. In this broader context which is the sum of many microcontexts, new leadership opportunities for women arise. Women have a critical role to play as leaders in a new social order to ensure that its goal, that is, the development of the potential of all people regardless of gender, ethnicity, social class, or religion, is achieved.

Although the contextual view may frustrate people who are looking for a quick and easy formula that makes them leaders, it explains aspects of leadership that other positions must either rationalize or note as exceptions (Borman, 1990). The contextual view encourages women to seek new leadership opportunities and take a leading role in the design of new contexts in which the social architecture of organizations and nations is not so much dominated by gender issues, but by human issues. Moreover, by understanding the different leadership contexts, whether in today's corporations, national and international communities, school systems, or reform movements, and the opportunities and constraints associated with each of them, women can acquire the skills and competencies to become instrumental as agents of change. By understanding the leadership context, women can become more influential in creating a climate more conducive to the acceptance of women leaders, and increase the demand for them as role models for both women and men.

2 Women Leaders in History

A singular exception ... a woman is often acknowledged the absolute sovereign of a great kingdom, in which she would be deemed incapable of exercising the smallest employment, civil or military.

Gibbons

INTRODUCTION

Many people see history as shaped by the leadership of great men. Images of the past are replete with male superheroes—the legendary kings and rulers, high priests, intellectual geniuses, and great artists who seemingly shook the world. The "great man" theory of leadership was originally espoused by Thomas Carlyle. In his essay on heroes, Carlyle (1813) reinforced the concept of the leader as a person who is endowed with unique qualities that capture the imagination of his or her followers. The author summed up his position when he said, "In all epoch's of the world's history we shall find the Great Man to have been the indispensable savior of his epoch—the lightening, without which the fuel never would have burnt" (Carlyle, 1813, p. 83). Similarly, according to William James (1902/1985), the mutations of society were due to great men who initiated movement and prevented others from leading society in a different direction.

The history of the world, for many commentators, is the history of great men who created what the masses desired to accomplish. As Bass (1959) observed, "From its infancy, the study of history has been the study of leaders. What leaders do and do not do matters enormously in the cause of human affairs" (p. 8). This position is clear in the writings of major exponents of leadership such as Thomas Carlyle and Max Weber, for whom leaders were the architects of history, as well as in the writings of determinists, such as Georg Hegel and Karl Marx, for whom leaders were only cogs in a wheel, controlled by powerful socioeconomic forces. Thomas Carlyle, for example, in the 1840s delivered a series of lectures on heroes and described them as "leaders of men—the modelers, patterns, and in a wide sense creators, of what the general mass of men contrived to do or attain" (1903, p. 1).

Women, with few exceptions, have had no place in history as leaders. Cora Castle (1913) conducted a statistical study of eminent women in history based on her research of biographical entries in major European encyclopedias. The search produced 868 entries of eminent women, famous and infamous, which Castle rank-ordered as follows: (a) queens, (b) politicians, (c) mothers, (d) mistresses, (e) beauties, (f) religious women, (g) women of tragic fate, and (h) women important only through marriage. Historically, eminent women fell largely into the latter six categories, since few women had established themselves as leaders in their own right. Even today, women's history is largely unexplored territory for many women because the subject is rarely taught.

Only recently have women rewritten history as "herstory" (e.g., Forfreedom, 1972; Sochen, 1975) recognizing that women, like men, need a sense of history to have their contributions valued. Much of the scholarship published by women and feminist historians since the 1970s has concentrated on restoring women to history, and history to women, by recharting women's contributions (Lewis, 1992). These scholars emphasized gender as a crucial concept for analysis. Kelly (1984), for example, argued that much of history was, for the most part, partial, distorted, and limited because questions about women had never been asked. Although the rewriting of history incorporating gender and deconstruction has produced some interesting work which draws on feminist theory and feminist work in other disciplines, women's history remains on the periphery of the male historical establishment's vision (Lewis, 1992). Considering the usefulness of gender as a category of historical analysis, Scott (1986) concluded:

> For the most part, the attempts of historians to theorize about gender have remained within the traditional social scientific frameworks using long standing formulations that provide universal causal explanations. These theories have been limited at best because they contain reductive or overly simple generalizations that undercut not only history's disciplinary sense of the complexity of social causation but also feminist commitments to analyses that will lead to change. (p. 1055)

In the 20th century, just as in the Mediterranean civilizations of 2000 B.C., there are no women on national security councils of any country, in top-level military commands, or among the top ecclesiastical authorities (who also historically had armies at their disposal), of any major religion (Boulding, 1992). However, the Episcopal Church has elected the first female bishops. In 1989, the Reverend Barbara Harris, a black woman, became the world's first female Episcopal bishop. Additionally, about 1,000 of the 14,000 Episcopal ministers in the United States are women (Aburdene & Naisbitt, 1992, p. 116). Other religions too, including Judaism and the Catholic Church, are beginning to change their hierarchial, patriarchal institutions to make room for women.

Writing from an historical perspective, Boulding introduced the concept of "underlife" to capture the subservient roles women have played throughout history. According to the author, "underlife" refers to women's sex-designated positions in society that historically kept them in the private domain, and outside of the public, visible structures of society which pattern the roles of men. The underlife concept implies and contrasts with the "overlife," which is populated and dominated by men. In addition to women, there are, of course, other groups— ethnic, racial, religious, and other minorities—who are examples of the underlife. Besides occupying the underside of history, women leaders who could not be erased from public consciousness were often declared frauds and heretics.

Building on the contextualist perspective presented in the first chapter, this chapter focuses on women leaders of the past. History, therefore, is a rich setting for the study of leadership. It provides a context that is not only temporally bound, but also constantly evolves and fluctuates, thereby creating opportunities for women (and men) to assume leadership at certain times in history while imposing constraints which prevent them from doing so at others. Moreover, in history, gender and contextual factors interact to produce the salient characteristics of an era (i.e., Louis XIV). Finally, history is an important context because leaders themselves are aware of the historical moment in which they lead. Once established in their roles, leaders often want to leave their personal marks on history by creating a legacy, which may take the form of monuments, constitutions, ceremonies, or works of art.

Historical leaders, both female and male, who were studied most in the past were often exceptional individuals—charismatic, saintly, dramatic, evil, or infamous. Women leaders have led (or led on) many great men acting as illustrious wives or notorious mistresses, courtesans, and concubines. Women accorded a leadership role in history often illustrated the statement made by the German poet Schiller who said that beside every great man, we can expect to find a beloved woman. Aspasia of Iona, for example, as Pericles' companion was the first lady of Athens during the Golden Age of Greece. She was a leader by example who created a unique civic culture, educated Athenian housewives, and served as political advisor to Pericles. Similarly, Olympia, wife of Philip of Macedonia and mother of Alexander the Great, played an active and aggressive role in her husband's crusade of liberating Macedonia from the Persian regime. In addition, she was instrumental in preparing young Alexander for world leadership. Other historical examples of great women/great men alliances included Cleopatra and Caesar, Josephine and Napoleon, Madame de Pompadour and Louis XV, Abigail and John Adams, and Eleanor and Franklin D. Roosevelt. Some of the women in these partnerships were leaders in their own right. Others became legends or sources of legends, while still others exercised leadership through their spouses or lovers.

This chapter presents selective portrayals of several historical women leaders who, in one way or the other, have shaped the course of history. The focus here is on women leaders in different historical periods, cultural traditions, and sociopolitical contexts. More specifically, women's leadership in this chapter is analyzed from three contextual perspectives: religious, political, and social. These contexts are particularly relevant from an historical perspective because of the continuity with which women have exercised leadership over time. The specific women leaders in these three contexts were chosen because: (a) they are recognized by historians as leading figures; (b) they were born into different cultural traditions; (c) they are from different historical periods; and (d) adequate biographical materials are available to assess the impact of their leadership. Finally, the women discussed in this chapter were selected to show that, in the past as well as in the present, we cannot talk or write about female leaders as a unitary category of exceptional women. Instead, their leadership is a tapestry consisting of many threads: gender, race, ethnicity, social class, religion, and sexual preference. Therefore, we must question the assumption that all women share a common past, and must weave threads of gender as central categories into historical and contemporary analyses of women's leadership. The sample of historical women leaders, although admittedly limited to women who were prominent figures in history, omits the long list of women who were effective leaders in a variety of unstructured contexts, such as families or local communities. However, it does reflect the diversity and multiplicity of women's experiences as leaders of churches, countries, revolutions, and social reform movements.

WOMEN LEADERS IN RELIGIOUS CONTEXTS

The deification of women throughout history has taken many forms, from the prehistoric mother goddesses and epic heroines like Helen of Troy or Penelope, to the medieval concept of courtly love. The first women leaders were found in the pantheons of many ancient cults as mother goddesses, female deities, and priestesses of either male or female gods. For example, Ishtar occupied a special position in the Sumerian pantheon, playing a leading role in rituals intended to stimulate the growth of crop and live stock. Similarly, in Egypt, Isis was a national divinity whose cult eventually spread throughout the Mediterranean world. On the island of Crete, the Minoan mother goddess was the center of a civilization that, according to many scholars, represented the golden age of matriarchy. As the goddess of land and sea, the symbol of female generative forces, the omnipotent mistress, the Mediterranean Great Mother predominated the Bronze Age cults of many civilizations, both Western and Eastern. She was known as Isis (Egypt), Atana (Crete), Inana (Sumer), and Ishtar (Babylon). Although there is no proof of the existence of matriarchies in the etymological sense, there are nevertheless indications that women in societies organized around female divinities enjoyed elevated social positions. They participated fully in the social life of their communities and were offered notable freedom and dignity (Beard, 1946).

In prehistoric societies, women often were assigned priestly functions. To our knowledge, they served as ritual leaders as early as the paleolithic period. During this period women were depicted as ceremonial leaders in numerous prehistoric societies from the Mediterranean basin to the Indus Valley. Neolithic artifacts such as cave drawings and fertility figurines indicate that a substantial amount of ritual activity performed by women occurred during this period. These artifacts suggest that the role of the priestess may have been one of the first specialized roles for women outside the domestic sphere.

In the trading town of Catal Huyuk, the largest neolithic site in the Near East (ca. 6000 B.C.), 49 shrines and sanctuaries have been excavated. The principal deity here was a goddess who is shown in her three aspects, as a young woman, a mother giving birth, or as an old woman, in one case accompanied by a bird of prey, probably a vulture. At this site, archaeologists found the most concrete evidence of the double life-and-death aspects of the mother goddess. The mother goddess' duality as a giver and a taker of life made her the terror and hope of the human race during the agricultural era and far into the age of the first great civilizations. As ritual leaders, women carried out a full range of priestly activities, which included the rites of human sacrifice. We also know that women as priestesses and representatives of the mother goddess presided over the sacrifice of young men and children culminating in the grisly mass sacrifices of the Phoenicians. The evidence for mass sacrifices among the Phoenicians is indisputable (Mellaart, 1965).

The presence of women in historical monuments also illustrates women's roles as leaders of religious ceremonies. For example, despite the prevailing notion that all human depiction in Maya subcultures was male, women are widely portrayed on Mayan *stelae*, which are oversized pillars engraved with inscriptions or designs. For example, one women, Lady Katun of Piedras Negras (Guatemala) appeared on a number of *stelae* from the classical period (ca. 700 B.C.), standing proudly in her royal robe and headdress. The text accompanying the *stela* speaks of Lady Katun performing her first bloodletting, a ritual done to honor a deceased king. On another *stela*, the text says that, for whatever reason, Lady Katun's own blood was used in one of these rituals, although the Mayans usually used the blood of the son of the deceased king in this ceremony.

In addition, women leaders acting as high priestesses performed a wide variety of duties, ranging from mummifying bodies to providing religious education for the community (Murray, 1908). In fact, in Egypt, women played a critical role in the administration of the temple centers from which all social, political, and community life flowed. Egypt, in all the long history of its classical period, never developed an urban infrastructure separate from the temple administration which ruled the country for the pharaoh. However, at some point in Egyptian history, as well as in other countries, the special women's government in the temples became associated with the palace and the royal alliance process, and eventually, women's roles as ritual leaders declined as the mother goddess was replaced by male gods in most civilizations.

According to several historians (e.g., Lerner, 1986; Woolger & Woolger, 1989) beginning with Hesiod, somewhere between 1600 and 700 B.C. a process took place in many cultures that shifted the power of creation from the mother goddess to patriarchal gods. In Greece, the ancient mother goddess Gaia, or Earth, was divided and replaced by a supreme male god of war and hunt. Hesiod, living approximately 700 B.C., detailed in *Theogony* the divine progression from female-dominated generations of deities, characterized by natural, earthy, emotional qualities, to the superior and rational monarchy of Zeus (Pomeroy, 1975).

In recorded history, the world religions created a new social unity beyond the family, tribe, and state which attracted women. Buddhism, Christianity, and later Islam were movements aimed at the destruction of the corrupt structures of the old civilizations and rebirth into new communities (Boulding, 1992). The rate at which women joined the new religious movements was a measure of their readiness to embrace new ways of thinking, social values, and lifestyles. For example, the institution of monasticism represented a new form of social order and social relations which eschewed both sexuality and politics. The convents of the Middle Ages, headed by abbesses, offered women the opportunity to become leaders of large organizations or communities dedicated to worship, learning, and service. Thus, the theoretical significance of religion lies in the rejection of political relationships of the past, a rejection which opened opportunities for leadership previously denied to women (Tucker & Liefeld, 1987).

A religious leader may be a Buddhist, Muslim, Christian, or Jew, with each religion having its own traditions and practices. Yet whatever the belief structure, most religious leaders have to grapple with some of the most intractable issues and problems of human existence. For many of them, leadership was an open-ended quest for the truth (Hutch, 1991). Regardless of the specific teachings of a religious doctrine, leaders in this context must deal with the ultimate concern of people. Any religion which hopes to survive must cope with problems of morality and suffering. On the one hand, organized religions offer standards of morality and world views filled with assumptions and prescriptions about how people should conduct themselves. In many societies they also offer ways for women to escape from oppressive home situations and achieve socially prestigious roles. On the other hand, however, organized religions have been the chief source of pain, suppression, and suffering for women. A large number of people, both authorized and unauthorized, have spoken in the name of religion targeting women as victims of persecution. The repressive, isolating, and negative influence religion historically has had on women is undeniable.

With the beginning of Christianity and other world religions, a phenomenon developed—the female leader whose strength and influence depended on her devotion to the divine (Saxonhouse, 1985). St. Paul's letters, for example, show that women were among the prominent and leading missionaries of early Christianity. Later, they participated in the church as deaconesses, abbesses, prophets, and preachers. Similarly, 13th-century Europe produced some leading women mystics, including Saint Clare of Assisi (1195–1253) who was the first woman in the West to write a rule for monastics, a document that gives insight into the kind of leader she must have been, and Mechthild of Magdeburg (1210–1297) whose extraordinary poetic gifts allowed her to communicate eloquently her own ''connective'' version of spirituality. These women mystics set the tone for a century during which feminine voices were raised, tolerated, and even revered (Flinders, 1993).

Ruether and McLaughlin (1981) argued that organized religions gave institutional space to women as leaders and teachers. According to these authors, religious institutions allowed women to teach, debate, promise cures, and exorcise in the early centuries of Christianity. During the emergence of the ''new'' Christian churches in America during the 18th and 19th centuries, women like Mary Baker Eddy, Lucy Wright, and Ellen Harmon White created space for leadership in the founding or renewal movements of Christianity. Beginning with the Shakers and continuing with the Quakers, Adventists, Christian Scientists, and Pentecostal sectarian groups, women were visible as founders and leaders of religious sects and congregations.

Christianity has been a powerful force which produced many charismatic religious leaders. Among the women leaders in this context were Joan of Arc, Teresa of Avila, who led the spiritual awakening during the 16th century in Spain, Ann Hutchinson, the religious dissident who led the first organized attack on the Puritan orthodoxy of the Massachusetts Bay Colony, Mary Baker Eddy, founder of the Christian Science religion, and Elizabeth Kuebler-Ross, the leading religious authority on death and dying. They are examples of religious leaders who attracted many followers, men and women alike. Many of these women experienced some form of spiritual transformation based on communications with a divine source which created visions that stirred them to extraordinary actions in the name of God.

PORTRAITS OF RELIGIOUS LEADERS

Joan of Arc (1412–1431)

Revered as the symbol of French nationalism and canonized by the Roman Catholic Church as a saint some 500 years after her death, Joan of Arc is one of the most prominent female leaders in history who has become a mystical figure over the years. Joan's leadership was shaped by her religious beliefs and the ecclesiastical affairs of the early part of the 15th century (Guillemin, 1970). Joan was convinced that God appointed her to restore the throne of France to her rightful king and reassert the supremacy of the French royal dynasty. She was to fight for her king, through her king, and beyond for the kingdom of God. This was her primary mission, which Joan pursued with both religious fervor and strategic vision.

Joan of Arc was born a simple shepherd girl at the height of the Hundred Years' War, when France was hopelessly mired in feudal divisions. She answered the divine summons to take up arms against the English invaders and lead the Dauphin to Reims to be crowned. Joan had visions and heard voices of archangels and the popular saints of her time, including the archangel Michael; St. Margaret of Antioch, an early Christian martyr; and St. Catherine of Alexandria, another virgin martyr, all of whom were prominent in medieval iconography. The voices came from her right, meaning that they were good rather than evil. They exhorted her to deliver the kingdom of France from its English invaders and to do battle against the Catholic Church; for this she was denounced as a heretic and burned at the stake. Joan had always insisted that she never told anyone of her vision, a fact which was used against her during her trial by the judges of Rouen.

When Joan was about 17 years old, her voices insisted that she assemble an army and join the Dauphin. In 1429 she was granted an audience with the Dauphin Charles. Suspicious of her intentions, Charles disguised himself and hid among his courtiers. However, Joan immediately recognized him and told him that she had come in the name of God to restore the French monarchy and have him crowned in Reims. She spent 3 weeks in Portiers proving the authenticity of her faith to theologians who interrogated her. Finally Charles ordered white armor, a sword, and a standard bearing the image of Christ and the French coat of arms for Joan and placed her at the head of his troops. "Give me a company of soldiers; they will do their part and God, in his turn, will provide the victory" was Joan's reply when her countrymen expressed disbelief that she could miraculously drive back the enemy by her mere presence (Duby, 1991). Granted the rank of Captain, she led her army to New Orleans where she defeated the English and forced them to retreat. The French saw the deliverance of New Orleans on May 8, 1429 as a clear sign of divine approbation and the turning point of the Hundred Years' War.

After this victory Joan became known as the Maid of Orleans. The battle of New Orleans was also the starting point of many decisive battles that Joan fought to free France from English domination.

Joan accomplished her mission in 1429, when the Dauphin was crowned King Charles VII in Reims as Joan stood by the altar. According to Dark (1969) the coronation in Reims Cathedral, in its mystic symbolisn, had a great influence on the French mind, as did the saving of Orleans (p. 72). According to Geis (1981), Joan believed that the coronation ceremony was crucial as God's recognition of Charles's kingship. After the coronation, Joan knelt before the kind and embraced his legs, weeping and saying,

> Gentle king, now is executed the pleasure of God, who wanted the siege of Orleans to be raised, and who has brought you to the city of Reims to receive your holy consecration, showing you that you are the true king, and the the kingdom of France belongs to you. (p. 112)

After the accomplishment of two important goals, the relief of Orleans and the coronation, Joan continued to fight for her king, although her voices foretold her that she would be captured. In 1430, she was taken prisoner by Burgundian troops. They sold her to the English, who charged her with witchcraft and heresy. The French saw this event as a sign of divine disapproval of Joan's conduct. It prompted many people to turn against her. Charles' advisors, for example, tried to show that the king was a puppet of diabolical forces, bewitched by the Maid of Orleans.

During her trial, Joan was interrogated by political and ecclesiastical authorities. She was forced to sign a statement renouncing her claim to divine inspiration, which she later retracted. However, she stood up to the wiles of the clergy jealous of her communications with divine forces. Since the clergy alone, by virtue of their office, were allowed to interpret the will of God, they believed that her revelations could have only come from the devil. Eventually, she was found guilty of having "trafficked with the devil" and condemned on a technicality—having disregarded an official order to put aside the male attire she had worn on the battlefields and during her imprisonment. According to the records of the Paris Parliament, a pointed hat was placed on Joan's head, bearing the words, "heretic, relapsed, apostate, idolator." In addition, a sign was fixed to the platform where she stood to hear the sermon and the sentence: "Jehanne, called the Pucelle, liar, pernicious, seducer of the people, diviner, superstitious, blasphemer of God, presumptuous, misbelieving the faith of Jesus Christ, braggart, idolator, cruel, dissolute, invoker of devils, apostate, schismatic, and heretic" (Geis, 1981). On May 30, 1431, at the age 19, she was burned at the stake by English authorities in the old market square of Rouen. Cardinal Beaufort ordered her ashes to be collected and thrown into the Seine.

Joan of Arc clearly identified her call to leadership with God. At least for a while, her contemporaries saw her as a divine instrument and heroine, with mysteriously redemptive powers. Her faith was the source from which her leadership flowed. Her leadership, motivated by her faith, was instrumental in accomplishing the reunification of France and the coronation of Charles VII. She raised the siege of New Orleans and won stunning victories over the English. According to Boulding (1992), Joan of Arc's significance lies in the fact that she enacted a major leadership role in a crucial period of French history because of an initial unawareness of the limitations that went with her status as a woman.

Mary Baker Eddy (1821–1910)

In a different time and culture, we encounter Mary Baker Eddy. Although female leaders abounded in the many radical sects that emerged during the 19th century, few women in history have founded formal, organized religions. Among them were Lucy Wright (1780–1821) and Anna White (1831–1910) of the Shakers, Ellen Harmon White (1827–1915) of the Seventh Day Adventists, and Mary Baker Eddy, founder of the Christian Science religion.

Mary was born in Concord, New Hampshire, where she spent her childhood as a sickly girl. She suffered from congenital spinal problems, chronic nervousness, and fevers, and was physically disabled all her life. She never attended public school, but was tutored at home by her favorite brother, Albert. After Albert's death and her marriage to his friend George Glover which came to an early end when Glover contracted yellow fever and died in 1844, Mary plunged into a state of utter despondency. Over the next 9 years her mother died and her father remarried, forcing family members and other relatives to share the burden of her care. In 1853, she married an itinerant dentist, Daniel Patterson, partly because of his charm and partly because he was able to administer the morphine required to relieve her physical pains. The marriage deteriorated because Patterson kept up his wandering travels in search of paying patients. After several years of separation, Mary and Daniel Patterson were divorced. At the age of 45, homeless, jobless, and penniless, she slipped on an icy sidewalk. She injured her fragile spine and was told that she would never walk again.

According to Eddy (1894), a miracle occurred when she had this accident which fundamentally changed her life. She reached for her Bible, turning to Matthew 9: 1–8. In this passage she read the account of a man cured of his suffering from palsy by the ministrations of Jesus. Upon reading this passage, Mary's back pain suddenly disappeared and she rose from her bed and walked. When she wrote about the fall later, she declared,

> that short experience included a glimpse of the great fact that I have since tried to make plain to others, namely, Life in and of the Spirit and this life being the sole reality of existence. (Peel, 1971, p. 197)

In *Health and Science*, she later said

> In the year 1866, I discovered the Science of Metaphysical healing, and named it Christian Science. God had been graciously fitting me, during

many years, for the reception of a final revelation of the absolute Principle of Scientific Mind-Healing. (Milmine, 1971, p. 75)

The immediate consequence of the fall was healing and the beginning of a new life. The fall on the ice prompted her to withdraw from society for about 3 years to ponder her mission, search the Scriptures, and find the science of the mind. She began to search for the spiritual meaning behind every passage in the Bible, from Genesis on. Since she believed that the mind can cure, she concluded logically that it can also afflict resulting in "mind crimes." Thus, "mind crimes" were a danger to which Eddy was constantly alert (Peel, 1971). She developed the central thesis of her work that God, Mind, and Good form a spiritual reality capable of controlling matter and obliterating the "unrealities" of sin, evil, sorrow, and sickness (Eddy, 1894).

After she experienced the miraculous cure from her fall on the ice, the event from which she dated the birth of Christian Science, Mary's life took on a significant religious momentum. She had dreams and visions which reflected her struggle with evil, since she was convinced that the only devil was the belief in a life apart from God. Her basic belief that a God-derived spiritual life is indestructible remained unshaken (Peel, 1966). Rebelling against her Calvinist upbringing, she developed a religious ideology that served her personally. It also appealed to the masses of 19th-century Americans who sought a philosophy that would ease their bodies as well as their souls (Tucker & Liefeld, 1987). Convinced that it was her own reading of the Scriptures that brought about her cure after the fall on the ice, Mary believed that this would also be the proper procedure for her followers. She set out to create a body of followers and supported them not only with a theology but with an ecclesiology—a structure of authority, shared rituals, and a communal identity (Wills, 1994).

After she established her Mother Church, the center of Christian Science religion in Boston, Eddy began to write her theories of spiritual healing and the use of the mind to restore physical health. As Peel (1966) saw it:

Mary wrote of mental molecules, molecules of faith, germs of truth, microbes of sin, the virus of hatred, and other such phenomena of inner experience. As she saw it, the invisible germ of doubt, suspicion, and hostility in unconscious thought were as much to be resisted as the evils of common existence. (p. 76)

Over the next decade, Mary produced a large body of publications. In 1875 her writings were published as *Science and Health*, a book which earned her over $400,000 in royalties and went through 381 successive printings. In 1908, at the age of 87, Mary founded the *Christian Science Monitor*, the prestigious secular paper. This magazine, the third of three she founded, distinguished itself through the excellence of its secular reporting and remains one of the most respected newspapers in the United States.

In addition to her writings, Eddy disseminated her theories of Christian Science and women's special roles in sickness and health through teaching, and public speaking. In fact, it was in teaching, rather than preaching, that Eddy's greatest gift lay (Peel, 1966). Nevertheless, she was an articulate speaker with a charismatic presence who attracted many followers. In 1881 she founded the Massachusetts Metaphysical College, where she taught for 8 years. Massachusetts Metaphysical College, as her biographer Peel (1971) mused, was a college with one faculty member (Eddy, who was also its president), one course (which lasted less than a week), and one textbook. Eddy was the college and the college was Eddy.

In 1895, loyal Christian Scientists gave to their foundress the endearing term "mother" which in 1903 was dropped and replaced by "leader." This change in title, according to Eddy (1906), was made in response to attacks by those both inside and outside of the Christian Science movement who claimed that Eddy regarded herself as a female divinity. Many of her followers from then on addressed her as my "precious" or my "beloved" leader. Oddly enough, Eddy's leadership was never more evident than in her dismantling of the organization she had built during the 1880s. Even as she "disorganized" the old church, Eddy took decisive steps to build on a new basis.

In 1877, Mary married Asa Gilbert Eddy who died 5 years later from an organic heart disease. After this death of her third husband, a student of hers and a successful practitioner of Christian Science spiritual healing, Mary carried on the propagation of Christian Science alone. In the years before her death she secluded herself from her followers, but continued to control the movement from her retirement home in Concord, New Hampshire. Peel (1971) commented on her retirement as follows:

> If an institution, as Emerson wrote, is the lengthened shadow of a man, Mrs. Eddy's shadow reached from Concord to Boston. The distance between the two cities symbolizes the separation between her private and public triumphs, but in one sense Boston was never more conscious of her presence than when she took refuge in Concord. (p. 294)

Mary Eddy died in 1910 of natural causes at the age of 89. Although Mary made no special provisions for a successor, the Christian Science movement continued to flourish and gain followers. However, despite her strong leadership, men dominated the movement after her death. Today, there over 3,500 branches of the Christian Science Church.

Few female leaders held such final authority in an organized religion as did Mary Baker Eddy. Her special role as the founder of Christian Science and church leader was unique because it allowed her to singularly dominate the movement during her lifetime. She tolerated no competition from other leaders, such as Augusta Stetson, one of her disciples, and who at one time was a rival for the leadership of Christian Science. After Stetson's excommunication from the mother church by Eddy in 1906, Stetson went on to found her own Christian Science movement (Stetson, 1913).

Mary Eddy was the spiritual leader of a Christian movement that under her leadership became a wealthy and respected middle-class church. Despite her lifelong struggle with spinal problems and other ailments, Mary was a strong woman who was convinced that she could and should govern the church. Out of her self-confidence, she insisted that her ideas about formal religion and the structure of the Christian Science Church presented no barriers to women practitioners (Ruether & McLaughlin, 1981). Like other female leaders of sectarian Christian movements, she was a charismatic and authoritarian woman who commanded absolute loyalty of her followers. Although not active in the suffrage movement, Mary also continually defended women's political and educational rights (Eddy, 1894).

Joan of Arc and Mary Baker Eddy were two truly remarkable women leaders in history. In both cases their leadership was fueled by a faith that helped them prevail over austere upbringing and debilitating illnesses. Both women also illustrate, as noted in Chapter 1, that leaders often are effective in more than one context. Joan of Arc was both a religious and a military leader, while Eddy led in a religious context and was also a shrewd business manager. Both women served as an example and inspiration to people regardless of their religious beliefs.

WOMEN LEADERS IN POLITICAL CONTEXTS

Historically, women often rose to positions of political leadership because they inherited tribes, states, kingdoms, or monarchies. In such cases, the legitimacy and entitlement of the woman occupying the leadership position was largely a function of legal inheritance, rather than the result of a personal quest or compelling vision to shape her state or nation. Since prehistoric times tribal kingdoms and monarchies followed the law that if a king died without sons, his oldest daughter succeeded to the throne. Cleopatra (69–30 B.C.), for example, took over the throne of Egypt which was left by her father, Ptolemy XII, to his two oldest children, Cleopatra and Ptolemy Dionysus whom she disposed of to seize the throne.

Historically, male-dominated societies were willing to accept female monarchs and rulers who came to power by succession. But more often, men have been reluctant to regard women as equals and give female leaders credit for their accomplishments. Today, dynasties are no longer found in political parties, but instead in families such as the Kennedys of Massachusetts or the Browns of California.

Throughout history, a number of women leaders have stood out in this context. Theodora (508–548), co-ruler of the Byzantine empire when Constantinople was a great mercantile center, completely dominated her husband, Emperor Justinian. Despite her deliberately sensational depiction by Procopius as a raging nymphomaniac (in his *Secret History*), Theodora was a woman with considerable insight into the political realities of her time. Although history has gloated over her sins, she was recognized for her courage, intelligence, and her ability to inspire genuine devotion in friends and followers.

Eleanor of Aquitaine (1122–1204) was a medieval queen of great influence and wealth who caused Louis VII's defeat in the Crusades. Isabella of Castile (1451–1504), co-ruler with Ferdinand of Aragon, personified the absolute monarch. Although she was illegitimate, her father Henry IV had acknowledged her as his heir, since he had no sons. Isabella played a significant role in reforming the clergy of Spain and expelling the Moors from their last Spanish bastion in Granada. In addition, she financed Christopher Columbus' expedition to the New World and brought Spain into the Renaissance. A deeply religious woman, Isabella has also been described as a "great general and even greater quartermaster" (Frazier, 1989). Her establishment of the Spanish Inquisition and her ruthlessness on behalf of a misguided vision of a "glorious, united, Christian Spain" is widely recognized by historians (Boulding, 1992).

Catherine the Great of Russia (1729–1796) was determined even as a young girl to rule an empire. She ambitiously planned her marriage to Karl Ulrich of Holstein, grandson of Peter the Great and heir to the Russian throne, and endured 18 years of silent humiliation under the rule of the Russian Empress Elizabeth before she was proclaimed empress in 1792. Nevertheless, from the first day she arrived in Russia from her native Germany, Catherine sensed that her only salvation lay in a constant effort to become naturalized. She identified with her new country politically and religiously and became fluent in Russian. Known to her admiring correspondent Voltaire as the Semiramis of the North, Catherine built a large empire, centralized power, unified and expanded territorial Russia, and acted as the spokesperson of Russian nationalism.

Boulding (1992) pointed out that each of the great women monarchs who ruled in the middle centuries of the second millennium had extraordinary levels of physical energy and moral courage. Moreover, they were of above-average intelligence and had a superb education in many subjects, including the study of languages, philosophy, and the arts; this was unusual for women of their times. Many of them lived their adolescence in insecurity and fear for their lives. They were, as we will see in Chapter 4, twice-born leaders.

In more recent times, Golda Meir (1898–1978) was the second woman prime minister (Indira Gandhi of India was first) to become head of state. Previously she had filled several political appointments, including first ambassador of the new state of Israel to Moscow, minister of labor and social security during the Ben-Gurion administration, and foreign minister of Israel. Meir rose to power and position not through hereditary privilege, but through her proven political savvy and acumen.

PORTRAITS OF POLITICAL LEADERS

Elizabeth I of England (1533–1603)

Elizabeth I was not only head of state, but as such, also head of the Church of England. She was the daughter of Henry VIII and his second wife, Anne Boleyn, who was beheaded on her husband's orders. As one of Elizabeth's biographers, Haigh (1988) has suggested, Elizabeth must have learned from her mother's fate that a woman in politics was at risk from emotional entanglements. She believed that a ruler of England, especially a female monarch, could easily be made a tool of court intrigues. She learned this not only from her mother's experience but also from her own ordeals.

For example, when her sister Mary I, aptly named Bloody Mary, was Queen, Elizabeth was sent to the Tower of London on suspicion of plotting to dethrone her sister and was imprisoned for 4 years. Every day of her imprisonment she faced the possibility of execution, since she posed a political and religious threat to Mary. Mary was a devout Catholic while Elizabeth publicly had aligned herself with Protestantism and preferred the Anglican hierarchy, with the throne at its head. When Mary died in 1556, Elizabeth ascended to the throne.

The dangers and hardships Elizabeth experienced taught her the skills she would need to rule her country: self-interest, deceit, patience, and diplomacy. Throughout her life, her political skills as a Tudor monarch would be tested because her gender raised major difficulties in a patriarchal society where there was no ideological basis for female authority (Haigh, 1988). According to Haigh, Elizabeth was confronted with three persistent gender-related problems: 1) gender complicated the problem of succession, because it was hard to find a father for her child without finding a husband for herself; 2) gender complicated her dealings with politicians and councilors, whom she had to convince of her profound knowledge and understanding of political, religious, and military affairs; and 3) gender complicated her relationship with her subjects, for she had to find an image of a monarch that was appropriate for a woman, yet at the same time promote obedience.

From the beginning of her reign, Elizabeth managed domestic and foreign politics very shrewdly. In an age of religious strife, characterized by plots and counterplots, Elizabeth's political strategy was to surround herself with experienced men. She met with her councilors in small groups and formed political, religious, and military alliances to advise her on the affairs of the state and the church. She never approached a political or religious crisis without studying the issue extensively, nor adopted a policy without consulting with each of her advisors individually. Yet she exercised an almost absolute authority over Parliament. Her approach to foreign policy was aimed at preventing Catholic hegemony both at home and abroad. Her foreign policy was reflected, for example, in a series of military maneuvers during which she used every card in her hand to avoid military conflict in the Netherlands. Here Protestant rebels were locked in conflict with the overlordship of Catholic Spain. After the defeat of the Spanish Armada which threatened to invade England in 1558, Elizabeth reviewed her army and, looking splendid on horseback, made the following speech to her troops:

> My loving people, we have been persuaded by some that are careful of our safety to take heed how we commit ourselves to armed multitudes, for fear of treachery. But I assure you, I do not desire to live in distrust of my faithful and loving people. Let tyrants fear. I have always so behaved myself that, under God, I have placed my chiefest strength and safeguard in the loyal hearts and good will of my subjects; and therefore I come amongst you, as you see, at this time, not for my recreation and disport, but being resolved, in the midst and heat of the battle, to live and die amongst you all, to lay down for my God, and for my kingdom, and for my people, my honor and my blood, even in the dust. I know I have the body of a weak and feeble woman, but I have the heart and the stomach of a king, and a king of England too, and think foul scorn that Parma or Spain, or any prince of Europe should dare to invade the borders of my realm; to which, rather than any dishonour shall grow by me, I myself will take up arms. I myself will be your general, judge, and rewarder of every one of your virtues in this field. I know, already for your forwardness you have deserved rewards and crowns; and we do assure you, in the words of a prince, they shall be duly paid to you. (Adair, 1989, p. 250)

Elizabeth maintained an aura of personal mystique that has had few parallels in history. Part of this mystique stemmed from the fact that she never married, since she refused to share power with a husband who would have seriously interfered with her omnipotence. Her subjects called her the Virgin Queen, a label she never denied. Elizabeth believed that she was endowed with special abilities such as courage and determination because she was God's instrument. To be His instrument, God must have made her as good as any man. According to Haigh (1988) as a virgin wife and mother, daughter of Henry VIII, instrument of God, and with the courage of a king, Elizabeth had risen above the limitations of her sex (i.e., the subservient wife and mother). As an unmarried female ruler,

Elizabeth contradicted the Tudor image of women and struggled all her life with the conventional ideal of womanhood. Nevertheless, she was a shining example of womanly virtues. These womanly virtues, combined with her sense of destiny and consciousness of divine favor, gave her the strength to beat the patriarchal system of her time (Haigh, 1988).

During her reign, Elizabeth I built a strong political power base which made England a premier world power. She enforced religious conformity because she believed that religious dissenters would weaken not only her position, but that of her country as well. Furthermore, she presided over an economically prosperous era and a flourishing culture. William Shakespeare, Edmund Spenser, Christopher Marlowe, and Francis Bacon were some of the intellectual and creative talents of her time, as was explorer Francis Drake. However, for all her political skills, extent of learning and religious conviction, Elizabeth I, like Isabella of Spain, displayed a ruthlessness which is part of the image that has come across the centuries (Boulding, 1992). For example, in 1587 she signed the death warrant for her Catholic half-sister, Mary, Queen of Scots, who challenged the authority of the Anglican Church and was beheaded for treason. During much of her rule, Elizabeth used the church as a political instrument. Although she was losing the devotion of her subjects toward the end of her reign, when war and failure abroad and poverty at home beset her regime, she was a popular and pragmatic monarch who led in an era named in her honor.

Catherine Breshkovsky (1844–1934)

Ekaterina Konstantinova Breshko-Breshkovskaya was the product of Russian nobility (her father) and Polish aristocracy (her mother). She was born in 1844, the year when Czar Nicholas I, the autocrat of all the Russian czars, was enthroned. While other girls of her social class went to "silly soirees," Catherine, or Katya, as she was called, preferred to read Voltaire, Rousseau, and Diderot and buried herself in the study of the French and German revolutions. Although her father treated their serfs with much more consideration than did most Russian landowners, Catherine, filled with young enthusiasm, favored the emancipation of the serfs. She began to think about reforms to ameliorate the inequality between the rich and the poor, and was convinced that revolution in Russia was imminent.

When she was 17, an edict was signed by Czar Alexander II which granted the 40 million Russian peasants freedom from serfdom. However, the so-called liberation of the serfs meant complete starvation in freedom instead of semi-starvation in bondage, since the government had driven the serfs off the land to which they had been tied. Under the old regime, the serfs had to cultivate their masters' estates, but were given a plot of ground on which they raised food for their own families. Now landlords ordered the serfs off their land, leaving them free but starving. Those who refused the Czar's order were lined up in the villages for flogging, first every tenth man, then every fifth man, and finally every woman, man, and child who remained on the land.

After her marriage to Count Breshkovsky, Catherine became increasingly interested in reform. While she was pregnant, she informed her husband that she had chosen to dedicate herself to a life of hardship and struggle for Russian freedom and justice. She knew that she could not be both a mother and a revolutionist. Therefore, she went to Kiev to stay with her widowed sister, with whom she left her son after he was born, and she joined a revolutionary group. One of the first Russian radical women, Catherine recalled the atmosphere of shock she produced, around 1870, by speaking out against the opinions of her male comrades (Breshko-Breshkovskaya, 1931).

In the summer of 1874, she began to put her ideas into practice. Together with two other socialist compatriots, she set out to launch the Russian Revolution. The trio traveled from town to town promoting Catherine's dream of a free Russia by sharing their ideas with peasants, reading to them, and distributing revolutionary pamphlets. Usually they traveled in disguise with false passports and took up quarters with peasants in the towns and provinces. When pressed by the police, Catherine could change herself at will into an old peasant woman.

Eventually gendarmes arrested her for her political activities and took her to the "black hole," a local prison. For the 2 years she was shuttled from one Russian prison to another, and then sent off into exile to a Siberia camp in Kara. However, instead of hard labor, she had to endure the even harder punishment of compulsory idleness. Later authorities transferred Breshkovsky to a bleak outpost in the Arctic Circle of Siberia, close to the Chinese border. In spite of all the hardships she endured in exile, nothing could break her spirit. She wrote, "I was never disillusioned; even as a child I learned from the biographies of great men that inspiration toward high ideals always leads to cruel penalties" (Marlow, 1979, p. 139).

Released from Siberia in 1896, Catherine returned to Russia to find her parents and husband dead and her son, educated in the ideas of the aristocracy, unsympathetic to his mother's revolutionary ideals. She went back to her revolutionary work and helped to found the People's Social Revolutionary Party. Baboushka, or the Little Mother, resumed her travels through the Russian provinces fighting for her dream of a free Russia. Her visit to America in 1904 was part of an effort "to enlist the sympathy of the world in the cause of a free Russia." She returned to Russia and to another term of exile in Siberia. In 1909, at the age of 65, the "stubborn little troublemaker" was sentenced to life imprisonment in Siberia where she spent the next 7 years "kept like a salted herring in a hogshead." On March 2, 1917, Catherine received a telegram announcing freedom: "Russia is free. Come home, baboushka" (Marlow, 1979, p. 140).

One of the first acts of the Russian provisional government was to declare an amnesty to all political prisoners and exiles. Together with her fellow political prisoners Catherine was transported from Siberia to Moscow, where leaders of the Kerensky government greeted her and celebrated her as a heroine. She paraded through the streets of Moscow in the gilded state coach of the former czar and received triumphant ovations. After Catherine was chosen a member of the Preliminary Parliament of Russia, she threw herself into her work, warning the Bolshevik government against peace with Germany. The little grandmother of the Russian Revolution saw the fulfillment of her dream. She spent her remaining years in voluntary exile in Prague where, at the age of 76, she opened a school for poor children (Thomas & Thomas, 1942).

Catherine Breshkovsky inspired the Russian Revolution and had undoubting faith in the righteousness of the cause. No price was too high to pay for her to see a free Russia. She spent 32 years in prison in Siberia, mostly in idleness. However, during her underground years between imprisonments, she frantically worked with revolutionary groups on the struggle for freedom. In her letters to Alice Stone Blackwell, she stated that her "greatest treasure was the infinite love for the people." Her whole life fulfilled the words she once wrote to an American friend:

> We ought to elevate the people's psychology by our own example, and give them the idea of a purer life by making them acquainted with better morals and higher ideals; to call out their best feelings and strongest principles. We ought to tell the truth, not fearing to displease our hearers; and be always ready to confirm our words by our deeds. (Stone Blackwell, 1917, pp. 329–330)

The women leaders discussed in the next section primarily defined themselves as political activists, but also played political roles in the social movements they led.

WOMEN LEADERS IN THE CONTEXT OF SOCIAL MOVEMENTS

Historically, most women leaders appeared in the political and religious contexts. Although women's organized efforts date back to the mid-1800s, it was not until the late 19th century that women began to emerge as leaders in social movements in larger numbers. During the 1800s and 1900s, known to historians as transition centuries, women formed alliance structures to share their social perception on common goals. After the Civil War, America saw the beginnings of a massive effort to win rights for women in politics, the legal and educational systems, church hierarchies, and professional employment. Women of the time who stood out for their leadership supported a decentralized, democratic, mass education, non-elite approach to revolution (Boulding, 1992). They demanded equal right to education and/or equal access to higher education, better property and inheritance laws, better marriage and easier divorce laws, vocational training, and better employment. They also sought work protection laws, economic rights including the right to unionize, and more civil rights, primarily the right to vote and the extension of full citizenship to women (Forfreedom, 1972).

Many of the women who led the way in the social reform movements, such as Florence Nightingale and Harriet Tubman, believed that they received a direct call from God to enter His service. Several of them also had a talent for prophecy. Harriet Tubman, for instance, reportedly foresaw the outcome of the Civil War in a dream several years before Fort Sumter was fired upon. As Ruether and Keller (1979) noted, many reforms pioneered by women began under religious auspices spurred by religious currents which provided a climate hospitable to social reform. Moreover, women were increasingly drawn into the newly developing field of social work. Through the various social reform movements—the women's suffrage, and abolitionist movements—women gained an increased sense of power and self-assurance. For decades they practiced the skills of fundraising, speaking in public, petitioning governmental bodies, managing their own reform institutions, editing and publishing papers devoted to reform issues, and writing articles, books, and memorials to legislatures and congressional bodies (De Swarte Gifford, 1981).

Social movements are one of the major vehicles for social change and have produced many colorful and charismatic leaders. Weed (1993) noted a leadership paradox in the history of social movements:

Social movements are by their nature a challenge to the conventional practices and institutional patterns in society. Frequently it is the individual with charismatic qualities of a strong sense of a moral mission, emotional appeal, self-confidence, and a willingness to ignore social conventions who becomes the leader of a social movement . . . The leadership qualities so important in creating a demand for reform and establishing an organization are not the leadership qualities that are conducive to sustaining an established organization. (p. 331)

Social reform movements have produced numerous outstanding examples of women (and men) who stood out for their leadership abilities and competencies. Pioneer feminists Susan B. Anthony (1820–1906) and Elizabeth Cady Stanton (1815–1902), who spearheaded the American suffrage movement, were models of grass-roots leadership. Susan B. Anthony became the driving force of the women's movement. She brought an extraordinary political acumen and deft organizational skills to an amorphous assemblage of liberals, radicals, libertarians, and reformers who rejected formal leadership. Florence Nightingale (1820–1910) renounced her affluent upbringing and refused a brilliant marriage to make a career of nursing, previously the domain of prostitutes, and transform it into a noble and reputable profession. Instead of accepting the comfortable and safe life, she decided to diverge from the conventional path of a woman of her upbringing and mystified and shocked her contemporaries by choosing to walk the grim corridors of army hospitals half a world away (Polster, 1992). A woman of iron discipline and great compassion for the conditions of the poor and the suffering, she became a highly efficient, take-charge administrator and great change agent—reforming army medical services, hospitals, and nursing education and instigating scientific, statistical methods in hospital management.

Many other women took leadership in the social reform movements. Dorothea Dix (1802–1887), mental health pioneer, teacher, writer, and religious poet, promoted human treatment for the mentally ill and criminally insane. In the United States as well as in Europe, Dix was recognized as the leading authority on mental illness. Eleanor Roosevelt (1884–1962), who revolutionized the role of women in American politics and government, was the first president's wife to pursue an independent career in public service. She supported the causes of women as well as blacks, and actively pursued issues of reform, education, the eradication of poverty and other controversial social issues. On the international scene, Rosa Luxemburg (1871–1918) was a towering figure in the socialist movement. Among the best revolutionary thinkers of her generation, Rosa fought for more democratic participation of the masses. She rose to international fame on the strength of her ideas about the revolutionary power of the proletariat and the forcefulness of her presentation of these ideas. These women, along with countless others, were inspirational leaders who, like Joan of Arc, were unshaken in their commitments to their beliefs and causes.

PORTRAITS OF SOCIAL MOVEMENT LEADERS

Harriet Tubman (1820?–1913)

Harriet Tubman, called the Moses of her people, was born a slave on the Brodas plantation in Maryland. Her parents, who were hard-working people with an exceptionally strong and loving relationship, provided their 11 children with care and affection. Harriet spent the first third of her long life in slavery. During these formative years, her family and her faith in God were the most powerful influences. According to Scruggs (1975), Harriet regarded the Divine Presence as a close friend, talking with God "as a man talketh with his friend." Bradford (1961/1897) noted that Tubman, rather than keeping a set time for prayers, preferred to share her problems with God as they arose. Her faith provided the moral basis for her yearning to be free.

When she was 15, she tried to stop the beating of a runaway slave and an overseer hurled an iron weight at her. The blow crushed her skull and left her delirious for 2 months. Harriet lingered near death for months reciting prayers for "the poor old master's conversion to a man of heart and Christianity" (Nies, 1977, p. 39). The injury marred her appearance and for the rest of her life she suffered periodic fainting spells, narcoleptic episodes, and other aftereffects.

However, the experience also liberated her and became the turning point of her life. After her mother nursed her back to health, Harriet worked in the fields, since she was not much good at domestic work. From this heavy physical labor, plowing, splitting timber, driving oxen, she developed stamina, endurance, and muscle strength which had beneficial effects on her health. When her master died in 1849 and the fortunes of the Brodas plantation began to go downhill, she begged her husband to run away to the North with her, but he refused. Of her escape north as a fugitive slave, a daring move from which her brothers turned back, she said to Sarah Bradford, her close friend and first biographer (Bradford, a white woman from Harriet's hometown, reproduced her dialect in Tubman's biography):

> I reasoned dis out in my mind: there was one of two things I had a *right* to, liberty or death. If I could not have one, I would have de oder, for no man should take me alive. I should fight for my liberty as my strength lasted and when de time came for me to go, de Lord would let dem take me. (Bradford, 1897/1961, p. 29)

Harriet escaped by herself and made her way to Pennsylvania, where she arrived in 1849. Once free, she resolved to go back for her family and help other slaves to gain their freedom. She became a "conductor" on the Underground Railroad—the term used to describe an organized network of people who helped thousands of slaves flee from the South to the free North and Canada. Hoover (1968) described the Underground Railroad with its legendary trappings: secret doors and rooms, code signals, and the grapevine telegraph. It was a mysterious organization with main lines and branches that stretched like a vast network over the country from the Mississippi to the coast. In actuality, however, the Underground Railroad was more like a guerilla operation, since leading slaves out of the South was essentially a military function.

Reportedly, Harriet Tubman returned 19 times to the South to lead emancipation expeditions which helped some 300 slaves escape. She was never captured, nor did she lose a single "passenger." Her contemporaries called her "Moses," the redeemer of her people from the Egypt-land of the South (Petry, 1955) because she used the songs of escape from Egypt as part of her signal system. She led the slaves in the hymn, "Go down Moses/Go down to the promised land" when she was conducting her sorties. Tubman's rescue expeditions made her a legend in the North. In the South, a $40,000 reward was posted for her arrest, probably the highest price placed on a woman's head in history.

In 1858, Harriet collaborated with John Brown, who addressed her as "General Tubman" in planning his raid on Harper's Ferry. It was inevitable that she and John Brown should meet, since both shared a messianic vision and both preferred action over words in the war against slavery. Their relationship was a fraternity, a brotherhood of doing (Woodward, 1953). At the time, Brown was preparing for a slave conspiracy and Tubman became an active recruiter for him. However, when Brown finally struck at Harper's Ferry in October, 1859, Tubman was ill in Massachusetts. She had a premonition that "Captain Brown was in trouble" (Nies, 1977, p. 48). And indeed he was. The day after the raid Brown and most of his men were arrested and Brown was later executed.

Harriet's resistance to slavery did not end with the outbreak of the Civil War. Governor Andrew of Massachusetts, an ardent abolitionist, asked her to serve in the Union army. She became an unofficial spy, scout, intelligence agent, and nurse for the Union army during the Civil War. She led many successful reconnaissance missions disguised as an old, hobbling woman, and was never suspected of being a Union spy. The skills that made her a highly successful conductor on the Underground Railroad also proved useful during the Civil War in military intelligence, reconnaissance, and medical support.

In 1864 she left the Union Army and went to her home in Auburn, New York. Ironically, it was on her way back home that she received the most cruel blow of her life when she was rejected from riding in a "for whites only" train. In Auburn, she opened a house for needy and elderly blacks and named the home after John Brown, whom she considered the quintessential symbol of freedom. This dream of her later life was finally realized in 1908 when the Harriet Tubman House was opened, a tribute to the energy and efforts of an 89-year-old woman (Conrad, 1943). To the end of her life, Harriet championed the rights of the oppressed. She belonged to the suffrage organization headed by Susan B. Anthony and Elizabeth Cady Stanton and often shared the speaker's platform with them. Although the struggle for female emancipation did not have the same urgency for Tubman as the struggle for black emancipation, she knew that blacks could not be really free while a large female population remained less than full, participative citizens.

Harriet Tubman was a heroine and leading figure in black history. She was eloquent in speech and song, although she could neither read nor write. Born a slave, she died a free woman who became the leader of her people. She escaped and could have lived on with her individual victory. But she went back to Southern plantations to lead caravans up north to freedom. By doing so, she accomplished more for the cause of black liberation than any other single individual. Scruggs (1975) wrote:

More than anything else, Tubman brought out of the slave community the will to resist all limitations on the rights of individuals to control their own destiny. To supporters of women's rights she became the symbol of woman freed from the restrictions of a male dominated society. To black people she symbolized the strength, patience, and faith of the generations of unsung black women who in their less dramatic but equally dedicated way overcame the obstacles of color and sex. Harriet Tubman spoke for them—indeed, for all the powerless—by her deeds and in her determination to be dealt with as a moral individual. (p. 121)

According to Wills (1994) the combination of qualities that made Tubman formidable were her mystical resignation to the form of liberation God would grant her, the certitude that she would be liberated in any case, and the ferocious reliance on her own strength to make one of the two forms of liberation happen here and now. Her behavior was bold and courageous, driven by the single-mindedness of her mission. Her success on the Underground Railroad as a rescuer of slaves, her support of John Brown's raid on Harper's Ferry, and her work with the Union Army in the South made her a central figure in the events which led to the Emancipation Proclamation in 1863. She was one of those rare cases where the legend—for she became transformed into Moses, Joan of Arc, and John Henry, all rolled into one dark body—far from exaggerating, scarcely caught up with the known facts (Bradford, 1897/1961). Polster (1992) summarized Tubman's role and accomplishments as a leader as follows:

Harriet Tubman is an excellent representative of the magnetism of kin-ship. She has been called the Moses of her people for bringing them out of slavery. She had escaped, and she could have lived on with her individual victory. But she went back again and again in disguise to Southern plantations to lead caravans of escaped slaves north to freedom. (p. 33)

Alice Paul (1885–1977)

A discussion of historical women leaders would be incomplete without a brief consideration of Alice Paul, who has been called the single truly charismatic figure in the 20th-century suffrage movement (Stevens, 1920). Many women provided leadership for the movement, including Susan B. Anthony, Elizabeth Cady Stanton, Lucy Burns, and Emily Pankhurst, but Alice Paul was the engine that powered the militant suffrage movement:

She has in the first place, a devotion to the cause which is absolutely self-sacrificing. She has indomitable will . . . She has a clear, penetrating, analytic mind which cleaves straight to the heart of things. She is a genius for organization, both in the mass and in detail. (Irwin, 1921, p. 31).

Irwin (1964) argued that when Max Weber wrote *The Sociology of Religion* in 1922, he might have used Alice Paul as his model in developing the concept of a charismatic leader. Such a person, Weber said, challenged the established order in ways both constructive and destructive, established boundaries by drawing on legitimacy from sources within him or herself, and disregarded public opinion (Weber, 1965). This, according to Irwin (1964), applied to Paul. When faced with a law or convention or law that, if observed, would have nullified a particular plan of action, Paul just commented on the "absurdity" of the existing situation (Irwin, 1964, p. 26).

Alice Paul, borrowing from the British, brought a militant strategy to the suffrage movement when it was at a standstill. By the time she arrived at the scene in 1912, the suffrage movement had lost its urgency and excitement. Susan B. Anthony and Elizabeth Cady Stanton were no longer active in the movement. Paul took over the reins of the National American Women Suffrage Association's (NAWSA) Congressional Committee and used the association as a forum for publicity to generate visibility for the movement. From the moment Paul assumed command of the Committee, she knew that the focus of its effort had to be the federal government, if the suffrage movement was going to succeed.

In 1919 she broke away from NAWSA and founded the National Women's Party. In 1923 Paul introduced the Equal Rights Amendment (ERA) which by 1944 had become a plank within the American presidential campaigns of both major parties. A Washington reporter noted:

> Every other woman in Washington I can imagine without a cause . . .
> Even over teacups I think of [Paul] as a political force, a will bound to express itself politically . . . I remember a long talk we had in 1921 when she was searching her mind for the next plan to advance the freedom of women. She was overwhelmed by the setting up of the League of Nations, which she regarded as a close corporation for deciding the fate of women and of the people. She burned with disgust for the inconsequential part women played in international politics. (Evans, 1924, p. 514)

For the rest of her life, Paul devoted herself to women's rights, and promoted the cause of women until she suffered a stroke in 1974. She was an absolute fanatic and nothing could shake her convictions. Paul lived to see the United States Congress pass an ERA amendment, but ratification was not won. Although Paul's ambition has yet to be realized, she did, by her unrelenting efforts, make equal rights a paramount political, social, and economic issue within her party and across her country (Lunardini, 1969).

Contexts such as religious, political, and social movements provide continuity for the analysis of women leaders, both past and present. In addition, among historical and contemporary female leaders, we find women (and many more men) who abused their leadership positions and power, committed mind crimes, or crimes of leadership, or implemented political or social policies divorced from moral principle that threatened to de-moralize their followers. Across the ages and cultures, people have been fascinated by the perversity of the misdeed, by the excitement of chaos, by the intellectual puzzle of who did it, how they got away with it, and how they were caught (Albrecht, Werns, & Williams, 1995). Cleopatra, for example, illustrates the dark side of leadership, because she primarily pursued her self-interests as Queen of Alexandria and produced largely negative outcomes for her followers. She fought wars designed not so much to expand the Egyptian empire, but rather to enhance her personal powers.

Some historians have called Cleopatra the wickedest woman in history, a sexual glutton, a politically decadent foreigner, and a consummate actress. Her relationships with Caesar and Antony were manipulative and calculating, motivated by ambition more than love. To some, Cleopatra was best known for her greed for territory, which drove her to undermine Antony's Persian expedition and prompted her to send the Egyptian fleet to Actium in 31 B.C. to meet the Roman ships. Even after Egypt became a Roman province after the battle of Actium, in Alexandria Cleopatra was beloved and revered, leading Anatole France to conclude that she could not have been as wicked as her enemies declared her.

CONCLUSIONS

Historical women leaders have been celebrated in biographies, novels, painting, poetry, music, and other forms of art. They have been folk heroines, priestesses, monarchs, rulers, church leaders, mistresses, and deviants. Historical periods provide a unique context for studying women leaders because leaders, like all of us, invariably are prisoners of their time (see Table 2.1).

What do the women leaders throughout history tell us about women? According to Boulding (1992) they proved that:

> Women could act on political goals, cultural values and prevailing religions as effectively as—or possibly more effectively than—men, given a chance to draw on all the resources a society has to offer. Their intellectual and social repertoire was a bit wider, perhaps, than that of most men. And in no way did they represent a feminine counterculture of nonmilitarism. They used the conventional sociopolitical tools that men used and more; they worked with the values available to them. (p. 100)

The historical leaders described in this chapter were truly extraordinary women. Yet in many cases, to paraphrase a Zen koan, a woman leader remains a woman first, regardless of how effectively she exercises leadership. She will be judged as a woman first, and her gender is often blamed if her leadership is less than effective. In that sense, little has changed since the dawn of civilization. Regardless of the roles women played in history as political, religious, social, intellectual, military, educational, and creative leaders, they were mostly viewed as exceptions. It is up to contemporary women leaders and the next generation of female leaders to redefine leadership for historians of the future. In Chapter 8 we will extend this discussion to contemporary women who are leaders and change agents in different contexts in our own as well as other cultures.

Table 2.1   Chronology of Selected Women Leaders in History

Leader	Context	Role	Leadership Accomplishments
Semiramis 810 BC	Political	Queen of Babylon	Rebuilding of Babylon after Assyrian rule; creation of Hanging Gardens, one of the seven wonders of the ancient world
Aspasia 450 BC	Community	Companion of Pericles	Enhancement of civic life; education of Athenian housewives; creation of literary and philosophical society in Athens during Golden Age of Greece
Olympia 440 BC	Political	Wife of Philip, ruler of Macedonia	Significant influence on husband's war against Persia; preparation of Alexander the Great for world leadership; ruled Macedonia after the death of Alexander the Great
Cleopatra 69–30 BC	Political	Queen of Egypt	Alignment of Caesar and Mark Antony for personal political agenda
Boudicca 1st century AD	Political	Revolutionary	Rebellion against Roman army to break Roman rule over Britain

Table 2.1 *Continued*

Leader	Context	Role	Leadership Accomplishments
Theodora 508–548	Political	Byzantine empress; co-ruler with Justinian	Expansion of Byzantine empire; restoration of power in Africa; instrumental in development of religious policies
Eleanor of Aquitaine 1122–1204	Political	Monarch	Defeat of Louis VII in the Crusades
Joan of Arc 1412–1431	Religious; political; military	Reformer; revolutionary	Reformation of Catholic church; liberation of France from English domination; restoration of French monarchy
Teresa of Avila 1515–1582	Religious	Spanish mystic	Reformation of Carmelite order; foundation of convents; spiritual writings
Isabella of Castille 1451–1504	Religious; political; military	Spanish monarch; co-ruler with Ferdinand of Aragon	Reformation of Spanish clergy; financing of Columbus' expedition to New World
Elizabeth I of England 1533–1603	Political; religious; military	English monarch	Elevation of England to world power; head of English church; defeat of Spanish Armada
Catherine the Great 1729–1796	Political	Russian monarch	Expansion of Russian territories; promotion of Russian nationalism
Dorothea Dix 1802–1887	Social movement	Mental health pioneer	Promotion of humane treatment of mentally ill and criminally insane
Susan B. Anthony 1820–1906	Social movement	Pioneer of feminist movement	Spearheading of American suffrage movement; driving force of women's suffrage

Table 2.1 *Continued*

Leader	Context	Role	Leadership Accomplishments
Florence Nightingale 1820–1910	Social movement	Reformer of nursing profession	Reformation of medical and hospital management
Harriet Tubman 1820–1913	Social movement; military	Leader in Underground Railroad; abolutionist	Setting slaves free; work with Union army in South
Catherine Breshkovky 1844–1944	Political	Political activist	Launched Russian Revolution
Rosa Luxemburg 1871–1919	Social movement; political	Revolutionary	Collaboration in creation of Communist Party; advocate of democratic participation of masses in political process
Eleanor Roosevelt 1884–1962	Social movements; political	Social activist	Social housekeeping; work for working-class women, Afro-Americans, and politically oppressed; social justice
Alice Paul 1885–1977	Political	Militant suffrage	Leader of American Women's Suffrage Association; founder of National Women's Party; introduction of Equal Rights Amendment

Contemporary Leadership Theories: The Conceptual Thicket

> If we could first know where we are and
> whither we are tending, we could better judge
> what to do and how to do it.
>
> *Abraham Lincoln*

INTRODUCTION

Much has been written concerning the what, when, why, how, and who of leadership, since every situation in which leadership occurs is a combination of at least five variables: the leader, his or her followers, the time, the place, and the circumstances. The strong tendency to explain both effective and ineffective leadership stems from the asuumption that many of us make, namely that organizational outcomes, both success and failure, are attributable to leadership. Thus, we are assigning causality to leadership based on the notion that leaders are in control of the organizations they lead.

Developing and testing theories of leadership consumes a large portion of the leadership literature. Neophytes and experts in leadership studies alike are struck by two basic observations: 1) the multitude of theoretical approaches, and 2) the consistency of inconsistencies across theories. Among the many existing perspectives are trait and contingency theories, leader-member exchange theories, normative decisionmaking theories of leadership, multiple linkage models, and stratified systems theory, to name a few. Even a cursory scanning of contemporary leadership theories, many of which have evolved during the past 50 years, leaves the reader in a state of helplessness and dismay. McCall and Lombardo (1978) expressed their frustration with the continuous proliferation of leadership theories when they stated:

> We need to rediscover the phenomena of leadership; the pursuit of rigor
> and precision has led to an overemphasis on techniques at the expense

of what is going on in a direct human way. As a result, we have masses
of findings that no one seems to be able to pull together—they simply
float around in the literature, providing nothing from which one can
push off to anywhere. (p. xii)

The authors go on to say that:

Already besieged by literally thousands of articles, books, pamphlets,
audio tapes, and films, students of leadership—academicians and practitioners alike—have no doubt discovered things: 1) the number of
unintegrated theories, prescriptions and conceptual schemes of leadership is mind-boggling; 2) much of the [leadership] literature is fragmen-
tary, trivial, unrealistic or dull: 3) the research results are characterized
by contradictions. (p. 3)

While this conclusion may appear overly pessimistic and is not always
supported by compelling evidence, a general disenchantment with the state of
leadership theories does permeate both the scientific and the practitioner community. Many of the existing leadership theories are built on two-dimensional
models, a practice which, as Rost (1991) observed, has become a major ritual.
Among these dichotomized approaches are initiating-structure-versus-consider-
ation, leadership-versus-management, transactional-versus-transformational leadership, structural-versus-functional theories, and content-versus-process
approaches. Obviously these two-dimensional models are oversimplified approxi-
mations of a complex and multifaceted phenomenon which cannot be adequately
captured by any set of bipolar dimensions.

The leadership theorist is not the only one disenchanted with the conceptual
thicket that characterizes the field of leadership theories. Practitioners who attempt
to put these theories to work for themselves also feel caught up in the jungle of
semantics. After all, theories are intended to provide guidance and direction for
the practice of leadership, following Kurt Lewin's (1951) famous dictum that
nothing is as practical as a good theory. The toolbox of the practitioner reflects
the lack of conceptual clarity of leadership theories and holds a wide array of
leadership programs, simulations, role-playing exercises, human relations training, programs for developing transformational leaders, "One-Minute-Managers,"
and whatever else the consumer market will bear at any given time.

Despite the plethora of past and present theories of leadership and the efforts
put forth by scholars and practitioners in the field, no universal theory has been
developed that would predict leader effectiveness across a wide range of tasks,
situations, organizations, and cultures. Many leadership theories, such as trait or
power and influence approaches, rest on a single underlying construct to explain
and predict a multidimensional phenomenon which is becoming increasingly
complex as workforce demographics and technologies diversify. Most of the

theories reviewed in this chapter assume that leaders and followers interact only face-to-face. However, this assumption is no longer tenable in a number of contemporary organizations where the nature of work has changed significantly as a result of new technologies. For example, industries such as airlines, insurance, and telephone companies often rely on computer-monitored performance evaluation, which greatly reduces the degree of face-to-face contact between subordinates and managers. In these settings, the "electronic supervisor," while not completely replacing the human manager, is partially executing a managerial function (see Chapter 4 for differences between leadership and management), namely the evaluation of subordinate performance (Klenke, 1991).

This chapter presents an overview of some of the major contemporary theories of leadership, along with some applications of these theories to real-life leaders or leadership situations. Theories of leadership, like their counterparts in other fields of inquiry, represent attempts to explain and/or predict the factors involved in the emergence of leadership and its effects, such as leadership effectiveness, follower performance and satisfaction. A popular way of grouping leadership theories is according to whether they focus on traits (most popular in the 1930s and 1940s), behaviors (the prevailing view of the 1950s), the situation (predominant in the 1970s), or some combination of the three. Underlying this rather simple classification system is a longstanding debate over whether leadership is produced by "great men/great women" (the person view of leadership) or "great times" (the situational view of leadership). Figure 3.1 presents an overview of the major contemporary leadership theories.

LEADERSHIP AS PERSONALITY: THE TRAIT APPROACH

> No amount of learning will make a man a leader unless
> he has the natural qualities of one.
> *Gerald Archibald Wavell*

The great men who shaped the character and direction of their eras historically were believed to consist of a rare and delicate mixture of hero, prince, and superman (Jennings, 1966). Early on in the study of leadership it was assumed that leaders possess certain physical and psychological traits that determined their rise to power and leadership positions. Also known as the "great man/great woman" theory of leadership, this perspective assumed that traits associated with effective leadership were inborn qualities.

According to House and Baetz (1990) a "trait" is defined as a distinctive physical or psychological characteristic of an individual to which her or his behavior may be attributed. Usually, traits are inferred from overt behavior, or from self-reported data provided by leaders and followers via interviews or

Great Man/Woman: Trait Approach

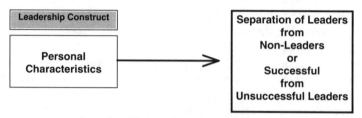

Leader Behavior Approaches

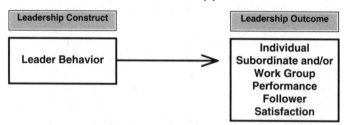

Contingency Approaches

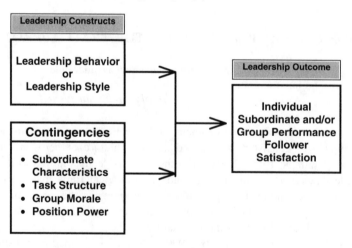

Figure 3.1 Overview of Theories of Leadership

questionnaires. Trait theorists adhere to the "leaders-are-born" school of thought, which is based on the premise that genes which determine traits such as height, dominance, and aggression are the driving forces which produce great leaders. Implicit in this point of view is the assumption that since the "right set of genes" is rarely found in the population in any great quantity, this rarity explains why there are so few leaders (Conger, 1992).

Three broad categories of traits have been identified in relation to leadership: 1) *physical traits*, such as height, weight, energy, and appearance; 2) *mental abilities*, such as intelligence; and 3) *personality traits*, including aggressiveness, extroversion, self-confidence, emotional control, and adaptability. For example, as early as 1915, it was found that religious leaders such as bishops were taller than their clergymen followers, and university presidents taller than college presidents. Similarly, the intangible element of self-confidence pointed out by Maslow (1954) is bolstered by the ability to look down on the world. Women have grown taller in the 20th century, but so have men. Therefore, Boulding (1992) concluded, the physical support for social equality continues to elude the female sex. In the 1984 presidential election, Democrats considered the height of their nominee—Geraldine Ferraro, 5'4", running for Vice President—to be a disadvantage against George Bush, who is over 6' tall. To avoid being looked down during the debate, the Democrats (over Republican objection) built a ramp behind the podium so that Ferraro would appear closer to Bush in height (Ferraro, 1985).

Dubin (1986) observed that leaders are persons with far-above-average energy levels. The author noted that he never encountered a lazy, lethargic, or lugubrious leader. However, he also made it clear that high-energy individuals are not necessarily leaders. He was only asserting that high levels of energy may be a characteristic that appears in a much higher than chance proportion in leaders. Because of the observed relationships between physical, mental, and personality characteristics, proponent of the "leaders-are-born" school of thought became preoccupied with measuring mental and personality traits by means of psychological testing procedures. They assumed that if an adequate battery of psychological tests could identify the cluster of personality and mental traits associated with leadership, they could make inferences regarding the causality of such traits (that is, propose that the presence of certain traits explains why certain individuals are leaders).

One of the first comprehensive reviews of the relationship between traits and leadership was conducted by Mann (1959). The author found that leaders tended to be more intelligent, extroverted, dominant, masculine, and taller than nonleaders. However, the author also reported contradictory evidence with respect to all of the traits studied, indicating that the possession of these traits does not guarantee leadership success. For example, successful salespeople are often described as extroverted, optimistic, energetic and enthusiastic; yet many women and men in sales do not display any of these traits or only one or two of them.

Stogdill (1948, 1974) conducted two classic reviews of the trait literature in an attempt to distinguish which traits would separate effective from ineffective leaders and leaders from followers. Although several of the traits examined appeared to be relevant for different kinds of leaders and were related to leadership effectiveness, Stogdill (1948) found that the results varied considerably from situation to situation, and did not produce a consistent constellation of traits which characterized most leaders. The author, therefore, concluded that "A person does not become a leader by virtue of the possession of some combination of traits . . . ; the pattern of personal characteristics of the leader must bear some relevant relationship to the characteristics, activities, and goals of the followers" (p. 64).

The later review (Stogdill, 1974), which covered the literature from 1949 to 1970, was somewhat more positive about the potential of personality traits in differentiating between leaders and nonleaders. In this review, Stogdill stated that:

> A leader is characterized by a strong drive for responsibility and task completion, vigor and persistence in pursuit of goals, venturesomeness and originality in problem solving, a drive to exercise initiative in social situations, self-confidence and sense of personal identity, willingness to accept consequences of decision and action, readiness to absorb interpersonal stress, willingness to tolerate frustration and delay, ability to influence other persons' behavior and capacity to structure social interaction systems to the purpose at hand. (Bass, 1981, p. 81)

From these findings, Stogdill concluded that personality is a factor in leadership differentiation, but insisted that this conclusion did not represent a return to the trait approach. Instead, Stogdill retained his views about the importance of the situation in the study of leadership, but attached greater significance to traits than in his earlier review. Summing up his position Stogdill stated:

> The reviews by Bird, Jenkins, and Stogdill have been cited as evidence in support of the view that leadership is entirely situational in origin and that no personal characteristics are predictive of leadership. This view seems to overemphasize the situational and underemphasize the personal nature of leadership. (1974, p. 72)

Stogdill's 1948 review has often been cited as a major reason for the disillusionment with the trait approach, although its author did not set out to debunk trait theory. One of the major reasons for the disappointing results of leader trait research is found in the methodologies employed in many of the trait studies. A great deal of this research was designed to determine who would emerge as the leader in leaderless groups. These groups were often artificially created in contrived settings, such as laboratories, or based on classroom observations and other environments with limited generalizability. The difficulty with this type of research is that the relevance of settings such as classrooms or experimental laboratories to real-life leadership situations is limited.

A second methodological problem common to many trait studies stems from the fact that much of this research is concerned with characteristics which distinguish effective from ineffective managers. As Yukl (1981) noted, between Stogdill's 1948 and 1974 reviews, both technical and administrative skills were added to the roster of leadership traits as the research shifted more to applied contexts. The "leaders" in applied industrial and military settings typically involved first-line supervisors, managers, or military officers at lower levels of the organization. For example, the American Telephone and Telegraph (AT&T) company in 1956 started a longitudinal study (Bray, Campbell, & Grant, 1974) designed to track the career progress of male employees who had been identified as potential candidates for managerial positions. The research evidence showed significant correlations between individual traits such as a need for advancement, energy, creativity and measures of managerial success. It is, however, debatable whether advancement to first- level supervisor or midlevel management is synonymous with leadership. Are leadership and managerial success the same? It is difficult in this area of research to make comparisons across studies in regard to "leaders," "supervisors," "managers," and "executives," since these positions are variously defined in different organizations but treated as synonymous leadership positions in research. This issue will be addressed in greater detail in the following chapter.

Although the assumptions that leaders are born and certain inborn traits are necessary to lead effectively have not been substantiated after six decades of research, the study of personality characteristics still has a place in the study of leadership. Recent studies (e.g., Kenny & Zacarro, 1983; Kirkpatrick & Locke, 1991) have confirmed the trait-based variance in leadership. Kenny and Zacarro, for example, reported that between 49% and 82% of leadership variance could be attributed to stable characteristics of the leader. Similarly, the current re-emergence of the trait approach is evidenced in research on charisma (e.g., Tichy & Devanna, 1987). Although charisma is more than an attribute of a leader, and therefore different from the leadership traits identified by the early trait theorists, it does include almost magical qualities ascribed to the leader. While it is now generally agreed upon that the possession of certain traits does not guarantee leadership success, there is evidence that effective leaders are different from ineffective leaders and followers, and that certain characteristics may improve a leader's chances of success.

House and Baetz (1990) suggested that the mixed findings obtained by Stogdill and others can be reconciled by consideration of the population studied, the measures of leadership used, or the results of more recent findings. The authors speculated about possible invariant characteristics of leaders. They noted, for instance, that since leadership always requires the presence of other people, social skills are likely to be always needed. Therefore, such skills as personal integrity, cooperativeness, and sociability are prime candidates for leadership traits. Although trait theory at best offers a partial explanation of what constitutes effective leadership, the trait approach accounts for some everyday observations of effective leaders.

Overall, the conceptualization of leadership as personality proved to be oversimplified, and did not provide much enlightenment. Although leaders in trait studies tended to be slightly superior on physical attributes, such as height, and scored higher on tests of intelligence, adjustment, extroversion, dominance, and self-confidence than did nonleaders, these differences were very small in magnitude, and did not converge to form a special ''leader personality'' profile. As noted earlier, this is not to say that personality traits have nothing to do with leadership. Rather, their significance must be evaluated in the context of other factors, including the situation in which these traits are displayed. House and Baetz (1979) discussed the situational nature of the traits themselves (i.e., leaders display certain traits in some situations, but not in others) and argued that situational characteristics determine the manifestations of traits. Blondel (1987) summed up the role of traits in leadership as follows:

> It would be inconceivable that qualities that compose the personality do not matter, assuming that leaders do make a difference in their societies. This seems to be true not only of exceptional leaders (good or bad) who have a personality well out of the ordinary, but of other leaders, who also need to possess special personal characteristics, whether of intelligence, determination, task orientation, sociability, or energy. The many findings, however disparate and discrete they may be, point in that direction. The ordinary characteristics that are required of leaders, have the effect of making these leaders different from most citizens. Precisely how much personality counts remains a matter of debate; but that the personality of the leader plays an important part in the ways leaders shape our lives is a subject on which there does not need to be a controversy. (p. 147)

Thus, while trait theory may not have produced unambiguous results, traits continue to resurface as explanatory constructs to account for effective leadership.

Application of Trait Theory: Margaret Thatcher

If we could conduct an exercise designed to identify a contemporary leader who embodies the largest number of personality traits included by traits theorists as predictors of effective leadership, undoubtedly Margaret Thatcher would be mentioned quite often. Thatcher, elected Prime Minister of England in 1979, defeated her own prediction, made years before, that the Treasury was as high as any woman would expect to go. For the next decade she dominated her country and her party like no other leader since Churchill. Her political message was a radical conservatism which bore her own name: Thatcherism.

In the evolution of Margaret Thatcher's political profile, personality traits such as aggressiveness, self-confidence, dominance, and pragmatism play a central role. No one has doubted the quality of her intellect. Thatcher's superior intellect is widely recognized among her colleagues who find her intellectual curiosity inspiring. In fact, several of her biographers believe that she saw her political struggles partly as a struggle of ideas.

Thatcher's verbal skills are reflected in her argumentativeness, and in office she was known to turn even a trivial conversation into a combat of words. Ironically, prior to her election, Thatcher had promised she would assemble a cabinet of like-minded colleagues because she could not waste time having internal arguments. According to one of her biographers, during her first year in office Thatcher established a pattern which was also discernable later, whereby the Thatcher character became the single most important factor in assessing a diplomatic position and forming a policy to deal with it. This Thatcher character was particularly evident in her foreign policies involving Rhodesia, Iran, Falkland Islands, Ireland, and the European Community. Thatcher's superb decisionmaking qualities and fortitude radiated during the Falkland War, which was a great triumph for her not only because it ended in victory but also because it took place away from home. After the Falkland War Thatcher's position as one of the world's foremost political leaders of her time was consolidated.

Other personality traits studied by leadership theorists which were manifest in Margaret Thatcher include her driving ambition and her moral certitude, which threw her opponents on the offensive. In addition, from her first to her last day in office, Thatcher brought a raw energy and unbridled enthusiasm to her political leadership. Thompson and Thompson (1994) described her as charismatic and successful but, at the same time, bossy, autocratic, overbearing, heavy-handed, domineering, and uncaring. These personality traits are captured in one of Thatcher's many nicknames, "Attila the Hen."

Margaret Thatcher was a woman leader in a man's world who neither demanded nor received concessions to her femininity. As she matured as a leader, she developed a powerful sense of self. According to Young (1989) she became shamelessly candid about her belief that nobody else could be expected to do her job as well as she was doing it. One of Thatcher's most widely quoted lines came at the conclusion of one of her speeches, when she cited Sophocles who said that once a woman is made equal to a man she becomes his superior. In the personality profile of the former British Prime Minister, then, we see the expression of a good number of traits that, at one time or another, trait theorists have associated with leadership.

LEADERSHIP AS BEHAVIOR: THE BEHAVIORAL AND LEADERSHIP STYLE APPROACHES

Behavioral theories of leadership dominated the field primarily during the 1950s, after the trait approach fell into disfavor. Instead of distinguishing between effective and ineffective leaders on the basis of personality traits, the focus shifted to leader behaviors. Rather than relying on innate (i.e., "leaders are born") mental and personality traits as prerequisites of successful leadership, the behavioral approach assumed that leadership is learned by acquiring a set of behaviors or leadership style necessary for effective leadership. The behavioral approach, associated largely with extensive research programs conducted at Ohio State University (OSU) and the University of Michigan, identified two broad dimensions of leader behaviors known as *initiating structure* and *consideration*. "Consideration" includes leader behaviors "indicative of friendship and mutual trust, respect for subordinates' needs and warmth while initiating structure refers to behaviors in which the supervisor organizes and defines group activities and his relations to the group" (Halpin & Winer, 1957).

The OSU leadership behavior studies resulted in the development of a series of questionnaires designed to identify task- or relationship-oriented leader behaviors critical to the attainment of group goals. The results of these studies, and many subsequent investigations of the relationships between initiating structure and consideration and criteria of leadership effectiveness such as group performance and follower satisfaction, may be summarized as follows: 1) leaders high on consideration tend to have more productive followers, who are also more satisfied with considerate leaders than leaders low on consideration; however, the relationship between consideration and leadership effectiveness varied substantially (e.g., Stogdill, 1974); 2) the correlations between initiating structure and leadership were less consistent (e.g., Bass, 1956); 3) studies combining the effects of the two behavior categories (i.e., leaders high on both initiating structure and consideration) showed that the effects of these behaviors on leader effectiveness depended on the situation, and that leaders high on both initiating structure and consideration did not always obtain optimal results (Larson, Hunt, & Osborn, 1976). The specific behaviors effective leaders displayed were determined by situational factors which, in turn, interacted with both leaders' and followers' abilities and needs.

Other researchers (e.g., Likert, 1967) created similar behavior typologies by distinguishing between a *job-centered leadership style*, which relies on close supervision, coercion, and reward to influence the behavior and performance of followers, and an *employee-centered leadership style*, which focuses on the needs of followers by creating a supportive work environment. As in the case of the OSU studies, this research, carried out at the University of Michigan, was designed to determine what leader behaviors lead to effective group performance. According to the evidence presented by Likert (1967), effective leaders 1) tend to have relationships which satisfy their followers' needs and enhance their sense of personal worth and self-competence; and 2) tend to set high performance goals. The findings of this line of research (e.g., Katz, 1960; Likert, 1961) have shown that behavior patterns or leadership styles that are follower-centered are related to supervisory effectiveness.

One important study by White and Lippitt (1960) used the concept of leadership style derived from observable leader behaviors. The authors identified three leadership styles which they labeled authoritarian, democratic, and laissez-faire. The results of White and Lippitt, as well as those of other researchers, showed that followers preferred a democratic leadership style, although not in all situations. Jago and Vroom (1982), for instance, reported that leaders use a democratic style when followers exercise initiative and autonomy, but a more autocratic style when followers are passive, depend on instructions, and need direction. Likewise, personal experience tells us that under certain circumstances an autocratic leader is likely to get the best results. The leading physician of an emergency room team or the quarterback of a football field seldom engage in democratic discussions of how to best complete the task at hand.

The leader behavior categories generated by the Ohio State and Michigan University studies essentially identified two broad dimensions. One was a task-oriented axis which emphasized task accomplishment, performance standards, and adherence to rules and regulations. The second category involved a relationship-oriented axis which focused on the leader's interpersonal skills, concern for mutual trust, and harmonious group interactions. These two dimensions are not mutually exclusive, since, theoretically, a leader can combine both task-oriented and relationship-oriented approaches. However, research has consistently failed to confirm the commonsense notion that effective leaders utilize both task- and people-oriented leadership styles (Stogdill, 1974). Equally disappointing were findings disconfirming the idea that leaders may be taught to exhibit high levels of both task- and relationship-oriented behaviors (Fleishman, 1953). The two most frequently discussed leadership styles, autocratic and democratic, are conceptually related to the two major behavioral dimensions, task orientation and relationship orientation, respectively. In other words, task-oriented (initiation of structure) leaders are likely to adopt an autocratic style while relationship-oriented (consideration) leaders prefer to lead in a democratic fashion.

The behavioral or leadership style approach departs from the notion that leader effectiveness does not reside within the person. In contrast to trait theories, behavioral perspectives suggest that leaders are not born, but that women and men can learn behaviors or a leadership style by observing a leader in action, participating in leadership situations, or engaging in leadership training (see Chapter 10). As in the case of the trait studies, the behavioral approach has numerous weaknesses, including inadequate conceptualizations of leader behaviors; overreliance on self-reported data rather than observations of leaders' actual behaviors in real settings; a lack of accurate measures; and a failure to attend to the role of situational factors.

LEADERSHIP AS SITUATIONALLY DETERMINED: THE CONTINGENCY APPROACH

Just as personality traits were not accurate in predicting leadership success, particular leader behaviors or leadership styles also failed to provide definitive prescriptions for leadership success across situations. Consequently, a number of situational or contingency theories were developed. Contingency approaches are defined as those theories which postulate that leadership effectiveness is dependent or contingent upon the interaction between certain leader attributes and the characteristics of the specific situation. These theories suggest that situational variables such as the characteristics of the task or the work setting moderate the relationship between leader behaviors or traits and leader effectiveness criteria.

Essentially, theorists adhering to this perspective argue that in order to predict which type of leader behavior will be most effective, we must know the relevant facets of the situation in which leadership occurs. The contingency approach emphasizes the importance of contextual factors, such as the nature of the task, the availability of human and material resources and organizational characteristics, and attributes of the followers, in order to determine leadership effectiveness. Contingency theories are based on the assumption that different behavior or trait patterns and different leadership styles are effective under different situational conditions and that the same pattern of behaviors or traits is not optimal in all situations (Yukl, 1989).

Among the various theories that fall into this category, two are discussed in this section: Fiedler's (1964, 1967) contingency theory of leadership and House's path-goal (1971) theory. These are among the more influential situational approaches in this category of theories.

Fiedler's Contingency Theory of Leadership

One of the leading proponents of situational leadership theories is Fred Fiedler who, along with his associates, carried out an extensive research program developing and testing his theory for over 25 years. Fiedler's model distinguishes between two leadership styles, *task-oriented* and *relationship-oriented* leadership, and rests on the construct of the *Least Preferred Co-Worker* or LPC measured by the LPC scale. This instrument was developed by Fiedler to assess the degree to which people rate the co-worker with whom they are least able to work along a number of bipolar adjectives. For example, followers rate their leaders as to whether they are supportive or hostile, helpful or frustrating, and rejecting or accepting. Low scores on the LPC scale are indicative of a task-oriented, structuring leadership style, while high scores reflect a relationship-oriented, considerate style. Fiedler argued that leaders preoccupied with task accomplishment are more directive than leaders whose primary concern is with the social welfare of their followers. The theory suggests that the high-LPC leader extracts superior performance in some situations while the low-LPC leader is successful in others. This idea is captured in the concept of *situational favorability*, which reflects the degree to which the situation is favorable or unfavorable to the leader. Situational favorableness, according to Fiedler's model, mediates the relationship between task- and relationship-oriented leadership and criteria of leadership effectiveness.

Fiedler and his colleagues proposed that these two leader orientations are associated with three situational variables or contingencies: 1) *leader–follower relations*, or *group atmosphere*, a variable which refers to the degree of confidence, trust, and respect followers have in their leaders; 2) *task structure*, or the extent to which the task performed by followers is routine (i.e., has clearly defined goals and specified procedures) or nonroutine (i.e., the task is unclear and ambiguous and the leader may not know more about the task than her followers); and 3) *position power*, which refers to the leader's authority to administer rewards and punishments and enforce compliance.

According to Fiedler's model, LPC and situational favorability interact in the way depicted in Figure 3.2. More specifically, if the situation is highly favorable or unfavorable for the leader (Situations #1 and #8 in Figure 3.3), directive or task- oriented leadership is most effective. This relationship between LPC and the situational variables in the model is based on the argument that when a situation is extremely favorable (or unfavorable), a leader can be directive because the task is clear, she has position power, and her relations with followers are good. Similarly, in highly unfavorable situations, a directive approach is also called for, because followers are likely to be in a crisis. This is due to the ambiguous nature of the task, the lack of the leader's position power, and her poor relationships with followers. In the middle range of the situational favorability continuum, conditions are moderately favorable for the leader; the leader lacks sufficient authority or power, the task is not quite clear, and leader-follower relationships are less than harmonious. Here, a relationship-oriented style (high-LPC) works best, because under these circumstances the leader has to get her job done through the followers by obtaining their cooperation, earning trust, or building commitment to reach the desired level of group performance.

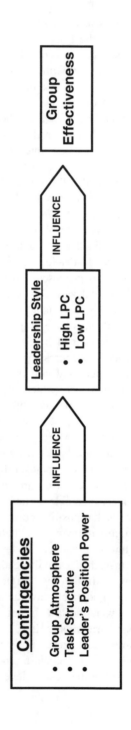

Figure 3.2 Fiedler's Contingency Theory of Leadership

Thus, two leader behaviors and the three situational variables produce eight different situations which vary in terms of their favorability, as shown in Figure 3.3. When the three situational factors (leader–follower relations, task structure, and leader position power) are either favorable (high) or unfavorable (low), according to Fiedler, the low-LPC leader is most effective. This is a task-oriented leader who works in a situation characterized by a harmonious group atmosphere and a clearly defined task and occupies a position of recognized power, factors which favor the accomplishment of the task. This is the most favorable situation for the low-LPC leader. If, on the other hand, the group atmosphere is good but the task unstructured, and the leader has little position power, as in Situation 4, we have a condition which favors the high-LPC leader; in order to get the task done, this leader must rely on her interpersonal skills. In the remaining situations, situational favorability varies depending on the specific combination of group atmosphere, task structure, and position power.

Like its predecessors, Fiedler's model has several problems. Although the LPC scale has played a central role in a large body of empirical research, critics have questioned its utility as well as interpretations of LPC scores. Much of the controversy surrounding the LPC scale stems from Fiedler's insistence that the LPC is a measure of the underlying needs and motives of the leader. Although Fiedler's high- and low-LPC leaders bear a conceptual resemblance to leaders high in consideration and initiating structure (defined as leader behaviors), respectively, the LPC as presented by Fiedler is conceptualized as a fairly stable personality disposition. In other words, leaders who rate their least preferred followers negatively in one situation are likely to do the same in all situations.

Despite a large body of empirical research (more than 400 validation studies), many of which support the basic premises of Fiedler's model, the conceptual meaning of the LPC remains unclear. Schriesheim and Kerr (1971) referred to the LPC as a measure in search of meaning. Even Fiedler expressed his frustration when he stated:

> For nearly 20 years we have been attempting to correlate it [LPC] with every conceivable personality trait and every conceivable behavior observation. By and large these analyses have been largely fruitless. (Fiedler & Chemers, 1974, p. 64)

In addition to the controversy over the meaning of the LPC construct, the validity of the model has also been called into question. While Fiedler (1967) interpreted most of the research evidence as supportive of the predictions derived from the theory, others (e.g. Graen, Alvares, Orris, & Martella, 1970) after re-analyzing Fiedler's validation data reached drastically different conclusions, asserting that the model lacks predictive validity. In general, Fiedler and his associates were more likely to obtain confirmatory evidence than were indepen-

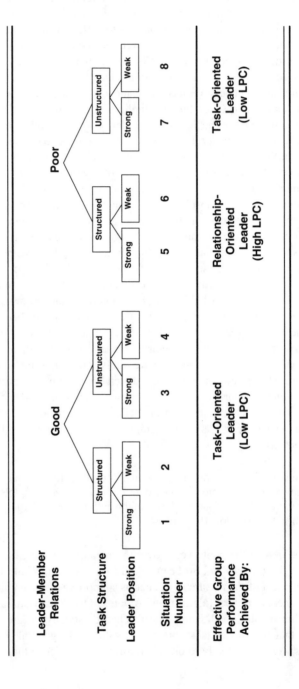

Figure 3.3 Fiedler's Continuum of Situational Favorability

dent researchers. Zaleznik (1990) concluded that the general problem with the contingency model is that it is too vacuous. The author argued that in everyday life everything depends on circumstances, but life is hardly a jigsaw puzzle which God as the Master Designer has provided.

House's Path-Goal Theory of Leadership

This situational theory of leadership originally stated by House (1971) focuses on the effectiveness of the leader in increasing the motivation of her or his followers along the path to a goal. It is called path-goal theory because the model emphasizes how leaders influence followers' perceptions of work goals, self-development goals, and paths to goal attainment. The basic premise of the theory, according to House and Dessler (1974) is that one of the strategic functions of the leader is to enhance the psychological well-being of followers, resulting in motivation to perform or satisfaction with the job. Because the motivational functions of the leader are stated in terms of paths, needs, and goals, the model was labeled path-goal theory.

Path–goal theory, depicted in Figure 3.4, makes two basic assumptions (House, 1971):

1. leader behavior is effective to the extent that subordinates perceive such behaviors as a source of immediate satisfaction or as instrumental to future satisfaction.
2. leader behavior is motivational to the extent that it makes satisfaction of subordinates' needs contingent on effective performance and that it complements the environment of subordinates by providing the guidance, clarity of direction and rewards necessary for effective performance.

In contrast to Fiedler's model, which identifies two leader behaviors, House's theory specifies four types of leader behaviors:

1) *directive* (i.e., letting followers know what is expected of them);
2) *supportive* (i.e., giving consideration to the needs and welfare of followers);
3) *participative* (i.e., consulting with followers and taking their opinions and suggestions into account); and
4) *achievement-oriented* (i.e., setting challenging goals and high performance expectations).

In addition, this model postulates two contingency variables. These variables are, first, *personal characteristics of subordinates*, which include followers' need for

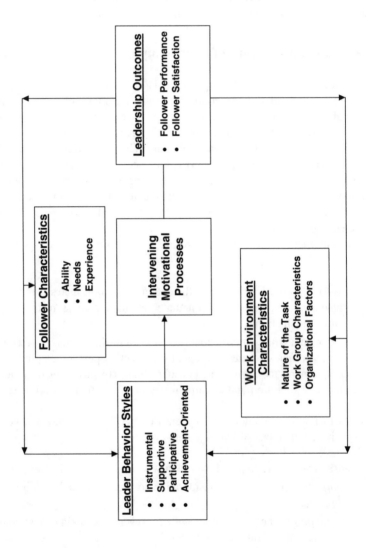

Figure 3.4 House's Path–Goal Theory of Leadership

autonomy, their abilities, and their task-relevant experiences. Path-goal theory, for instance, predicts that the higher the degree of followers' perceived ability or experience, the less likely those followers are to accept a directive leadership style. On the other hand, followers with a strong need for autonomy will perform best under a leader who emphasizes participation or achievement orientation.

The second situational variable involves *characteristics of the task and/or the work environment*, such as the nature of the task, work group characteristics, or organizational factors. It is proposed that these two situational variables moderate the effects of the four leader behaviors on follower motivation which, in turn, is predicted to influence follower satisfaction and performance.

Path–goal theory also includes three moderator variables: 1) effort–performance expectancy; 2) performance–reward expectancy; and 3) valences. The motivational variables were adopted from expectancy theory of work motivation (e.g., Porter & Lawler, 1968) which holds that if employees' believe that exerting high levels of effort will lead to high performance (i.e., known as effort–performance expectancy). High performance, in turn, results in the expectation that such performance will be rewarded (i.e., performance–reward expectancy). Finally, the theory suggests that in order to motivate employees, it is important to know what kinds of organizational rewards, such as higher pay, promotion, or recognition have value (known as valence) for employees (see the box in the center of Figure 3.4 labeled "Intervening Motivational Processes").

Path–goal theory, then, proposes that the effects of leader behaviors on follower performance and satisfaction depend on the situation, described in terms of characteristics of the task and characteristics of followers. These situational moderator variables determine both the potential for increased subordinate motivation and the manner in which the leader must behave to maximize performance outcomes and subordinate satisfaction. Unlike Fiedler, who believed that it is easier for a leader to change the situation than her or his leadership style (i.e., shifting from being a high-LPC leader to a low-LPC leader, or vice versa), House assumed that a leader can practice different leader behaviors (directive, supportive, participative, and achievement-oriented) at varying times and in different situations.

In contrast to Fiedler's contingency theory, which has been widely tested through empirical research, investigations of path-goal theory are limited to partial tests of House's model. For example, hypotheses have been tested concerning the tasks performed by followers, while measures of the intervening motivational processes (i.e., follower expectancies) were not included in many empirical studies. Similarly, most of the research focused on directive and supportive leader behavior, but excluded participative and achievement-oriented leadership. Moreover, House himself, as well as other investigators, used the scales developed at Ohio State University to measure initiating structure and consideration to operationalize the leader behaviors in path-goal theory. However, the degree to which instrumental and supportive leader behaviors in path-goal theory can be equated with initiating structure and consideration, respectively, in the behavioral approach, remains an empirical question. Validation studies of path-goal theory suffer from the same measurement problems (i.e., extensive use of questionnaires measuring subordinate perceptions of leader behavior and effectiveness) that plague other theories of leadership. Overall, although there is some support for certain tenets of path-goal theory, the existing evidence is mixed. Inconsistent findings, problems of causality, and failure of path-goal theory to predict performance across a variety of situations suggest that important moderator variables are missing from the model (Schriesheim & Schriesheim, 1980).

Application of Path–Goal Theory: Debbie Fields

Debbie Fields started her cookie company, Mrs. Fields Cookies, with her husband Randy in Park City, Utah. In just 4 years, they had established a business that has more than 500 company-owned stores in over 40 states selling what Debbie calls a "feel-good feeling." While that might sound a little hokey, in 1987 her company sold more than $90 million worth of cookies, a jump from $37 million in 1986.

When Debbie started the company, she had a vision of how organizations in the future might be more effectively run by computers (achievement-oriented leadership). With microcomputers helping manage the paperwork, Debbie had time to personally control widely dispersed operations (directive leadership), something which most small companies find difficult to achieve. In the management structure that she built, computers didn't just speed up administrative practices, they altered them. The technology gave Debbie the ability to project her influence into more stores that she could never reach effectively without computers. It also enabled her to focus on the major goal: having managers stay close to employees and customers (supportive leadership), not doing administrative work. How does her system work?

Richard Lui is the store manager for Mrs. Fields Cookies on Pier 39 in San Francisco. On a typical morning, after Lui opens the store, he boots up the computer, calls up the Day Planner, plugs in the sales projections for the day (based on year-earlier sales adjusted for growth) and answers a couple of queries the program presents him with. What is the day of the week? What type of day: normal day, sale day, school day, holiday, other? Say, for example, it is Tuesday, a school day. The computer goes back to the Pier 39 store's hour-by-hour, product-by-product performance on the last three school day Tuesdays. Based on what his store did over those three days, the Day Planner tells him what he can expect today, hour-by-hour, cookie-by-cookie, to meet his sales projections. It tells him how many batches of cookies he'll have to mix and when to mix them to meet the demand and to minimize leftovers.

Each hour, as the day progresses, Lui keeps the computer informed of his progress. Debbie and Randy designed software systems linking the cash register and the Day Planner. After every sale, the computer constantly updates projections in the Day Planner and sends Lui hourly updates. These hourly goals help the managers run their stores efficiently (intervening motivational processes).

Several times a week, Lui communicates with Debbie via phone and e-mail. Besides interacting through these messages, Debbie visits each store to learn firsthand the problems that store managers encounter (supportive leadership). Debbie believes that she must consider managers' needs and goals if the company is to grow profitably (leadership outcomes: follower performance and satisfaction). Her philosophy is that managers should make their people feel special, needed, and capable of doing anything. To communicate this message to each store manager, she believes that personal contact is essential. She also believes that good people join a growing business because it offers them the opportunity to be creative. To foster creativity she constantly encourages employees to make suggestions on how to improve store operations—or to come up with a recipe for a new cookie.

LEADERSHIP AS CHARISMA AND VISION: THE TRANSFORMATIONAL APPROACH

> Don't let the vision be shot through with holes, but be damned sure some of your best and brightest are shooting at it—with bazookas as well as with snipers' rifles.
>
> *Tom Peters*

During the past 20 years, there has been a flurry of research on a new generation of leadership theories referred to by various scholars as visionary, charismatic, transformation, inspirational, and post-heroic leadership (e.g., Bass, 1985; Bennis & Nanus, 1985: Bryman, 1992; Conger, Kanungo, & Associates, 1985; Huey, 1994a; Kotter, 1990a; Sashkin & Rosenbach, 1993). In contrast to previous theories, which were based on assumptions about scientific management, rational decisionmaking, positivist epistemology, and behavioristic psychology, this newer generation embraces a more descriptive, naturalistic phenomenology of leaders in action (Starratt, 1993). The essence of these perspectives is captured by the terms transformation, vision, empowerment, self-development, and social responsibility; they impart notions of leaders elevating the goals of followers, sharing power with them, converting followers into leaders, and being shaped by the followers. Bennis and Nanus (1985) described this approach to leadership as follows:

Leadership is "causative" meaning that leadership can invent and create institutions that can empower employees to satisfy their needs. Leadership is morally purposeful and elevating, which means, if nothing else, that leaders can through deploying their talents, choose purposes and visions that are based on key values of the work force and create the social architecture that supports them. Finally, leadership can move followers to higher degrees of consciousness, such as liberty, freedom, justice, and self-actualization . . . The end result of the leadership we have advanced is empowerment and an organizational culture that helps employees generate a sense of meaning in their work and a desire to challenge themselves to experience success. (p. 218)

Charisma is a concept underlying, either implicit or explicit, the current generation of leadership theories. The word "charisma" is derived from the Greek and literally means "gift of grace." The concept has been known since Biblical times and refers to a number of charismatic gifts such as the ability to prophesize, rule, teach, convey wisdom, and heal. Although the term has been used since antiquity, it was the German sociologist Max Weber (1947) who formally developed the concept of charisma in relation to his conceptualization of authority. The term charisma, Weber writes,

will be applied to a certain quality of an individual personality by virtue of which he is considered extraordinary and endowed with supernatural, superhuman, or at least exceptional powers or qualities. These are such as are not accessible to the ordinary person but are regarded as divine in origin or as exemplary, and on the basis of them the individual concerned is treated as a leader. (p. 149)

Weber used the term "charisma" to characterize self-appointed leaders who attract followers in distress or times of crisis. Followers of charismatic leaders believe in the leaders' extraordinary qualities. These qualities, according to Etzioni (1961) included magical abilities, revelations of heroism, power of mind, and speech. For Weber, the link between charismatic leaders and their followers is direct, since the followers constitute a congregation (*Gemeinde*) that is not mediated by established organizations, institutions, or rituals. Charismatic leaders evoke their claim to leadership not on the basis of office, but rather upon the belief in the direct and unmediated possession of grace. Later, the social sciences converted charisma into an endowment of spiritual grace from God bestowed upon leaders by their followers (Bass, 1991).

Over the last 15 years or so, a substantial body of literature and empirical evidence has been accumulated on charismatic leadership. Numerous theorists (e.g., Bass, 1985; Bennis & Nanus, 1985; House, 1977; Tichy & Devanna, 1986) have provided us with conceptualizations and descriptions of leaders who have been alternately called charismatic, transformational, inspirational, and visionary. At times, some of these terms, such as "charismatic" and "transformational leadership," have been used synonymously (e.g., Conger, 1989). On other occasions, leadership theorists have attempted to draw distinctions between them. Yukl (1989), for example, argued that charismatic leadership is more narrowly defined, referring specifically to followers' perceptions that the charismatic leader (but not the transformational leader) possesses divinely inspired gifts and is somewhat larger than life. Similarly, Bass (1985) used "transformational" as more than just another word for "charismatic" and believed that charisma is a necessary but not sufficient condition for transformational leadership.

Despite variations in conceptualizations of charismatic, transformational, or visionary leadership, leaders who exemplify this type of leadership stand out from other kinds of leaders in their force of powerful personal characteristics; their ability to appeal to ideological values and to expect self-sacrifice from their followers; and their intensely personal relationship with their followers (House & Howell, 1992). This unique relationship invokes powerful images: the Greeks conceding to Alexander the Great, who claimed to be a descendant of Heracles; Florence Nightingale, transforming the army medical service and nursing education during the Crimean War; Susan B. Anthony, campaigning feverishly to improve women's status in society by obtaining women's legal right to vote; Reverend Jim Jones, seducing his disciples to drink cyanide-laced punch in the mass suicide ritual of Jonestown; and most recently, Davidian cult leader David Koresh, a 33-year-old self-proclaimed "Anointed One" awaiting God's instructions in the sect's compound in Waco, Texas.

Charismatic and transformational leaders are usually described in terms of the extraordinary effects they have on their followers. These effects include commanding unquestioning obedience and loyalty; inspiring followers to identify with and emulate the leader, and idolize the leader as a superhuman hero or spiritual figure; communicating values that have ideological significance for followers; elevating followers to higher levels of morality; and transforming the needs and values of followers from self-interest to collective interest (Bass, 1985; Burns, 1978; House, 1977; House & Howell, 1992). Conger and Kanungo (1987) added to these effects a set of behaviors which included radicalism, unconventionality, risk-taking propensity, vision, and entrepreneurial spirit. Transformational and charismatic leaders have been found in many contexts including politics, religion, business, science, and social movements. Examples include religious leaders such as Christ, Gandhi, the Ayatollah Khomeini, and Mother Teresa; business leaders, such as Mary Kay Ash, Lee Iacocca, and Eva Peron; political leaders such as Cleopatra, Franklin Roosevelt, and Churchill; scientific giants, including Marie Curie, Freud, and Einstein; and leaders of social movements such as Gloria Steinem, Martin Luther King, and Malcolm X.

Theories of charismatic, transformational, and visionary leadership raise a number of important theoretical and empirical issues. First, they add a new dimension to the historical debate over personal versus situational views of leadership. It is generally acknowledged that personal characteristics and selected behaviors are part of the charismatic process. Willner (1984), for example, suggested that personal traits and relational dynamics between leaders and followers are responsible for charismatic leadership. Likewise, proponents of the situational perspective of leadership point out that charismatic and transformational leaders are most likely to emerge in crisis situations that require fundamental changes in the social or political fabric of organizations and society. For example, Blau (1963) argued that social and historical events are critical elements in the emergence of charismatic leadership. Boal and Bryson (1987), on the other hand, proposed that charismatic leaders emerge not only in crises, but also as a consequence of the vision of the charismatic leader and the way this vision is articulated and communicated to create a sense of need for action among followers. These authors suggest that charismatic leadership begins with an ideology and moves to action, while crisis-induced charismatic leadership begins with a solution to a problem and then seeks ideological justification for the solution. The rise to power of historical charismatic leaders from Alexander the Great to Fidel Castro, Cleopatra to Margaret Thatcher, may therefore be accounted for in terms of crisis-induced charisma. According to the situational point of view, sociopolitical turbulence, natural catastrophes, revolutions, and counterrevolutions create a set of contextual factors which favor the emergence of charismatic leaders.

The second theoretical issue deals with the question of the conditions that produce functional or dysfunctional charismatic leaders. In the wake of leaders like Hitler or Jim Jones, followers let themselves be led into a consenting and loyal submission resulting ultimately in destruction. On the other hand, leaders like DeGaulle and Mother Teresa motivated followers beyond the call of duty toward exceptional acts. Obviously, the potential for damage and destruction of charismatic leaders is significant. What forces propelled the demonic Attila the Hun, compared to the relatively humanistic Alexander the Great, into the leadership role? Among religious charismatic leaders, how do we account for Christ's pacifism and Khomeini's repression? Being able to differentiate the charismatic leadership of Martin Luther from that of Joseph Stalin is important. Under what conditions, then, is charismatic leadership functional rather than dysfunctional, transforming rather than negatively transforming?

Bass (1985) suggested that leaders like Hitler or Jones keep their followers weak and dependent and instill personal loyalty rather than a commitment to ideals. Burns (1978) went further and argued very strongly for a moral basis of transformational leadership. According to Burns's definition, leaders are transforming followers by elevating them to higher moral ground. This is one of Burns' most significant contributions to theories of leadership, since prior to

1978 a moral/ethical component was not included in such theories. Burns (1978) noted that:

> [the] ultimate test of moral leadership is its capacity to transcend the claims of the multiplicity of everyday wants and needs and expectations, to respond to the higher levels of moral development, and to relate leadership behaviors—its roles, choices, style, commitments to a set of seasoned, relatively explicit, conscious values. (p. 46)

Empirically, theories of charismatic and transformational leadership were developed using either descriptive and qualitative research or questionnaire data. Tichy and Devanna (1986), for instance, formulated a theory of transformational leadership centered around three themes: 1) recognizing the need for revitalization, which centers on the leader's attempt to alert the organization to growing threats from the environment; 2) creating a vision; and 3) institutionalizing change or transformation. Using this framework, the authors selected leaders who were personally involved in a major overhaul or transformation in organizations and who defined themselves as change agents. They conducted in-depth interviews with leaders such as Lee Iacocca of Chrysler, Jack Welch of General Electric, and Jerry Campbell of Burger King. Not surprisingly, the only woman who appeared in this sample of transformational leaders was Mary Ann Lawlor of the Drake Business Schools of New York.

These leaders created powerful visions of desired states of their organizations which served as conceptual maps for what they dreamed the organization to be in the future. These visions, expressed in the companies' mission statement, became powerful vehicles for mobilizing the commitment of followers and the entire organization to institutionalize the envisioned change.

A second example of the qualitative approach to charismatic, transformational, and visionary leadership is found in Burt Nanus' (1992) recent book entitled *Visionary Leadership*. The book was written to help leaders develop both personal and organizational visions. According to Nanus, four specific leadership roles—direction setter, change agent, spokesperson, and coach—define the job of the visionary leader. Consulting with leaders of corporations, universities, and government, Nanus identified a number of properties of powerful and transforming visions:

1) appropriateness of the vision for the organization and the time;
2) standards of excellence and noble ideals reflected in the vision statement;
3) clarity of purpose and direction;
4) inspiration of enthusiasm and commitment to the vision;
5) articulation and communication of the vision; and
6) ambitiousness of the vision.

The book then presents a step-by-step approach to help leaders to develop power-ful and transforming visions. Neither the framework developed by Tichy and Devanna nor that of Nanus have been empirically tested.

Qualitative descriptions and retrospective analyses have been augmented by questionnaires designed to measure transformational, charismatic, and visionary leadership. Most of the research of Bass' (1985) theory of transformational leadership, for instance, is based on the Multifactor Leadership Questionnaire (MLQ), which was designed to differentiate between transformational, charis-matic, and transactional leadership. According to Bass, transformational leader-ship consists of three components or factors which he labeled charisma, intellectual stimulation, and individualized consideration. Charisma, as noted earlier, is a necessary but not sufficient condition for transformational leadership. Intellectual stimulation, according to Bass, is the process wherein leaders increase followers' awareness of problems, while individualized consideration (similar to the consideration dimension in the Ohio State leader behavior studies) refers to the leader providing support, encouragement, and developmental experiences for followers. Bass proposed that these three factors, charisma, intellectual stimula-tion, and individualized consideration, interact to produce changes in followers, and their combined effects distinguish between transformational leadership and charismatic leadership. Thus, Bass and his associates treat charisma as an im-portant dimension of transformational leadership, particularly in terms of out-comes such as effectiveness, follower satisfaction with the leader, and the amount of extra effort followers are prepared to expand (Bryman, 1993).

The MLQ was designed to distinguish the transformational from the transac-tional leaders who "mostly consider how to marginally improve and maintain performance, how to substitute one goal for another, how to reduce resistance to particular actions, and how to implement decisions" (Bass, 1985, p. 27). The distinction between transctional and transformational leadership goes back to Burns (1978) who identified these as two distinct types of political leadership: transactional and transforming. Bass (1985) applied Burns' ideas to organiza-tional management.

Burns (1978) stated that transactional leadership occurs when one person takes the initiative in making contacts with others for the purpose of an exchange of something valued; that is,

> transactional leaders approach followers with an eye toward exchanging one thing for another: jobs for votes, or subsidies for campaign distribu-tions. Such transactions comprise the bulk of the relationship among leaders and followers, especially in groups, legislatures, and parties. (p. 4)

Transactional leaders, then, motivate followers by appealing to their self-interest, while transformational leaders motivate followers by appealing to collective interests. The transactional leader concentrates on trying to maintain the status quo by satisfying followers' psychological and material needs, while the transformational leader creates new visions. Transformational leaders create new cultures; transactional leaders live in existing cultures.

The relationships between transactional leaders and their followers and those of transformational leaders and their followers, then, are considerably different. Transactional leaders engage their followers in a relationship of mutual dependence, in which the contributions of both side are acknowledged and rewarded. Transformational leaders, on the other hand, achieve more than obtaining the compliance of their followers; they are able to shift the needs, values, and beliefs of their followers. In other words, transformational (and charismatic) leaders gain influence by demonstrating important personal characteristics, including self-confidence, dominance and a strong conviction in the moral righteousness of their beliefs or causes; this elevates followers and may convert them into leaders (Burns, 1978; Kuhnert & Lewis, 1987).

In its most recent version, transformational leadership, according to Avolio, Waldman, & Yammarino (1991) is achieved by employing one or more of the four "I's." *Individualized attention* refers to a developmental orientation the leader has toward her or his followers. It is seen when leaders assign increasingly challenging tasks to followers which allow for personal growth. The second "I" of transformational leadership refers to *intellectual stimulation*. Here the leader offers or suggests new ways of looking at things, novel ideas, and creative solutions, instead on focusing what has worked previously in similar situations. The remaining two "I's" refer to idealized influence and inspirational motivation. *Inspirational motivation* involves leader behaviors that motivate and inspire followers by providing meaning and challenge to their work, while *idealized influence* refers to the leader's ability to serve as a role model which followers desire to emulate. The model of transformational leadership offered by Bass and his associates differs from Burns's conceptualization in that the latter treats transactional and transformational leadership as opposite poles of a continuum, while Bass argued that transformational leadership is different, but not necessarily the opposite, of transactional leadership.

Empirical studies of charismatic leadership using the MLQ have been largely consistent with the tenets of the theories. Clover (1989), for example, found that United States Air Force Academy cadets indicated that they wanted to emulate those squadron commanders whom they described as highly charismatic as measured by the MLQ. Similarly, several investigators reported high correlations between followers' ratings of the charisma of their leaders and leadership effectiveness (e.g., Waldman, Bass, & Einstein, 1985), as well as correlations between charisma and self-actualization, indicating that charismatic leaders were perceived as encouraging self-actualization in their followers (Seltzer & Bass, 1987).

Finally, although it is difficult to operationalize charismatic or transformational leadership in laboratory settings, a few experimental studies have been conducted. One of these studies (Howell & Frost, 1989) operationalized the charismatic leadership by having "leaders"—actually professional actors—articulate an overarching goal, communicate high performance expectations, empathize with the needs of followers (undergraduate students), and project a powerful and dynamic presence. In addition to charismatic leadership, the researchers also employed structuring and considerate leadership behaviors to assess the effects of these three orientations on task performance.

As hypothesized, the results showed that individuals working under the charismatic leader achieved higher performance on the task and greater satisfaction than did individuals working under the considerate leader. Charismatic leaders were also able to overcome group pressures for low task productivity and generate group pressures for high task performance. The authors of the study concluded that their results supported the theoretical literature, which suggests that charismatic leaders, by force of their personal qualities, are capable of inducing follower performance beyond ordinary limits (Bass, 1985; House, 1977).

Charisma is an enigmatic word which has been attributed to powerful political leaders as well as leading rock stars and silver screen goddesses. Theoretically, charismatic and transformational leadership remain elusive phenomena. Nevertheless, Rost (1991) argued that transformation should be the cornerstone of what the author called the postindustrial school of leadership. The author asserted that our present theories of leadership are caught up in an industrial paradigm that treats leadership as good management. While many of us have experienced transformations to a postindustrial paradigm, i.e., restructured our work to take advantage of technologies, these shifts are not captured in existing leadership theories. According to Rost, the cataclysmic and momentous events in Eastern Europe of 1989–90 are one of the many indicators of a massive paradigm shift. Therefore, the theory and practice of leadership must be radically transformed to explain the transitions and extensive changes in values experienced by people all over the world. Yukl (1989) concluded that theory development of charismatic and transformational leadership is at an early stage. This development rests largely on retrospective analyses, qualitative and descriptive studies, and questionnaire data, and has not yet produced sufficient empirical research to test the various versions of charismatic, transformational, and visionary leadership in different contexts. Nevertheless, this form of leadership has a certain "sex appeal," and is an intoxicant which has fascinated scientists and laypeople alike for centuries.

Application of Charismatic Leadership: Candy Lightner

Candy Lightner is the charismatic founder of Mothers Against Drunk Driving (MADD). MADD, like other social movements, emerged from a crisis situation.

On May 3, 1980, Cari Lightner, the 13-year-old daughter of Candy Lightner, was killed while walking in a bicycle lane on her way to a church carnival near her home. The driver of the car, Clarence Bush, released from jail just 2 days before, was arrested 4 days after the accident. In addition to his previous arrest, Bush had been held on charges of a hit-and-run drunk driving crash and had been previously convicted in two other drunk-driving incidents. Candy Lightner expected her daughter's killer to be sentenced to prison, but was told by the investigating officer that any jail time for Bush was unlikely because "that's the way the system works."

In August 1980, Candy Lightner started MADD with her own money and volunteer help from friends. This marked the beginning of a crusade in which Lightner was able to rally large numbers of concerned mothers behind her desire to make cracking down on drunk driving a national policy. It resulted in the creation of a well-funded national organization, which Lightner led singlehand-edly for 5 years; she then found herself embroiled in a conflict with the Board of Directors that eventually led to her replacement (Weed, 1993).

Candy Lightner illustrates many characteristics of a charismatic leader. She identified a cause in which she firmly believed and with which other mothers easily identified. She vigorously pursued her cause and her underlying belief in the moral righteousness, justification, and legitimacy of promoting the anti-drunk driving movement. During the early days of MADD, Lightner' leadership style almost fit Webster's definition of charisma as "a personal magic of leadership arousing special popular loyalty" (Guralnik, 1976). Her followers, who were mothers of other victims as well as other concerned parents, believed in the ideas Candy Lightner stood for because it was she who advanced them. In other words, it was not necessary for Lightner's followership to test the truth or plausibility of her ideas. Candy's relationships with other concerned individuals and organiza-tions illustrates a fundamental aspect of charisma, namely the extraordinary, intensely personal relationship between charismatic leaders and their followers. The unqualified emotional support of her followers allowed Candy Lightner to build a solid foundation for MADD. As Weed (1990) pointed out, the victim status became a basis of legitimate authority for Candy Lightner and other local MADD leaders.

CONCLUSIONS

Twenty-five years ago, Gibb (1968) stated that the concept of leadership has largely lost its value for the social sciences, although it remains indispensable to general discourse. Meindl (1990) echoed Gibb's statement when he stated that, despite the sheer volume of theory and research devoted to the study of leadership, we have been unable to generate an understanding of leadership that is both intellectually compelling and emotionally satisfying. Leadership remains a slippery phenomenon. Wildavsky (1989) refers to this state of the art as "leadership in a stew" when he notes:

> As ontology was once said to recapitulate phylogeny, with each individual passing through all stages of the species, so each approach to leadership ends up, willy-nilly, by incorporating the others. Each conceptual nationalism becomes its own research imperialism. Every native dish turns out to be a stew. (p. 90)

In this chapter, several "native dishes" were sampled, including trait, behavior, contingency, and charismatic/transformational leadership. Each of these models carries its own set of assumptions about the leader, those who are led, the situation, and the spatial and temporal boundaries that constrain these theories. For example, trait theories have been appealing when leadership was primarily studied through the narrow lenses of single disciplines, such as social psychology, which perceived leaders as historical or political actors possessing certain physical and psychological traits that explained their rise to power. The jungle of theories leaves many people with the impression that leadership theory is a confusing, disorganized, discrepant, and unintegrated field of study; some are so disgusted with the mess, contradictions, and inconsistencies they perceive that they consider leadership studies as an academic discipline to be a bad joke (Rost, 1991).

As noted earlier, each theory relies on a limited set of concepts, such as leadership traits, behaviors, or situations which are usually applicable to only one level of analysis. For example, House and Dessler (1974) confine their hypothesis testing to four individual leader behaviors, while Fiedler (1967) seems to concentrate on group performance. Moreover, the review of the theories presented here indicates that the majority of our models involve oversimplified dichotomies, such as autocratic versus democratic, transactional versus transformational, or task-oriented versus relationship-oriented leadership which rely on "either-or" categories. That is, leader is either task or relationship, either transactionally or transformationally oriented, but does not vary these dichotomized behaviors in different situations.

Two other ingredients that leave a bad taste in the mouth of the consumers of the "leadership stew" are measurement problems and the issue of causality. Much of the research reviewed here is based on static correlational data derived from questionnaires. A few, such as Fiedler's LPC scale and the Ohio State measures, have played a dominant role in leadership research for over 40 years. Many others, developed for specific populations or purposes, have questionable reliabilities and validities, and have produced findings which are not replicable and in which we can have little confidence. Closely related to the measurement problems are definitional ambiguities, lack of conceptual clarity and coherence, poor design and execution, statistically significant findings which have little practical meaning, and problems arising from convenience samples. Finally, in the majority of empirical investigations, concern with the study of real leaders—as opposed to managers, students, or hypothetical scenarios describing leaders—has not been a priority for many researchers, although there are some exceptions.

The need, as Immegart (1992) pointed out, is not for quantification and scientific rigor, as such, but for analytic schemes that fit the design and conceptualizations of leadership we employ. Many existing efforts, as the author noted, are merely attempts to theorize *about* leadership, as opposed to serious work aimed at developing models for leadership that are useful to the practitioner. Immegart concluded:

> Studies have revealed the complexity of leadership, the situational nature of leader behaviors, and the importance and effect of an increasing number of variables. . . . Indeed, current efforts in terms of rigor and sophistication are clearly of a different order than the early subjective or simplistic "studies" of leadership. The prevalence and continuation of the latter kinds of studies—two variable investigations, endless replications and endless repeated pursuits, and conceptually and methodologically inadequate efforts—do cloud the situation and serve to mask the advances that have been realized. That the developments do not sufficiently inform practice or represent major breakthroughs or increments to knowledge also should not detract from the positive nature of developments. (p. 267)

The second "bad taste" concerns the issue of causality. Is leadership a cause, an effect, or both? Direction of causality, whether unidirectional or reciprocal, is important in scientific research. Do leaders support productive followers, or are followers productive because they have a supportive leader? Are there other variables that mediate the relationship between follower productivity and leader support? Traditionally, the only way to establish causality in the social sciences was through laboratory experimentation. Now leadership researchers are beginning to employ other methodologies, ranging from sophisticated quantitative techniques to qualitative methods such as ethnographic studies, to tackle the question of causality from different perspectives.

Have we made progress at all in the development of theoretical models of leadership? Despite the considerable degree of dissatisfaction, frustration, and gloom, there is reason for optimism. Early leadership models have evolved from unidimensional individual-centered approaches (e.g., traits) to multidimensional conceptualization, which takes the individual, the group, the situation, and the larger environment into account. More importantly, the field of leadership studies is becoming increasingly more multidisciplinary, with the goal of moving toward interdisciplinary integration. Whereas the last 50 years of leadership theory and research were essentially dominated by the social sciences, today anthropology, education, philosophy, and feminist theory are contributing to our understanding. The theories and methodologies germane to these disciplines offer new, rich and provocative opportunities for cross-fertilization. In the future, there will be a plurality of models with "different strokes for different folks." The "different folks" we are concerned with here are women.

4 Women Leaders and Women Managers

> People cannot be managed; inventories can
> be managed; people must be led.
> *Ross Perot, 1993*

INTRODUCTION

Leaders lead and managers manage. We have been told that good leaders need to be good managers but managers are not always good leaders. Socrates, the great Greek philosopher and intellectual leader, for example, was an atrocious manager in every sense of the word. His lack of managerial competence was evident in both his public and private life. As Popper (1989) observed, in the end he even managed to get himself condemned to death by a court of 500 of his fellow Athenians for criminally mismanaging the moral education of young citizens of Athens who adored him.

Mary Kay Ash is known as an inspirational leader who articulates a vision; Janet Reno manages the office of Attorney General efficiently (see profiles in this chapter). Judging from historical accounts and popular movies, Cleopatra was a charismatic leader while Elizabeth I, dogged by the fact that she was a woman, prudently managed her political skills knowing that they would be constantly tested during her reign. Organizations in the United States, both private- and public-sector companies, are said to be overmanaged and underled. Bennis and Nanus (1985), for instance, wrote:

> The problem with many organizations, and especially the ones that are failing, is that they tend to be overmanaged and underled. They may excel in the ability to handle the daily routine, yet never question whether the routine should be done at all. There is a profound difference between management and leadership, and both are important. "To manage" means to bring about, to accomplish, to have charge of or responsibility for, to conduct." "Leading" is "influencing, guiding in direction,

87

course, action, opinion.'' The distinction is crucial. Managers are people who do things right and leaders are people who do the right thing. The difference may be summarized as activities of vision and judgment— effectiveness—versus activities of mastering routines—efficiency. (p. 21)

The authors expressed their fear that without better leaders, America will become a ''mega-banana republic.''

The quote above reflects an attempt to draw a distinction between leadership and management after years of confusion during which the two were often treated synonymously. In fact, leadership and management have been confused by scholars and laypeople alike. Much of our scholarly knowledge of leadership has been gathered by investigating managers, from first-line supervisors to executives, from military officers to hospital administrators. For example, the research underlying the Ohio State Leadership Studies (see last chapter) does not easily distinguish between leadership and management because it treated managers and supervisors in industry and elsewhere as leaders. One of the ironies that permeates the leadership literature, as Tosi (1991) observed, is that while it is *leadership* (i.e., the process) which is the focus of our interest, we study *managers* (i.e., the person), quite often in very low-level jobs. However, we cannot assume that research on managerial behavior informs our understanding of leadership.

The relationship between leadership and management is complex and often a source of confusion. Before examining the different positions scholars have taken on this issue in more detail, and looking at representative women, a brief discussion of the nature of managerial work is necessary.

THE NATURE OF MANAGERIAL WORK

Management has been defined as ''an authority relationship between at least one manager and one subordinate who coordinate their activities to produce and sell particular goods and services'' (Rost, 1991, p. 21). Many studies have focused on what managers do, how they spend their time, and what roles they perform. Probably the most detailed and best known investigation into the nature of managerial work was conducted by Henry Mintzberg (1973) who asked five executives to keep diaries (known as diary studies) to describe their days at work. The picture which emerged from this study suggests that managers hardly conform to the common perceptions of reflective planners, organizers, and rational controllers painted by Fayol (1906/1950).

Mintzberg found that the jobs of managers are remarkably alike. Managers engage in many discrete activities such as attending meetings, handling conflict, directing subordinates, and organizing operations in the course of a day. Their activities are not only discrete, but also varied and fragmented. Most of the managers' activities were completed in less than 9 minutes and only one tenth of them occupied more than an hour. A manager may, for example, go from a budget meeting in which decisions about millions of dollars are made, to a discussion of how to fix a broken water fountain (Sayles, 1979). According to Mintzberg, managerial work is characterized by brevity, variety, discontinuity, and fragmentation. Managers work long hours, spend a great deal of time in meetings and on the telephone, prefer face-to-face communication over written documents, and generally favor the verbal mode in most of their interactions. Moreover, Mintzberg noted that the managers he studied strongly gravitated toward the active elements of their work—activities that were current, specific, and well-defined. The author concluded that managers are oriented toward action, not reflection. Unlike leaders, who derive much of their power from followers, control and information seem to be the primary sources of power for managers.

Mintzberg found that a number of different functions, including planning, organizing, communicating, controlling, evaluating, coaching, rewarding, and budgeting, are at the core of managerial work. In his description of managerial work, Mintzberg concluded that the manager's job can be described in terms of 10 roles within 3 areas: 1) interpersonal; 2) informational; and 3) decisional. According to Mintzberg, these roles are common to the work of all managers, and account for most managerial activities. Thus each activity—telephone calls, meetings, mail processing, talking to a subordinate in the hall, teambuilding, troubleshooting—can be categorized in at least one of the ten roles. These roles cover the interpersonal behavior of managers (figurehead, leader, liaison), information-processing behavior (monitor, disseminator, spokesperson), and decisionmaking behavior (entrepreneur, disturbance handler, resource allocator, negotiator).

In the interpersonal role category, the *figurehead* has no executive powers or leadership responsibilities but serves as a symbolic head who is obliged to perform legal or social duties as seen in organization ceremonies. Many monarchs, both past and present, are essentially figureheads. In contemporary organizations, the figurehead role involves signing documents, receiving visitors, and participating in ceremonies and other rituals.

In the second category, which captures the *informational* role, a manager as a *monitor*, seeks and receives information about the organization and the environment and is responsible for information input, output, and processing. Mintzberg (1973) reported that managers exercising the monitor role pass some of the information received on to subordinates (disseminator role) or to outsiders (spokesperson role).

Finally, as an example of a manager playing a role in the *decisional* category, the manager as a *resource allocator* is in charge of scheduling, budgeting, and programming of subordinates' work. Mintzberg suggests that by retaining the power to allocate resources, the manager exercises control over strategy formation and "acts to coordinate and integrate subordinate actions in support of strategic objectives" (Mintzberg, 1973, p. 65).

Many studies have focused on how managers spend their time, what work they do, and what roles they play. Basically this research has supported the generalizability of Mintzberg's managerial roles to both public- and private-sector organizations, as well as at different levels of management (Alexander, 1979). Mintzberg (1980) suggested that differences in managerial work are the result of the relative importance of the roles across hierarchical levels (i.e., lower, middle, and upper management) and the manager's functional specialty, such as human resource management or strategic planning. For example, CEOs focus their attention on external roles (e.g., liaison, spokesperson, figurehead) which connect the executive with the larger environment in which the firm operates. At lower levels of management, on the other hand, where work is more focused on internal affairs, the internal roles of negotiator and disturbance handler are more important. Research by Pavett and Lau (1983) showed that hierarchical level does indeed contribute to differences in the rated importance of Mintzberg's ten managerial roles. An interesting finding of this study was that lower-level managers rated leadership as more important for successful performance than did either middle or senior managers. The explanation advanced to account for these results was that lower-level managers are closest to actual supervision and need the interpersonal skills demanded by the liaison, leader, and figurehead roles in order to be effective.

The work on managerial roles and the nature of management is important not only because it defines the domain of management, but also because provides a basis for distinguishing management from leadership. However, the potential value of capitalizing on the possible distinctions, suggested by the work of Mintzberg and others, is not always realized. Sally Helgesen, for example, in *The Female Advantage: Women's Ways of Leading* (1990) applied Mintzberg's diary studies methodology to a sample of four women executives. They included Frances Hesselbein, formerly the National Executive Director of the Girls Scouts of the U.S.A.; Barbara Grogan, founder and President of Western Industrial Contractors; Nancy Badore, Executive Director of the Ford Motor Company's Executive Development Center; and Dorothy Brunson, owner and President of Brunson Communications, which owns several radio and TV stations. These women are described as leaders who, according to Helgesen, exemplify a unique, feminine leadership style (see Chapter 5). Helgesen attempted to show that these women have superior leadership skills. The author uses these four examples to show that there is a "female advantage" when it comes to leadership.

Despite the similarity in the methods used in the work of Mintzberg and Helgesen, there are some important differences in these two sets of diary studies, in which managers themselves recorded their various activities in terms of their duration, place, and interactions with subordinates. Mintzberg's five male executives worked in established corporations, while Helgesen's female executives were entrepreneurs. In addition to arbitrarily labeling the four women leaders, Helgesen also is prone to confusing leadership and management in her writings. For example, she states that "comparing elements in the diary studies can help us draw a concrete, empirically based picture of the different ways in which men and women approach the diverse tasks of management" (p. 19). Moreover, the author says that she is not concerned with corporate women, but with women leaders. Women who own companies, according to Helgesen, have a freer hand in setting policy and defining administrative tasks; thus, their businesses are especially reflective of women's values. This study of four women, whether leaders or managers, can hardly provide a concrete, empirically based picture of women's leadership. Finally, although the four participants in Helgesen's diary studies are called leaders, the description of their leadership as "defining administrative tasks" puts them into the realm of management. Thus it becomes difficult to assess which, of the four women studied, is a leader, and which is a manager. In either case, these four women are hardly representative of women leaders, women managers, or executive women.

LEADERSHIP AND MANAGEMENT: THREE PERSPECTIVES

Three perspectives which have addressed the relationship between leadership and management have emerged. These perspectives suggest, respectively, that 1) leadership and management are synonymous; 2) leadership and management are fundamentally different; and 3) leadership and management complement each other.

Leadership and Management as Synonymous Processes

The ease with which leadership has been treated as a synonym for management, and, for that matter, for administration and supervision as well, is puzzling and paradoxical. In leadership research the practice of equating leadership with management—more often than not, with *good* management—has a long tradition; it was quite pervasive until the 1980s. Stogdill, in his early attempts to discern unambiguous traits which permitted discrimination between leaders and nonleaders, indicated that the distinction between leadership and management did not matter when he said: "The question of whether leaders or executives are being studied appears to be a problem at the verbal level only" (Stogdill & Startle, 1948, p. 287). Thus, early on, researchers were inclined to treat all kinds of people, including managers and supervisors in prima facie leadership positions, as leaders, confusing not only leaders and managers, but also leadership and management. This is a process distinction which we will return to later in this chapter.

More recently, Smith and Peterson (1988) also commented from a leadership-as-management perspective when they stated that "leadership which contributes to effective event management can be defined as actions by a person which handle organizational problems as expressed in the events faced by others" (p. 80). Likewise, Yukl (1989), in a popular textbook entitled *Leadership in Organizations*, informs his readers that he is using the terms "leaders" and "managers" interchangeably. Fiedler, whose well-known theory of situational leadership was discussed in Chapter 3, has also asserted that leadership and management are the same, a position he basically maintained into the 1980s:

> Our research thus far does not demonstrate the need for this distinction. Leadership, as we use the term, refers to that part of organizational management that deals with the direction and supervision of subordinates rather than, for example, inventory control, fiscal management, or customer control. (Fiedler & Garcia, 1987, p. 3)

Gardner (1987) also rejected the distinction between leadership and management when he suggested that effective managers must have the clarity of purpose and motivation of effective leaders:

> Every time I encounter an utterly first-class manager, he turns out to have quite a lot of leader in him . . . even the most visionary leader will be faced on occasions with decisions that every manager faces: when to take a short-term loss to achieve long-term gain, how to allocate short-term resources among important goals, whom to trust with a delicate assignment. (p. 7)

Gardner does make a distinction, however, between the leader-manager and the routine manager. The leader-manager emphasizes vision, values, motivation, and renewal. The author summed up the leader-manager's task as envisioning the group's goals, affirming values for the group, and serving as a symbol.

Peter Drucker, another well-known writer on management, also embraced the position that leadership and management are synonymous when he contends that good leadership is "mundane, romantic, and boring" (p. 16). According to Drucker, good leaders are managers who successfully accomplish three primary tasks: 1) selecting and developing quality personnel; 2) setting goals, priorities and standards; and 3) establishing trust through consistent action. Likewise, Tosi (1985) expressed agreement with this perspective when he noted:

> With few exceptions, behind the popular charismatic image, the leader

acted as a manager. A good deal of time was spent acquiring resources, making decisions, assigning responsibilities, and so forth. These managerial practices may account for as much of the individual's success as do personal qualities, which are the base of charisma. If this is so, then any theoretical construction of leadership influence which does not include managerial elements is likely to be far too inadequate. (p. 225)

Even in recent discussions, the lack of conceptual clarity between the two concepts is obvious. Howell and Avolio (1992), for instance, contend that charismatic leaders are celebrated as heroes of management. The authors go on to say that by turning around ailing corporations (a la Lee Iacocca), revitalizing aging bureaucracies (a la Jack Welch of GE), or launching new enterprises (a la Sandra Kurtzig, founder of the ASK company, one of the nation's largest software firms and the highest-profile woman in Silicon Valley), these leaders are viewed as the magic elixir to cure organizational woes and change the course of organizational events. Again, we see leadership infused into management as if one has no legitimate existence without the other.

One of the consequences of confusing leadership with management or equating leadership and management is that leaders are typically treated as the "good guys" while managers are the "bad guys" (see Table 4.1). In other words, we tend to ennoble leadership and denigrate management. Abraham Zaleznik, in his book *The Managerial Mystique: Restoring Leadership in Business* (1990) pointed out that the managerial mystique is the bad guy at the root of business problems in the United States. Leadership, on the other hand, is the good guy, and restoring leadership in American corporation is the solution to business problems.

The degradation of the role of the manager is echoed by Jacques and Clement (1991) who suggested that the basis of the confusion of management and leadership is that leadership is endowed with virtue, strength, and creativity whereas management and administration are concerned with mundane, dull, and tedious everyday work routines. More specifically, the authors point out that:

> The separation of "manager" from "leader" has reinforced the modern-day tendency to debase the idea of the managerial role. A manager is seen as "boss"; and a boss is seen as someone who has hierarchical authority and hierarchical authority has had a bad name for a long time as autocratic and coercive domination of others. A leader, however, is not seen as a boss but as someone who gets things done exclusively by a good personality without exercising a "nasty," one-way downwards, oppressive authority. (pp. 20–21)

This sentiment was also captured in a hypothetical "Help Wanted" ad: "Wanted: Corporate Leaders: Must have the ability to build corporate culture. Mere managers need not apply" (Howell & Avolio, 1992) or article titles such as "Wanted:

Table 4.1   Let's Get Rid of Management

People
don't want
to be managed.
They want
to be led.
Whoever heard
of a world
manager?
World leader,
yes.
Educational leader.
Political leader.
Religious leader.
Scout leader.
Community leader.
Labor leader.
Business leader.
They lead.
They don't manage.
The carrot
always wins
over the stick.
Ask your horse.
You can **lead** your
horse to water,
but you can't
manage him to drink.
If you want to
manage somebody,
manage yourself.
Do that well
and you'll
be ready to
stop managing
and start
leading.

Source: Copyright 1984, United Technology Corporation. Reprinted with permission.

Leaders who can make a difference'' followed by the qualifier "Mere management isn't good enough anymore" (Main, 1987).

This good guy/bad guy analysis is evident in the language connected with leadership and management. The language of leadership is poetic, mystical, creative, and full of images and metaphors. Leaders are heroes, spellbinders, lone rangers. They are phoenixes rising from the ashes, corporate visionaries, champions of change, the chosen ones. They have personal magnetism, thrive on fantasy, and bring about great self-sacrifice. The language of management, on the other hand, is pragmatic and down-to-earth. Here, creative expressions and ambiguous terms are handicaps rather than assets, because they foster chaotic thinking and may force us to learn new ways to think and feel about a phenomenon. Words such as "trust" and "commitment," which defy a clear-cut definition, are often used by leaders, but are not in the language repertoire of managers.

Viewing management as the "bad guy" is to overlook some important facts. First, many subordinates enjoy and appreciate working for a well-organized manager and dislike being supervised by a disorganized manager. Organizations are dependent upon competent management for survival. Second, leadership is not always good and effective. As Dubin (1979) observed, "Effective organizations can be managed and supervised and not led, while some ineffective organizations can be led into their difficulties without the benefit of management and supervision" (p. 225).

Even charismatic leaders do not always produce positive and beneficial outcomes for their organizations. Conger (1990) discussed examples of charismatic leaders whose behavior became exaggerated, who lost touch with reality, or who became concerned only for personal gains. One of the examples quoted by Conger involves Ross Perot. After Ross Perot joined General Motors (GM) and was elected to the board, he became one of the company's most outspoken critics. His style and outspokenness were so much at odds with the GM culture that the company offered him $700 million in stock to resign from the board of directors.

Charismatic leaders sometimes are not welcome because they have a distaste for the status quo. History has shown that charismatic leaders may even go further and cause great harm to their followers. Historical examples of flawed leadership include the Reverend Jim Jones of the People's Temple, a self-proclaimed social visionary and prophet, who offered his followers an alternative to lives of desperation, isolation, and humiliation. Another charismatic leader was the Ayatollah Khomeini, the self-denigrating, ascetic leader of the Iranian revolution. As for most charismatic leaders, the source of Khomeini's leadership and authority was derived from his personal characteristics and his relationship with his followers. However, in contrast to Adolf Hitler, also a charismatic leader, Khomeini's charismatic leadership was legitimated by religion. Thus, charismatic leadership is not always good or effective, but has a dark side that may result in poor collective judgement on part of the followers and social upheaval.

Many people would agree with Rost (1991) that the down with management and up with leadership approach is not always a good idea. As the author suggested, any concept of leadership that devalues management and ennobles leadership has to be defective.

Leadership and Management as Distinctively Separate Processes

The opposing perspective, which treats leadership and management as fundamentally different processes, is held by Zaleznik (1977, 1990). In a widely quoted *Harvard Business Review* article, Bennis (1993) highlighted some of the critical differences between leaders and managers:

- the manager administers; the leader innovates.
- the manager is a copy; the leader is an original.
- the manager maintains; the leader develops.
- the manager focuses on systems and structure; the leader focuses on people.
- the manager relies on control; the leader inspires trust.
- the manager has a short-range view; the leader has a long-range perspective.
- the manager asks how and when; the leader asks what and why.
- the manager has an eye on the bottom line; the leader has an eye on the horizon.
- the manager accepts the status quo; the leader challenges it.
- the manager is the classic good soldier; the leader is his own person. (p. 214)

Similarly, looking at management and leadership from a personality standpoint, Zalesnik (1977) suggested that managers tend to be more rational and controlled. They require efficiency, are persistent, tough-minded, hard-working, and intelligent. Leaders, on the other hand, are brilliant, lonely people, who first gain control over themselves before they lead and motivate others. Similarly, according to Vail (1988), "Leadership is the articulation of new values and the energetic presentation of them to those whose actions are affected by them. Management is the discovery of value conflicts and the invention of processes for working through them" (p. 55).

Distinctions between management and leadership may be made based on a number of dimensions, including management as structure versus leadership as process; management position versus leadership role; and span of control versus span of commitment. It has often been said that management is driven by structure and leadership is driven by process. "Structure" here refers to the formal pattern of how people and jobs are grouped together in an organization. "Processes," on the other hand, are the activities that give life to the structure. Leadership processes include motivating followers, creating a vision, and affirming values.

Management is usually defined by the position or level the manager occupies in the organizational hierarchy. Leadership, on the other hand, as pointed out in Chapter 1, has a role that is independent of position. In contrast, managerial positions are deeply embedded in the structure of the organization and often arranged in vertical relationships. For example, we speak of lower, middle, and upper management. This hierarchical arrangement of managerial positions creates the organizational hierarchy.

Roles and role expectations, on the other hand, according to role theory (Katz & Kahn, 1978) of leaders and followers and the prescriptions and proscriptions associated with these roles, are determined by the context in which members of a role set find themselves. In contrast to management, leadership is not determined by structure or positions. Rather, it is a role individuals assume independent of their position in the organizational hierarchy. Leadership is a role relationship and a set of processes shaped by the reciprocal interactions between the leader and the led as well as by the context. According to Rost (1993) leadership is a process in which people other than managers can be leaders, and a process in which people intend real changes as opposed to a process in which they achieve organizational or group goals. In contrast to managers, who typically work in a single context (i.e., the formal organization), leaders assume their roles in different contexts.

Another dimension along which leaders and managers may be distinguished involves the concept of span of control versus span of commitment. According to classical management theorists (e.g., Barnard, 1939; Taylor, 1911) managers have a "span of control," a term referring to the number of people one manager can effectively supervise. Classical theorists argued in favor of a small span of control of five to seven subordinates per supervisor, and showed a bias in favor of close supervision; arguing that the number of people reporting to a single manager should not be so large that it creates problems of communications and coordination. Coordination, according to management theory, is most effectively accomplished when a manager is responsible for a restricted number of subordinates. Jaques and Clement (1991) pointed out that the concept of span of control has had a widespread and devastating effect, doing more to produce too many organizational layers than any other factor except pay and grading systems. According to these authors, a small span of control produces an excessive number of organizational and managerial levels, resulting in "delegation disease."

Today, many organizations are flattening their hierarchies by eliminating layers of management. Similarly, information technology has taken over tasks such as inventory control or production scheduling, previously performed by first-line supervisors or middle managers, thereby shrinking the organizational pyramid. The role that information technology plays in the structuring of work and organizations allows managers to increase their span of control.

Narrow spans of control are no longer essential for effective management. Many of today's knowledge workers, for example, are geographically dispersed and accomplish their work by telecommuting. In information technology-intensive organizations, managers often have a much larger span of control than that advocated by classical management theory. Since leadership is not linked to position or authority relationships, span of control is not an issue for leaders and followers. Instead, leaders have a span of *commitment* to values such as honesty, justice and integrity, to vision and change, and to sharing the tasks of leadership with followers by empowering them.

Anita Roddick, founder and managing director of the Body Shop and a business leader of an almost-all-natural cosmetics and bath products empire, illustrates the multiple and multidimensional commitments a leader may embrace. Flying in the face of conventional wisdom by refusing to advertise, Roddick has succeeded "in an industry rooted in vanity and superficiality by making customers and employees feel good about purchasing and selling Body Shop products" (*Current Biography Yearbook*, 1992, p. 479). Roddick uses her business as a vehicle for social and environmental change. She says that her company has not just to do with products but with the transformation of ideas, self-education, and a sense of love (Roddick, 1991). With more than 1,100 stores in 45 countries, Roddick asks each of her franchisees to contribute to a national campaign on social issues such as AIDS education, voter registration, and women's and environmental issues.

As a business leader, Roddick is committed:

- not to use materials in her products that involve cruelty to animals or threaten species
- not to cause unnecessary waste
- to develop service and community projects (each shop must have one)
- to make people part of instead of adjunct to the business process
- to educate and use the workplace as a center of social change.

Roddick and the Body Shop are committed to and have supported numerous social causes. They have become symbols of the politically correct "Green movement" when they teamed up with Greenspan's lobbying efforts against the dumping of hazardous waste in the North Sea. This campaign was followed by others: to "Save the Whale," to save the rain forest in South America, and to renovate orphanages in Rumania and Albania. Roddick also started a London newspaper, called The Big Issue, which is sold by homeless people. She conveys her social messages by using window displays in her shops around the world and by monitoring her products and practices for environmental safety. In addition, each of her franchisees is required to conduct two or three national campaigns a year, which are developed in-house. Roddick is also contemplating using her shops as information centers for human rights abuses (Conlin, 1994). Social activism, one of Roddick's passions, is an issue on which she constantly works to make a substantive difference to society and which she develops at the core of her organization.

Roddick's span of commitment casts a net around a wide range of social causes. Its focus presently is on the empowerment of communities in the Third World. The Body Shop, unlike other multinational corporations, does not exploit the Third World as a source of cheap labor. Its overseas workers are paid wages comparable to those earned by British employees. It is this commitment to social change which sets Roddick apart from her competitors. As the Body Shop and its products have flourished, copycat imitations of natural cosmetics have proliferated. Roddick claims that there are at least 33 American copycats, including Estée Lauder and Leslie Wexler, founder of The Limited, Inc., who launched a chain called Bath and Body Works which advertises itself as dedicated to preserving the earth (*Current Biography Yearbook*, 1992). Imitators turn Roddick off and she is prepared to defend her trademark. She complains that imitators offer ointment and ecobabble, but never change the underlying values—meaning her genuine commitment to social change (Brock, 1993).

Roddick, in an interview with Gaines (1993) described the culture of the Body Shop as "genuinely global, responsible, accountable, pro-active, concerned, lateral, enthusiastic, ethical, honest, open, and committed to action" (p. 354). In addition to her commitment to social issues, Roddick sees vision as a prerequisite for leadership, and calls for authority to be grounded in moral vision.

Leadership and Management as Complementary Processes

According to this perspective, which represents an intermediate position, leadership and management are different processes, both of which are necessary for organizational success. This perspective is consistent with Bass's (1985) theory of transactional and transformational leadership, as well as with the work of Kotter (1990) and Jaques and Clement's (1991) stratified systems theory. Jaques and Clement's response to the question of whether a manager should also be a leader is that managers carry leadership accountability by the very nature of their roles. The authors make it clear that the role is that of a manager and the role relationship is manager-subordinate. They also point out that "part of [the manager's] work role is the exercise of leadership but it is not a 'leadership role' anymore than it would be called a telephoning role because telephoning is also part of the work required'' (p. 17). These authors see no conflict between management and leadership, since all managers carry leadership responsibility. Good management includes good leadership as an integral part of its function without which management per se cannot exist.

The notion of management and leadership as complementary processes is also captured in one of the most influential contemporary theories, transactional and transformational leadership, as discussed in the previous chapter. Bass (1985) proposed a two-dimensional model which distinguishes between transactional leadership and transformational leadership, but treats the latter as an extension of the former. Burns (1978), on the other hand, who first distinguished between transactional and what he called transforming leadership, argued that in transactional leadership (which is often equated with management), followers are motivated by appealing to their self-interest, whereas in transforming leadership, leaders seek to raise the consciousness of their followers by appealing to higher values such as liberty, justice, and peace. According to Burns, transactional and transformational leadership are separate and mutually exclusive. The more common type of leadership is transactional:

> The relations of most leaders and followers are transactional—leaders approach followers with an eye to exchanging one thing for another: jobs for votes, or subsidies for campaign contributions. Such transactions comprise the bulk of the relationships between leaders and followers. (Burns, 1978, p. 4)

The transactional exchange between leaders and followers is basically a cost-benefit or social exchange approach. Followers exchange pay and other organizational rewards for efforts expended. Although transactional leadership may achieve loyalty, commitment, and high levels of performance, transforming leadership inspires followers to transcend their self-interest for the sake of the team, organization, and society. Burns described the superior powers of transforming leadership as follows:

> Transforming leadership, while more complex than transactional leadership, is more potent. The transforming leader recognizes an existing need or demand of a potential follower. But, beyond that, the transforming leader looks for potential motives in followers, seeks to satisfy higher needs, and engages the full person of the follower. That people can be lifted into their better selves is the secret of transforming leadership. (p. 4)

Burns argued that although leaders and followers can raise one another to higher levels of motivation and morality, since uplifting oneself and others is a moral goal of leaders and followers, most leadership is transactional. Burns challenges leaders when he stated:

> The great bulk of leadership consists of day-to-day interaction of leaders and followers. But the ultimate test of moral leadership is the capacity to transcend the claims of multiplicity of everyday wants and needs and expectations, to respond to higher levels of moral development, and to relate leadership behavior—its roles, choices, style, commitments—to a set of reasoned, relatively explicit, conscious values. (p. 46)

Bass (1985), building on the work of Burns, argued that transactional and transformational leadership represent two anchors of a single dimension. Transactional leadership, according to Bass and his associates, consists of two basic management practices: management by exception and contingent reward. It emphasizes the transaction or exchange between leaders and followers, which is based on the leaders discussing with the followers what is required and specifying the conditions and rewards to be received if they fulfill those requirements. Transformational leadership, on the other hand, includes charisma—the ability to inspire, arouse emotions, enliven, or even exalt—which is one of the elements separating ordinary managers from true leaders.

Kotter (1990b) also explained the difference between management and leadership from a complementary perspective by suggesting that leadership involves coping with change, while management entails coping with complexity. Unlike managers, who often try to maintain the status quo because it prevents turbulence in the organization, leaders do not fear change, but often embrace it. Kotter also proposed (1990b) that leadership and management are two distinctive yet complementary systems, each with its own functions and characteristic actions. For example, since one the important functions of leadership is to produce change, setting the direction of that change is instrumental to leadership. However, as the author pointed out, setting direction is not the same as planning. Planning is a management process designed to produce orderly results.

In addition to "creating change" as a major leadership function, Kotter also stresses the importance of articulating a vision, communicating it to followers, and having the ability to rally followers around that vision as central aspects of leadership. Management, on the other hand, is more about organizing people, controlling work flow, allocating resources, and solving problems. In contrast to leadership, management by itself can never produce significant change. According to Kotter, leadership complements management instead of replacing it. He proposed four major dimensions to including creating an agenda, developing a network of people for achieving the stated agenda, execution, and outcomes to organize the differences between leadership and management. Kotter suggests, for example, that good management produces order and consistency for organizations, but leadership creates movement. However, this does not mean that leadership is never associated with order, but simply that change is the essence of leadership.

WOMEN MANAGERS AND WOMEN LEADERS

What makes a manager? What makes a leader? Managers have been described as rational, controlled problem-solvers who require efficiency, while leaders have been portrayed as brilliant, lonely people who first gain control of themselves before they attempt to control others. For example, Zaleznik (1977) in his now classic article titled "Leaders and Managers: Are They Different?" described managers as follows:

> A managerial culture emphasizes rationality and control. Whether his or her energies are directed toward goals, resources, organizational structures, or people, the manager is a problem solver. It takes neither genius nor heroism to be a manager but rather persistence, tough mindedness, hard work, intelligence, analytical ability, and perhaps most important, tolerance and good will. (p. 127)

Comparing managers and leaders in terms of personality, Zaleznik made a distinction based on the leader's and the manager's sense of self by adopting two personality types described by William James (1902/1985) in *The Varieties of Religious Experience* as once-born and twice-born personalities. According to James, once-born personalities have linear, straightforward developmental experiences, while twice-borns struggle and have many ups and downs caused by parental losses and other personal trauma. As a result, once and twice-borns derive their sense of self from different sources. For the once-born, according to Zaleznik (1977), his or her sense of self stems from being in harmony with the environment. For the twice-born, on the other hand, the sense of self develops based on feelings of separateness, being apart from the environment. Leaders, in contrast to managers, have a capacity for loneliness which has been long documented in the literature. Many leaders are heroes and lone rangers, out front and alone. They were described by Cooper and Kingsley (1985) as self-defined loners.

According to Zaleznik (1977), managers are once-borns, while leaders are twice-borns. Leaders are said to be twice-borns because they develop by mastering painful conflicts during their formative years, refashioning themselves after each of these experiences. As Zaleznik put it, leaders turn inward in order to re-emerge with a created, rather than inherited, sense of identity. The author (Zaleznik, 1990) described the differences between the two as follows:

Managers and leaders . . . differ in what they attend to and in how they think, work, and interact. Above all [they] have different personalities and experience different developmental paths from childhood to adulthood . . . Managers perceive life as a steady progression of positive events, resulting in security at home, in school, and at work. Leaders are twice-born individuals who endure major events that lead to a sense of separateness, or perhaps estrangement, from their environments. As a result, they turn inward in order to re-emerge with a created rather than an inherited sense of identity. That sense of separateness may be a necessary condition for the ability to lead. (p. 9)

Mant (1983) referred to this process as withdrawing so that one may better re-enter. Managers, on the other hand, see themselves as regulators of an order with which they identify. They have a strong sense of being part of a group or an organization and comply with organizational protocols.

Women's access, albeit a limited access, to senior management positions has produced a cadre of female managers who are widely recognized and admired in their respective industries. Shareholders admire them because they deliver healthy profits and boost the values of their stocks; customers admire them because they develop and market top-notch products; their subordinates admire them because they show them how to do their jobs better; and their communities admire them because they further the greater good. Among this group of outstanding female managers are Lillian Vernon, a marketing maven who made it on her own in the man's world of mail-order retailing. Others include Georgette Mosbacher, cosmetic executive, and Linda Wachner, Chair and President of the Warnaco Group, which produces more than one-third of all women's intimate apparel sold in department and specialty stores. Wachner is the only female CEO in the Fortune 500 and one of the most successful women in retailing. Oprah Winfrey, Chair and CEO of Harpo Entertainment Group, not only dominates the TV talkfest, but is a business leader in her own right.

Also in the league of top-notch female managers are Jill Barad, Loida Lewis, Katherine Graham, and Katherine Hudson. Jill Barad, President and Chief Operating Officer (COO) of toymaker Mattel, who was behind the resurgence of Barbie, worked her way up from product manager to junior executive and finally to her current position. She was promoted 11 times at Mattel, an average of once for every year she has been with the company. She now is second in command of a Fortune 500 company with annual revenues exceeding $2 billion.

Another example, Loida Lewis, is the CEO of TLC Beatrice International, a food processing and distributing company which is also the largest minority-owned firm in the country. Lewis, a Philippine-born lawyer who is fluent in four languages, developed her intimate knowledge of the workings of the company she heads when she served as her husband's informal advisor and confidante during their 24-year marriage. She is known as a no-nonsense boss determined to take her company to new heights.

Media magnate Katherine Graham, who recently turned over the helm of the *Washington Post*, was a domineering figure in the context of the media. Graham came to her position as President and CEO with previous publishing experience (her father initially groomed her for the CEO position, but turned the *Post* over to Phil Graham after his marriage to Katherine); she developed her managerial skills on the job. One of her most important moments came in 1971, when she decided to publish the Pentagon Papers about the Watergate scandal. Felsenthal (1993) commented on this decision, noting that risking the store and publishing the Pentagon Papers is routinely cited as Katherine Graham's finest hour. Making risky and difficult decisions, taking responsibility for these decisions, and being able to surround herself with effective and extraordinary male colleagues were important skills Katherine acquired while running the Post.

Katherine Hudson is also a remarkable manager who made a name for herself in the male-dominated context of information systems at Eastman Kodak, where she was the highest-ranking woman in the company. Along with Bill Gates and H. Ross Perot, she has been acclaimed by *Computerworld* as one of 25 people who most changed the computer industry. At Kodak, Hudson started in finance and finished at the head of a $2.5 billion Kodak information systems division where she championed the outsourcing of all of the companys' data processing to IBM. She quickly became a celebrity because of her quirky management techniques, such as awarding gold-plated crabgrass cutters to employees who ''rooted'' out useless company procedures (McCormick, 1995).

Hudson recently took over the helm as CEO of W. H. Brady Company, a midsize manufacturing firm with 13 factories and sales offices in foreign countries. She contends that the kayak has replaced the ladder as the most serviceable metaphor for one's career. ''Sometimes you're in the rapid, at other times you are in placid places,'' she says. ''It's ok to explore the ebbs and flows—to slow down, to speed up.'' Her message to women is long on accountability, but short on victimization (McCormick, 1995, p. 47).

To bring the differences between a woman leader and a woman manager to life, consider the following profiles of two women whose accomplishments and achievements have been nationally and internationally recognized. The two profiles also highlight the importance of context in shaping individual behavior: the world of politics, in the case of Janet Reno, and the world of high-profile corporations, in the case of Mary Kay Ash. Context is not only established by characteristics of the tasks and the organizations where leaders and followers are found. It also involves the relationships they value and the complex network of people they interact with who contribute and give meaning to the leadership experience.

Profile of a Woman Manager: Janet Reno

On March 12, 1993, Janet Reno was appointed the 78th attorney general and confirmed by a 98-0 Senate vote. She is the first woman to hold this position. Although some contended that she was selected primarily because of her gender rather than her legal standing, Reno brought a strong record of experience with high-profile cases to the federal Justice Department. Previously, she had been a high-profile prosecutor for 15 years in crime-plagued Dade County, Florida which serves the greater Miami area. With 900 employees, including 238 attorneys, the Dade County prosecutor's office was the largest in the state. It handled more than 120,000 cases a year on a budget of $30 million. Reno took over this unwieldy engine of justice at a time when racial tension, drug trafficking, and illegal immigration from the Caribbean were on the rise (*Current Biography Yearbook*, 1993). As the head of the prosecutor's office, Reno became known for her tough mindedness and efficient handling of a number of controversial issues, including police brutality and prosecutions in one of the most racially volatile cities in the country; the death penalty; and abortion. Although Reno is personally opposed to the death penalty, she stresses that she has not shied from seeking it. In fact, Reno has asked for the death penalty as much as any other prosecutor in the country and secured it. Under her direction, the Dade County prosecutor's office won 80 capital punishment convictions.

Reno's life and rise to a position as the nation's top law enforcement officer followed the pattern of once-borns. She was born in Miami in 1938 and attended public school in Dade County, where she showed early achievements as a state debating champion in high school. Reno admits that she owes her independent spirit in large measure to her parents. Her mother, Jane Reno, an investigative reporter for the Miami News, has been described as a genuine eccentric who, according to local legend, would wrestle with alligators in one minute and recite poetry the next (Current Biography Yearbook, 1993). Her father, who for more than 40 years worked as a police reporter for the Miami Herald, provided a stable environment when he settled his family onto a remote homestead not far from the Everglades. Here the family built a rustic home that quickly became a landmark of Dade County.

Reno went on to Cornell University, where she was president of Women's Student Government and earned a degree in chemistry in 1960. In 1963, she earned a law degree from Harvard University, one of 16 women in a class of more than 500 men. Although Reno has never married and has no children, she remains close to her two brothers, one sister, and her nieces and nephews.

Family, education, and the physical environment served as the pivotal anchor during Reno's formative years. Even today, Reno describes herself as an outdoorswoman who is at home with nature. She is known to go out on a canoe through the Florida waterways to reflect on life. After her appointment as Florida

State Attorney General in 1978, Reno continued to live in the family house with her mother, who is still described as a hard-drinking, chain-smoking eccentric who instilled in her daughter a reverence for the environment.

Reno is described as organized, strong-willed, efficient, bossy and, at 6 feet 2 inches, a physically imposing boss who is self-confident, aggressive, and tough. Her toughmindedness and aggressive pursuit of justice are seen in her crackdown on absent fathers, making them pay financial support for their abandoned children. Her image as a tough, decisive, and zealous prosecutor was reinforced when Reno ordered the use of tear gas against members of the Branch Davidian cult led by David Koresh in Waco, Texas in 1993. This decision led to a confrontation with federal authorities that lasted several weeks and finally resulted in an inferno that left 86 cult members dead. She is technically competent, with extensive experience in complex issues involving civil and constitutional law, and politically savvy. In fact, President Clinton claimed that it was Reno's political skills more than her gender that favored her selection as Attorney General.

Profile of a Woman Leader: Mary Kay Ash

Mary Kay Ash, founder and chairwoman emeritus of Mary Kay Cosmetics, presents a different profile that sets her apart from a manager. She provides inspiration and motivation in addition to handling day-to-day management tasks. According to Kotter (1990a), Mary Kay Ash is a charismatic leader with impressive oratorical skills. Mary Kay herself takes a more modest view:

> People are often amazed at how I can talk about the firm so naturally and spontaneously, without any notes. What they don't realize is that it has taken me years to get to this point where I can do this as well as I do. Oh, I'm sure I have some natural ability but that's only part of it. (Mary Kay Ash, quoted in Kotter, 1990a, p. 12)

Ash is an effective leader who believes that the best results are achieved when employees are treated as individuals, rather than as subordinates who are expected to follow orders.

Mary Kay Ash founded Mary Kay Cosmetics, Inc., a privately held company that manufactures and distributes more than 200 premium skin care, cosmetic, and toiletry products through a worldwide sales force of more than 375,000 independent beauty consultants. The products are sold under the company's trademark color, pink, which extends to Mary Kay's pink house, pink Cadillacs, and pink nail polish on her dog's nails. A complementary pink Cadillac for high-performing consultants serves as both a trademark and sales-incentive status symbol. Beauty consultants are self-employed, independent agents, each of whom defines her goals and rewards. The company prides itself in having more women earning more than $50,000 per year than any other organization.

Once-divorced and twice-widowed, Mary Kay is a twice-born. From the age of 7 she kept house in Hot Wells, Texas, and cooked and cared for her father, who was bedridden with tuberculosis. After her first husband left her for another woman, she dropped out of the premed courses she was taking at the University of Houston and began selling full-time to support her three children. Her second husband, an executive in the vitamin industry, collapsed with a heart attack a month before she launched her own company. According to Mary Kay, he just fell into his plate, and his face turned purple. Her third husband, Mel Ash, a retired manufacturing representative, died in 1980 after 14 years of marriage. Before she started her business with $5,000, Mary Kay worked for 25 years in a male corporate world. Underpaid and repeatedly passed over for promotions, nothing made her angrier than training a man only to see him become her superior. She gambled her $5,000 life savings to launch Mary Kay Cosmetics from a 500-square foot Dallas storefront, a gamble that paid off big-time. After 25 years, Mary Kay took the risk of going out on her own.

Today, Mary Kay beauty consultants are found all over the world. Recently, Mary Kay discovered that Russia is a fertile market since women there have limited career opportunities. Mary Kay Russia now has over 5,000 independent beauty consultants, many of whom are highly educated women such as former lawyers, physicians, and teachers who earn $300-400 a month—about 3–4 times the average monthly salary they made in their former professions (Dukess, 1995).

One of the important leadership tasks in which Mary Kay Ash is heavily invested is building, transmitting, and nurturing a corporate culture, which is manifested in the ubiquitous use of the color pink. The organizational culture of Mary Kay is obvious at corporate headquarters in Dallas, the annual sales convention, and the stories about the company that are circulated among new recruits. The first floor of Mary Kay headquarters in Dallas is a shrine dedicated to her. Also on display at Mary Kay headquarters are larger-than-life photographs of the company's sales directors, which according to Kotter (1990a) say more about the firm's competitive strategy than some corporations are able to say in their annual reports.

Similarly, the annual sales meetings in Dallas, to which thousands of beauty consultants flock every year, make a statement about corporate culture. Correspondent Kristine McMurran (1985) captured the spirit of the convention when she described the beauty consultants as assembled in "full plumage with brows arched, false eyelashes aflutter, and cheeks abloom. En masse they bristle with enough flawlessly polished, razor sharp fingernails to puncture a Goodyear blimp and tear it to tatters" (p. 58). At these meetings, Mary Kay Ash, rather than serving as an anonymous figurehead, promotes the mission and vision of her company and motivates her sales force. Top saleswomen are lavishly praised and rewarded with diamond baubles, mink coats, and pink Cadillacs. And Mary Kay Ash stands out as "a sort of mascaraed Moses leading her chosen people to a promised land brimming with personal pride and her trademark pink Cadillacs" (McMurran, 1985, p. 58).

Finally, the culture of Mary Kay is transmitted through stories about the company which are recounted and shared with new recruits. In *A Passion for Excellence* (Peters & Austin, 1986), the authors discovered that many leaders rely on stories and storytelling to perpetuate important company values and transmit the culture of the organization. At Mary Kay, successful beauty consults are rewarded with a 14-carat pin shaped like a bumblebee. The story, that goes with the bumblebee, is that this bee has a body too large for its wings and therefore should not be able to fly. But it does. And that is what is transmitted to new recruits, and what Mary Kay is all about.

The culture of Mary Kay Cosmetics rests on commitment to customer satisfaction, a pillar built through quality, value, convenience, innovation, and personal service (Ash, 1981). It is transmitted through company symbols, motivational seminars, pep talks at Mary Kay's home, birthday cards for each consultant, diamond-studded bumblebees, generous incentives, and an organizational structure that promotes individual achievement, economic independence for women, and the notion of the company as an extension of the family. The company's leitmotif, another visible symbol of a strong organizational culture, is the Golden Rule: "Do unto others as you would have them do unto you." Not only is this rule taken seriously in company decisions, but it is also the obvious way for Mary Kay to motivate and lead. She leads by example. The statement "The speed of the leader is the speed of the gang" is often heard at directors' meetings. Inspired by her own example, Mary Kay Ash is dedicated to selling women on themselves. She has very strong ideas about the roles of women in the work force and has gained a national reputation as a forceful supporter of women's rights.

CONCLUSIONS

The distinction between leadership and management, while conceptually important, may have limited practical utility. Most people recognize that a balance between leadership and management is necessary and that organizations need both to survive and prosper. In contrast to leaders, a manager's authority, power, and responsibility come by fiat: by position in the hierarchy, control over decisionmaking, dispensation of reward and punishment, and allocation of resources. A leader's power, on the other hand, comes from her followers. Leadership and management are not incompatible, no more than leadership and followership are at odds with one another. Managers produce orderly results, concentrate on the short run, seek consistence, and solve problems. Leaders by contrast produce significant change, develop long-term visions, establish new directions, and produce innovative and creative opportunities. Managers thrive on order and control, while leaders embrace chaos and empowerment. Managers tend to avoid conflict, while leaders find creative value in conflict. The profiles of Janet Reno and Mary Kay Ash portray two accomplished, yet very different women, one a once-born manager, the other a twice-born leader. Business leader Anita Roddick illustrates the complementarity of leadership and management as interlocking modes of action. An effective balance between leadership and management is essential for organizational survival and success.

5 Women Leaders in the Media and Popular Literature

> Men are from Mars, women are from Venus.
>
> *John Gray*

INTRODUCTION

The media—newspapers, magazines, radio, television, video, movies—play a pervasive role in our lives, today more so than ever before. For the Greeks, the epic poem was a popular medium of communication for mythmaking. In our contemporary culture, the mass media play a major role in framing lessons about values that have been preserved or are being produced (Creedon, 1994). The sheer number of media with which we come in daily contact is growing rapidly. In addition to the familiar TV networks and radio broadcasts, technology is constantly creating new communication channels and people worldwide are saturated with media. Wireless communication networks, video-on-demand, and online computer bulletin board services over telephone and television networks allow the user to selectively create her or his own "infoworld."

In addition, multimedia which combine text, graphics, sound, animation, and motion video are used as an enhanced user interface to a computer-based application (Del Greco Wood, 1995). They are being developed for home and business environments. Within the next few years, we will have access to more than 500 TV channels, and news will travel over fiber optics faster than ever before. Today our primary context is still largely one of words but, according to DePree (1992), global communications threaten to enslave us to the media, since the consumer will grow increasingly dependent on a multitude of information and communication vehicles.

The last decade has not only witnessed an unprecedented growth in the level and type of media coverage, but more importantly, the media have taken an active, sometimes aggressive role in shaping events. The media, like leaders, transmit values and culture. The role of mass communications in shaping views of ourselves and the world around us has been widely recognized. The mass media, which here refers primarily to TV, newspapers, and magazines, MTV, and radio, have a powerful influence in determining what issues are important; they often set the agenda for what the public thinks about. They not only transmit information and knowledge but, more significantly, reinforce or alter existing beliefs, influence public opinion, and cultivate perceptions of social reality (Paisley, 1981).

The media achieve this, in part, by using a barrage of decontextualized statistics. The credibility of the media is often predicated on their claim to empirical superiority and political impartiality (McDermott, 1995). For example, according to the media, single women in their thirties and forties who give priority to their professions are doomed to get what they deserve, a life without a spouse and full of loneliness. Likewise, armed with equally alarming statistics, the media predicted a mass exodus of managerial women trading their organizations for full-time motherhood. However, as Faludi's (1988) reassessment of media statistics, indicated the projected doom for women in their thirties and forties and the saga of mothers' return to the hearth ignored a more significant pattern. Recent data published by the Institute of Women's Policy Research (1993) revealed that in the early 1990s, a majority of women with young children were employed in the workforce. Some of these full-time working mothers would have preferred part-time work or job-sharing if these options were available, and many more would like to see a more equitable distribution of childrearing and domestic responsibilities. The media, disregarding these latter statistics, enjoy what Rhode (1995) called a blissful freedom from footnoting, and are able to spin numbers to support their coverage.

With unparalleled immediacy and sometimes frightening candor, the media brought national and international events into our living rooms: the Thomas–Hill hearings of 1991, the Challenger disaster, the Persian Gulf War, widespread starvation in Somalia, and ethnic cleansing in Bosnia. Take the Clarence Thomas–Anita Hill hearings as an example. A Supreme Court nomination, once a dignified affair, became a media circus. We watched on our sets at home and at work how law professor Anita Hill accused nominee Clarence Thomas of sexual harassment during his tenure as chairperson of the EEOC during the 1970s. Cameras captured the testimony of Hill and Thomas before the Judiciary Committee, which was unable to reconcile images of Clarence Thomas as a presidential nominee for the Supreme Court and a sexual harasser; as being both dignified and judicious and capable of exerting hostile power and control over women; as being both good and bad (Noumair, Fenichel, & Fleming, 1992).

During the hearings, the media dramatically featured Thomas's rise from the poverty of his childhood in Pin Point, Georgia, to the pinnacle of responsibility as nominee for the Supreme Court. In the economy of the Thomas–Hill discourse,

Lubiano (1992) suggested a set of tropes mobilized on Thomas's behalf, among them the culture-of-poverty discourse. Moreover, class position and status came into play to marginalize Hill at the same time that the class position of Thomas was ignored.

Thomas received the worst ratings the American Bar Association had ever given to a Supreme Court nominee. Yet the media did not make much of these unsatisfactory ratings, looking for gaffes of any kind instead, and exploited the explosive potential of the sexual harassment charges. Thomas knew, when the confirmation hearings reopened and Hill came forward and went public with the allegations, that he was not only playing to the senators on the Judiciary Committee but, also to a nationwide audience watching him live on TV. He expressed his disdain by calling the hearings a travesty, a high tech lynching of uppity blacks.

Instead of treating the Thomas–Hill hearings as a political process, the media played up the event as a courtroom trial filled with political posturing. The public, overwhelmed after watching Hill's and Thomas's conflicting testimony, was lost as to whom to believe. At the same time, the audience was inundated with sensational tidbits such as Thomas's alleged sexual prowess and the infamous question he allegedly asked, "Who put pubic hair on my Coke?" Similarly, Hill's alleged tendency to sexual and romantic fantasies about men who rejected her was played up by the media. Then there were reports of a former Oral Roberts law school student who reportedly signed an affidavit stating that he and two other students received graded papers from Hill with pubic hair between the pages. Because blacks in our culture are often viewed and stereotyped as promiscuous, it is not surprising that at various times during the hearings Thomas and Hill were accused of being both oversexed and undercontrolled (Noumair et al., 1992). This kind of news stimulated more discussion among the audience than the issues at hand, and so did Thomas's Long Dong Silver and Hill's erotomania. By focusing on sexual innuendos, the media trivialized the hearings, which were in fact charged with power and racial issues.

During the televised hearings, the camera reminded viewers that the Senate Caucus room had not only been the scene of the demise of a previous Supreme Court nominee, Robert Bork, but also of some of the most important investigations in American history including post-mortems of Pearl Harbor, Vietnam, and Watergate. The camera analyzed every word selected and every gesture and emotional display of the two protagonists, from Hill's primness and calmness to Thomas's forceful appearance and passionate denial of the charges at the reopening of the hearings.

The media clearly went beyond objective reporting; they were aggressive in their "spin control," interpreting the events for the audience, offering explanations, filling the gaps, and passing judgments. In her compelling coverage of the hearings, Lubiano (1992) analyzed the photographic presentations in the *New York Times* and called attention to the male power behind this nomination which was evident in the pictures. In a central *Times* story published on October 12, 1991, when the outcome of the hearings was still undecided, photographs of Thomas and Hill being sworn in appeared side by side. The next day, however, new photos of Hill and Thomas showed the two of them in the "missionary"—male on top, female on the bottom—position (Lubiano, 1992). Whether conscious or not, according to Feagin (1992) this placement of the photos implied a representation of gendered power relations, the visual sign of the discovery by men in the Senate and the media of a new American "hero." According to Lubiano (1992) Thomas occupied almost a mystic ground in the hearings; he articulated and seemed to embody the Horatio Alger success myth, the ultimate American individual. Countless commentators reminded the audience that he did.

The role of Senator Kennedy in the confirmation hearings was an other example of media interpretation extending beyond the simple presentation of facts. Kennedy, who could have been a forceful voice in support of Anita Hill, chose not to play an active role in the hearings. To account for his conduct, the cameras took viewers back to Martha's Vineyard, where a young woman died in Kennedy's car. They also took viewers back to Palm Beach, where local newspapers reported stories about a bottomless senator romping around the Kennedy compound the evening his nephew Willie Smith allegedly raped a young Florida woman. The message the media was trying to convey during the Thomas–Hill hearings was that because of his own indiscretion and dubious personal sense of morality, Senator Kennedy was in no position to question another man's integrity.

Likewise, on October 15, 1991, when the Senate finally voted to approve Thomas by a vote of 52 to 48, the media offered their explanations for decisions made by individual senators to vote for or against Thomas—or to believe or not to believe Hill. Senator Charles Robb of Virginia, married to the daughter of former President Lyndon B. Johnson, told reporters that his vote for Thomas was influenced by his personal experience with false accusations. Flashbacks appeared on TV reminding the audience of Robb's alleged affair with beauty queen Tai Collins. TV also brought back Robb's presence at a beach party with people involved in drug trafficking. TV, with its ability to traverse time and place, captured images of earlier events and presented viewers with other information from which to make judgments, this at a point in time when many people were unable to form their own opinions.

The Hill–Thomas hearings are just one of many examples of media presentation and interpretation of public events. Boutlier and San Giovanni (1983) pointed out that regardless of the truth of an event, it is often the media's interpretation that shapes our attitudes and values about the event. For example, in the context of women leaders in sports (see Chapter 8), women have revolutionized their performance records in many sports and developed outstanding skills and expertise in competitive sports. Nevertheless, the media are now only beginning to acknowledge the existence of female athletes and remain mostly myopically focused on male athletes (Cohen, 1993). One clear message sent in the Thomas–Hill hearings was that the moral and ethical problems encountered by some members of the Judiciary Committee influenced their judgement. These personal problems prevented some senators from challenging nominee Thomas on questions of character. Polls taken immediately after the approval of Thomas showed that most people polled believed he was speaking the truth.

In this chapter, we look at the portrayal of women leaders and leading women in the mass media and the presentation of women and leadership in the popular press. For each communication medium discussed in this chapter, the messages conveyed about women in leadership roles are examined, as well as the extent to which the mass media reflect and/or shape dominant ideologies. Gitlin (1980) has shown that the media is more than a simple conduit for the transmission of dominant ideologies. The author goes on to say that if it were simply that, then the propaganda function of the media would be transparent for all to see, stripping them of their veneer of objectivity and thus reducing their legitimacy. Rather, the media provide frameworks of meaning which, in effect, selectively interpret not only the events themselves, whether athletic, political, or social, but also problems and controversies surrounding the events.

THE CONSTRUCTION OF LEADERSHIP IN THE MEDIA

The mass media, more so than any other type of organizational system, has a romantic affair with leadership, illustrated by a concept proposed by Meindl, Ehrlich, and Dukerich (1985) known as the romance of leadership. The authors suggested that the social construction of organizational realities has elevated leadership to a lofty status and imbued it with mystery and near-mysticism. As they pointed out,

> One of the principal elements of this romanticized conception is the view that leadership is a central organizational process and the premier force in a scheme of organizational events and activities. It amounts to what might be considered a faith in the potential, if not the actual efficacy, of those individuals who occupy the elite positions of formal organizational authority. (p. 79)

This romanticized conception of leadership is reflected in the mass media by the tendency of newspapers, radio broadcasts, and TV to attribute the world's successes and failures to leadership. Meindl (1990) stated that the romance of leadership notion calls attention to whatever realities regarding the ''true'' impact of leaders and leadership exist, and these concepts are often glamorized in our analyses of organizations.

Chen and Meindl (1991), in an analysis of the media presentation of Donald Burr, CEO of People Express, found that the business press reconstructed an image of Burr so as to account for the performance decline the airline experienced. At the same time, the CEO was described as possessing many positive characteristics which fitted his mission and made him an ideal and charismatic business leader. The authors described the reconstruction of Burr's image as a process that began with highly positive features but "ended not with a denial or replacement of these endowments, but with a revised image in which these endowments were portrayed as being responsible for his demise. The downside of Burr's idealism and motivation gradually came into relief for news readers and writers as the performance drama of his firm unfolded" (p. 546). The authors went on to say that the media develop

> constructions of leadership regularly and widely for our consumption . . . These images feed and expand our appetites for leadership products, appealing not only to our collective commitments to the concept but fixating us in particular on the personas and characteristics of leaders themselves. (p. 522)

Because of the effects of the mass media on the public's perceptions of leadership, the term *pseudo-charisma* has been introduced to refer to the media's manufacture of charismatic leaders through selective coverage. We can observe daily the manipulation of propaganda techniques and the use of opinion polls to create an image of leadership: "The procedures employed are no different from those used in the creation of movie, theatrical, or TV plays" (Bensman & Givant, 1975, p. 606).

As stressed throughout this book, an important influence on leadership arises from the context in which leaders, followers, and their interactions are embedded. Contexts important to the study of the practice of leadership include the historical, social, political, economic, and cultural environments in which leadership occurs. The media furnish yet another context, with its own characteristics, including the diversity of message channels, the brevity of fleeting images, dramatic use of language and metaphors, and the speed with which information becomes obsolete. Tuchman, Daniels, and Benet (1978) pointed to some characteristic features of TV when they reminded us that "this medium does not require literacy from its audience and, unlike radio, TV can show as well as tell. Each of these characteristics is significant in itself, the constellation of medium-specific characteristics endows TV with a dangerously seductive credibility" (p. 245).

In the media, contextualism is one of the primary modes of analysis. Contextualism stresses the situational nature of inquiry and reporting. Pettigrew (1985) distinguished contextual analysis from other modes of inquiry when he stated:

> One of the core requirements of a contextual analysis is to understand

the emergent, situational, and holistic features of an organism or a process in its context. This central feature of contextualism—the mutual nature of inquiry, the balance between involvement and distance, the notion that knowledge is created through a process of making rather than discovered through a process of knowing, the importance of the situational and multifaceted character of meaning. . . . the study of emergent processes in particular and changing context are some of the constants that contextualist research is likely to bring to the process of inquiry. (p. 228)

The mass media utilize the contextualist approach in their construction of leadership. The mutual nature of the inquiry process is illustrated in the relationship between the media and the audience in which involvement and distance fluctuate. Since the media achieve their impact through the audience, they have to show allegiance to viewers or readers. News selection and treatment have to take into account the viewing and reading behavior of the audience and be responsive to its needs and expectations (Kennan & Hadley, 1986). Yet the interpretation of information presented by the media is not passive reception of data or facts. Instead, as several researchers (e.g., Dervin, 1981; Swanson, 1981) have noted, it involves interaction with the material read or viewed, building on pre-existing cognitions and attitudes, previous and current expectations, and the nature of the perceived context.

Knowledge is created every time we turn on our TV sets and learn about the latest accomplishments and failures of world leaders. For example, in the fall of 1993, American citizens knew little about Vladimir Zhirinovsky. He headed the Liberal Democratic party of Russia which emerged as the strongest antireform group in Russia's parliament under Yeltsin after the demise of Communism. When his party captured 24% of the vote, Russian newspapers projected that Zhirinovsky's Liberal party, together with other antireform groups, would capture two-thirds of the parliament's lower house. All over the world, the media catapulted Zhirinovsky into the position of a world leader, portraying his rapid rise in the Russian parliament, focusing on his extreme nationalistic position, as well as his racist and anti-Semitic statements. The media provided dramatic commentaries of how Zhirinovsky's early years of pain shaped his extremist position. They informed people all over the world about his lonely, sad childhood, and exposed in vivid detail the humiliations he endured during his boyhood and his unsuccessful attempts as a student at Moscow State University to develop intimate relationships. The message conveyed was that politics eventually became the substitute for friendship and love.

The case of Zhirinovsky is an example of how the media enhance and legitimize the status of those to whom they call attention. In our society, one of the highest status roles is that of the leader. Lazarsfeld and Merton (1948), in a now-classic paper, identified "status conferral" as one of the major functions of mass communications. The status-conferring function of the mass media has been illustrated on many occasions. In 1969, the media covered the beginnings of the women's movement, spotlighting the leaders who burst into the headlines with the Miss America contest in September 1968. Protesters crowned a live sheep Miss America to make the point that the contestants were being judged like animals in a county fair (Davis, 1991). The media focused on the radical feminists—Kate Millett, author of *Sexual Politics*, appeared on the cover of *Time* magazine, and Gloria Steinem, founder of *Ms.* magazine, became better known for her miniskirts than the message she was trying to get across to the audience.

The mass media thrive on the perpetuation of images and portraits of leaders. They characterized leaders of the women's movement such as Betty Friedan and Bella Abzug as strident, aggressive, masculine types through news editing and picture selection (Miller, 1975). Betty Friedan, the founder and leader of the women's movement, for example, was described as "Mother Superior," a "double-chinned, badgering eccentric" whose theories reflected her own unhappy marriage and interpersonal failings (Douglas, 1994, p. 228).

Rhode (1995) analyzed newspaper reports of the early women's movement and recounted the way in which the media described it, once they began to pay attention to it at all. Essentially, the media focused on individual "extremist" women such as Kate Millett and Betty Friedan. For example, Rhodes quoted *Time* magazine's coverage of the women's movement during the 1970s and 1980s (*Time*, 1970a, p. 93; 1970b, p. 16) as a representative sample of common media characterizations of feminists: "strident," "humorless," "extremist," "lesbian," "hairy-legged," and, of course, "bra-burning." Even in the 1980s, in a cover story on women's issues, *Time* reported that "hairy legs haunt the feminist movement as do images of being strident and lesbian" (Douglas, 1994). Rhode (1995) asserted that in *Time's* rendering, the leaders of the "Women's Lib" movement had a "penchant for oddball causes—from ban-the-bra to communal child-rearing—which leave the majority of women cold. Moreover, *Time's* coverage failed to mention the movement's substantive achievements or grassroots-organizing efforts and capped it all with a ludicrous cartoon of Kate Millet" (p. 693). This biased coverage is unfortunate, since many women and men have only learned about the women's movement from information provided by the press.

In the portrayals of the leaders of the women's movement, the messages of the media tended to undercut the movement's messages. The leaders were portrayed in such a way that women in the audience were unlikely to identify with them (Tuchman et al., 1978). Apfelbaum and Hadley (1986) argued that a systematic study of the way the mass media depict women leaders would show that the typical presentation of female leaders as exceptions may actually discourage, rather than promote, any role identification by stressing the exceptionality of women in leadership roles. As the authors noted, mass media presentations of women leaders are rarely neutral. Instead, they insist on or confound the exceptionality of such cases.

As in other spheres of private and public sector life, the mass media underrepresent women in leadership roles. Instead, they often show women as wives and companions of powerful or famous men who wield political, economic, and social influence. Although producers of prime-time TV series and heads of advertising agencies with time have become less resistant to giving women lead roles or casting female characters with authority over men, women in general and women leaders in particular still do not appear very frequently in the mass media. For the fifth year in a row, the 1993 *Media Report to Women* found that not only in coverage, but also in reporting, women were significantly underrepresented in newspapers across the country and on the network nightly news. The report indicated that men wrote 66% of the front page articles of 20 newspapers surveyed and 74% of the opinion pieces. Women appeared in 34% of front pages. However, despite the continued underrepresentation of women's issues and women leaders in the media, the growing number of women journalists and TV anchors are beginning to make a difference. Coverage of women's issues, including women leaders, is slowly increasing. In addition, as Rhode (1995) observed, "dramatic events like the Hill-Thomas hearings or the Tailhook scandal can create a sudden cottage industry of commentary on issues that for centuries have gone unchallenged and unchanged" (p. 688).

When the media cover women leaders, they are often portrayed in a stereotypical manner. Stereotypes are evident in the disproportionate number of males to females portrayed, the gender specificity of traits assigned to each gender, and the limited number of behavioral roles (wife, mother, helpmate) assigned to women compared to men. Women also are employed in a more limited number of occupations in media presentations. Moreover, few women appear in realistic positions of authority. When women do hold positions of authority and propose fundamental political, economic, or social changes, the media frequently call them into question, both as women and as leaders. In the media, such questioning is typically very public, very emotional and often very "dirty" in nature. For example, Edith Cresson's appointment as prime minister of France by President Mitterand carried the charge of upgrading France's economic position to match Germany's and leading France into a single-market Europe (see Chapter 9). Instead of detailing the political and economic challenges facing the new prime minister, the media dredged up stories and circulated rumors about an affair between Mitterand and Cresson. The audience could not help concluding that Cresson must have slept her way into this important political appointment.

In the advertising world, males make up 90% of the narrators of advertisements. Similarly, in a study which content-analyzed the portrayal of women and men in TV commercials, Bretl and Cantor (1988) found that in commercials that had narrators, 91% were male and 8% were female; in 1% of the cases the sex of the narrator was not clear. These findings are consistent with earlier studies which have shown that the "voice of authority" in TV commercials has consistently and overwhelmingly been male and has remained relatively unchanged over the years. Thus, although women and men now appear in approximately equal numbers as primary characters in prime-time TV advertisements, women are largely underrepresented as narrators. Advertisers continue to use male narrators because "they believe that a male voice on TV sounds more authoritative and, therefore, more convincing, than a female voice" (Bretl & Cantor, 1988, p. 605).

In the movie industry, women film directors were virtually unknown until recently. According to Naisbitt and Aburdene (1990) of the 7,332 feature films made in Hollywood between 1939 and 1979, only 14 were directed by women, although more recently women have begun to gain status as directors. Partly due to pressure from the Directors Guild of America (DGA), and partly because talented women directors can no longer be overlooked, the numbers have improved a little. In 1990, according to the DGD, women directed 23 of the 406 feature films produced under guild contracts (Schickel, 1991). More importantly, Schickel notes, "the range of the work of female directors belies the conventional wisdom that holds that women can be entrusted only with delicately nuanced films dealing with intricate personal relationships" (p. 75). Among the leading women directors are Martha Coolidge (*Rambling Rose*), Kathryn Bigelow (*Point Break*), Barbra Streisand (*The Prince of Tides*), and Jodie Foster (*Little Man Tate*; *Nell*). In radio broadcasting, on the other hand, only few women serve as general managers of radio stations or other positions in which they can influence programming. The number of nationally syndicated female talk show hosts can be counted on one hand, and several of them are practicing therapists like Joyce Brothers (*Media Report to Women*, 1994a).

Even on MTV, a fairly recent addition to the mass media, gender stereotyping is obvious. In the late 1980s, the world of MTV depicted few or no women politicians, scientists, athletes, or business executives, mirroring the results obtained by researchers of prime-time TV shows. Seidman (1992) reported that MTV showed both male and female characters in gender-typed occupations. It portrayed males as more adventuresome, domineering, aggressive, and violent than female characters. On the other hand, MTV depicted women as being affectionate, dependent, and nurturing. Moreover, many women on MTV wore revealing clothes, while little attention was paid to male clothing. An earlier study by Vincent, Davis, and Bornszkowski (1987) revealed that women were put down and kept in their place by men in almost three-fourths of the rock video programs analyzed in the study. Hansen and Hansen (1988) concluded that MTV is a force in the perpetuation of stereotypes that continue to exist about how women should behave, work, and act, as well as what they should believe.

Lewis (1990), in her book *Gender Politics and MTV*, showed how gender inequality and discrimination persist within the same rock music institutions that at one time enabled women to overcome past repression. MTV, according to the author, by indications of design, goals, and history, appeared poised to perpetuate, or reactivate, the structure of values and strategies of differentiation that have historically defined female musicians as inferior.

PORTRAYALS OF WOMEN LEADERS IN THE MASS MEDIA

Across the mass media the message is clear—female leadership across a variety of contexts including politics, sports, and arts and sciences, is tangential to male leadership. Except for world leaders like Indira Gandhi, Golda Meir and, more recently, some key women in the Clinton administration, the mass media have largely ignored women in leadership roles. The appointment of Turkish Prime Minister Tansu Ciller (see Chapter 9), who has risen to the top leadership position of her country on the basis of sheer merit, did not make front page news of many major national or international papers in 1993.

When women leaders move into the media spotlight, the press is often hostile and negative. Press coverage of Janet Reno's appointment to Attorney General included innuendos about her lifestyle and sexual orientation which often over-shadowed her accomplishments as a tough prosecutor. When Representative Marjorie Margolies-Mezvinsky became Pennsylvania's first and only congress-woman in 1993, the media discovered that she left something off her resume. Specifically, she was accused of withholding her authorship of a steamy novel called *The Girls in the Newsroom* published in 1983. The novel, replete with graphic sexual scenes that unfold as three TV anchorwomen compete for an anchor spot, had the news media aflutter, and the discovery topped the front page news.

Newspaper Coverage of Women Leaders

Leadership of women simply is not front-page material. Instead, stories about women leaders are often found in "women's pages," implying that this material is less important than other topics presented in the general news sections and only appropriate for women. As every newspaper editor knows, the placement of a story makes a difference between public notice and oblivion, since categoriza-tion by section (i.e., front page, general news, sports, women's news) makes a large difference in how the messages are heard and experienced (Tuchman et al., 1978). Unless the news is negative, newspapers relegate stories about female leaders to lesser "inside" positions. Thus, the Zoe Baird saga was splashed across the front pages. However, appointments of women to important cabinet posts—examples include Hazel Rollins O'Leary, Secretary of the Department of

Energy, or Madeleine Korbel Albright, Ambassador to the United Nations—were featured somewhere inside the paper. Likewise, a meeting of Hillary Clinton with women of the House on February 24, 1993 appeared in the Styles section of the *Washington Post* instead of the paper's news section.

As in other mass media, newspapers and news magazines continue to under-represent women and women leaders. For example, *USA Today* (Equal Writes, 1992; see Figure 5.1) reported statistics on the coverage of women in three major business magazines, *Newsweek, Time,* and *U.S. News and World Report* which indicated that although women make up over 50% of the workforce, they receive relatively little coverage. The percentages of women mentioned were 10% in *U.S. News and World Report,* 11% in *Time,* and 18% in *Newsweek.* Moreover, sometimes newspapers publish data that clearly contradict public opinion. For example, newspapers reported that 58% of a national sample of women and men felt negatively about the possibility of having a woman president. Several public polls, on the other hand, have shown that the majority of Americans have positive attitudes toward a female president and women leaders in high political offices. For example, Aburdene and Naisbitt (1992) predicted that by 2008 U.S. women will hold at least 35% of governorships and a woman will be electable, or already elected, as U.S. president (p. 3).

Executive Female conducted a survey among daily newspapers and business magazines which replicated these findings. Women's representation was low in both the general media (newspapers) as well as in business magazines. Only one-tenth of experts and sources named in these publications were women (Wheeler, 1994). Conversely, when an anonymous factory worker was pictured, or a welfare recipient quoted, women were chosen (see Figure 5.2).

Like other forms of the mass media, newspapers judge women leaders who exhibit leadership styles congruent with prevailing gender stereotypes more favorably than they do women who "lead like men." The *New York Times* (1994, September 14) presented a profile of the progressive Norwegian Prime Minister Harlem Brundtland and labeled her "a bit of a nitpicker and occasionally self-righteous." According to the *Times,* "her directedness and aggressiveness" have offended many of her Labour colleagues in a country where confrontation is a dirty word.

Hillary Clinton became a prime symbol of the media's confusion over the coverage of women in leadership roles who deviate from stereotypes ascribed to their gender. Early newspaper coverage of the 1992 presidential election campaign focused on her career and accomplishments as a lawyer and social rights activist. As the campaign progressed, coverage shifted to her clothes, hair, public gaffes, and chocolate chip cookies. For every serious analysis of Hillary's position on a wide range of national issues, there was a host of stories about Hillary as the overbearing yuppie wife who learned the hard way to act meekly and wear pastels. Since the media and presumably the public prefer a "traditional"

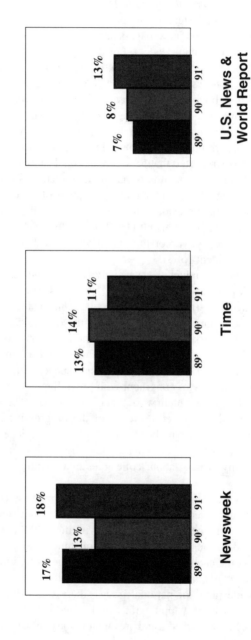

Figure 5.1 Coverage of Women in News Magazines

Source: From "Equal Writes" 1992, April 16, *USA Today*, 1A. Copyright 1992, USA Today. Reprinted with permission.

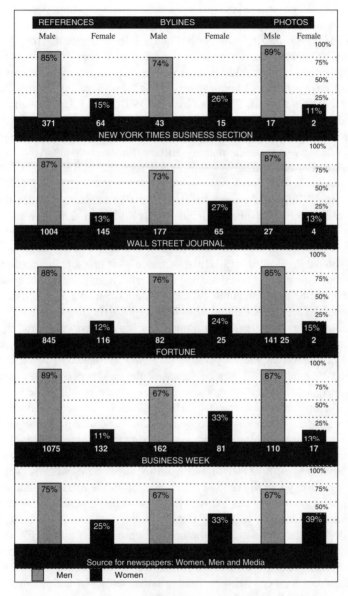

REFERENCES		BYLINES		PHOTOS	
Male	Female	Male	Female	Msle	Female

NEW YORK TIMES BUSINESS SECTION
- Male References: 85% (371)
- Female References: 15% (64)
- Male Bylines: 74% (43)
- Female Bylines: 26% (15)
- Male Photos: 89% (17)
- Female Photos: 11% (2)

WALL STREET JOURNAL
- Male References: 87% (1004)
- Female References: 13% (145)
- Male Bylines: 73% (177)
- Female Bylines: 27% (65)
- Male Photos: 87% (27)
- Female Photos: 13% (4)

FORTUNE
- Male References: 88% (845)
- Female References: 12% (116)
- Male Bylines: 76% (82)
- Female Bylines: 24% (25)
- Male Photos: 85% (141 25)
- Female Photos: 15% (2)

BUSINESS WEEK
- Male References: 89% (1075)
- Female References: 11% (132)
- Male Bylines: 67% (162)
- Female Bylines: 33% (81)
- Male Photos: 87% (110)
- Female Photos: 13% (17)

- Male References: 75%
- Female References: 25%
- Male Bylines: 67%
- Female Bylines: 33%
- Male Photos: 67%
- Female Photos: 39%

Source for newspapers: Women, Men and Media

☐ Men   ■ Women

Figure 5.2 IN THE EXECUTIVE SUITE, BUT NOT IN THE EXECUTIVE PRESS

Source: Reprinted with permission from *Female Executive*, the official publication of the National Association for Female Executives.

first Lady, Hillary subjected herself to a culinary confrontation, competing with Barbara Bush for the best chocolate chip cookie recipe. Furthermore, Hillary was forced into apologizing publicly and said: "I deeply regret that my comments about baking cookies and having tea was taken out of context. There is nothing in my life or work that could be construed as disparaging women who stay at home and raise a family. I honor them. Those are the choices my own mother made" (quoted in Carroll, Clift, & Fineman, 1992, p. 31). On the battleground of symbolic politics, as Howell (1990) pointed out, cookies served as a metaphor for a broader set of societal issues. Once the debate was framed in terms of "policy-making versus cookie-making, Hillary Clinton could not avoid alienating some substantial constituency, whatever her response" (Blumenfeld, 1994, p. 213).

The media dubbed the term "Billary effect" to capture the idea that Bill Clinton ran on a two-for-one (Bill and Hillary) platform. The term refers to a husband-and-wife partnership that bridges boardroom and bedroom. They called it a dilemma of the 1990s and raised the concern of the public about nepotism focusing on the President's wife. Hillary Clinton's leading role in the administration's health care reform pushed her into a powerful, highly visible policy-making role, although she holds no public office; this kept the media on a roller coaster.

Women like Hillary Clinton who lead aggressively are labeled "bossy," "obnoxious," "overbearing," and "ambitious" in newspaper reports. If, on the other hand, they continue to adhere to stereotypic female socialization patterns and lead in a nurturant and cooperative way, they are labeled "weak," "sensitive," and "unambitious." The confusion of the newspapers over how to deal with women leaders who do not conform to female gender stereotypes was pointed out in a statement made by Harriet Wood, president of the National Women's Political Caucus. At a Freedom Forum roundtable in Washington, DC, Wood pointed out that Hillary Clinton is suffering from being used symbolically as a whipping boy for what the media perceive as the difference between the conservative women of America and mainstream working women. Yet, many women see Hillary Clinton as the embodiment of all the roles they are trying to juggle in their own lives, and many believe she is being punished for being too smart and too successful (O'Brian, 1994).

In 1993, Hillary Rodham Clinton reached stardom on Capitol Hill when she testified to Congress, lobbying for her husband's proposed health care reform package. The media compared Hillary Clinton to Eleanor Roosevelt in the 1940s and praised her for her intelligent, authoritative selling of the administration's health care plan. Many of the members of the House and Means Committee, which in the fall of 1993 consisted of 36 men and 2 women, did not know what to make of the Yale-educated lawyer and chief architect of the President's health care reform plan. The media either put out lavish and complementary reports on her performance, or ridiculed her. Media coverage of Hillary Clinton changed from describing her as heavy-handed, Bill's wife, a meddler, an overachiever, domineering, radical, and a fashion nerd to being politically savvy, Bill's advisor, political insider, competent, outspoken, role model, and trendy (Hill, 1993). Media coverage emphasized her appearance and style over substance and made it clear that the American public was not ready for a his-and-her presidency (Eagan, 1992). The astonishing and often exasperating publicity surrounding Hillary Rodham Clinton epitomizes the struggle over the social construction of feminine and masculine identities, as do controversies over other highly visible women such as Margaret Thatcher and Madonna (Van Zoonen, 1994).

Other women in history who tried to reshape the role of first lady—by custom, the nation's model wife—did not fare better in the media. They too came under fire and public scrutiny. For example, Mary Todd Lincoln's loyalty was questioned because of her Confederate kinfolk. Dolly Madison became the target of a congressional investigation after purchasing a $40.00 mirror. Eleanor Roosevelt wrote a newspaper column and accepted money for speaking engagements, both of which the media objected to. Even before her husband's inauguration, newspapers editorialized against Mrs. Roosevelt, admonishing her to keep her opinions to herself. Betty Ford lobbied for ERA and Rosalyn Carter attended cabinet meetings. Both women came under media scrutiny for their involvement in these activities. Each of them established a distinct identity different from that of her husband. Nevertheless, the media continued to treat them as appendages of their spouses.

Wintermantel and Christman (1983) analyzed newspaper coverage of women and men in recognized leadership positions. The authors found that, in contrast to male leaders, descriptions of female leaders made more reference to leadership traits (i.e., dominance and self-confidence), making it appear as if the possession of such traits was self-evident in men while requiring special mentioning for women leaders. In the descriptions of female leaders, their leadership traits were stressed because these characteristics differentiated them from the gender-role cliché. Conversely, descriptions of male leaders called attention to other attributes and roles, such as interest in sports, their personal leadership philosophy, and their role as fathers. Newspaper descriptions of women leaders illustrate the "male-as-norm" principle, which serves both as a frame of reference for newspaper descriptions of female leaders and as a standard for judging their adequacy.

Thus, the world of newspapers as one important mass communication vehicle remains largely a man's world. Few women hold senior management positions or own newspapers. When women do occupy senior executive positions—two examples being Margaret Pynchon, owner and publisher of the *Los Angeles Tribune*, or Katherine Graham, former CEO and chairwoman of the *Washington Post*—readers are quickly reminded that these women usually inherited their leadership positions from their spouses.

Women Leaders and Leading Women on Television

Television is the most powerful medium of mass communication simply by the sheer number of people it reaches. TV provides the sole source of news for over 40% of Americans, since the majority of Americans feel that TV news is more deliverable than newspapers. Information conveyed via TV is perceived as more immediate, easier to receive, and more intimate with the benefit of attractive and persuasive messengers (Driscoll & Goldberg, 1993). All types of people, regardless of race, national origin, social class, gender, and age, watch TV.

The amount of TV viewed by the average American is considerable and has increased steadily over the years. The average American household is tuned in to a TV over 7 hours a day. During their school years, children spend more time watching television than they do in the classroom. Among the mass media, TV is the most popular and powerful cultural medium, one which broadcasts programs that are replete with potential meanings (Fiske, 1987).

Because of the size of its audience and the frequency with which it is watched, TV has been credited with an unprecedented ubiquity that makes it potentially more effective than any other mode of mass communication. Gerbner and Gross (1974) said of TV's pervasiveness:

> [We] cannot emphasize too strongly the role of TV in standardizing and sharing with all as common norm what had before been more parochial, local, and selective cultural patterns. We assume, therefore, that TV's standardizing and legitimizing influence comes largely from its ability to streamline, amplify, ritualize, and spread the conventional capsules of mass produced information and entertainment. (p. 6)

TV not just transmits information, it transforms it. In doing so, this medium has become a major system of social regulation or as Smith (1980) called it, the machine of social regulation. Janis (1980) also suggested that TV acts as a socializing agent by providing models or scripts of action in society. Thus TV is being credited with being the great socializer in American society. It teaches us what is believed to be important. It teaches children how to behave. It may also teach violence and sex-role stereotyping. As a result, the role of TV in sex-role socialization has become the topic of a good deal of research.

As a socialization agent, TV promotes traditional stereotypes and plays a role in the development of children's values regarding gender-appropriate behavior. Because watching TV involves the observation of the behavior of others and its reinforcement contingencies, TV is considered an important vehicle through which people, particularly children, learn about gender-appropriate behavior (Rak & McMullen, 1987). Since children watch TV anywhere from 3 to 7 hours a day (e.g., Bretl & Cantor; Furnham & Bitar, 1993), they can easily acquire stereotypic views by the time they enter first grade. Numerous studies (e.g., Kolbe, 1991; Macklin & Kolbe, 1984; Morgan, 1982, 1987) have demonstrated children's active involvement in the construction of gender-typed TV attitudes as well as the role TV plays in the occupational socialization of young viewers. Moreover, McGhee and Frueh (1980) found that increased TV viewing correlated with children's stronger beliefs in gender stereotypes. Because TV messages must be easily comprehended by the viewer, producers often use roles and situations that are readily identifiable by the audience and in agreement with cultural values, particularly those regarding gender-appropriate behaviors (Manstead & McCulloch, 1981).

News, according to Fiske (1987) is a high-status TV genre because it claims objectivity and independence from political or governmental agencies and therefore is believed to be essential for the workings of a democracy. Here again, women leaders and women in leading roles, such as newscasters or anchorwomen, are short-changed. Based on a survey of female correspondents on TV news, Sanders (1993) concluded that although a few women cover the White House and a handful of other visible government departments, many others do not get on the air. With the exception of a few well-established female correspondents such as Andrea Mitchell or Barbara Walters, and the gains several other women have made in network television news reporting, many other anchorwomen appear on TV news paired and overshadowed by older men, or their stories are relegated to non-prime-time programming or to syndication.

Media Report to Women (1994b) found that men reported 86% of the stories on ABC, CBS, and NBC. According to other sources (e.g., Carmody, 1993; Durka, 1990) men hold 90% of upper-level Hollywood executive positions, play two-thirds of the leads in prime-time TV, supply 90% of the narrator's voices in TV commercials, and monopolize 90% of televised sporting events. In addition, men host most of the top nationally broadcast talk shows on politics and current affairs. They appear on the more powerful stations, get better time slots, and broadcast more hours each week. For example, on PBS's "McNeill-Lehrer," 87% of the experts interviewed were male; on ABC's "Nightline," 89%. Female opinion leaders, on the other hand, are rarely consulted for these shows, which are anchored by men (Driscoll & Goldberg, 1993). Although there has been an increase in the presentation of women, they are depicted in a much narrower range of roles on TV news shows. TV prime-time drama presents a similar picture. In the 1987–1988 season, only 3 of 21 primetime dramas featured female leads, and only two of these were adults (Faludi, 1991). In addition, on TV as in other media, women often lack the competitively achieved occupational power ascribed to men (Vandeberg & Streckfuss, 1992).

The pervasive use of TV, and the potential of televised portrayals of female and male leaders to influence and shape the audience's perceptions of leadership, justifies the concern for the way gender roles are played out in this medium.

Figure 5.3 Television: News Show Averages Correspondents & Interviewees
Source: Copyright 1994, Media Report To Women. Reprinted with permission.

After decades of depiction as sex objects, dumb blondes, naive virgins, or wise-cracking tarts, women finally began to appear in strong leading roles in the mid-1980s. Examples include top-ranking shows like ''Roseanne'' (who cannot easily be labeled a sex object) and ''Murphy Brown.'' These shows which, probably not coincidentally, were created by women, became instant hits. In addition, Oprah Winfrey, Sally Jesse Raphael, and Joan Rivers appeared on our sets as hosts of talk shows and moved to the top of a field once almost exclusively dominated by men. Finally, the morning news shows added high-visibility women including Joan Lunden, Paula Zahn, and Katie Couric, who, in most cases, helped their networks ratings.

Despite these gains, many researchers (e.g., Davis, 1990; Signorielli, 1989) argue that despite dramatic changes in the outside world, TV programs have been remarkably stable in their portrayal of women and men, resulting in the underrepresentation of women leaders in the mass media. Davis (1990) concluded that ''while changes have been made in television's treatment of Blacks, Hispanics, and others, little change has occurred in portrayals of women'' (p. 330). Thus, many of the demographics characteristics (e.g., age, physical appearance) relating to women imply that traditional gender-typed roles still form the basis of the portrayal of women on TV.

Women leaders, in contrast to some leading women (on TV), receive little coverage on TV, partly because leadership is defined by the media in the narrow context of formal positions or political leadership. Adjectives used to identify women's contributions tend to be gender-specific, and accounts of women's leadership styles aired on TV reinforce prevailing stereotypes. The language used to describe women leaders is carefully selected to evoke and reinforce gender stereotypes. TV commentators, for example, are more likely to make reference to the emotional qualities of women leaders than to those of their male counterparts. In an analysis of references to emotions in a transcript by the three commercial networks and PBS conducted immediately after the 1984 debate between vice presidential candidate Geraldine Ferraro and George Bush, Shields (1987) found nearly twice as many references to Ferraro's emotions (both presence and absence) as to Bush's.

TV also reinforces stereotyped perceptions of leadership styles. In the review of behavioral theories of leadership in Chapter 3, we noted two broad dimensions: task-oriented and relationship-oriented leadership styles. Based on this people-versus-task dichotomy, it is generally assumed that women leaders are relationship-oriented, while men prefer the task-oriented style. On TV, this assumption plays itself out in the person of Ted Koppel, of ABC. Koppel comes across as a strictly task-oriented anchor, while Katie Couric of NBC is more concerned with building interpersonal relationships with staff and interviewees.

George Gerbner, professor of communications and dean emeritus of the University of Pennsylvania, in an interview with USA Today (Gable, 1993, p. 4D), referred to the underrepresentation of women and other minorities on TV as ''out-of-focus casting'' which he called the tip of the iceberg. Gerbner said, ''When you have a cast like that (referring to the more than 1,300 characters studied of which 84% were white and 63% were male), you can tell more stories about power, conflict, and violence and that's what sells.'' The out-of-focus presentation of women on TV, according to Faludi (1991), produced a backlash resulting in a significant shrinkage of TV audiences. Faludi reported that since 1987 TV network ratings dropped sharply and the audience shrank by more than 25% with women accounting for much of the shrinkage.

WOMEN LEADERS IN THE POPULAR LITERATURE

In contrast to TV and newspapers, which either pay little tribute to women leaders or minimize their contributions, the popular literature which includes books, women's magazines, and newsletters of women's organizations like the National Association of Female Executives is celebrating women's leadership. Headlines like "Men who (Gasp) Manage Like Women" and labels such as "feminine leadership" are intended to reverse the long-held belief that men are uniquely qualified for leadership. The popular literature emphasizes certain female advantages. Instead of men's command-and-control style of leadership, which emphasizes hierarchy, dominance, control, and competition, popular accounts characterize women's leadership style as cooperative, nurturant, empowering, and team-oriented. Tom Peters (1990) articulated this reversal of leadership superiority as follows:

> It is perfectly obvious that women should be better managers in today's topsy-turvy business environment. As we rush into the 1990s, there is little disagreement about what business must become: less hierarchical, more flexible, and team-oriented, faster and more fluid. In my opinion, one group of people has an enormous advantage in realizing this new vision: women. (p. 216)

The popular literature dispenses notions such as *Feminine Leadership: Or How to Succeed in Business without Being One of the Boys* (Loden, 1985) and *The Female Advantage: Women's Way of Leadership* (Helgesen, 1990). Loden's book was one of the earliest books acclaiming women's superior leadership potential. The author maintains that there is a masculine mode of leadership based on high control for the leader, hierarchical authority, and analytic problemsolving. Women, on the other hand, prefer a feminine leadership model built on cooperation, collaboration, low control for the leader, and intuitive problemsolving. According to Loden, the core characteristic of the "feminine" leadership style is the reliance on emotional as well as rational data. The author asserted that feminine leaders see the world through two different but concurrent lenses and, as a result, respond to situations on both thinking and feeling levels. Since feminine leadership favors personal over position power, women embracing this type of leadership create a climate of cooperation, participation, and shared accountability.

Helgesen (1990) in her book *Female Advantage: Women's Ways of Leading* takes a similar position. She describes the differences between male and female leaders by using two images: the hierarchy and the web. The author asserts that women form flat organizations rather than hierarchical ones. Their leadership style is characterized by frequent contacts with staff members and sharing of information. Helgesen argued that the integration of female values into the leadership situation creates a web of inclusion, a circular system interconnected by an exchange of power and information. The web structure puts a premium on affiliation and flexibility. At the center of the web is the woman leader, who stresses the importance of accessibility and maintains an open-door policy.

Like Loden, Helgesen suggests that women embrace a participative, empowering, consensus-building style of leadership. She insists categorically that being a woman is not a handicap when it comes to leadership. Instead, it is an advantage. To illustrate the essence of the "female advantage," Helgesen quotes a statement by Anita Roddick, who believes that business practices can be improved if they are guided by feminine management principles. These principles involve sharing, making intuitive as opposed to rational decisions, having a sense of work as part of one's life, rather than separate from it, and putting your labor where your love is. Like the women in Helgesen's book, Roddick is said to operate from the center of the web.

In a controversial article entitled "Ways Women Lead," Rosener (1990) suggests a leadership style characteristic of women which the author calls "interactive leadership." After interviewing 355 female executives who served as heads of large corporations, and 101 male executives matched for position, type, and size of organization, Rosener concludes that men employ the command-and-control style of leadership, whereas the hallmarks of women's leadership style are getting their followers to transform their self-interests into those of the group, sharing power, and enhancing other people's self-worth. Rosener calls this leadership style, which bears some resemblance to transformational leadership, "interactive" because the women in her sample actively worked to make their interactions with subordinates positive for everyone.

The article was controversial because academics attacked the survey on methodological grounds while proponents of the "vive la différence" position on gender differences in leadership styles hailed it as a significant piece of evidence documenting women's superior leadership abilities. Although Rosener employed a much larger sample then Helgesen, the fact remains that the women participating in the survey represented a highly selective group of managers. The average profile described a 51-year-old executive in the service industry with an annual income of $140,000, married to a corporate manager or attorney with no children at home. Typically, the female executive was employed in a medium-sized organization which had experienced rapid growth and change. The sample, therefore, was hardly representative of women in upper management in general. In addition, the synonymous treatment of management and leadership discussed in the last chapter also applies to Rosener's article.

Most recently, Carol Edlund (1993), following the tradition established by the writers quoted above, proposes what she calls a humanistic model of leadership, based on the assumption that all people possess both feminine and masculine traits. The author highlights the differences between feminine and masculine styles of leadership as depicted in Table 5.1.

Central to Edlund's model, which is based on a survey of 850 female managers in the public sector, are notions of the importance of the "open door" policy for women; the idea that success for women is not material in nature;

TABLE 5.1   Feminine and Masculine Models of Leadership

Characteristic	Feminine	Masculine
Operating Style	Cooperative	Competitive
Organizational Structure	Team	Hierarchy
Basic Objective	Quality Output	Quantity Output
Problem-solving Style	Intuitive/Rational	Rational
Key Characteristics	Low Control Empathetic Collaborative	High Control Analytic Strategic

team orientation in women's style of leadership; and the need to balance personal and professional lives. What is less clear is how these factors were measured and how they correlated with indices of leadership effectiveness.

Thus, the popular literature portrays two types of leadership, one predominantly feminine and the other predominantly masculine. According to Tannen (1990), for women the world is a network of connections in which support and consensus are sought and confirmed. For men, in contrast, the world is made up of individuals in a hierarchical social order in which life is a competitive struggle for success, the gaining of independence and advantage over others, and avoiding the loss of power. According to Nelson (1991) these two types of leadership are the result of two different kinds of experiences: those of men in the military and on the playing field, and those of women managing the home and nurturing husbands and children.

Taken together, popular descriptions of successful female leadership add to existing leadership paradoxes. They also add other two-dimensional models of leadership based on gender differences. The popular literature implies that women's ways of leading are more effective and should perhaps be the norm desirable for men as well. In fact, it has been suggested that women's collaborative, flexible leadership style will play a vital role in managing our heterogeneous, culturally diverse workforce. However, ironically enough, the skills and traits women were once told had no place in boardrooms are the very same which now give them a leadership edge. After half a century of male-oriented research, leadership in the popular press is presented as a highly gendered domain of a different kind, with women leading more effectively because prevailing female gender stereotypes are now touted as providing an advantage. As Cantor and Bearnay (1992) noted, instead of exhorting women to put aside their femininity and manage like men, the popular press praises and celebrates feminine attributes. However, many of the characteristics ascribed to "feminine leadership" are not limited to women, but also exhibited by men like Thomas Watson of IBM or Edwin Land of Polaroid.

CONCLUSIONS

This chapter chronicled the frequent absence of women leaders in, on, and behind the media. The importance of the media in constructing the social reality of leadership and shaping our perceptions and attitudes toward women leaders has been widely recognized by social scientists and media analysts. The media do not simply provide facts and information, but serve as socializing agents by giving meaning to events. The Clarence Thomas–Anita Hill hearings were cited as an example here to illustrate how the media construct events for the audience and perpetuate the dominant values and ideology of our culture. They also illustrate the media's own selective vision of social and political issues.

Sanders (1993), in a survey designed to monitor gender issues in the media, stated:

> Just as we [women] were so obviously absent from the Senate Judiciary Committee hearings on Clarence Thomas, just as we were barely visible in President Bush's cabinet, just as we are tokens on the boards of corporate America, so we are largely unseen and unheard in the newsrooms of this nation. (p. 171)

Many people became accustomed to looking at the media as a source of expert knowledge. Yet typically, in descriptions of women leaders, the media fail to accurately reflect the demography of the occupations, social, and organizational life of our society and a specific subset of it, namely the women who occupy leadership roles. An examination of the portrayal of women leaders on TV, in newspapers, business magazines, and the popular press reveals an interesting paradox: women leaders are either treated as a scarcity, or are labeled ineffective because cultural stereotypes hold that they lack important leadership attributes or they are heralded as possessing the keys to effective leadership. However, as Cohen (1993) pointed out, the responsibility for the media as a socialization agent should not be construed as a mandate to act as conservators of the status quo.

In contrast to newspapers and TV, which treat women leaders as exceptions and often trivialize their contributions, popular literature thrives on claims that women are uniquely prepared and qualified for leadership. By doing so, the development of new stereotypes is encouraged by continuing to label one form of leadership feminine and the other masculine. Stereotyping women leaders as different-superior is just as limiting as stereotyping them as different-inferior.

Although more women now hold high-profile positions in the media than they did 20 years ago, and many would agree that there has been a change for the better in the coverage of women leaders and that more women are cast in leading roles on news shows and prime-time TV, few women are presented in leadership roles carrying authority and high status. Moreover, few women are found in leading positions as CEOs of TV networks, newspaper publishing houses, or radio stations. Those who have succeeded had to fight negative stereotypes and biased coverage to gain respect and credibility. This underrepresentation of women leaders raises the question whether the changes in the representation of women leaders in the mass media has been sufficiently large to give women leaders the same visibility and exposure to the public enjoyed by their male counterparts.

6

Leadership and Gender in the Scientific Literature: How Real Are the Differences Between Women and Men?

> The superiority of the male is indeed overwhelming: Perseus, Hercules, David, Achilles, Lancelot, the French warriors Du Geslin and Bayard, Napoleon—so many men for one Joan of Arc.
>
> *Simone de Beauvoir*

INTRODUCTION

Are women and men really as different in how they think about leadership, how they practice it, and how they are perceived as leaders by others? As the last chapter suggested, the mass media and popular literature in their portrayals of female and male leaders claim they are. Basically, these media convey the message that women and men bring different approaches to leadership. Moreover, by pointing to the different ways in which women and men lead, the media legitimize the different expectations the public may have when dealing with or interpreting the leadership of women and men.

Gender and the categories of male and female have been central to Western thought, entering virtually every domain of human experience and structuring human relationships. Gender categories are used to organize our experiences, since they allow us to define and rank individuals (Hare-Mustin & Marecek, 1990a). Our language tells us that women and men are "opposite sexes." Theories of leadership offer gendered concepts, such as democratic and autocratic leadership styles. Moral philosophers describe differential paths of moral development of boys and girls, which suggest that men achieve higher levels of moral reasoning.

Likewise, historians and anthropologists have asked the question of why women everywhere and through the ages have been labeled the "subordinate sex," as reflected in the long record of male leadership and dominance. As

135

Boulding (1992) pointed out, historically, dominance systems have organized most of our political and economic lives. Moreover, because they are also *male* dominance systems, they cast a shadow over the lives of women, both in the public and domestic spheres. Gender differences in the form of male dominance and female subordination have prevailed throughout history, from the Judaic Biblical account of the creation of the human race to the theories of Freud. The visible world, as Boulding (1992) notes, continues to be male.

In this chapter, we will examine the scientific evidence (or lack thereof) regarding gender differences in leadership. In contrast to the media and popular literature, which do not claim to be objective or unbiased, empirical research of gender differences in leadership is conducted in the name of science. However, this does not mean that research in this field is always objective and free of biases, since leadership is both an art and a science. It only implies that leadership researchers have applied methods which allow them to produce a body of knowledge derived from empirical work, as opposed to anecdotal evidence, that is replicable and becomes accumulative with those replications. This type of research is conducted primarily for the sake of advancing knowledge and understanding phenomena related to leadership.

The scientific study of leadership shares many of the same methodological problems which besets research in most of the social sciences. Since much of the research in the scientific literature is derived from leadership theories, operational definitions of the variables of interest (i.e., defining concepts by the steps used to measure them), such as leadership style or leadership effectiveness, are always problematic. How do we operationally define an effective leader as opposed to an ineffective one? Operationally defining concepts is one of the requirements of science which is necessary if science is to provide communicable knowledge. Thus, although the scientific approach promises control over extraneous variables, operational definitions of theoretical concepts, and reproducibility of observations, leadership researchers often have to compromise, since different requirements of the scientific method are difficult to attain in a single study.

GENDER AND GENDER DIFFERENCES

Before discussing the nature and evidence of female-male differences in leadership, it is necessary to distinguish between two terms, "sex" and "gender," which are often used interchangeably. This leads to the belief that differences in traits and behaviors of male and female leaders are due to biological differences when, in fact, they may have been shaped by culture. The tendency to confuse sex and gender is illustrated by the number of terms that gender research has generated to describe sex-linked and gender-related phenomena. These include concepts of sex roles, sex typing, sex-role norms, and sex-role identity. All of these terms have also been used in conjunction with gender; thus we find the terms gender roles, gender typing, gender stereotypes, and gender-schematic (i.e., sex-typed) behaviors in the literature.

Distinction Between Sex and Gender

Basically, sex is a biological variable, while gender is a matter of cultural relativity. For more than 100 years geneticists and social scientists have attempted to determine to what extent nature (genes) and nurture (environment) are responsible for the physical and psychological differences between women and men, but have not been very successful in providing definitive answers reflecting the respective contributions of heredity and environment. Today, relative contributions of genes and environment to leadership traits are not much better understood than at the beginning of the last century, when psychologists first started studying individual differences.

Some traits like aggression or dominance which have been linked to leadership are also believed to be sex-linked. In other words, American men presumably are more aggressive than American women. The biological basis of aggression is derived from the presence of the Y chromosome and the sex hormone testosterone, both of which convey maleness. However, behavioral manifestations of aggression in boys and girls, or men and women, can also be explained culturally and socially, since both sexes display a variety of aggressive behaviors ranging from aggressive verbal acts to criminal behavior. Eagly and Steffan (1986) asserted that gender differences in aggressiveness may also be attributable to the distribution of women and men in social roles. Since men occupy high-status level positions in organizations more often than do women, men are presented with greater opportunities to wield power. Conversely, occupants of low-status positions, that is, the majority of women, typically do not possess sufficient power to intimidate others, and therefore often behave in nonaggressive ways. Nevertheless, even for behaviors such as aggression and dominance, which are believed to have a genetic basis and which consistently have shown male-female differences, biology or sex account only for 5% of the variability between people (Hyde & Linn, 1986).

Biological sex is a highly visible, salient feature of a person which immediately triggers different behavioral expectations for both men and women. As Deaux (1984) pointed out, whether an individual is a woman or man is an important determinant of impression formation and social judgments. Since biological sex is a dichotomized category, there is a tendency for people to align psychological attributes, including personality characteristics, leadership styles, and competencies, with being female or male.

Gender, on the other hand, is used to designate social relations between sexes. As Unger and Crawford (1992) suggested, gender is what culture makes of the raw material of biological sex. According to Scott (1986), the word "gender" implies the explicit rejection of biological determinism implicit in the use of such terms as "sex" or "sex differences." Instead, "gender" refers to a set of assumptions about the nature and character of biological differences between women and men. These assumptions are manifest in a number of ideas and practices that have a predominant influence upon the identity, social opportunities, and the experiences of women and men as leaders and followers.

As defined in Chapter 1, gender in this book is treated as a significant, if not the most significant, component of culture. It denotes the cultural descriptions and proscriptions that society ascribes to biological differences and the social construction of appropriate roles of women and men. Van Zoonen (1994) suggested that:

> Gender is a volatile, almost meaningless category that can be filled with meaning according to individual preferences, social conditions, cultural peculiarities or historical contingencies. It may obscure the power relations in which gender is embedded and the very terminology of gender may conceal that "masculinity" often implies a discourse of power and centrality, whereas "femininity" is commonly related to powerlessness and marginality. (p. 150)

Although many disciplines have participated in the discourse on gender differences, psychology in particular, with its long tradition of studying individual differences, has developed an area of specialization within the discipline variously known as the "psychology of sex differences," "psychology of women," or "feminist psychology," which is dedicated to ascertaining the ways men and women differ. As part of a critical analysis of their discipline, psychologists began to examine the gender biases of their theories and research findings that provide the foundation of our knowledge of differences between women and men. They called attention to the androcentric or male-centered nature of many psychological theories. For example, Kahn and Jean (1983) pointed out:

> There was widespread agreement about [psychology's] faults: that women were studied from a male-as-normative viewpoint; that women's behavior was explained as a deviation from male standards; that the stereotype of women [as passive and dependent] was considered an accurate portrayal of women's behavior; that women who fulfilled the dictates of the stereotype are viewed as healthy and happy; that differences of the behaviors of women and men are attributed to differences in anatomy and physiology; and that the social context which often shapes behavior was ignored in the case of women. (p. 660)

Research on gender was an idea whose time had come (Deaux, 1985). This interest in gender research took place in a social context characterized by changing roles of women and the women's liberation movement of the 1970s, when social scientists began to rethink their assumptions and beliefs about women. They challenged major theoretical frameworks, from Darwin and Freud to recent developments in cognitive psychology. Some, particularly feminist psychologists, believed that a radical change in psychological theorizing about gender was needed. Consequently, feminist psychologists took on the task of deconstructing their discipline by analyzing the implicit assumptions about women embedded in psychological theories and research practices (Unger & Crawford, 1992).

Just as biologically based sex differences give rise to stereotypes, gender stereotypes emerge as the differential distribution of women and men in social roles (Hoffman & Hurst, 1990). Whenever we hold expectations that are prescribed according to biological sex, we are engaged in gender-role stereotyping.

Gender stereotyping occurs most frequently when people know little about individuals except their sex. Thus, the degree of gender stereotyping of female and male leaders depends on the extent to which people acquire information about these leaders. If little other information is available, men are typically seen in high-status authority roles (leaders) and women in low-status subordinate roles (followers). In other words, when little information other than the leader's sex is available, people are more likely to evaluate women leaders based on conformity to socially sanctioned sex roles.

Gender is a knot that consists of pieces of biology, psychology, sociology, and culture—the complex interplay of which is difficult to unravel. Unlike other individual difference variables, such as spatial ability or mathematical achievements—which are theorized to account for the small number of women found in professions such as architecture and engineering—gender has no explanatory power. Instead, its effects must be explained by other constructs, such as the lack of opportunity structures for women in male-dominated occupations. The term "gender" calls our attention to the role that social, environmental, and cultural factors play in shaping women's and men's leadership. Gender, therefore, is construed as a set of overlapping and sometimes contradictory cultural descriptions and prescriptions referring to sexual differences (Van Zoonen, 1994).

Because of the tangled meanings of sex and gender, distinctions between the two concepts are important. Distinguishing between these two concepts is important because the differential use of "sex" and "gender" guides our choice of vocabulary and language. Van Nostrand (1993) discussed "4 Ds" of gender stereotypes in language when she pointed out that men try to maintain privilege and entitlement in conversations by *dominating* or *detaching* and *distancing* themselves from the group. Women, on the other hand, tend to accommodate by *deferring* to others or *diagnosing* dysfunctional group processes. The author argued that each of these behaviors—dominance, detachment, deference, and diagnosis—represents patterns of speech through which men and women attempt to gain control over group processes. Paying attention to the 4 Ds can sensitize us to the self-defeating nature of behaviors attached to gender roles, and to the ways in which these behaviors create power imbalances between men and women. They also show that men frequently use language to gain and maintain status, while women communicate to create connection, resulting in "report" talk of men and "rapport" talk of women (Van Nostrand, 1993).

Furthermore, the choice of language, at least in part, drives our assumptions about causality. Thus, when we talk about sex differences in leadership, we are implying differences between men and women caused by biological factors. The reliance on the trait paradigm has led to attributions of sex differences to innate factors, such as intelligence and aggression, and these attributions have in turn provided a rationale for viewing women as temperamentally unsuited or inferior for leadership. On the other hand, if we frame differences between female and male leaders based on gender, culture becomes the focus of analysis when seeking explanations for female-male differences.

LEADERSHIP AND GENDER

Many interpretations have been advanced to explain behavioral differences between women and men, including biological determinism, culturally and environmentally derived theses that include the notion that women are not different at all from men. As in other areas of gender research, when leadership is the subject of investigation, studies have been framed through the eyes of men, resulting in biased portrayals of women leaders. Most research conducted prior to the 1980s emphasized differences between female and male leaders, and often these differences have been used to support the belief in superior male leadership qualities.

Findings showing or implying differences in the ways women and men lead produced two streams of evidence: one minimizing gender differences in leadership, and the other maximizing them. These two approaches were labeled, respectively, beta and alpha biases (Hare-Mustin & Marecek, 1990b). Beta bias is the tendency to minimize or ignore gender differences, while alpha bias refers to the tendency to maximize or demonstrate the existence of such differences. Researchers in both camps have cited empirical evidence and proposed theoretical explanations to bolster their respective positions. As a result, both streams of research have led to widely held and divergent representations of the role of gender in leadership.

Research on gender differences in moral reasoning and judgment (e.g., Gilligan, 1982; Kohlberg, 1981), which have been linked to both gender development and leadership, illustrates alpha bias. This line of research is relevant to the study of leadership because of the importance of morality that underlies conceptualizations of leadership (e.g., Burns, 1978). At what level of morality, asked Burns, must leaders operate to fulfill a critical leadership task, namely, elevating follow-ers to higher levels of moral reasoning? According to Burns, the ultimate test of morally responsible leadership is "the capacity to transcend the claims of multiplicity of everyday wants and needs and expectations, to respond to higher levels of moral development and to relate leadership behaviors to a set of reasoned, relatively explicit, conscious values" (p. 46).

Gilligan (1982) suggested that individual differences exist between the princi-ples employed by women and men as the basis of their moral reasoning. The author explained gender differences and the divergent paths of moral development followed by girls and boys in terms of differences of experience, or "different voices." In her book entitled *In a Different Voice*, Carol Gilligan tried to show how women's moral development was devalued and misrepresented by male researchers, particularly Lawrence Kohlberg.

According to Kohlberg, moral development unfolds in a series of six stages, during which process our capacity for moral reasoning becomes increasingly differentiated and complex. More specifically, Kohlberg proposed a six-stage theory of moral development divided into three phases—preconventional, conven-tional, and postconventional. These three stages, in turn, are divided into three sublevels: the punishment-obedience and instrumental relativist orientation (pre-conventional), the interpersonal concordance and "law and order" orientation (conventional), and the social contract and ethical principle orientation (postcon-ventional). In other words, the moral choices of children and few adults are based on fear and punishment (preconventional) while most adults apply "law and order" reasoning to moral dilemmas and choices (conventional). At the highest stage of moral development which, according to Kohlberg, only few adults attain, moral reasoning is determined by universal ethical principles and values such as equality of human rights and respect for individual dignity (postconventional). At this stage, individuals whose moral thinking is based on internalized, universal principles may break laws they believe to be unjust.

Moral reasoning is assessed by presenting individuals with a number of moral dilemmas which reflect the different stages of moral development of Kohlberg's model. An example of a moral dilemma used in Kohlberg's interview procedures is the question "Should a man steal a drug to save his wife?" A male child might answer "no" to this question, seeing the possibility of being hurt oneself as worse than the possibility of someone else dying. A female child, on the other hand, might say "no" because the man has a responsibility to keep himself out of jail and help the rest of his family. As Arinder (1993) noted, despite substantially different answers, and the different means used to arrive at those answers (abstraction of the problem versus consideration of the man's specific family situation), both children exemplify Kohlberg's preconventional stage of moral development, with the male child at Stage 1, punishment–reward orientation, and the female child at Stage 2, instrumental relativist orientation (personal needs first, with the needs of others good if achievable in consequence). Kohlberg concluded that boys and men achieve higher levels of moral reasoning, whereas women have a less mature and less developed sense of morality.

Numerous criticisms have been lodged against Kohlberg's stage theory of moral development. Critics, including Gilligan (1982), quoted gender, cultural, and methodological biases arguing that what constitutes "more advanced" moral reasoning, according to Kohlberg, is oriented toward male views of moral problems, and underrepresents an equally valid approach to morality that women more frequently embrace. Gilligan argued that when faced with a hypothetical, Kohlberg-type moral dilemma, girls and women are at a disadvantage simply because Kohlberg's dilemmas pose conflicts of justice in which the rights of different people clash. Since women, according to Gilligan, see morality as a problem of care rather than justice, they are ill-prepared to reason about the focal issue involved in the moral dilemma (Colby & Damon, 1983).

Gilligan stressed women's concern with caring in moral choices and construed it as an essentially female attribute. One of her first specific statements about female moral development is that "Women's judgments are tied to feelings of empathy and compassion and are concerned with the resolution of real, as opposed to hypothetical dilemmas" (Gilligan, 1982, p. 69). Gilligan goes on to say that "The conflict between the self and others thus constitutes the central moral problem for women, posing a dilemma whose resolution requires a reconciliation between femininity and adulthood" (p. 71). She argued that Kohlberg's theory emphasizes an orientation to justice ("rules are rules," "fair is fair") which should be contrasted with women's orientation to caring, rather than their concern with being treated fairly and justly. Thus, according to Gilligan, gender differences in moral development and moral reasoning are the result of women preferring the moral principle of caring, while men prefer the principle of justice.

Thus, as Arinder (1993) stated:

> Gilligan's stages of moral development in women are based on the evolution of the individual of the supposed guiding ethic of femininity, that of care. From an initial, perhaps "female-preconventional" stage, in which care is extended only to the self, women evolve to a second, "female-conventional" stage. In the second stage, care for personal interests is denounced as selfish and extended to others only. However, awareness of the inadequacy of the second position comes to women, for whom the third stage, possibly designated as "female-postconventional", entails an awareness of a matrix of relationships into which a woman fits herself and which is not merely personal but universal. (p. 7)

According to Gilligan, then, male moral development, and, therefore, the traditional model of human moral development, is conflict- and evaluation-based, while female moral development is based on relationships and communication.

Gilligan asserts that for men, justice is defined abstractly by balancing individual, often competing, rights, while for women, moral judgments stem from interpersonal connections. They are influenced by considerations of care, responsibility for others, and the personal-social context in which moral choices are made. Accordingly, women at the highest level of moral development make moral choices by resolving dilemmas between their own and others' needs. Rather than judging women as "morally deficient" by Kohlberg's standards, Gilligan suggested that women are capable of the highest level of moral thinking, but reach that stage through different, but equally valid, ways. Her theory suggests that when it comes to moral reasoning, women focus on care and responsibility and men on right and justice. If Gilligan is correct, there are two separate dimensions of moral justification: one used by women who base their moral decisions on obligations to care and avoid hurting others, and one used by men who view moral conflicts as abstract, logical problems concerning rights and rules.

Gilligan's book became one of the most widely quoted and influential works of the 1980s, representing the "most famous emblem of scholarship on women's difference" (Faludi, 1991). Both Kohlberg and Gilligan illustrate alpha bias in their research, since both proposed gender-linked theories of moral development. Like Kohlberg's research, Gilligan's work has been challenged on a number of grounds, including methodological biases. Researchers supporting the no-difference perspective presented evidence reflecting beta bias. For example, Friedman, Robinson, and Friedman (1987) tested the hypothesis that women are more likely to resolve moral dilemmas by means of care-oriented choices, while men draw on justice-oriented principles. A sample of college students responded to four moral dilemmas by rating the importance of 12 different statements reflecting care and justice orientations; in this study, gender was not associated with care-based or justice-based moral judgments. As Walker (1984) has pointed out, Gilligan failed to provide acceptable empirical support for her model. So far, the main evidence comes from studies using traditional measures of moral reasoning, such as Kohlberg's interview procedures. Based on two reviews of this literature (Rest, 1979; Walker, 1984), Friedman et al. (1987) concluded that there is little evidence that supports Gilligan's prediction that scoring procedures based on Kohlberg's theory will lead to the assignment of women to lower stages of moral development. In the final analysis, both Kohlberg's and Gilligan's theories of differences in moral development may be interpreted as perpetuating traditional stereotypes (e.g., Colby & Damon, 1983).

GENDER DIFFERENCES IN LEADERSHIP: HOW REAL ARE THEY?

Research on gender differences in leadership may be seen as a subset of a larger field of inquiry into male-female differences conducted in a variety of areas, including the study of physical differences in height, psychological differences in spatial, verbal, other cognitive abilities, and social behaviors, and differences in communication competence of men and women. The language used to describe these differences conveys a sense that these differences are fixed, built on a series of dichotomized dimensions such as reason–emotion, fact–value, good–evil, male–female (Culler, 1982).

One problem inherent in these dichotomies stems from the fact that in each pair, the contrasting terms take their meaning from the opposition or difference from the other. In addition, as Nehamas (1987) pointed out, the first member of each pair is considered more valuable (i.,e,, male norm) than the other. When gender is represented by dichotomized traits, behaviors, values or attitudes, the possibility that each component of the dichotomy may contain elements of the other is usually not taken into account. Moreover, any given set of gender dichotomies such as autocratic versus democratic, or task-oriented versus relationship-oriented leadership style, is likely to prompt observers to interpret the same behavior differently, depending on the gender of the actor. Hare-Mustin and Marecek (1990b) noted that dividing human characteristics along gender lines is also likely to increase the attention we pay to particular behaviors displayed by men and women, as well as the possibility of exaggerated selective judgments. Shields (1987), for example, found support for this hypothesis. Her findings showed that observers were more likely to look for, and explicitly note, emotional behaviors in women but not in men. Similarly, female aggression still carries a stigma, and is considered unacceptable and deviant behavior for women. Evidence that any of these stereotypes reflect reality is far from convincing.

The premise of the overriding importance of context, which predicts an increasing unpopularity of emphasizing differences between female and male leaders, was derived from two observations: 1) the time-bound nature of research on gender differences in leadership; and 2) the role of methodological artifacts in producing such differences. First, earlier studies of gender differences in leadership conducted prior to the 1980s (an arbitrarily set date) are more likely to report significant differences in leadership styles of men and women, evaluations of female and male leaders, follower satisfaction with male and female leaders, leader effectiveness, and performance of female and male leaders. More recent findings, on the other hand, tend to report rather small or insignificant differences.

Just as leadership theories are bounded by their temporal (and, for that matter, spatial) context, so is research on gender differences in leadership. A chronological split of the studies of gender differences into an earlier set (prior to the 1980s) and a more recent set of findings shows a temporal split between alpha and beta biases. This is not to say that all early studies show differences between female and male leaders or that all later research fails to report such differences. Rather, just as the results of some earlier studies (e.g., Butterfield &

Powell, 1981; Osborn & Vicas, 1976) favored the null hypothesis of no differences between male and female leaders, some later studies (e.g., Dobbins, 1985; Van Fleet & Saurage, 1984) continue to support the existence of differences. Despite these apparent inconsistencies, the importance of temporality, and the additional context time provides for research on gender differences in leadership, is critical. In the 1970s, for example, organizations were reluctant to allow female executives to travel with their male colleagues. Today, women and men traveling together on business no longer raise eyebrows or become the butt of jokes. Working on the premise of a temporal split does not, however, imply that we have evolved from an emphasis on differences between male and female leaders to an assumption of *no* differences and, therefore, equality. Thus the greater preponderance of small or no differences in no way represents an evolutionary progression toward more egalitarian values in our society at large.

Second, the chronological split is confounded by important differences in the research methods used in earlier versus later studies. More specifically, one particular methodology that has gained increasing popularity is meta-analysis. Meta-analysis is a quantitative technique designed to integrate and synthesize research across studies and reconcile inconsistent findings which may stem from statistical and methodological factors. It enables the researcher to summarize many different and independent studies testing the same hypothesis—in this case, testing for gender differences of some aspect of leadership. While earlier studies relied largely on narrative reviews and correlational approaches, later studies are more likely to employ quantitatively more sophisticated techniques, such as meta-analysis. However, as I noted elsewhere (Klenke, 1994), meta-analytic studies of leadership are not a panacea for resolving inconsistencies and contradictions. Instead, they sometimes introduce additional elements of confusion associated with this particular methodology, such as the lack of standardized procedures for conducting meta-analyses.

Time and methodologies, then, provide yet another context which shapes the study of gender differences in leadership. It is not only vital to understand how leadership works through categories like gender (and class, race, and ethnicity) but also how a contextualized view of leadership, in addition to the contexts discussed so far, sensitizes us to the temporal and methodological embeddedness of leadership concepts. Singling out one specific variable like gender is not a fruitful way of studying leadership, especially since it has been shown that social status incongruences based on class, power, racial, and ethnic differences override gender differences.

In the discussion of the scientific evidence of gender differences between female and male leaders, I have focused on three particular clusters of research: 1) female-male differences in leadership style; 2) differential evaluations of female and male leaders; and 3) follower satisfaction with male and female leaders.

Gender Differences in Leadership Styles

Leadership styles are frequently dichotomized along gender lines. These styles have been variously labeled instrumental versus expressive, production-oriented versus people-oriented, task versus socioemotional, and initiating structure versus consideration. Early leadership theorists representing the trait and behavioral traditions assumed that a leader exhibits a single style which she does not vary in response to different situational contingencies.

The distinction between these leadership styles is often made on the basis of one of the several instruments developed in the Ohio State University studies, such as measures of consideration and initiating structure, or using instruments developed at Iowa State University to measure democratic and autocratic leadership styles (see Chapter 3). Early studies (e.g., DiMarco & Whitsitt, 1975; Petty & Bruning, 1980) reported that women supervisors were more likely to display consideration than initiation of structure. These findings are consistent with stereotypes of women as being less goal-directed and more interpersonally oriented. However, as noted before, early findings of gender differences are not always consistent. For example, Kushell and Newton (1986), on the other hand, reported the results of an experiment in which female autocratic leaders were not perceived negatively. Likewise, Donnell and Hall (1980) concluded that male and female managers, based on their responses to the Style of Management Inventory, which measures managers' values and practices concerning task and social demands, did not differ in the way they managed the organization's technical and human resources. In addition, there were no overall differences in subordinates' perceptions of the leadership styles preferred by male and female managers.

Other studies have used arbitrarily defined leadership styles such as "acting like a man versus acting like a woman." Watson (1988) found that women who enacted the "masculine" leadership style which I refer to as counter-stereotypic in a role-playing simulation were found less influential than were women who enacted a "feminine" style in a problem-solving situation. Most of the studies which have dichotomized leadership style suggest that consideration (or leading democratically, or being interpersonally oriented) is an adequate base for leadership of women. They also suggest that leadership style and the masculine gender role correspond very closely.

More recent research, on the other hand, particularly studies employing meta-analytic techniques, suggests that the two dimensions of leadership style are more interactive than independent. As a result, in these studies, gender differences in leadership style are much smaller than earlier studies reported. Representative of a meta-analysis of gender and leadership style is a study by Eagly and Johnson (1990) which reviewed 162 studies of leadership styles of men and women using instruments such as the Leader Behavior Description Questionnaire, Supervisory Behavior Description Questionnaire, or Fiedler's Least Preferred Co-Worker scale. The results of this quantitative review indicated near-zero differences for interpersonal versus task oriented-leadership styles. It did show, however, a tendency for women to adopt a more democratic and participative leadership style when compared to men. Nevertheless, as Eagly et al. cautioned us, we should refrain from interpreting the tendency of women to lead more democratically as either an advantage or disadvantage, since a democratic leadership style may enhance leader effectiveness under some circumstances, while the autocratic style may facilitate a leader's effectiveness under a different set of circumstances. In practice, then, leadership styles dichotomized along gender lines are less obvious. Concern for people (consideration, democratic style) may only become appropriate and acceptable to followers once attention to the task has established the leader's credibility and defined a context for the interaction between leaders and followers.

Evaluations of Female and Male Leaders

It has been proposed that women leaders are evaluated differently because people use different cognitive structures when they assess the effectiveness of women and men in leadership roles. Evidence of gender differences in evaluations of female and male leaders, however, is mixed. As in the case of leadership style, earlier studies supported alpha biases favoring men in leadership positions. For example, Patterson (1975) found that female leaders received lower ratings of their performance and promotability. Likewise, Rice, Instone, and Adams (1984) obtained similar findings, indicating that female leaders were rated as having less capacity for increased responsibility, less ability to organize and coordinate the efforts of others, less initiative, forcefulness, and aggressiveness, and less ability to adjust to new or changing situations and stressors than were male leaders. On the other hand, although the authors tested for gender differences in leader behaviors, leader-follower relationships and leader success, no significant effects for gender were obtained.

Again, two recent meta-analytic studies (Eagly, Makhijani, & Klonsky, 1992; Swim, Borgida, Maruyana, & Myers, 1989) shed a somewhat different light on evaluations of male and female leaders. Eagly et al. (1992) investigated the question of whether or not women are evaluated less favorably when exercising leadership, even though in some objective sense their performances are equivalent. These researchers found small differences, with women leaders being evaluated slightly more negatively than their male counterparts. However, more important than this small difference were findings of selective devaluations of women leaders. For example, women were more likely to be evaluated negatively when they exhibited a masculine leadership style than when they exercised leadership in a more stereotypic female way (i.e., task versus interpersonal orientation). The

implications of this research are that behaviors that violate gender role expectations will elicit penalties such as social rejection and negative evaluations.

In addition, in the Eagly et al. (1992) study negative evaluations of women
leaders were stronger when female leaders occupied male-dominated roles and
when the evaluators were men. Finally, respondents favored female leaders over
male leaders with male subordinates, but favored male leaders over female leaders
with female subordinates. While Eagly et al. (1992) confined their review of
gender effects in leader evaluations to studies in which the leader's sex was the
manipulated variable, Swim et al. (1989) used studies in which participants rated
behaviors such as job performance or articles written by a hypothetical male or
female expert. Their results essentially replicated Eagly's findings, revealing only
slight differences favoring men in the evaluations.

Independent researchers (i.e., Brown & Geis, 1994) also showed a pro-male
bias in leadership evaluations and attributions of competence to male and female
leaders. The Brown and Geis (1994) study showed that the male leader was
personally backed by the group's supervisor and approved by fellow group
members, and the female leader had neither of these advantages. When the
advantages were reversed, however, the evaluation bias was also reversed. Since
evaluators assume that the reality determining their evaluations is the performance
itself and effectiveness of the leader, discriminatory biases in evaluations of
equally competent female and male leaders result in distortions of women's
contributions and competence.

Follower Satisfaction with Female and Male Leaders

Because women in leadership positions have to deal with other women as well
as men in follower positions, the potential effects of leader sex on follower
satisfaction are of interest. Several studies have shown that sex of the leader has
effects on follower performance (e.g., Donnell & Hall, 1980) and satisfaction.
Petty and Lee (1975), for instance, reported a tendency for male subordinates to
be more dissatisfied with male superiors who were high on initiating structure
and to be more satisfied when both male and particularly female supervisors
showed consideration. In this study, initiating structure by female supervisors
was negatively related to satisfaction for male subordinates, but positively or
not related to satisfaction for female subordinates. High initiation by female
supervisors, whether real or imagined, apparently clashed with sex-role stereotypes and produced the interaction effect between subordinate satisfaction and
leadership style. Bass and Avolio (1990) theorized that women leaders may be
judged more leniently by their followers because they are expected to do poorly
because of negative stereotypes. Conversely, male leaders may be seen as not
living up to followers' expectations and are judged more severely. Moreover, it

has been suggested that male leaders are more attuned to focusing on failings of their followers rather than to caring about them as individuals, as women leaders appear to be more likely to do (Brockner & Adsit, 1986).

CONDITIONS FOSTERING GENDER DIFFERENCES

The foregoing section probably raised more questions than answers about gender differences in leadership. However, a closer look at some of the factors embedded in these studies reveals that certain conditions foster alpha bias or contribute to male-female differences. In this section, I discuss four of those conditions: 1) the research setting; 2) the measures used to assess leadership-related variables; 3) situational characteristics, such as the nature of the task; and 4) the role of power in studies of gender differences.

Gender Biases Inherent in Research Settings

Gender bias may systematically enter empirical investigations according to certain methodological decisions made in the design of empirical research. One such decision involves the research setting in which the data are collected. The studies discussed in this category basically fall into one of two types of settings: those conducted in the laboratory, and those conducted in the field. In laboratory studies, research participants are strangers who interact with other strangers or with paper-and-pencil, hypothetical descriptions of male and female leaders for brief periods of time in contrived settings (Terborg, 1977). A recent variation in lab studies used video technology in lieu of paper-and-pencil descriptions of male and female leaders. In field studies, on the other hand, respondents evaluate leadership styles or leadership effectiveness of their leaders in real-life organizational settings.

Looking at these two different types of settings, research has shown that gender effects are much more likely to be found in the lab than in the field (e.g., Dobbins & Platz, 1986; Osborn & Vicas, 1976; Ragins, 1991). Ragins, for example, reviewed 21 studies of subordinate evaluations of male and female leaders and found gender effects in only 9.5% of the field studies, compared to 38% of the lab studies. Similarly, Eagly and her associates in their meta-analysis of leadership style found that gender differences for organizational (field) studies were significantly less pronounced than were those obtained in lab studies. Again, the gender differences observed in contrived settings tended to be more in line with gender stereotypes than those obtained in real-life contexts. Studies of men and women in actual leadership situations, on the other hand, show that leaders who perform similar functions do not differ much in terms of leadership style or effectiveness (e.g., Dobbins & Platz, 1986; Donnell & Hall, 1980; Nieva & Gutek, 1981).

A number of factors specific to field and lab settings account for these findings. In lab studies, research participants are typically undergraduate students who, in the absence of information or personal knowledge of the leader other than sex, base their evaluations upon readily available stereotypes. Moreover, as Wallston and O'Grady (1985) suggested, young adulthood (i.e., the developmental phase of traditional undergraduate students) appears to be the age when differences between the sexes are maximized. The choice of undergraduate students as subjects to study gender differences in leadership may result in inadvertent overrepresentation of the differences between men and women. The authors also noted that the relationship between the specific topic studied and the sex of the respondents chosen for study further obscures the situation. Males, for example, are more likely to be chosen for research on aggression, whereas females are more likely to be chosen for studies on affiliation and cooperation. Thus, conclusions about gender differences in aggression may be based on a great deal of information about men, but on only a small amount about women.

Whereas practicing leaders often indicate that there are no differences between male and female leadership styles, students hold the opposite to be true. For example, Brown (1979) reported that gender differences in leadership were most likely to result when measuring attitudes of students in laboratory experiments. Experience at work and frequent interactions with women, on the other hand, modifies the attitudes of practicing managers toward women leaders, making them less likely to subscribe to traditional sex-role stereotypes. The notion that experience and familiarity dissipate stereotypic attitudes toward male and female leaders was discussed by Maccoby and Jacklin (1974) in their comprehensive work on *The Psychology of Sex Differences:*

> The dominance relations between the sexes are complex: in childhood sex segregation of play groups means that neither sex frequently attempts to dominate the other. Among adult mixed pairs or groups, formal leadership tend to go to males in the initial phase of interaction, but the direction of influence becomes more sex-equal the longer the relationship lasts with division of authority occurring along the lines of individual competencies and division of labor. (p. 353)

Finally, laboratory experiments are conducted to show cause-and-effect relationships and the statistics used to detect such relationships focus by design on differences rather than on similarities. In the typical lab experiment with its experimental group and control group, the logic of the design and the statistical analyses performed call for comparisons between the two groups to determine whether the average difference between them is statistically significant. Some consider this choice of language unfortunate since "significance" to many laypeople implies importance. To statisticians and researchers, however, the term means that the differences observed between two groups is unlikely to be due to chance. It is therefore important to remember that even large statistical differences do not automatically translate into practical or social importance.

When looking only at the influence of gender, it is easy to forget that in real life, other characteristics such as education and experience also contribute to differences between male and female leaders. Students who are asked to act out or simulate a particular leadership style, respond to paper-and-pencil leaders, or rate simulated or described leader behaviors may have no other choice than to react on the basis of those gender stereotypes that are most familiar to them (Kruse & Wintermantel, 1986). As a result, gender is a more salient cue in laboratory experiments and tends to exaggerate male-female differences. On the other hand, in realistic settings where leaders and followers engage in long-term, ongoing interactions with multiple opportunities to observe each others' behaviors and engage in informal performance evaluations, there has been a frequent failure to find differences between male and female leaders. In other words, laboratory experiments, in contrast to field studies, strip leaders of their social roles by treating sex as the single most important variable on the basis of which leader evaluations are made.

Gender Biases Inherent in Leadership Measures

As mentioned earlier in this chapter, most of the measures used in research on gender differences in leadership relied on questionnaires such as the Leader Behavior Description Questionnaire, the Supervisory Behavior Description Questionnaire measuring initiating structure and consideration, and the Least Preferred Co-Worker scale developed by Fiedler to assess task- versus relationship-oriented leadership. Most of these scales are formatted and scored in a bipolar fashion. Requiring people to endorse one or the other end of a bipolar continuum (e.g., initiating structure or consideration) forces them to adopt an "either-or-fallacy" (Brown, 1979) which precludes notions of implied equality and potential integration of apparent opposites (Bobko, 1985). Based on these instruments, women have often been found to score high on consideration and relationship-oriented leadership, while men score high on initiating structure and task-oriented leadership. Helmich (1974), for instance, surveyed 550 company presidents and found that men tended to be more task-oriented while women were more people-oriented. However, these measures with their gender role polarities create demand characteristics (i.e., research participants behave in a particular way because they believe that the demands of the situation—the experiment—calls for certain behaviors) because a) they imply that there are two distinct leadership styles, and b) each pole of the dichotomized pair reinforces the popular belief that the two leadership styles are gender-linked, with female leaders supposedly being more considerate and supportive and male leaders more task-oriented. Thus, the consideration or relationship-oriented leadership dimension is seen as being congruent with female gender stereotypes, while the initiating structure or task oriented dimension is considered congruent with male gender-role expectations.

There are, however, problems with the use of these measures in the study of gender differences. As Hollander (1978) pointed out, the two dimensions, consideration-versus-initiating structure or task-versus-relationship orientation, are not logical opposites of each other. Moreover, both sets of behaviors are indicative of effective leadership. As suggested in Chapter 3, instruments based on leadership theories which operationalize theoretical constructs as dichotomies are problematic because they do not capture the full range of complementary behaviors and capabilities a leader may display in any given situation. Instead, they polarize leader behaviors along gender role expectations which may or may not be working in any given leadership situation. Statham (1987), for example, found that women managers in her sample were not simply relationship-oriented. As one woman put it, "Efficiency is the most important thing. If people don't love me at the other end, that's OK" (p. 417). The female managers in this study exhibited both sets of behaviors and focused on task accomplishment, using their person orientation to this end. Similarly, an emphasis on task orientation at the expense of socioemotional concerns may result in negative consequences for both sexes. Several investigators (e.g., Bartol, 1974; Bartol & Wortman, 1979) argued that leadership style based on leader behaviors such as consideration and initiating structure can be construed to be more a matter of individual differences than of gender differences. By removing the bipolarity inherent in most measures of leadership, we avoid splitting these instruments into a good/bad, active/passive, or strong/weak polarity and may pave the way for the emergence of new constructs and measures. In the long run, effective leadership requires a balancing and simultaneous mastery of seemingly contradictory or paradoxical capabilities— decisiveness and reflectiveness, broad vision and attention to detail, bold moves and incremental adjustment, and a performance as well as a people orientation (Hart & Quinn, 1993).

Gender Differences Resulting from Situational Factors

Many tasks in the workplace are gender-typed. Construction work is typically considered "men's work," while clerical work is considered "women's work." Therefore, we may expect that the nature of the task is likely to have an effect on the performance or effectiveness of male and female leaders. More specifically, we would expect that males are more likely to assume leadership roles when dealing with "masculine" tasks while women are more likely to take the lead in situations involving "feminine" tasks. Whether a task is gender-linked or neutral is likely to influence people's evaluations of their leaders. Empirical evidence essentially bears out these predictions. For example, Bass (1965) found that directive (defined as giving orders with or without explanation) and persuasive wives were acceptable as leaders when working with their husbands on household tasks, but were unacceptable as leaders when the task involved organizational activities of the companies their husbands worked for.

The nature of the task as a potential source of bias is but one of many situational factors. Other factors that play a role in moderating the relationship between gender and leadership outcomes include the sex composition of the group (i.e., same sex versus mixed-sex groups), the private or public domains in which men and women function as leaders, and other situations in which gender may obstruct and act as a filter for evaluating women's and men's leadership. These situational variables call for a broader conceptual analysis of leadership situations, since the various contexts in which women and men lead continue to expand against a changing social ecology.

The Role of Power in Gender Differences in Leadership

As in the case of leadership, gender is a primary field within which, or by means of which, power is articulated. In other words, to the extent to which references to gender imply unequal distributions of power and differential control over access to material and symbolic resources, gender becomes implicated in the perception of power itself (Scott, 1989). For men, as Nichols (1994) reminded us, the path to power and leadership is straightforward: join the usual clubs, board of directors, civic associations, visible charities, or national leadership groups; then leverage ties with financiers, power brokers, ranking politicians, competitor CEOs, opinion leaders, or possible venture partners to establish a power base. For women, on the other hand, access to power and leadership is still limited. Thus, as Miller and Cummins (1994) stated, "an individual's power is defined almost exclusively in structural, hierarchical, and interpersonal terms; whoever has the money, wins the fight, or controls another person's choices is the powerful person" (p. 416).

Although women's roles and status are gradually changing, the stereotypic notion that women and power are mutually exclusive is hard to overcome. Hillary Clinton, according to one writer, is a "virtual Rorschach test for contemporary ambivalence about powerful women" (Kaye, 1993, p. 53). Generally, it is assumed that women have less positional power in organization than do men. One factor that inhibits women from attaining this power is that they themselves tend to have mixed feelings about it. As Kaye (1993) noted, we are often less preoccupied with the question of how to obtain power than with the grimmer question of how much it will cost. As a result, power continues to be a dirty word when it comes to women. The only power acceptable to many women is power exercised behind the scenes, recalling the old adage that behind every successful man is a forceful, strong woman.

In reviewing empirical research on gender differences in leadership, surprisingly few studies have tried to test simultaneously the role of power in both the construction of gender and in gender differences in leadership. Yet it has been shown that power is positively related to evaluations of leader effectiveness (e.g., Trempe, Rigny, & Haccoun, 1985). Changing definitions and conceptualizations of power, as well as power differences between men and women, are bound to contribute to gender differences in leadership. For example, subordinates may respond not so much to the leader's gender, but to differences in power presumably held by male and female leaders. Therefore, power perspectives of gender and leadership may provide an important key to understanding why followers react differently to female and male leaders when exposed to similar leader behaviors.

In the social sciences, definitions of power take one of two forms. One set of definitions captures the ways in which men, more often than women, experience power in our culture in the form of wealth, resources, influence, and control. This definition describes power in terms of "power over" which may express itself in the use of reward, coercion, and expertise (French & Raven, 1959). According to this definition, power is defined almost exclusively in structural, hierarchical terms. At each level of social rank, "power over" means a differential distribution of power to men and women, children, old people, racial, ethnic, and religious minorities. In hierarchical models of leadership, the leader is someone who has authority and controls resources in order to achieve a particular objective. By definition, this person exercises power over those he or she leads. Feminist scholars treat power over as a masculine attribute that helps to perpetuate male dominance over women. Adrienne Rich (1976) suggested:

> Power is . . . a primal relationship under patriarchy . . . the identity, the very personality of the man depends on power and on power in a certain sense: that of power over others, beginning with a women and her children. (p. 64)

The other face of power advocates the use of power in the form of *empowerment* instead of control. Here, power is something to share, something to use for the advancement of others. The definition of power as empowerment treats it as an expandable resource that is produced and shared through interactions between leaders and followers. Empowerment or "power to" does not imply domination of others. Rather, it deals with developing power over oneself (Leong, Snodgrass, & Gardner, 1992). This definition is endorsed by feminists who, like Joan Rothschild (1976), argue that the experience of women's work in the family has been based on a set of power relations different from those experienced by men. These differences are captured in the "power over" versus "power to" definitions of the concept. According to Rothschild, women view power as "energy, potential, competence of oneself, rather than power over others. Women will seek to achieve and maintain such power through personalized and cooperative means" (p. 6). This other face of power, then, suggests that an effective leader is one who empowers others to act in their own interest, rather than one who coerces others to behave in a manner consistent with the goal of the leader. Burns (1978) stated:

> Our main hope for disenthralling ourselves from the emphasis on power [power over] lies . . . in seeing that the most powerful influences consist of deeply human relationships in which two or more persons engage with one another. It lies in a more realistic, a more sophisticated understanding of power, and of the often far more consequential exercise of mutual persuasion, exchange, elevation, and transformation—in short, of leadership. (p. 11)

In one of the few studies that controlled for both gender and power, Ragins (1991) found that perceived power accounted for 59% of the variance in leadership evaluations, while leader gender accounted for only 1%. This study suggests that in evaluating gender differences in leadership, we must remain alert to dimensions of power. Recognition of the role played by the differential power of men and women helps us to put empirically observed gender differences in perspective.

Kanter (1977) argued that many apparent gender differences in power are the result of the relative powerlessness of women in positions of authority. The author suggested that gender differences in the behavior of organizational leaders are the product of different structural positions held by men and women in the organization. If power structures and opportunities were the same for men and women, according to this argument, gender differences in the exercise of power, and gender stereotypes about gender and power, would disappear. In the meantime, women are supposed to adapt themselves to male power-holders. Boulding (1992) suggested that women are highly skilled at converting what power they have derived from rendering important personal services to men, a special privatized "underside" of power that gives women more leverage than formal analysis of their roles would suggest.

THEORETICAL PERSPECTIVES ON GENDER DIFFERENCES IN LEADERSHIP

A number of reasons have been advanced to account for gender differences in leadership, several of which are drawn from role theory (Katz & Kahn, 1978) which use gender stereotypes and gender-role socialization as explanatory concepts.

Gender stereotypes are based on the assumption that women lack the attributes, abilities, skills, and motivation required for leadership roles. Behaviors such as emotionality, dependency, and sensitivity associated with the female gender stereotype are perceived as incompatible with requirements for leadership. Not too many years ago, Rosalind Rosenberg (1986), a noted expert in women's history, testified for Sears Roebuck in a sex discrimination suit. She stated that "Women are more relationship centered than men, derive their self image from their role of wife and mother and tend to be more interested than men in the cooperative, social aspects of the work situation" (p. 763). The author went on to say that women who choose "jobs typically pursued by men often experience doubts about their ability to do well; women, in general, are less competitive, less aggressive and less able to behave as leaders than men largely because they have not had men's extensive experience in competitive sports" (p. 765). The judge agreed with this argument and interpreted the evidence presented by the Equal Employment Opportunity Commission on statistics dealing with selection and promotion rates at Sears as an indication of women's avoidance of certain jobs rather than of a pattern of discrimination exhibited by the company.

Traditionally, women in our society have been socialized to become nurturing, likeable, affectionate, soft-spoken, warm, yielding, selfless, gentle, compassionate, and dependent rather than ambitious, aggressive, dominant, self-reliant, strong, individualistic, and independent (Butler, 1976). According to the gender stereotype, the attributes and behaviors typically ascribed to women are opposite of what is expected of a leader. Moreover, these commonly held stereotypes imply that women who want to be successful leaders should adopt manlike qualities and learn to lead like a man. This "male managerial model" (Terborg, 1977) has been endorsed and confirmed for both men and women.

Instead of using gender stereotypes as the main explanatory construct, the concept of gender-role congruence refers to the extent to which leaders behave in a manner that is consistent or congruent with gender role expectations (Schein, 1973). The gender-role congruency hypothesis (Nieva & Gutek, 1981) predicts that gender-role congruent leader behaviors will be evaluated more favorably than gender-role incongruent behavior. Furthermore, this hypothesis posits that leader behavior consistent with gender stereotypes is more positively related to followers' satisfaction than is leader behavior incongruent with gender stereotypes. More specifically, considerate leader behavior, which is more consistent with the female stereotype, is predicted to correlate positively with subordinate satisfaction with female leaders, whereas initiating structure, a style congruent with the male stereotype, is positively associated with subordinate satisfaction for male leaders.

The gender-role congruency model implies behavioral consequences for women leaders who choose one of two options: 1) adopt a "feminine" leadership style congruent with role expectations of women, or 2) lead in a "masculine" way, which deviates from and is incongruent with women's prescribed gender roles. Domineering, aggressive, or competitive behaviors are incongruent with the female gender role and therefore are counter-stereotypic. Several studies (e.g., Eagly et al., 1992; Watson, 1988) which reported that women were negatively evaluated when they embraced a "masculine" leadership style have been quoted in support of the gender-role congruence model. On the other hand, men who employed a "feminine" leadership were evaluated in the same way as their female counterparts, suggesting that men may have greater freedom to vary their leadership styles without encountering negative reactions.

However, other research presents contradictory evidence. Petty and Bruning (1980), for example, failed to obtain support for the gender-role congruence hypothesis in a study which showed that consideration was effective for both male and female leaders. The authors suggested that followers' needs for a considerate leadership style may override stereotypical expectations of gender-appropriate leader behavior of men and women in an environment characterized by turbulence and recent changes in leadership. In such contexts, leaders, regardless of gender, must help followers to deal with the stress of the situation. Leaders achieve this by showing concern for their followers and by helping them to adjust to the demands of the situation.

A variant of role theory focuses on the conflicts believed to be inherent in the role of woman and the role of leader. According to this model, role conflict is particularly difficult for women enacting both a gender role (i. e., wife and/ or mother) and an organizational role (i.e., leader). Because of this dual role, the theory predicts that women are particularly vulnerable to role conflict and the negative consequences, such as stress, associated with it. The dual role dilemma is stressful because as "good girls" women learn behaviors appropriate to the role of wife and mother. Later, however, when they are in leadership positions, women are confronted with a set of conflicting expectations. Even women leaders who have resolved this conflict at an intrapersonal level still have to cope with the conflicting expectations held by colleagues, subordinates, and society. Eagly and Karau (1991), in their research on leadership styles, suggested that women who lead in a "feminine" style may escape the role conflict they would otherwise experience, while women who lead in a "masculine" style may exacerbate their role conflict. Thus, leader behavior congruent with gender stereotypes protects women from stress generated by role conflict, while counter-stereotypic behaviors lead to additional stress.

Role theory implies the existence of a hierarchical relationship between the roles ascribed to men and women, with one gender (men) dominant and superior and the other (women) subordinate and inferior. The theory, in its different versions, assumes that legitimation of the leadership role does not arise from job titles such as chief executive officer, president, manager, or supervisor, but rather from specific role-related characteristics of the leader. According to role theory, gender differences in leadership result from a variety of role-related phenomena, including gender role expectations, differential socialization experiences, and the extent to which leadership situations differentially create role conflict for male and female leaders. Role theory, and its variations, retains the basic dualism and with it a worldview sustained by gender-related polarities. The gender hierarchy implicit in role theory suggests that female leaders threaten or upset the traditional relations between men and women, leading to a devaluation of the female leader based on role-linked attributes.

Gender-role socialization perspectives suggest that socialization agents such as families, schools, and peers teach women as little girls to be emotionally oriented and reserved in interactions with others, while little boys are taught to be outgoing and achievement-oriented. It is through this process of gender-role socialization that children, from infancy, learn about the relationship between biological sex and social roles. This learning is shaped by societal, cultural, and ideological beliefs about what girls and boys, women and men are, what they should be, and what they should do. To this day, in many situations and child-rearing practices, the biological sex of the child frequently determines which activities she or he will be exposed to or permitted to experience. In other words, sex determines both opportunity and experience. As a result, many socialization practices represent a type of systematic discrimination based on unfounded beliefs about gender (Greendorfer, 1993). By the time boys and girls reach middle childhood, gender stereotypes play an instrumental role in shaping their perceptions of female and male leaders.

According to gender-role socialization theory, observed differences between female and male leaders result from differential child-rearing practices. Henning and Jardim (1977), for example, argued that girls lack experience with team sports, which later on, as women, puts them at a distinct disadvantage. The authors believe that playing team sports teaches little girls the key elements of management, how to plan strategies, how to work with people regardless of personal feelings, and how to compete. Because girls are less likely to engage in team sports, they do not learn these skills, and consequently may not possess the abilities that lead to managerial success.

The premise underlying this perspective is that socialization practices have encouraged the development of personality characteristics and behavior patterns in women which are antithetical to leadership. The socialization perspective predicts that without specific training to eliminate gender effects, gender will continue to affect leader and follower behavior in stereotypic ways.

A different explanation has looked for the source of gender differences in leadership in the ways men and women learn from experience. According to this view, women and men experience work differently because they bring different histories, perceptions, and behaviors to the workplace. Belenchy, Clinchy, Goldberger, and Tarule (1986), for example, suggested that women do not learn well in a competitive or adversarial milieu. Similarly, Keith (1987) found that women do not benefit as much as men from the so-called advocacy mode in which every point must be debated and defended. In one study (Van Velsor & Hughes, 1987), which addressed how gender differences in learning occur, male and female managers' descriptions of lessons from experience were content-analyzed. The results indicated that even when men and women worked at similar organizational levels, women focused more than men on learning who they were as individuals, finding their niche, and integrating themselves with the environment. About one-third of the important lessons of experience quoted by women focused on their capacity to learn about self in relation to the organization as well as learning from other people. Male managers, on the other hand, stressed their mastery of specific business skills, and lessons learned from turning a business around or starting a new venture. The authors concluded that women may employ a different set of learning strategies or make sense out of their experiences in ways that are qualitatively different from men. Moreover, based on interviews with these high-potential executives, the authors felt that women's opportunities for learning from a diversity of experiences were limited, even though they learned a great deal from the organizational environment. Thus, even organizations which attempt to provide equal developmental opportunities may not provide equivalent experiences.

When we look at the two different bodies of literature, the popular literature and the images of women leaders portrayed by the mass media and empirical research on gender differences in leadership, different conclusions may be drawn; these are summarized in Table 6.1. Rather than attributing gender differences in leadership to differences in personality or leadership styles, the writings in the popular and empirical studies reviewed in Chapters 5 and 6 suggest that different contexts including different times (i.e., historical periods) favor women, while others favor men.

CONCLUSIONS

Based on the review of the literature on gender and leadership reviewed here, empirical evidence of female-male differences in leader behaviors, leadership styles, and evaluations of female and male leaders is fragile at best. When we conflate leadership with gender, we imply that there are women's ways of leading and men's ways of leading. The review of the scientific evidence of gender differences in leadership leaves us with some perplexing questions. In contrast

Table 6.1   Summary of Gender Differences in Leadership

No Differences	Stereotypic Differences Favoring Women
*In most recent empirical research female leaders do not differ significantly in terms of personality, goals, leadership styles, or leadership effectiveness	*In most of the popular literature women leaders are depicted to have a distinct "female" advantage based on female gender stereotypes of care and nurture
Stereotypic Differences Favoring Men	**Counter-Stereotypic Differences**
*Early research derived from trait and behavioral theories reported that men are more effective leaders based on personality traits stereotypically ascribed to men and task-oriented leadership styles preferred by men	*Women adopting a leadership style that is incongruent with gender stereotypes; studies showed that women embracing a "masculine" leadership style are negatively evaluated as leaders compared to women who practice a "feminine" leadership style

to popular writers, leadership researchers generally seem to agree that there are few and negligible gender differences in actual leader behavior. Moreover, the scientific evidence fails to support the notion of a distinctive "feminine" leadership style portrayed by the popular literature. Denmark (1977) summed it up by stating that:

> Many of the assumptions that women managers are basically different from men are just not supported by data. The one difference investigators generally agree upon is women's greater concern for relationships among people and this should be considered a plus in terms of leadership effectiveness. Alleged sex differences in ability, attitudes, and personality have been based on sex role stereotypes rather than empirical observations of women leaders. (pp. 110–111)

Bass (1991) echoed this opinion when he concluded:

> When it comes to traits underlying the potential to lead, women are favored by having slightly better verbal skills, but differences in cognitive skills are generally hard to find. With reference to personality traits, women may suffer from a lack of self-confidence, but this trait, along

with other personality differences in needs, values, and interests that are of consequence to leadership, appear to evaporate for those women who move up the corporate ladder. (p. 723)

Research which, because of methodological and temporal constraints, has shown gender differences is likely to have undesirable consequences for women. It perpetuates unfounded stereotypes of women leaders as either behaving too much like women (i.e., being too dependent, emotional, passive, or sensitive) or too much like men (being too aggressive, ambitious, outspoken, or competitive). Analyzing research on gender differences chronologically reveals that the time when the data were collected and/or the study was published needs to be considered as a qualifier when interpreting gender differences in leadership.

Taken together, it seems that the belief in enduring, deep-seated gender differences does not fare well when tested against the behaviors of men and women leaders in different contexts, at different times, or in methodologically diverse studies, giving gender differences a "now you see them, now you don't quality" (Unger, 1981). As Deaux (1984) concluded in her review of the leadership literature:

Main effects of sex are frequently qualified by situational interactions and the selection of tasks plays a critical role in eliciting or suppressing differences. Furthermore, the amount of variance accounted for by sex, even when main effects are reliable, is quite small. Thus, when any particular behavior [such as a leadership style] is considered, [gender] differences may be of little consequence. (p. 108)

Realistically, as Eagly and Johnson (1990) noted, male and female leaders presumably are selected by organizations or select themselves into organizations, according to some relevant organizational criteria. Applying these criteria, rather than gender stereotypes, to female and male leaders is likely to decrease the probability that women and men, once they occupy leadership roles, differ substantially in their leadership styles, performance, and effectiveness as leaders and their interactions with their followers. The notion that organizational roles override gender roles is consistent with Kanter's (1977) structural interpretation of the behavior of women and men in organizations. In other words, for both men and women, their behavior as leaders and followers is structured by organizational roles. Socialization that sanctions only certain roles and behaviors for women, and a culture that reinforces these limitations, is only one side of the difference equation (Driscoll & Goldberg, 1993).

At the bottom of the gender-differences-versus-no-differences argument we must assume that leadership, like many, if not most other behaviors, knows no gender. Yet, it seems that someone always will call out "Vive la différence." Dobbins and Platz (1986) recognized the fruitless search for reliable, gender differences in leadership when they called for a moratorium on research that simply compares male and female leaders along dimensions such as initiating structure or consideration. Even those who support the notion of distinctive male and female leadership styles recognize that leadership is first and foremost a social phenomenon, defined and validated in many different contexts—social, political, corporate, and religious, to name a few—by followers, peers, supervisors, the media, and others. As a result, more research needs to be carried out using women in actual leadership positions. More important than the question of substantial differences in female and male leadership styles, or in evaluations of male and female leaders, is research on female leaders which focuses on their social and societal impact. Feminists, for example, hoped that women acting as political leaders would radically change public policy, only to find out that prime ministers Margaret Thatcher or Indira Gandhi offered little hope to those who looked to their office to advance feminist issues.

Gender stereotypes continue to persist, despite the clear evidence that male and female leaders are similar in many personality traits and job-related behaviors (e.g, Brown, 1979; Powell, 1993). The damages caused by stereotypes are detrimental to both women and men because they reinforce a set of beliefs about each group which, even if it is statistically valid, inaccurately characterizes many individuals within each group. Therefore, it is useful to remember that gender stereotypes constitute normative beliefs to which people tend to conform or are induced to conform (O'Leary & Ickovics, 1992).

The focus on gender differences in much of the early research on leadership reflects the tendency of traditional Western epistemology to dichotomize the experience of women and men. The experiences attributed to women and portrayed as contributing to their nature (i.e., exercising a nurturing, caring leadership style) are not timeless and universal but socially, historically, and politically located (Bohan, 1993). To believe that all women lead in a manner congruent with gender stereotypes denies the context that frames leadership. Women construct their leadership style based on different personal, social, and organizational experiences, in part because they lack realistic role models. One alternative to emphasizing gender differences is found in the pursuit of equality. As Alexis de Tocqueville pointed out in 1848:

> The gradual development of the principle of equality is . . . a providential fact. It is universal, it is lasting, it constantly eludes all human interference . . . All men have aided it by their exertion, both those who have intentionally labored in its cause and those who have served it unwittingly. (p. 56)

If the passion for equality is a significant evolutionary force, as Tocqueville contends, I tend to agree with Boulding (1992) who argued that the future of equality will depend on the social values and enabling structures that will come to prevail over the next decades and centuries. Yet, for women, despite greater equity in the workplace, the social values and enabling organizational structures that make up the leadership fabric that would reinforce equality will continue to emerge at a very slow pace as long as the debate about women's qualifications for leadership is deeply entrenched in gender stereotypes, perceptions, and attitudes, rather than in actual experiences with women leaders.

7 Visible and Not-so-Visible Barriers To Women's Leadership

> To dream the impossible dream, to fight the
> unbeatable foe, . . . to run where brave dare
> not go, to reach the unreachable star! This is
> my quest.
>
> *Don Quixote,*
> *Man of La Mancha*

INTRODUCTION

Taken together, the previous two chapters suggest that both the popular literature and scientific research require careful scrutiny before we can make provocative references to a superior ''feminine'' leadership style, a ''female advantage,'' or similar generalizations about women in leadership roles based on modest, if any, gender differences in key characteristics pertaining to leadership. Scientific studies have shown that we cannot answer the question whether it is better to be led by a man or by a woman without a contextual analysis of the leadership situation in which male and female leaders find themselves. History and much of the existing leadership literature does not permit us to judge the superiority of one gender over the other.

Contexts, rather than gender, provide the framework on which both women and men build their leadership models. Educational institutions, for example, tend to be more liberal in their attitudes toward women than do business organizations. They have been known to embrace ideologies which support the so-called ''feminine style'' of leadership. In contrast to corporations where the leadership role is often identified by position titles such as Chief Executive Officer (CEO), Astin and Leland (1991) labeled the leadership experiences and styles of a group of women as ''nonpositional leaders'' (p. 6). These women exercised their leadership in educational and research settings, producing scholarly works that affected the lives of others and created knowledge central to social change. Their leadership style was characterized by collaboration, sharing, listening to and empowering others, and accomplishing desired changes through collective efforts.

While this leadership style was effective in context of educational and research institutions, a multinational corporation may require a different approach.

Previously, we also saw how some of the attributions and judgments made about women in leadership roles are contained in the female gender stereotype which transcends history and continues to persist. In her discussion of the history of women's subordination, Boulding (1992) takes us back to an era when

> embattled champions of the downtrodden sex put forward the enslave-ment concept which invokes the image of the helpless, food-gathering, child bearing female in the hunting and gathering society who is both protected and victimized by the brute strength of the male, who gains brief respite as mother, goddess, and matriarch after the invention of agriculture in a world of dwindling animal prey, who then loses all claims to power and status as man invents the plow and takes over farming and the gods. (p. 30)

The gender stereotype embedded in this description of prehistoric women is actually not that different from the characteristics ascribed to women leaders, which also use gender as the salient category for social classifications.

Stereotypes are descriptive shortcuts applied to categories of people: women and men, blacks and whites, poor and rich. They rest on oversimplified generaliza-tions, leading to categorized judgments about people. Although stereotypes may, in fact, often be based on a grain of truth, in reality they more often conceal than they reveal (Cohen & Bradford, 1989). One irony of the leadership literature is that the overdefinition and polarization of stereotypes is not only common among popular writers, but is also fostered to some extent by leadership research-ers. The development and use of gender stereotypes scales (i.e., instruments measuring task- and people-oriented leadership styles) in leadership research is an example of their role in defining, fixing, and perpetuating gender-role stereotypes (Eichler, 1980).

Despite the gains women have made over the past two decades, negative attitudes and stereotypes of women leaders prevail. Early studies focused on differences in leadership traits and styles as well as stereotypical expectations associated with men and women. These stereotypes imply that, with respect to their leadership abilities, men are better fit for the leadership role than women. Bowen, Worthy, and Greyser (1965), for example, surveyed male executives and reported that 44% of the men sampled expressed mildly unfavorable to strongly unfavorable attitudes toward women executives. Similarly, Aries (1976) found that men tend to emerge more often than women as leaders in mixed-sex groups. Other studies (e.g., Bartol & Butterfield, 1976) found that women in positions of authority were evaluated as less competent than men, even when their performance were equal by some objective measure. Brown (1979) concluded that "one of the popular reasons given for the differential treatment of women in management stems from stereotyping women as ineffective leaders'' (p. 595). Still other research (e.g., Eskilon & Wilson, 1976) found that not only were women generally seen as less likely to be leaders, but women themselves reported that they were less inclined to see themselves as leaders or seek leadership roles.

Most stereotypical descriptions of female leaders present them in a negative light. Hammer (1978), for example, discussed four negative stereotypes of female managers. The *earth mother* brings home baked cookies to business meetings and keeps the communal aspirin bottle in her desk, while the *manipulator* relies on her feminine wiles to accomplish her goals. The *workaholic* cannot delegate responsibility, and the *egalitarian* manager denies the power of her leadership by treating her subordinates as colleagues. Kanter (1977) discerned a similar set of stereotypes about women in leadership roles. Again, we have a *mother* who provides solace and comfort; a *pet* who is the little sister of the group; and a *sex object*, who fails to establish herself professionally in the leadership role, while the *iron maiden's* status as a leader is recognized but she is seen as a tyrant by her subordinates. These different sets suggest that women in leadership roles are categorized according not to one but to several different stereotypes, each of which carries its own assumptions and biases.

One widely quoted study (Rosenkrantz, Vogel, Bee, Broverman, & Broverman, 1968) showed that men, but not women, were characterized as aggressive, objective, active, dominant, competitive, and decisive whereas the traits attributed to women clustered around gentleness, emotionality, passivity, dependency, and submissiveness. Moreover, the same study reported that the stereotypic characteristics of men were preferred and considered desirable attributes by both men and women. However, only for men were gender-congruent characteristics considered acceptable in all situations. Women, on the other hand, were perceived as ''real'' women only in some situations, namely those in which they acted in accordance with the gender stereotypes. In other situations, women's behavior is seen as out-of-role according to prevailing stereotypes, and easily becomes subject to perceptual biases. By exhibiting out-of-role behaviors that are incongruent with the female stereotype, women run the risk of being negatively evaluated as leaders. Jago and Vroom (1982), for example, compared autocratic and participative leader behaviors of male and female managers and found that women who were perceived as autocratic leaders received negative evaluations, whereas male managers exhibiting the same leadership style were positively evaluated. Hence, ambiguity with respect to how to evaluate the leadership style of women seems to result in greater reliance on gender stereotypes as the basis for assessment. Despite the increasing number of women in management and some leadership positions, gender stereotypes have not changed significantly over the past 15 years (Powell & Butterfield, 1988). Instead, these stereotypes are maintained by perceptual and cognitive processes which generate gender-related attributes and schemata for women in leadership roles, but develop leadership-related attributes and schemata for men in similar positions.

Additionally, switching or adopting the behaviors stereotypically associated with the opposite gender seems more problematic for a woman serving in a leadership capacity than it does for her male counterpart. In fact, in some situations, the gender bias seems to have an inverse effect when women behave in a masculine way and are successful in doing so. In these situations, their success becomes magnified and is treated as an anomaly. Abramson, Goldberg, Greenberg, and Abramson (1977) labeled this effect as the "talking platypus phenomenon" because "after all, it matters little what the platypus says, the wonder is that it can say anything at all" (p. 123). Hence, career success can be a stigma for women, especially in their relationships with men. "I bet she gives instructions in bed" was one male executive's comment about a women who performed well in a management role (Morrison, White, Van Velsor, & the Center of Creative Leadership, 1992). As Figure 7.1 shows, many of the prevailing stereotypes continue to exist. When asked for their preferences of toys they hope to receive for Christmas, little, boys mentioned electronic games and sports equiment most often, while little girls had fashion dolls and toy animals on their wish lists.

A Supreme Court case involving Price Waterhouse, a law firm which denied Ann Hopkins a partnership, illustrates the effects of a woman's failure to meet stereotypical expectations of gender-appropriate behavior. Hopkins was the only woman of 88 candidates who were considered for partnership that year in a bid to join 662 partners—only 7 of whom were women. She sued the company for alleged discrimination, since she had a performance record with more billable hours than any other colleague proposed for partnership yet was denied for promotion. The firm claimed that Hopkins had problems with interpersonal skills and described her as macho and overcompensating for being a woman. Thus, although women have made gains over the decades since Title VII was implemented, the association between gender stereotypes and requisite leadership characteristics has not diminished much. In the selection and promotion of women, attributes of the candidates not directly related to job qualifications, such as female gender, overwhelm job-relevant attributes. Larwood, Szwajkowski, and Rose (1988) predicted that these less obvious discriminatory practices will continue to occur as long as they remain grounded in stereotypical expectations about women. (See Figure 7.1.)

Once in a while we catch a glimpse of stereotypes being challenged or questioned. Indianapolis Judge Paula Lapossa recently wept during the sentencing for a brutal rape and was asked by the defendant's lawyer to recuse herself. The appeals court ruled that compassion and emotion exhibited by a woman did not equal bias (Kim, 1993). By and large, however, sex-role stereotypes persist and continue to form the basis for social classification. As a result, people construct

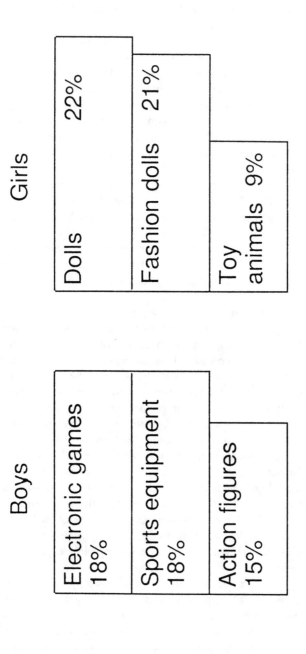

Figure 7.1 Persistence of Gender Stereotype

Source: Adapted from: Dear Santa Toys that Girls and Boys Would Most like to Receive for Holiday Gifts, USA Today, 1994

separate categorical structures of leadership of men and women. Lord and Maher (1991) argued that gender-related information processing occurs when females are in a minority in leadership positions and gender becomes the salient basis for social categorization. Instead of reacting to women in terms of leadership-related categories (i.e., motivation, goal achievement, or influence) people do so in terms of gender-related categories (i.e., warmth, friendliness, or nurturance). Furthermore, leadership within the female category, because of the small number of women at the top, is often defined and evaluated in comparison with leadership in the male category, thereby reinforcing gender-based social categorizations.

Although these stereotypes have little basis in reality and are largely myths, they are, nevertheless, used by people to assess and subsequently distinguish leaders from nonleaders. Perceptions are subject to biases and inaccuracies, which factor into decisions and judgments people make. Because of the lack of an appropriate reference group for women—there are no female counterparts of Franklin D. Roosevelt, John F. Kennedy, or Martin Luther King—people fall back on stereotypes and may conclude that women are born to be followers or cannot be successful as leaders without acting in a masculine way. The few women who make it to the top are itemized by those who wish to set them apart and put them in their place; trivialized by those who assume they cannot accomplish the task; scrutinized by those who may covet their positions; criticized by those who envy their talents; categorized by those who see women as being in the wrong place; and stigmatized by those who continue to believe that female attributes and leader attributes are mutually exclusive (Van Nostrand, 1993). Thus, stereotypes and biases derived from social categories tend to be largely unfavorable to women seeking leadership.

In addition to being faced with negative gender stereotypes, it has been suggested that one of the reasons women do not reach their leadership goals is because they do not dream of greatness. Young boys grow up dreaming of role models, heroes, sport idols, supermen, and other charismatic leaders they admire. They talk about succeeding beyond their wildest dreams or dreaming that the world would never end. Women, on the other hand, do not have such sandbox dreams while growing up. Instead of dreaming of becoming a great artist, athlete, politician or missionary, the stuff women's dreams are made of presumably focuses on love, marriage, and family. Former ambassador to the United Nations Jeane Kirkpatrick, a respected political scientist, was asked in an interview at what age she decided to be president. She countered that girls don't dream of becoming president. Psychologist Daniel Levinson (1978), in his theory of male lifespan development, proposes that dreams (Levinson refers to them as the "Dream") play a crucial role in the transition into adulthood. Levinson argues that the Dream is an indication of the kind of life boys want to lead as adults. A central developmental task, according to Levinson, is to give the vaguely articulated notions of greatness expressed in dreams a more precise definition and to live out the Dream. In Levinson's discussion of female lifespan development, the Dream does not exist.

The absence of sandbox dreams, along with other explanatory concepts, have been discussed in this and the previous chapter to account for the underrepresentation of women in leadership. Factors such as gender stereotypes, lack of congruence between the perceived roles of woman and leader, and the differential distribution of power among women and men in organizations are factors that operate largely at the individual level of analysis. Additionally, in Chapter 5, we saw how the perception that ''woman must be different from leader'' is aggravated by the media and popular writings, which depict women possessing traditional sex-typed characteristics or tout the advantages of female gender stereotypes and feminine sex-role socialization for women in leadership. In this chapter, we will take a closer look at organizational and structural barriers that reinforce the notion that a ''woman leader'' is an oxymoron or anomaly requiring exceptional treatment.

Although overt discrimination on the basis of race, gender, color, or ethnic origin is prohibited by Title VII and monitored by EEOC, other, more subtle forms of discrimination exist in organizations which make it difficult for women to advance to leadership positions. For example, although women are now admitted in equal proportions to men to medical schools, women trail men in medical school tenure. Miller (1995) reported that after about 11 years in faculty positions, 23% of men had achieved the rank of full professor, compared to 5% of women. Moreover, female faculty were less likely than their male counterparts to have access to the same resources such as dedicated laboratory space, grant support, or protected time for research.

More subtle forms of discrimination may also take the form of segregation within a particular field. For example, women in corporations tend to congregate in staff positions in departments such as human resources and community relations, career paths which rarely lead to the executive suite. Or, as Kroeger (1994) observed, changing technologies cause a job to become too much like ''women's work'' for men to want to do it anymore, thereby also creating occupational segregation. Declining wages often accompany a gender shift in occupations or professions; for example, bank tellers in the past were largely male until this job became feminized. This process also adds to the segregation of women in female-dominated occupations and prompts employers increasingly to turn to women to fill vacancies. In addition, an organization's physical surroundings, status symbols, hidden promotional criteria, jokes that are told at meetings, the information loop, and the corporate culture itself all represent potential barriers that must be examined when trying to understand why these factors may make it difficult for women to assume leadership roles. These subtler forms of discrimination are more difficult to detect and cannot be litigated away. It is the software of training, as Joyce Miller, executive director of the Department of Labor's Glass Ceiling

Commission put it, the informal stuff that separates women and men (U. S. Department of Labor, 1991).

Among these specific organizational and structural barriers are the much-talked-about "glass ceiling," the solo or token status of women in leadership, work-family conflicts, and the exclusion of women from informal networks in organizations. These barriers are more difficult to overcome because, unlike legal barriers, they are less visible. They are linked to cultural and organizational norms which continue to identify leadership as "men's work," or to male-normative and societal expectations that keep women from having the same sense of power that men have.

THE GLASS CEILING

In 1987, the Department of Labor published a report—*Workforce 2000*—that brought dramatic attention to the changes taking place in our economy and in the composition of the work force. Significant among these was the increased importance of minorities and women to the competitive status of the American economy. Since the publication of *Workforce 2000*, ample evidence has been generated to show that minorities and women have made significant gains in entering the workforce. But there is also significant evidence from research conducted by universities, non-profit organizations, executive recruiters, and the Department of Labor that documents a dearth of minorities and women at management levels—the so-called "glass ceiling." The glass ceiling, where it exists, hinders not only individuals but society as a whole. It effectively cuts our pool of potential corporate leaders by eliminating over one-half of our population. It deprives our economy of new leaders, new sources of creativity—the "would-be" pioneers of the business world. If our end game is to compete successfully in today's global market, we then have to unleash the full potential of the American workforce. The time has come to tear down, to dismantle—the "glass ceiling."

Lynn Martin, former Secretary of Labor
(U.S. Department of Labor, 1991, pp. 1–2)

The metaphor of the glass ceiling has become a popular explanation of why few women attain leadership positions, why they do not appear to move up the organizational hierarchy as rapidly as men, and why they tend to be faced with more stringent promotion requirements than are their male counterparts. The term "glass ceiling" has been used to describe an invisible barrier that is transparent, yet strong enough to stymie access to leadership for women and other minorities. Although the glass ceiling exists at different levels in different organizations or industries, the term is typically used to suggest a barrier to entry into top management positions (Powell & Butterfield, 1994). The scarcity of women in the very top positions in private sector organizations suggests that although efforts to satisfy organizational needs may have positive effects on women in management overall, these effects may be different for higher levels of management (Blum, Fields, & Goodman, 1994).

Breaking the Glass Ceiling: Can Women Reach the Top of America? (Morrison et al., 1987, 1992) was first published in 1987 and has spurred a lively discussion among laypeople and researchers in the academic, trade, and popular press. In the original Glass Ceiling Project, 76 female executives were interviewed to identify the barriers that kept them from rising above a certain level in corporations. According to the authors, the glass ceiling is not simply a barrier for an individual woman; rather, it applies to women as a group who are kept from advancing higher because they are women. Morrison et al. concluded that in order to reach high-level positions, women are expected to have more strength and fewer faults than their male colleagues.

The government too has adopted the glass ceiling concept, with its *A Report on the Glass Ceiling Initiative* undertaken by the Department of Labor. This initiative began in 1989 with a study involving compliance reviews of EEOC guidelines of nine federal contractors. The study (U.S. Department of Labor, 1991), by the former Labor Secretary Lynn Martin, showed that not only was the glass ceiling a reality in companies doing business with the federal government, but it was present at much lower levels than was first thought. Much of the earlier literature focused on the glass ceiling at the executive level; it was presumed that women at lower levels of management were not confronted with impenetrable barriers. However, the barriers identified in the *Report on the Glass Ceiling Initiative* included lack of opportunities for women and people of color to enroll in employer-sponsored, advanced education programs; an absence of career-enhancing assignments such as rotations through the various functional departments, such as human resources and management information divisions within an organization; and a lack of accountability for equal opportunity within the leadership ranks.

The Office of Federal Contract Compliance Programs (OFCCP) was charged with the enforcement of laws and regulations that prohibit government contractors and subcontractors from discriminating in their employment practices against women and minorities. Such practices include an organization's personnel selection system, performance evaluations, assignments to training programs, and salary and benefit systems. Organizations, including those of federal contractors, are required by law to make good-faith efforts to attract, develop, and retain women and minorities. Through the compliance review process, OFCCP was able to collect empirical evidence of barriers to upward mobility. The agency documented a growing disparity between the large number of women in entry-level and middle management posts and the few women who rose to executive leadership (Dominguez, 1992).

Among the specific findings described in the *Report on the Glass Ceiling Initiative* were:

- Existence of a glass ceiling - a level beyond which very few women and minorities had advanced in any of the nine companies reviewed by OFCCP.
- The ceiling was lower than expected. Much of the literature reviewed for this effort had focused on the executive suite. This study found a glass ceiling well below that level.
- Although all contractors were believed to be in compliance with Title VII and EEOC, their employment practices and processes proved the contrary.

OFCCP continues to review corporate employment practices and to reach out to all federal contractors before they are audited. The agency is also engaged in a large-scale campaign to increase public awareness of equal employment issues, and publicly recognizes organizations with progressive employment practices which promote a diverse workforce. Dominguez (1992) concluded that "shattering the glass ceiling is no longer a matter of persuasion or legal compulsion, but a matter of competitive economic necessity" (p. 391).

In the private sector, too, similar observations were made. For example, a study conducted jointly by Korn/Ferry International, a headhunting firm, and the University of California, Los Angeles, Graduate School of Management canvassed Fortune 500 industrial corporations and service firms in 1990. This survey revealed that women and minorities held less than 5% of senior management positions in the participating firms (Korn, 1989). Similar results were obtained by Campbell and Ritchie (1993) who studied 1,633 women at AT&T. These women were identified as having high managerial potential in 1973 and 1974 on the basis of their performance on a series of psychological tests. By 1982, many of these women had reached management positions; but in 1990, only 3% were in upper management positions. Overall, during the past decade, there has been only a 2% increase in the number of women and minorities in top executive positions in America's largest firms. Furthermore, predictions are that women will not hold a much greater percentage of top jobs at major corporations in the near future. In a survey of 400 female managers reported in *Business Week* (Anon, 1992), for example, 70% of the managers polled saw the male-dominated corporate culture as significant block to their success. More importantly, nearly one third of the sample believed that the number of women managers promoted into executive ranks will either stay the same or drop over the next 5 years. However, although there has only been a slight increase of women in leadership positions, the women who make it to the top of corporations as business leaders today tend to be younger and more highly educated, compared to women vying for leadership several years ago.

Cracking the glass ceiling may be easier said than done. After all, of the top five Fortune 50 companies, General Motors, Ford Motor, Exxon, IBM, and General Electric, only IBM had female executives. Morrison (1992) argued that after breaking the glass ceiling, many women realize that they are still not on the road to the top; that they are hemmed in even more than they were; and that the support that was helpful in the past suddenly becomes scarce because of the fierce competition for the few leadership positions at the top. The barriers behind the glass ceiling have been dubbed the "glass wall." Statistics attest to the continued existence of the glass ceiling:

> In the two decades since significant numbers of women began entering managerial careers, many companies have succeeded in building large pools of high-potential women. Yet most of these companies have been less successful in moving women into top levels and in retaining those who reach the executive suite. While a small percentage thrive, many come away frustrated by their own attempts to succeed. (Morrison et al., 1992, p. 157)

Despite a few cracks in the glass ceiling here and there, Heilman, Block, Martell, and Simon (1989) concluded:

> Assumptions of progress as a result of social, legal, and organizational changes are unwarranted; today's male managers persist in viewing women in general as far more deficient in the attributes for success as a manager than men in general. (p. 941)

The most recent glass ceiling report (e.g., Stone & Lee, 1995) based on a bipartisan federal panel investigation indicated that few women and minorities pass through this barrier into top levels of business. While white men make up 43% of the workforce, they hold 95% of senior management positions. In addition, women and minorities who make it to the top continue to earn less than their male colleagues. Labor Secretary Reich commented on these recent finding by saying, "This should be an eye-opening for everyone who believes we have succeeded in eradicating discrimination. Women and minorities still have a long way to go" (Stone & Lee, 1995, 4A). Reich goes on to say that the "glass elevator" which confines women and minorities to traditional jobs limits their career options and career paths.

Although it is difficult to break through the glass ceiling, a number of women have been successful in doing so. Hellwig (1992) recently provided a list of 50 female executives who have crashed through the glass ceiling. The list included Jill Barad, President and Chief Operating Officer of Mattel, Inc.; Lucie Fjeldstad, VP and General Manager of IBM's multimedia division; Karen Horn, Chairwoman and CEO of Bank One; and Linda Wachner, Chairwoman, President, and CEO of Warnaco, Inc., to name a few. Instead of occupying VP- or senior

VP-level jobs in supporting staff roles such as human resources, public relations, and community affairs, which rarely lead to the top, these women are found in positions which have traditionally served as launching pads for CEO positions (Wachner already holds that title). However, the not-so-good news emerging from this profile of leading businesswomen includes the fact that most of these women reported having been passed over for a promotion at least once, and many felt that gender is still a barrier to the executive suite.

In the small business sector, women may have shattered a glass ceiling of a different sort. Specifically, there are now over 4 million female entrepreneurs who started their own companies in the United States. Since 1991 the number of businesses owned by women jumped 20%, and these firms now employ more workers in the U.S. than Fortune 500 companies do globally (United States Small Business Administration, 1993). This growth of female entrepreneurs may, in part, be attributed to the continued existence of the corporate glass ceiling, which remains rigid to advancing women into business leadership positions. Thus, although women are getting a crack at new businesses and start-up efforts, they are often overlooked for key assignments in upper management. At this level, women continue to see the top; but they cannot get through to it.

How can women overcome the glass ceiling and glass walls? Ann Morrison, in her recent book, *The New Leaders: Guidelines on Leadership Diversity in America* (1992) reported the findings from a study which examined organizations with good records of promoting women and minorities. The author found that the attention of the CEO was the single most important factor in eliminating the glass ceiling. Other factors included accountability of top management for diversity; internal advocacy groups; targeting women in the leadership succession process; providing opportunities for start-up and troubleshooting assignments, both domestically and internationally; and deliberate attempts on the part of senior management to counter institutional barriers to women's advancement.

In order to crack the glass ceiling, it is not only necessary that women come to the attention of the CEO, but that men and women understand the perceptual and cognitive mechanisms that perpetuate stereotypic characterizations of male and female leaders, despite overwhelming similarities in leader behaviors. Since much information about women leaders seems to be encoded in terms of gender categories, rather than leadership categories—especially for females—''women in leadership situations may trigger extensive gender-related knowledge, but little knowledge related to leadership of specific individuals'' (Lord & Maher, 1991, p. 98).

WOMEN LEADERS AS TOKEN MINORITIES

Beginning with Kanter's (1977) groundbreaking work on women managers, *Men and Women of the Corporation*, numerous studies have asserted that the underrepresentation of women in leadership positions is essentially a function of the structure of their positions in the labor force. This author suggested that when members of a particular gender or ethnic category comprise less than 35% of a group, they have "token" or "solo" status. Not only are dominant group members the defining group, but they are taken to be the highest category—the best—and all other groups must be defined and judged solely according to majority group standards (Keto, 1989). Kanter, who based her work on the analysis of organizational environments in which men greatly outnumbered women in positions of authority, chose the term "token" for the underrepresented member in a mixed-sex group to highlight the special characteristics associated with that position. According to Powell (1988):

> Tokens are not merely people who differ from other group members along some particular dimension; they are people who are characterized on the basis of an easily recognizable characteristic such as sex (race, ethnic group, age). This characteristic carries a set of assumptions about the traits and expected behaviors of people in the category. Tokens exist only in small numbers, and the rest of the group puts them in the position of representing their category, whether they want to or not. (p. 112)

Women in leadership roles share many of the structural characteristics of tokens: they are highly visible, public individuals who attract attention with anything they do; as such, they are stand-ins for all women, symbols of how women behave and perform as leaders. As tokens, women leaders are different in status from other members of their work group. The pressure of being a minority sets women apart by gender even before anything is said or done.

Token leaders find themselves in the organizational limelight; their actions and moves are constantly scrutinized, and they are faced with pressures that result from the application of performance standards that are only applicable to tokens. Many token women have reported that they must work twice as hard as their male colleagues to be considered competent. In addition, token women usually are treated as representing women as a group because there are only a few others to share the leadership role. The smaller the number of tokens, the greater the chances that those leaders are isolated and evaluated on the basis of gender stereotypes. As tokens, women are not only scrutinized more closely, but also pressured to side with the (male) majority against "their kind," and expected to conform to the prevailing stereotype (O'Leary & Hansen, 1982).

The numerical imbalance, especially in the composition of the leadership echelon in an organization, calls attention to the uniqueness of token women, heightens their visibility, and creates the dynamics of tokenism. These dynamics involve attention-producing, polarizing, and assimilating processes that result in the token dynamics of performance pressure, social isolation, and role entrapment (Kanter, 1977). "Attention-producing" means an increased visibility of women in leadership roles, which translates into a disproportionate amount of scrutiny. The dynamic of polarization occurs when members of a work group exaggerate the differences between the numerical majority and the token.

Polarization typically results in social isolation of the woman with solo status. Because differences between the token and the rest of the group are exaggerated, the token has a difficult time gaining acceptance and is often excluded from group activities. Token women leaders have difficulties gaining the trust of their co-workers and followers, especially men, because they are frequently excluded from informal networks.

In assimilation, characteristics of the token are distorted to fit the stereotype of his or her category. This dynamic is also known as negative stereotyping. Assimilation of tokens into the stereotype of their group in turn leads to role entrapment. Kanter (1977) used this term to describe the limits placed on tokens when she stated: "Stereotypical assumptions about what tokens must be like, mistaken attributes and biased judgments, tend to force tokens into playing limited and caricatured roles" (p. 230). Thus, women in leadership become entrapped in stereotyopic roles such as "mother," "seductress," or "pet." At the executive level, on the other hand, women often find themselves entrapped in the role of the "Iron Maiden."

Crocker and McGraw (1984), in an empirical study of tokenism, worked with three types of groups: *token female groups*, consisting of five males and one female; *mixed groups* (three males and three females); and *token male groups* (five females and one male). The purpose of this research was to determine the number of times that male and female participants were identified as group leaders. As predicted, overall, male group members were almost twice as likely to be selected as group leaders than female participants. Even more interesting was the finding that the token women never perceived themselves as group leaders, whereas men in the solo status situation identified themselves as group leaders 30% of the time. Finally, the researchers noted that gender was invoked most often as an explanation for behavior in groups with a women token, but least often when men had solo status. The authors suggested that tokens with higher status (i.e., males) are more easily integrated into a group as leaders, thereby producing effective group performance. In the case of token females, on the other hand, gender may emerge as the salient issue and the presence of a female leader—a double deviant (Laws, 1975) because of her lower social status as well as her minority status as a woman—may disrupt group functioning and create dissatisfaction among the majority members of the group.

Fairhurst and Snavely (1983) pointed out that the problem with tokenism is that the token's perceived power in relation to a majority member is seen to be low by both the token and members of the majority. Tokenism is not just something that a majority group "does" to a person with solo status; instead, it is contingent on the token's compliance with the role expectations of the dominant majority (Katz & Kahn, 1978). Consequently, when ''tokens are treated on the basis of class membership, they tend to accept this definition of the situation more frequently than they reject it'' (Fairhurst & Snavely, 1983, p. 293). Taylor (1981) suggested a cognitive, rather than a power or motivational, explanation for the token phenomenon when he concluded that the focus on women is due to their uniqueness rather than their minority status in organizations.

Both the glass ceiling and tokenism represent structural barriers which limit women's leadership opportunities and power in organizations. Alleviating the numerical imbalance of women in leadership roles alone will neither remove the glass ceiling or reduce tokenism. Tokens can increase their power, and thereby their status, by taking advantage of their visible positions, which often increase their accessibility to important people in the organization or to other valued resources. Moreover, since women in leadership positions are often exceptional, both in terms of general competence as well as specialized expertise, their knowledge base may serve as an important source of power, especially if the group is dependent on the expertise possessed by the leader.

As in the case of the glass ceiling, we would expect that tokenism will gradually decline as more women take on leadership roles and positions, although this seems to be a very slow and protracted process.

WORK–FAMILY CONFLICT OR INADEQUATE CAREER SYSTEMS?

For many women and men today, not only are the employing organization and the family the central institutions in their lives, but in many cases the work and personal spheres are inextricably linked. The dilemmas, trials, and tribulations of women who attempt to combine family and work roles have been well documented and described elsewhere (e.g., Burke & Greenglass; Greenhaus & Parasuraman, 1987; Zedek & Mosier, 1990). As long as the world of work was defined as the place where instrumental (masculine) roles are played out, and the world of the family as the setting where expressive roles were played out, a legitimate framework existed that justified the relegation of men's priorities to work and women's priorities to the family (Thompson, Thomas, & Maier, 1992). The changing demographics of the past two decades, the changing contexts of women's work, their career choices, together with the increasing number of dual-career couples in which both husbands and wives hold jobs that are highly salient, have a developmental sequence, and require a high level of commitment as well as considerable investments of time and energy, have made it clear that the integration of work and family roles is a critical task for contemporary couples. Work, family, and leadership roles have developmental sequences that involve a series of transitions—for example, moving from middle management to the executive suite, or dropping out of the management race to devote more time to the family—which require occasional restructuring or recycling of these roles. Gender differences in the outcomes of multiple career transitions accumulate over time to produce large differences between men and women at later career stages (Ragins & Sundstrom, 1989), including differences in leadership success.

Realistically, few women are convinced that they can integrate their various roles and be effective simultaneously in each of them without experiencing stress or conflict. As one woman said:

> I am not really sure if it is possible for most of us to fuse the personal and professional into one smooth, charming, comfortable, and competent whole—doing everything our mothers did, and everything our fathers did as well. (Cosell, 1985, p. 135)

Multiple and often competing demands from major life roles almost invariably create conflict and stress, among them work overload and conflict stemming from discrepancies between societal and personal norms. According to Greenhaus and Beutell (1985), career-family conflict is most likely to occur when both work and family have high salience for the individual. Although men are participating more in household tasks, sex-role distinctions persist when it comes to the division of labor at home, with women continuing to handle the lion's share of domestic and childrearing obligations. Cowan (1989) in a poll conducted for the *New York Times*, found that 78% of the women in her sample of dual-career couples prepared most of the meals; 74% did most of the cleaning; 69% did most of the food shopping; and 65% handled most of the childrearing. Among the wives with children under 18 working full-time, 42% indicated that their husbands did less than their fair share of household chores. Even women without children who hold high-powered positions sometimes find it difficult to maintain a marriage or relationship with a significant other. However, compared to 10 years ago, when only 40% of women executives were married and 40% had children, the survey by Korn/Ferry and the University of California (Korn, 1986) found that 60% of the senior women managers were married and 57% had children. Although the number of female executives (vice presidents and up) in the survey was relatively small and their compensation was less than two-thirds of male executives' salaries and bonuses, Richard Ferry, chairman and CEO of Korn/Ferry, commented that senior women executives have made monumental gains in both their professional and personal lives over the past decade. A more realistic interpretation of this data is that women executives may be less willing to sacrifice family for the boardroom. But juggling family and work obligations continues to take its toll: 77% of the women surveyed indicated they wanted to retire before the age of 65, compared with 30% of their male counterparts. As Senator Dianne Feinstein of California, who helped release the survey, noted: although there has been a piercing of the glass ceiling, the shattering remains to be done. Clearly, this most recent survey of women executives shows that they have not achieved parity with men.

The skill with which women balance work, leadership responsibilities, and family demands depends not only on the organization's attitudes about family but women's own feelings about their jobs, as well as the fundamental life choices they make. Felice Schwartz is founder and president of Catalyst, a nonprofit organization specializing in research on women in corporations and work-family issues. In a highly controversial article, Schwartz (1989) claimed that the cost of employing women is greater than that of employing men (because of maternity leaves and maternity-related turnover). In order to reduce this cost, corporations should provide more flexible employment arrangements for women who are not willing to make significant sacrifices in their personal lives.

Schwartz distinguished between a "career-primary" and a "career-family" group of executive women. According to the author, these choices represent fundamental lifestyle orientations which reflect the relative priority of family or career. Women with a career-primary orientation have accorded top priority to their career progress and advancement and allocate family and social life to a secondary status. They are willing to forego marriage and/or family to reach for the top. On the other hand, women with a "career and family" orientation pursue careers but allow work-related choices such as working hours, compensation, or advancement to be determined and constrained by family demands and obligations. This orientation became known as the "mommy track" (a term coined by the media, not by Schwartz), which made front page news immediately. Initially, the mommy track, separate and unequal, was believed to permanently derail women's careers, making them second-class citizens and confirming the prejudice of male business leaders (Ehrlich, 1994).

Schwartz argued that organizations value the career-primary group as potential leaders and top executives. For career and family women, on the other hand, organizations have fewer opportunities for promotions and advancement. Moreover, the author suggested that organizations treat high-potential, career-primary women, most of whom will be childless, the same as high-potential men. In fact, the article was seen as playing into the hands of the current generation of male business leaders, who are only too happy to have their perceptions of career women confirmed (Hall, 1990).

The article hit a nerve and stirred a controversy because it implied that there are two classes of corporate women, only one of which (career-primary) makes it to the top. It was also criticized for giving male executives an easy excuse for not promoting women, appearing to place all the responsibilities for family care on women, and not acknowledging women's options to shift gears and increase or decrease work commitments at different stages of careers and life-cycles (Hall, 1990). Indeed, women may change career-primary or career/family orientations from time to time. Following childbirth, career-primary women may shift their lifestyle to a career and family orientation to accommodate the needs of the family. Similarly, the opportunity to move into a leadership role may require a transformation of the basic lifestyle orientation. Because of the salience of both career and family, and the interdependencies that exist between work and family domains, women often resent having to choose one over the other. Such choices are determined by a host of individual, organizational, and other factors including marital status, career stage, timing of parenthood, division of homework and child care, the nature of work, leadership opportunities, and the trade-offs women are willing to make to achieve leadership success. The fact that career and family involvements are interdependent in itself is not so problematic. However, as Crosby (1987) pointed out, the gender asymmetries underlying work-family interdependencies are both unfortunate and inequitable.

Business Week (1989), in a cover story, claimed that "across the country, female managers and professionals with young families are leaving the fast track for the mommy track" (Ehrlich, 1989, p. 128). Although women are often faced with conflict between career and family, contrary to the "mommy track" idea, most female managers are leaving the organization because of perceived limits on their career, rather than because of work–family conflict (Tashjian, 1990). Similarly, Stroh and Brett (1993) reported turnover rates of 615 male and female managers from different companies. Although women had higher turnover rates than men, for them, leaving the organizations was not so much caused by the demands of combining work and family, but by a variety of individual and organizational factors, including gender bias and job dissatisfaction.

Although leading companies such as DuPont and Merck have corporate policies designed to balance work and family life by offering child care, elder care, parental leave programs, and alternative work schedules, career systems in most organizations lack the flexibility to promote the integration of work and family lives. Career success in many contemporary organizations is defined as a sequence of linear, vertical steps up the corporate ladder. Leadership opportunities are offered to those men and women who rapidly obtain the series of promotions necessary to move them into leadership positions. The status positions at the top continue to be the ultimate symbol of success. Women executives who decide to take extended family leaves (more than 2 years) are penalized not only by a discontinuous salary history, but by being passed over for advancement once they return to work full-time. As long as career systems in organizations are designed around hierarchical progression, the integration of work, family roles, and leadership roles will remain problematic.

As a result of these trends, there have been increasing pressures on organizations to acknowledge that family life and work life are no longer separable (Auerbach, 1988). Thus, although restructuring work to help a woman assume leadership responsibilities and raise a family has been alien to corporate orthodoxy, some companies are beginning to embrace work-family initiatives as good for the company. First and foremost among these initiatives are child care benefits and workplace flexibility (Goodstein, 1994). Murray (1994) argued that the best explanation for the latest cultural shift is the demise of guaranteed corporate paternalism in exchange for unquestioned employee loyalty. Therefore, a growing number of companies are experimenting with telecommuting, leave programs, and subsidies for child and elder care to retain their investment in executive women.

EXCLUSION OF WOMEN FROM INFORMAL NETWORKS

The final structural barrier which impedes women's access to leadership is the informal networks that exist in organizations. Informal networks tend to be more fluid than the formal relationships depicted on the organizational chart which defines reporting relationships, leadership positions, power, and job responsibilities. Informal networks, on the other hand, involve more discretionary patterns of interactions, where the content of the relationship may be work-related, social, or a combination of both (Ibarra, 1993). Dubek (1979) argued that informal social networks dominated by men function on a basis of trust rooted in assumptions of shared characteristics between key actors. The more unlike those actors outsiders appear to be, the more likely they will remain on the periphery. Women, in a male circle of leaders, therefore have an immediate disadvantage, based on their visible difference.

Most women leaders do not share a traditional "old boy" network because they are often on their own. They often have to create alternatives to substitute for what informal networks accomplish. Networking is an informal process which serves critical functions in career development and advancement. Among the benefits of networking are information exchange, career planning and strategizing, professional support and encouragement, increased visibility, and upward mobility. Although the networks of women and men appear to be of similar size, both sexes tend to interact in separate spheres; two examples being men playing golf together and women joining female business networks in their local communities. In fact, in some organizations, sex segregation of the informal structure is more severe than that of the formal structure, with women lacking access to many of the informal groups, such as male clubs or sports. Limited network access creates multiple disadvantages for women, including restricted knowledge of what is going on in the organization and difficulty in forming alliances which, in turn, are associated with limited mobility and the glass ceiling effect (Brass, 1985; O'Leary & Ickovics, 1992). As long as male networks are the more powerful informal groups with greater access to political, financial, legal, and professional resources that flow through the informal tributaries, the structure of organizations will continue to serve as a barrier to women's leadership.

Often, networking includes the establishment of mentoring relationships. Mentoring, of course, is nothing new; the original Mentor can be traced to Greek mythology. Mentor, in the disguise of Athena, provided encouragement and support for Odysseus' son Telemachus while his father was fighting the Trojan War. Like all good mentors, Athena imbued Telemachus with a sense of courage and morality and set him off on a journey to explore his leadership potential. With his mentor's support, Telemachus developed leadership qualities similar to those displayed by his father.

Mentor has been immortalized by the attachment of his name to an organizational process that pairs a younger person with a more experienced individual who provides support and guidance through the maze of organizational policies and politics. While mentoring itself is not new, what is a relatively recent phenomenon is women serving as mentors to other women and organizations implementing formal mentoring programs to help women along the leadership path.

Kram's (1985) research on mentoring showed that mentors serve both career and psychosocial functions. Career functions include those aspects of the mentoring relationship that prepare protégés for career advancement and involve activities such as nominating the protégé for career-enhancing projects, lateral moves, appointments to organizational task forces, and promotions. Among the psychosocial functions performed by a mentor are serving as a role model, conveying acceptance and support, and modeling behaviors and attitudes consistent with the culture of the organization. By exercising these functions, the mentor enhances the protégé's sense of competence, work-role effectiveness, and assimilation into the organizational culture. Kram suggested that the greater the number of functions performed by the mentor, the more beneficial the relationship with the protégé. Mentoring relationships which provide the full range of career and psychosocial functions are categorized as classic or primary mentoring relationships.

Mentoring has a number of benefits, including enhancement of career progress; promotional decisions; motivation; job performance; and retention rates. Roche (1979), for example, reported that two-thirds of the executives in his study had mentors, and that these executives received higher salaries, bonuses, and total compensation than their counterparts without mentors. Similarly, Riley and Wrench (1985) reported that women with mentors were more satisfied with their jobs and had greater success on the job than women without mentors. Not only do individuals benefit from mentoring but, as Zey (1988) pointed out, both the employee and the organization can profit from these relationships by promoting the development of corporate leaders, integrating employees into the organization, fostering creativity and commitment, and keeping the lines of communication open. According to Keele and DeLaMare-Schaefer (1984), the most successful mentoring relationships are those in which the benefits accrued to the protégé also accrue to the mentor, including opportunities to advance, increased control over the work environment, access to a variety of resources, enhancement of status, and personal satisfaction.

In addition to the benefits accrued by the mentor and his or her protégé, mentoring systems play an important role in developing or modifying the culture of the organization. As noted in Chapter 1, organizational culture is a constellation of basic values and beliefs shared by members of the organization which give it its identity. Culture manifests itself in slogans, language (i.e., IBM–speak), dress codes, and company rituals. Just as in historical societies, where folklore and fables with their morals were passed down from generation to generation, mentors can pass on organizational myths and legends. Mentors can be trusted sources who lend credibility to organizational stories, put organizational myths into perspective, and enlighten the junior person as to their deeper meaning (Wilson & Elman, 1990). In this capacity the mentor performs a leadership function, because building an organizational culture, shaping its evolution, and reshaping its meaning is a unique and essential task of leadership (Schein, 1991). Bennis (1988) in *Why Leaders Can't Lead* discussed four specific leadership competencies that effective leaders must show. These are management of attention through vision; management of meaning through communication; management of trust through reliability and constancy; and management of self through knowing one's skills and developing them effectively. Effective mentors possess each of these four competencies and develop them in their protégés.

Mentoring relationships may be particularly important for women seeking leadership roles, since they face gender-related obstacles to advancement. While men often have mentors who guide them through the behavioral minefield of the workplace, for women, mentors are not always easy to find (Driscoll & Goldberg, 1993). Mentorships are important because they help aspiring leaders to develop a sense of self-efficacy through which initiative, thought, and independent judgment are encouraged and reinforced. However, since young girls traditionally have not been brought up with the networking/mentoring mentality, women until recently seemed reluctant to join these types of male structures; having a mentor, especially of the opposite sex, was perceived as risky.

The widely publicized mentoring relationship between Mary Cunningham and William Agee at Bendix illustrates some of the pitfalls encountered in cross-gender mentoring. In 1980 William Agee, chairman and chief executive at Bendix, one of the largest auto suppliers, appointed Mary Cunningham, just 15 months after graduating from the Harvard Business School, to the position of Vice President of Strategic Planning. Although Agee denied at a corporate meeting that their personal relationship had anything to do with Cunningham's promotion, gossip about a romantic involvement would not subside. The relationship between Agee and his protégé generated an avalanche of media coverage which fueled the rumor mill even more when Agee divorced his wife of 23 years. Cunningham resigned under the pressure of publicity and her resignation further spurred sexual innuendos and speculations about the nature of her relationship with Agee. While both Cunningham and Agee saw the controversy as sexist and Cunningham felt victimized, this mentorship highlights some of the problems that may occur when men mentor women. Although many senior men are effective mentors, the complexities involved in mentoring women may limit the usefulness of such relationships (Parker & Kram, 1993).

Men Mentoring Women

Although mentorship is important for women, and empirical evidence (e.g., Dreher & Ash, 1990) suggests that there are no gender differences in the frequency of mentoring, several studies (e.g., Kram, 1985; Noe, 1988) have shown that women have more difficulties establishing mentoring relationships, both when mentoring other women (same-gender mentorships) and when being mentored by men (cross-gender mentorships). Both types of mentorship have their pros and cons. However, because of the lack of female role models, especially in traditionally male-dominated occupations, most mentors in the past were men.

Noe (1988) suggested that the development of cross-gender mentorships may be inhibited by a number of perceptual and situational factors, including women's lack of access to informal networks, socialization practices, power differences, tokenism, and social norms regarding cross-gender relationships between superiors and subordinates. Women who do not have a mentor because they lack access to informal networks may not be visible to organizational decisionmakers and therefore may reduce their chances of being selected for leadership roles. Similarly, male managers, because of the way they have been socialized, may avoid building a mentoring relationship with a female employee because they perceive the roles of women and manager to be incompatible, or believe that women are not interested in career advancement. For example, Fitt and Newton (1981) found that male mentors were less likely to believe that women were competent managers, and deferred establishing developmental relationships with women protégés until they had proven themselves.

Having a mentor of the opposite sex may also raise concerns over the public image of such relationships, as the Agee-Cunningham situation has shown. Concerns over the public image of a cross-gender mentoring relationship are likely to emerge, especially in view of the often intense and frequent personal interactions between the mentor and his protégé, since these interactions center on work tasks as well as on concerns or problems of a personal nature. As a result, some managers avoid mentoring women because they perceive the relationship as risky, a potential threat to their job security, or possibly damaging to their own careers because of the closeness and intimacy involved in the psychosocial functions of mentoring.

Women Mentoring Women

Same-gender mentoring relationships have a different set of potential problems. To begin with, the shortage of women in leadership roles results in a shortage of women mentors. Moreover women are often perceived as not having the legitimate authority or power to serve as a mentor, especially when they hold such supervisory staff positions as heads of human resource or public relations departments, which are not always seen as central to the goals of the organization. In order to be attractive as a mentor, women need to be placed in positions that promote their credibility. Finally, women may lack the willingness to mentor other women, a reason that may be related to the Queen Bee syndrome ("I got to where I am without help, why should I help her?") or because they may be too busy themselves trying to break through the glass ceiling.

Parker and Kram (1993) discussed the barriers to same-sex mentoring in terms of disconnections that exist between women. The authors argued that, paradoxically, the common experiences women share in the workplace, which are the attraction and glue for a mentoring relationship, are often not discussed by a female executive and her junior protégé. These discussions may not take place because of differences in career stages, unwillingness to self-disclose or unrealistic expectations regarding the nature of the relationship. Junior women looking for a mentor, for example, may assume that their common experiences as women will create an automatic bond with the female executive that overrides differences in career stages, power, and authority inherent in any mentoring relationship. And finally, as Ragins and Cotton (1991) pointed out, given the limelight focused on the token women, the failure of a protégé is a much greater risk for a woman executive than it is for a man. Performance and success of the protégé are often viewed as a direct reflection of the mentor's judgment and competency (Zey, 1984). Mistakes made by women mentors in guiding the careers and advancement of other women are often evaluated more harshly. Nevertheless, at least one organization is offering a "womentoring" program which links women interested in leadership with successful female mentors. This program provides leadership training and opportunities, educates participants about gender issues in leadership, and promotes the understanding of leadership in different contexts.

Same-gender as well as cross-gender mentoring are sources of personal growth for the mentor and provide opportunities for the development of leadership potential in both the mentor and the protégé. Women and men mentoring women are involved in developmental relationships of increasing levels of psychological complexity, especially in the upper echelons of formal organizations where most leadership is institutionalized. At this level, one aspect of the mentoring role is the sharing of the mentor of his or her vision to establish a continuity of leadership. The other aspect of the mentoring role is to encourage the protégé to develop his or her own vision to promote organizational change and inspire organizational renewal.

CONCLUSIONS

While many of the legal barriers to women's participation in the workforce and access to leadership positions in corporations have been removed through legislation, changing demographics, and women's increased level of education and experience, women still face many obstacles on the path to leadership. Although it is no longer politically correct to be overtly gender-biased, subtle forms of discrimination continue to exist. As long as gender stereotypes provide a major framework for organizing information about women leaders, and as long as social categorizations based on gender (or other status characteristics such as race, ethnic background, education, or wealth) play an important part in judging women's fitness for leadership, we need to scrutinize the effects of stereotypic perceptions and expectations which drive the assessment of leaders, especially those who deviate from the prevailing male model.

The effects of the glass ceiling; the dynamics of tokenism; the persistence of cultural norms which identify leadership as men's domain; the unwillingness of senior male and female leaders to establish mentoring relationships with female organizational novices; the lack of access to or exclusion from informal networks; and the collusive role men play in perpetuating these structural and organizational barriers all serve to impede women's leadership opportunities. Mentoring plays an important role in this process because mentors act as transfer agents of organizational leadership. Women's exclusion from male informal networks prevents them from developing an intelligence or communication base which could spread a mantle of authority over their positions in the informal structure. The resulting handicap activates a vicious cycle which women leaders frequently do not have the resources to break (Horner, Nadelman, & Nortman, 1989). Leadership is in the eyes of the led, and is embedded in organizational contexts which impose unique barriers and constraints on women and other minorities who pursue leadership opportunities. Organizations willing to promote leadership in an increasingly diverse, heterogeneous population must analyze the visible and invisible effects of these barriers and constraints and take a hard, critical look at how they influence the way we educate, train, and develop leaders for the 21st century.

8 Contemporary Women Leaders in Different Contexts

> The most notable fact that culture imprints on women is the sense of our limits. The most important thing one woman can do for another is to illuminate and expand her sense of actual possibilities.
>
> *Adrienne Rich*

INTRODUCTION

The central theme of this book is the notion that much of leadership is contextual, shaped by situational, historical, temporal, and spatial factors. We have examined a number of different contexts thus far. In Chapter 1, we looked at several contextual factors, such as federal legislation in the form of Title XII, executive orders, the Equal Pay Act, etc. that have facilitated women's leadership in recent history. In Chapter 2, we focused on one specific context, history, as a frame for analyzing women's leadership across different spheres including politics, religion, and social movements. In Chapter 4, formal organizations and management provided the context that allowed us to examine the differences between women leaders and women managers.

The study of leadership from a contextual perspective builds on the idea that at any given time and in any given place, leaders are very much the product of their particular era and the organizational or community setting in which they exercise leadership. Furthermore, the contextual perspective calls our attention to the fact that successful leadership in one context—whether business, grassroots organizations, or the military—does not necessarily guarantee success in another field. By neglecting the context, be it historical or situational, we run the risk of failing to understand what makes a strong religious leader, cultural leader, intellectual leader, reform leader, or sports leader.

In this chapter, the premise that leadership is contextual is applied to contemporary women leaders. Each context defines leadership differently. Formal organizations, for example, frequently define leadership as a position in the hierarchical structure of the organization. Community organizations, on the other hand, define leadership using such criteria as effective coordination of interdependent, interlocking citizen groups, or achievement of harmony and consensus. Communities celebrate their leaders for their commitment to the common good, altruism, and willingness to forego personal interests for the welfare of their communities. Thus, communities seek or develop different types of leaders than those sought in business and other contexts.

In the context of religion, despite the roles women have played as founders of churches, convents, leaders of congregations, and lay voices, it is undeniable that women have been excluded from institutional church leadership. Pope John Paul II, for example, recently reaffirmed that women cannot become priests in the Catholic Church. Yet Jesus appeared first to Mary Magdalene after his resurrection, and the apostle Paul chose Lydia, a businesswoman, to establish the first church in Europe. Women were also active as disciples during the ministry of Christ and participated in religious preaching and ceremonies before male-dominant forces took over the control of the Church.

In our society, women who petition to be admitted to the priesthood, ministry, or rabbinate of their respective religion are no longer willing to settle for subordinate and indirect access to their God (Polster, 1992). Instead, according to Pagels (1979), women seek to revise

> what religious rhetoric assumes and that men form the legitimate body of the community while women are allowed to participate only when they assimilate themselves to men. (p. 49)

Ruether and McLaughlin (1979) assessed women's religious leadership as follows:

> Women today have the possibility of playing roles in the institutional and ordained leadership of more and more branches of Western religion. No longer do they have to validate the possibility of leadership through roles marginal and subversive to the institution. Women must therefore ask themselves not only what they gain by these new developments but also what they may lose. Is it enough simply to be incorporated into paradigms of ordained ministry shaped by males for many hundreds of years in hierarchical molds intended to exclude women? Or must women, by their very presence, reshape the ministry into forms that are more open, pluralistic and dialogic? In gaining the leadership of office, will they abandon insights gained through the authority of holiness and charisma? Women, excluded from the institutional church leadership, have continued to represent forms of leadership that derive from a church

shaped by direct religious experience, millennial hope and marginality within established social forms. (p. 28)

Since women comprise the bulk of fellowship of most denominations, Reynolds (1994) believes that it is only a question of time until women tire of second-class citizenship in their churches.

Leadership also plays itself out in yet another context, the realm of the arts and the sciences. Wills (1994) argued that intellectual leadership is as rare as intellectual influence is common. Although we are influenced by Einstein's theory of relativity and Freud's theory of the unconscious, intellectual leaders do not mobilize their followers toward a goal as business or political leaders do. Against the many male intellectual giants—Socrates, Voltaire, Hume, Russell, Wittgenstein, James Watson, and Schlesinger, to name a few—only a few women leaders like Marie Curie and George Eliot (Ann Marie Evans) stand out. Among contemporary women leaders in this context, Bernardine Healy, former President of the American Heart Association and Director of the National Institutes of Mental Health under the Bush administration, was the first woman to hold both offices. Healy, in addition to her fetal tissues research, played a leading role in correcting the longstanding bias against women's health issues.

In this chapter on contemporary women leaders, I have chosen two contexts which, more than others, have remained strongholds of male leadership. Although the glass ceiling and the glass wall remain factors of organizational life, women have made visible progress in the business and corporate sector. Historically, from the early leaders of the women's movement—Lucretia Mott, Susan B. Anthony, Elizabeth Cady Stanton, Emmeline Silvia Pankhurst—to Margaret Sanger, founder of Planned Parenthood, and Candy Lightner, founder of Mothers Against Drunk Driving (MADD), women leaders have been at the core of many social reform movements. Many of the women in these movements were and are charismatic leaders who present their message and mission with passion and zeal, emphasizing familiar values and sentiments in order to create a legitimate rationale for action in our society (Weed, 1993).

Politics and sports, on the other hand, are contexts in which the number of women leaders has yet to reach a critical mass. These two contexts share common themes. In both contexts, as many researchers (e.g., Cantor & Bearnay, 1992; Stangl & Kane, 1991) have argued, the reasons for the low level of representation of women in leadership positions are found in the power structure and male hegemony characteristic of these settings. Moreover, in both contexts, individual inadequacies such as women's lack of experience or competence in these settings have been blamed for the small number of women leaders. However, structural factors, such as the absence of support groups, lack of role models in visible leadership positions in politics and sports, and the power structure of these contexts represent the more critical obstacles facing women.

This chapter makes no attempt to provide in-depth biographical treatments of contemporary women leaders. Rather, the intent is to show how contextual, personal, organizational, cultural, and environmental forces merge and interact in determining the leadership of influential contemporary women in two arenas which are resistant to female leadership.

WOMEN SPORT LEADERS

Sports Leadership in Context

The world of sports has produced a few outstanding women leaders like Lottie Dodd, Gertrud Edule, Aileen Riggin Soule, America's oldest living gold medalist, Deion Sanders, and Babe Didrikson Zaharias. Zaharias, for example, is perhaps the best all-around female athlete in the history of American sports. Zaharias excelled in running, swimming, javelin-throwing, diving, high jumping, baseball, boxing, rifle shooting, and golfing and became a legend and role model for many women athletes. Described as crass, crude, colorful, competitive, and controversial, her fans nicknamed her after the athletic world's idol Babe Ruth. She dominated women's sports for a quarter of a century, accumulating an unparalleled list of victories, records, and accolades (Hicks, 1975). More importantly, perhaps, she had considerable social impact, providing encouragement and inspiration for women to venture into a field in which they were presumably at an inherent disadvantage.

In the context of sports, star athletes are heroes. Carlyle (1813), in his classic work on heroes, wrote that the moral character of heroes may be something less than perfect, and courage may not be the essential ingredient, yet fans follow their heroes, admire them, and obey them to the point of worship. Carlyle's observation, made more than 180 years ago, seems to be as valid today when we consider sports heroes like Mike Tyson and O.J. Simpson.

In sports, hero worship involves the admiration of the idol's physical prowess and strength, and for many adoring sports fans the hero is a source of inspiration. Sports fans not only worship male players, but also their managers, umpires, team owners, and stadium builders. People are willing to go the extra mile to protect their heroes, as the recent case of O.J. Simpson has shown. Even if these heroes fall from status, their followers revere them. Yet, as Wills (1994) pointed out, admiring and imitating a hero is not the same as following a leader. Fans of sports leaders typically do not share their leader's motives (i.e., playing to win, making money, becoming famous, being idolized, etc.), since a unified commitment and common purpose do not exist to bind sports leaders to their followers.

Creedon (1994) defined *sport* as a cultural institution and *sports* as activities or games that are óne part of the institution of sport. Several authors (i.e., Birrell & Cole, 1990; Kane & Parks, 1992) have argued that perhaps more than any other social institution sports perpetuates male superiority and female inferiority by equating physical superiority with social superiority. The arguments presented by these authors suggest that sports represents a potent medium through which biological or physical differences interface with social and cultural interpretations of gender-role expectations (Creedon, 1994). Based on physical differences between men and women, people perceive male athletes to be better qualified for many sports leadership roles. As a result of the presumed inferior performance capacity of women and women's presumed psychological unsuitability for sports competition, few female athletes have access to leadership in sports.

Sports is an important context because it teaches many leadership skills and lessons; the benefits resulting from participation in sports have been well documented. Individual and team sports build self-confidence, courage, patience, humility, stamina, and persistence. The world of sports, like the military, is considered valuable training for leadership and organizational success because it provides images for teamwork and tough competition (Acker, 1990). In addition to muscles, as Nelson (1991) writes, "Athleticism builds self-esteem so athletes are better prepared than other women to think on their feet and, when wise, fight back" (p. 129). In addition, team sports offer their participants rewards that are not only pertinent in the world of sport, but also in other settings. For example, through team sports, players learn and come to value cooperation, consensus-building, negotiation, and conflict resolution, which are valuable in political and business contexts as well. Many authors have described the camaraderie and intimacy which characterize male sports teams as something unparalleled and not found in any other context (Whitson, 1990). At the same time, team sports teach competition, perseverance, and endurance. Team sports are also seen as vehicles for cultivating and displaying community and national values and identities (Jansen & Sabo, 1994).

Sports is a context that is rich in rituals, metaphors, and symbolism. The locker room, with its emotionally charged atmosphere and jock culture, conjures up images of gladiators, national pride, post-game stripping, and bawdy drunkenness. Likewise, in football, symbols of patriotism, militarism, violence, and meritocracy are all dominant themes (Messner, 1988). Much of the imagery of leadership employed in other contexts, such as business or politics, has its origins in the world of sports, which in itself contains images from other sources, such as the military. For example, consultants and supervisors advise women managers to "play hardball," "crunch" the enemy, "don't show your trump card." Jansen and Sabo (1994) noted the convergence and conflation of the vocabularies of sport and war. They pointed out that by the time the Watergate tapes were produced during the Nixon administration, football imagery had become the root metaphor of the American political discourse. More recently, a widely quoted example of sport/war imagery during the Persian Gulf War was provided by General Norman Schwarzkopf. He characterized the strategic plan of the ground war as "the Hail Mary play in football" (Janson & Sabo, 1994, p. 3). Sports metaphors are also commonly used in business, often to the chagrin of women. For example, the CEO who turns on the old half time speech—"Just take the ball, put your head down, and run right thru them"—may not reach women with this message. Through images, language, metaphors, and cults, sports provide symbolic and tangible "proof" of the physical superiority of men, which, in turn, predisposes them to social superiority. Messner and Sabo (1990) wrote:

> Sport is without doubt one of the most masculine institutions. Sport, it is argued, is an institution created by and for men. As such, it has served to bolster a sagging ideology of male hegemony and has helped to reconstitute masculine hegemony in the 19th and 20th centuries. Yet women's movement into sport (as athletes and as spectators) has challenged the naturalization of gender difference and inequality which has been a basic aspect of the institution of sport. (p. 9)

Similarly, Hoch (1972) labeled sports a "school for sexism," while Naison (1972) saw it as an institutional source of the "ideology of male domination" (p. 108). Whitson (1990) takes the position that sport as a social institution helps to reinforce men's power over women. The author argues that despite women's recent movement into sport, it continues to bolster hegemonic masculinity by ritualizing the aggression, strength, and skill of the male body and linking it to competitive achievement. The major games "Monday Night Football" or "Hockey Night in Canada" continue as social institutions through which the perpetuation and reinforcement of male hegemony are actively pursued.

Sabo (1987) compared games such as football to a social theater with an all-male, intergenerational cast. In this theater, the major actors and the relationships between the older coach and his younger players is defined as a testing ground for adult manhood. Similarly, as basketball was transformed from a mere pastime to an important cultural and patriarchal symbol, it was necessary that it be defined as completely masculine (Ferrante, 1994). According to Dunning (1986), the games are institutions which celebrate the physical and fighting skills of men and in which male solidarity and intimacy play a critical role. The rituals and cults surrounding the games unfold in sex-segregated contexts such as the locker room or playing field. As women become stronger economically and socially, men retreat more into the world of athletics, where fans revere their superiority.

Sabo and Runfola (1980) described how the media capitalized on the boundless male interest in sports to build a huge listening, reading, and viewing audience. The authors stated:

A symbiosis has developed between sports and the mass media. Sports are used to promote newspaper sales, to sell advertising space, and to win lucrative contracts for TV and radio time. In turn, the media help to sell spectator sports and attendant sports related consumer products to the public. (p. 161)

Finally, sports is a provocative context for the study of women's leadership because, in many ways, women's position in sports is a reflection of the changing role of women, not only in this particular context, but society in general. According to Messner (1988), women's movement into sport represents a genuine quest by women for equality, control of their own bodies, and self-definition, and, as such, represents a challenge to male hegemony in athletics and larger society. Thus, women's quest for equality in society has its counterpart in the world of sport. Until two decades ago, sport was sex-segregated, with one set of programs and policies provided for girls and women and another set for boys and men. For the latter group, competitive athletics were designed around a military model; women's sport programs were built on a distinctively different philosophy which stressed cooperation rather than competition. Boys and men treat sport as serious activity, but when played by girls and women it is seen and portrayed as a social, leisurely, and recreational enterprise.

Women's place in many sports evolved from invisibility to a sex-segregated and trivialized position, often characterized by sexual innuendos (Oglesby & Shelton, 1992). Women's lower participation rates in sports, particularly competitive intercollegiate sports, have been attributed to a confluence of factors including physical characteristics such as women's lower upper body strength, negative attitudes towards female ''jocks,'' and less opportunities to develop themselves as athletes. The scholarly literature (i.e., Blinde, Taub, & Han, 1993; Kunesh, Hasbrook, & Lewthwaithe, 1992) holds that factors other than gender determine whether women will participate in sports.

The progress women have made in sports was largely a result of Title IX of the 1972 Education Amendments Act. In the year Title IX was enacted, only a handful of college athletic scholarships were available to women. This legislation facilitated the integration of women into athletics. Title IX requires that no person shall, on the basis of sex, be excluded from participation in, denied the benefits of, or subjected to discrimination under any education program or activity receiving federal financial assistance. One of the major concerns of Title IX is the opportunity afforded to women athletes to develop themselves through participation in sports of interest to them. As Greenlaw and Kohl (1982) argued, following the usual logic applied to questions of equity, the number of opportunities for athletic participation open to women would be expected to be proportionate to their numbers in the student population. However, many NCAA Division I schools do not meet this definition of equity. Nevertheless, the congressional enactment of Title IX made discrimination against girls and women in secondary school and college sports illegal and provided the legal basis from which to push for greater equity.

The passage of Title IX brought about a wave of optimism about female participation in sports and resulted in greater funding for women's sports in colleges and high schools. This legislation, the gender-equity law, leveled the playing field for women by providing both athletic scholarships for women and by affording women to participate in emergent sports including archery, ice hockey, and water polo. Colleges and universities had to revamp their physical education and athletic programs; they were pressed to increase sports opportunities for women if current funding and opportunities are deemed inequitable.

However, as in business, legislation and equal opportunity under the law did not translate into equity or equal gains for women athletes. In fact, sports has remained a strong male bastion, honored and reinforced by a male value system in which force, aggression, conflict and a win–lose mentality are critical elements. Sports defines strength, muscularity, and competitiveness as "masculine." Women who exhibit these characteristics present an unacceptable side of femininity (Matteo, 1988). Therefore achieving parity with their male counterparts remains an uphill battle for women athletes. This is, for example, reflected in the gender gap of coaches' pay. According to the Women's Basketball Coaches Association, in 1994 the average base salary for men and women who coach women's basketball was $44,961; for men's coaches, it was $76,566. The same survey also found that 75% of women's coaches had contracts, compared to 92% of men's coaches. The average budget for a woman's program during the same year was $148,194, compared to $252,922 for a men's team (Becker, 1994, p. 1C).

Other recent statistics on female athletes speak to the continuing inequality of women's representation in sports. For example, the National Collegiate Athletic Association (NCAA) reported that the 288 schools in the NCAA's Division I enrolled 13,700 female athletes and 25,138 male athletes as freshmen in 1990–1992 (Gartner, 1994, p. 11A). In 1990–91, Division I schools offered an average of 42.3 scholarships to women, compared with 95.7 to men according to an NCAA study. The NCAA also reported that in 1993 the graduation rate for female athletes was 68%, compared to that of 52% of their male counterparts. While good male athletes have some chance of obtaining a high-paying job without a degree, women athletes do not have this option, since they cannot plan on an athletic career beyond college. Therefore, women athletes have greater incentives to complete college, which partially accounts for their higher graduation rates. Nevertheless, women have a long struggle ahead of them as they seek equal opportunities in sports.

As of 1993, for example, no woman has been hired as an umpire in major league baseball. Pam Postema, who worked in the minor leagues for 13 years

and was most likely to make the jump, said of her battle to break into the
major leagues:

> I'll never understand why it's easier for a female to become an astronaut
> or cop or fire fighter or soldier or Supreme Court justice than it is to
> become a major league umpire. For Christ sakes, it's only baseball.
> (Postema & Wojciechowski, 1992, p. 255)

Postema's (1992) autobiography chronicles her trials and tribulations during 13
years as umpire in the minor leagues. In 1988, the National League considered
her as a candidate for one of two openings created by the death of one umpire
and the retirement of another. Pitcher Bob Knepper of the Houston Astros, after
a game against the Pittsburgh Pirates which Postema umpired, made the comment
that umpiring is the wrong calling for women:

> I just don't think a woman should be an umpire. It has nothing to do
> with her ability. I don't think women should be in any leadership position.
> I don't think they should be presidents or politicians. I think women
> were created not in an inferior position, but in a role of submission to
> men. (p. 180)

The following year the National League made no attempt to invite Postema to
the 1990 spring training, but offered her a minor-league supervising job instead.
In 1990, the Triple A Alliance dropped her, citing as the reason for her dismissal
the policy that if after 3 years an umpire is not recruited by the major leagues,
he or she is released. It was then that Postema said good-bye to umpiring
and baseball.

In the context of sport, an important leadership role is that of the coach who,
over an extended time, develops an intense and personal relationship with the
players. Although individual styles of coaches vary from authoritarian to participatory, coaches exert considerable control over their players, since most insist on
some degree of conformity (Coakley, 1986). The low level of representation of
women in coaching and other leadership positions, according to Staurowsky
(1990), speaks to the strength of the connection between gender and sport. This
connection between sport and masculinity is established in sport systems through
the higher valuation of male qualities, especially physical strength of the male
body, since men are believed to be stronger, tougher, and faster.

Although research (e.g., Hasbrook, Hart, Mathes, & True, 1990) has shown
that female coaches are at least as well qualified, and sometimes better qualified,
than their male counterparts, given their coaching experience and professional
training, the number of women in coaching positions is small. In fact, as women's
sports became more popular and lucrative, men have claimed more leadership

positions, especially as coaches in the post-Title IX era. According to data provided by Nelson:

The executive director of the Women's Tennis Association is a man, as are the heads of the Ladies Professional Golf Association and the Ladies Pro Bowlers' Tour. The United States Olympic Committee has 105 members on its executive board: 91 are men. Of the 38 governing bodies of sport (such as the U.S. Figure Skating Association), 34 have male presidents. Male corporate representatives dispense endorsements. Information about women athletes is filtered through male writers, photographers, sportscasters, and publishers: approximately 9,650 of the nation's 10,000 print and broadcast journalists are men. Women now play in "men's" gyms, under male rules, male officiating, male coaching and, too often, male harassment. (1991, p. 5)

Knoppers (1989) pointed out the benefits men derive from the absence of women in coaching. Not only is the size of the competition for these positions automatically reduced because of the small number of female coaches available for these positions, but the status of the coach remains high, instead of being lowered by the entry of a large number of minorities. Therefore the "maleness" of the coaching professions maintained.

Outstanding female coaches are the exception; two examples are Old Dominion University's basketball coach Ann Donovan, one of the most decorated players of the sport, male or female, who in 1995 was inducted in the Basketball Hall of Fame, and Tara VanDerveer, head coach of the 1992 national champion women's basketball team at Stanford University. VanDerveer in particular typifies the contemporary female sports leader. Her leadership is different from other kinds of leadership found in the context of sport. Owners of teams, for example, are business leaders, rather than sports leaders, since they market a product that portrays male athletes as heroes. VanDerveer, on the other hand, is a women leader of a leading women's basketball team. She attributes her successes—as of 1993 she had won 322 games—to her players and assistant coaches. Highlen (1994) described VanDerveer not only an exceptional basketball coach, but also a superb strategist and visionary for the future.

Female participation in athletics is, in part, limited by the effects of gender stereotypes concerning what is and is not appropriate sport activity for women. Not surprisingly, sports commentators typically consider individual sports, such as tennis, ice skating, gymnastics, and swimming, which are labeled "low contact" sports, more appropriate for women than team sports or sports which involve heavy body contact. Sport typing, that is, labeling certain sports "masculine" and others "feminine," as Kane and Snyder (1989) pointed out, is essential for minimizing and controlling women's athletics, because it allows our culture to restrict women's involvement to certain kinds of sports.

At the heart of the notion of gender-appropriateness of a sport is, according to Metheny (1965) what female athletes do with their bodies. If they use their bodies in aesthetically pleasing ways (gymnastics), or use light instruments to overcome light objects (tennis, golf), the female body is essentially performing in a "nonphysical" (in the sense of "nonpowerful") way. If, on the other hand, the female athlete uses her body as an instrument of physical power—by subduing an opponent through the use of physical force (football, rugby)—she is behaving in "a typically male" and thus gender-"inappropriate" fashion (Kane & Snyder, 1989, p. 81). As Boutlier and San Giovanni (1983) noted:

> Girls and women continue to receive social acceptance for individual sports more readily than for team contests. Social approval for sports such as tennis, golf, and gymnastics is high. As non-contact individual sports, they offer the dual "benefits" of continued segregation of female athletes from team mates and continued confirmation of participants' femininity. (p. 43)

Kane (1987), tested this hypothesis and showed experimentally that gender-role conformity had an important influence on attractiveness ratings of women athletes. In this study, the researcher found that attractiveness ratings of pictures of female athletes matched with a sex-appropriate sport such as volleyball dropped significantly when compared with ratings of pictures of the same athletes associated with a sex-inappropriate sport, such as body building or wrestling. Oglesby and Shelton (1992) provided the description of gender-typed characteristics of male and female sports activities depicted in Table 8.1.

Del Rey (1978) noted that female athletes must emphasize that they are feminine to reduce the cognitive dissonance they experience as a social anomaly. Unlike men, women in sports have to choose between being a successful girl or woman and being a successful athlete. Women's athleticisms has been viewed as conflicting with the conventional ethos of femininity (Lefkowitz-Horowitz, 1986). In fact, if we were to believe the media, being feminine as well as athletic is often an oxymoron. In contrast, sports participation for young men confirms masculinity.

Several explanations have been proposed to account for the small number of women leaders in sports. Lerner (1986), for example, suggested that gender acts as a metaphor for power relations, since sport has historically served as a vehicle for reproducing male power. The author described sports as a setting in which power relations, along with the various intersections of race, class, and sexuality, are played out. The gender metaphor in sports is based to a large extent on the assumption that men are physically stronger than women. As a result of this biology-is-destiny assumption, women are in the minority in the power structures of organized sports, even though their participation rates have increased considerably.

Table 8.1   Characteristics of Male and Female Sport Activities

MEN'S SPORTS	WOMEN'S SPORTS
Business-oriented	Education-oriented
Star/spectator focus	Participant/mass focus
Specialized/particularistic	In balance with other life interests
Institutional support	Limited to self-support
Risky	Safe
Active	Passive
Aggressive	Cooperative
Dominant	Subordinate

Source: Carole C. Oglesby and Christine M. Shelton, "Exercise and Sport Studies" in C. Kamarae, C., & D. Spender (Eds.), *The Knowledge Explosion: Generations of Feminist Scholarship*, (New York: Teachers College Press (p. 184). Reprinted with permission.

Birrell (1988) also used power as an explanatory concept and speculated that athletes, especially in organized team sports, are motivated by the need for power. The author argues that it is this group of sports in particular, dominated by male participants, that allows athletes to exercise their power directly, satisfy their need for power, and see the immediate and direct results of their power. Women, on the other hand, who are largely excluded from participation in team sports, are denied the opportunity to wield their power directly. When they are more powerful than their opponents, women's competitive efforts are billed as a "battle of the sexes." This was the case in the 1973 match between Billie Jean King (then 29 years old and happily married to Larry King) and Bobby Riggs. King defeated her 55-year-old opponent and "quickly disposed of the former champion to the glee of the feminists and the chagrin of the chauvinists" (Lumpkin, 1982, p. 525). Duncan and Hasbrook (1988) argued that sport is not merely a reservoir of social attitudes, norms, and values, but also has the potential for modifying larger social practices. According to these authors, a more equitable balance of power in sport can lead to a fairer balance of power in other social spheres.

MacKinnon (1987) has argued that the "problem" of sport is not simply one of gender differentiation, but of gender hierarchy. In other words, the critical concern is not that females and males are defined differently in relationship to sports, but that males are perceived as better than females within an athletic context. Ultimately, this physical, biological, "natural" supremacy of males in sport becomes translated into natural supremacy of males in the larger social order (Clark & Clark, 1985; Kane & Snyder, 1989; Theberge, 1988). Since women and men are seen as dialectical opposites in sports, media coverage of athletes focuses on contrasting images of female and male athletes (Hillard, 1984).

In the cultural institution of sport, the mass media play a major role in the portrayal of women athletes as inferior by maximizing rather than minimizing male/female differences. Although the coverage of women's sports has increased over the past 15 years, it is not proportionate to women's participation. Women sports coverage that does exist, according to Boutilier and San Giovanni (1983), can be classified in three ways: 1) less coverage than men's sports; 2) greater coverage of "feminine," gender-appropriate sports, such as golf and tennis; and 3) coverage of athletes according to sex-role stereotypes rather than according to sports roles. Women usually receive greater social acceptance and media coverage in "feminine" sports, such as gymnastics and figure skating, which are characterized by graceful and fluid movements, rather than by competitive spirit and physical prowess. Similarly, the media devote a disproportionate amount of coverage to men's sports, especially men's team sports such as basketball and football, and to "male-appropriate" individual sports such as body-building, wrestling, and surfing. This leaves women's sports with a negligible amount of air time (Duncan & Hasbrook, 1988).

On the other hand, the media seldom show women in team sports, even sports such as field hockey, volleyball, and softball in which women are highly involved (Lumpkin & Williams, 1991). When women's team sports events such as basketball are televised, Duncan and Hasbrook (1988) found that broadcasts of women's games were ambivalent because they lacked analysis of both the game and the play of the team. Based on their review of the televised 1986 NCAA women's and men's basketball championships, the authors argued that TV coverage of women's team sports is a symbolic denial of the sport as well as the team. Denial of the team occurs when coverage lacks technical analysis and technical commentary in the women's championships. Instead, broadcasters focused on women's movements, describing them primarily in aesthetic terms. Focus on individual players, rather than the team, in the women's game distorted the basic nature of basketball as a team sport. In the women's championship between the University of California "Lady Trojans" and the University of Texas "Lady Longhorns," rather than introducing USC to the audience as a team seeking its third national title, TV commentators pointed out that Cheryl Miller was "seeking her third NCAA title in four years" (CBS Television Network, 1986a). In contrast, during the men's game between the Duke Blue Devils and the Louisville Cardinals, no comments were made about individual players (CBS Television Network, 1986b).

Not only are female athletes often excluded from media presentations and coverage of organized sports events, they are also often depicted in tangential and subservient roles. Across a variety of sports, the media frequently portray women as sex objects. *Sports Illustrated*, for example, the leading sports magazine which comprehensively covers all sports, fully exploits the "T and A" motif of soft pornography to produce its annual swimsuit issue, where women models, not women athletes, make the sports scene (Sabo & Messner, 1993). Similarly, TV coverage of the 1988 Olympics sexualized Katerina Witt's ice skating performances by closing in on parts of the female anatomy, body proportions, and making reference to Witt's physical attractiveness. In their analysis of men and women's surfing competitions, Duncan and Hasbrook (1988) showed how the camera fragmented women reducing them to faces, bikinied torsos, breasts, and buttocks. Instead of riding waves, the camera captured women in passive poses—lying on the beach, carrying their surfboards through the sand, or meditating. In football, the spotlights, cameras, and the eyes of the fans focus on the display of brute force by male players. The only females seen anywhere near the football field are scantily clad, leaner-than-lean cheerleaders (Jansen & Sabo, 1994).

The message to the viewing audience in all these instances is clear: women are, as a class, decorative objects, not serious competitors. Sabo and Messner (1993) concluded that the liberating potential of sport to empower women's bodies and minds is in danger of being coopted by the media, distorted by homophobia, and ignored by the sexist legacy of the men's locker room. Messner (1988) echoed a similar sentiment when he stated:

> Organized sport, as a cultural sphere defined largely by patriarchal priorities, will continue to be an important arena in which energizing images of active, fit, and muscular women are forged, interpreted, contested, and incorporated. The larger socioeconomic and political context will continue to shape and constrain the extent to which women can wage fundamental challenges to the ways that organized sports continue to provide ideological legitimation for male dominance. And the media's framing of male and female athletes will continue to present major obstacles for any fundamental challenge to the present commercialized and male dominant structure of organized athletics. (p. 208)

Scrutiny of media presentations of female athletes is important, because it has been shown that the social sanctions embedded in media coverage shape women's participation in sports (Metheny, 1965). For the Greeks, the epic poem was a popular medium of communication for myth-making. In our contemporary culture, the mass media play a major role in framing lessons about values, as seen in the coverage of organized sports (Creedon, 1994).

The social institution of sport, then, as Whitson (1990) suggested, is very much a gendered cultural space. By that the author means that "gender is a dynamic, relational process, and can be interpreted as a fundamental theoretical category in understanding the historical and contemporary meaning of sport'' (p. 17). Each sport, from rugby to surfing, wrestling to gymnastics, has its own gender-dominated subculture. Trailblazing female athletes such as Billie Jean King and Martina Navratilova in tennis, Nancy Liebermann in basketball, and Jackie Joyner-Kersee in the heptathalon, have shown that women do perform as well, and occasionally better, than men in many sporting events. They also demonstrate that highly trained female athletes are very similar to highly trained male athletes in their physiological capacity for sport and exercise (Jarratt, 1990). Instead of attributing the differential performances in sports that do exist between men and women to inherent sex differences, female athletes should be judged not on the basis of their physiological characteristics, but by their athletic talents and performance, personal integrity, and character.

WOMEN LEADERS IN AMERICAN POLITICS

Political Leadership in Context

Leaders and leadership have held a place of importance in politics throughout history. People are fascinated with and by their politicians, regardless of whether they are good or bad leaders. Biographies of current political figures, such as Hillary Rodham Clinton, become instant bestsellers. Political leadership is intriguing because it is highly visible and, ostensibly, at least, highly important. This is so because if we reduce politics to its bare bones, it is the national political leaders, both at home and abroad, who are the most talked-about elements of political life (Blondel, 1987). We find political leaders not only at the national level, but at all levels of government (i.e., local, state, and regional). They achieve office by election, appointment, revolution, or assassination. Political leadership also occurs in a broader context; examples include serving as principal of a school or superintendent of a school system; minister of a church; university president; or the president of a local Chamber of Commerce.

What is political leadership? Katz (1973) defined a political leader as an individual who has the authority to commit the resources and select the goals of a political unit and, in turn, to affect its policies. Political leadership is different from other leadership contexts, although no clear and widely agreed-upon definition of political leadership exists. Kellerman (1986) provided a fairly comprehensive definition of political leadership which states:

> Political leadership means control over policies that affect public welfare. Political leaders may derive their power from the position they hold in

a legally sanctioned state office. That office bestows upon them the authority to choose among alternative courses of action. However, not all political leaders hold political office. Leaders of sociopolitical movements—Martin Luther King, Jr., for example, are empowered by their ability to transform a strong political sentiment into a personal crusade. (p. xiii)

Leadership has been, more often than not, defined as political leadership. Many historians (e.g., Tucker, 1981) hold that politics is the essence of leadership, or at least attempted leadership. The public expects political leaders to lead and serve their constituencies. The political process involves taking into account the needs and demands of diverse constituencies, weighing the realities of power, calculating consequences, and negotiating and bargaining (Gardner, 1990). In this process, regular elections are the primary institutional mechanisms that tie political leaders to their followers. As Jones (1989) noted:

It is assumed that politicians want to win elections and that they maximize the number of votes in order to do so. Hence, the wishes of followers have substantive policy content (that is, followers want certain policies from the democratic process) but the wishes of the leader do not. Leaders are vote maximizers; that is, their welfare that is derived through the political process is entirely determined by how many votes they can get in the upcoming election. (p. 42)

In addition, the issues and the nature of the office occupied by a political leader, that is, legislative or executive, influence leadership in this context and determine the behavior the public expects from the leader. Mayors, governors, presidents, and other executives, for example, can get away with actions that run counter to public preference more readily than can legislators (Sigelman, Sigelman, & Walkosz, 1992). Thus, political leaders need to understand the rules that structure political action, as well as understand and respond to the needs of their followers.

Political leaders are alluring in part because of the intricate interplay between politics and power. In politics and in political science, power and leadership are closely linked. Janda (1960), for example, argued that political leadership is a particular type of power relationship. Similarly, Burns (1978) wrote, "To understand the nature of leadership requires understanding the essence of power, for leadership is a special form of power" (p. 6). Millett (1970) whose book *Sexual Politics* became a classic of the women's movement, defined politics broadly as "power-structured relationships, arrangements whereby one group or person is controlled by another" and argued that "sex is a status category with political implications" (p. 23). Likewise, Blondel (1987) defined political leadership as power exercised by one or a few to direct members of the nation toward action.

The author contended that political leadership is manifestly and essentially a phenomenon of power. Thus, many definitions of political leadership include or imply the concept of power. Yet, as Gardner (1990) pointed out, we must distinguish between political leaders and power-holders. The author holds that

> Leaders always have a measure of power, but many power-holders have no trace of leadership. Some power-holders, for example, who are very generous contributors to political campaigns, may be able to lead politicians around by the nose, yet themselves have no capacity for genuine leadership. (Gardner, 1990, p. 56)

Power, like sports and politics, is a gendered concept. Research revealed a consistent difference favoring men in accessibility to, and utility of, resources for power (Ragins & Sundstrom, 1989). In their review on gender and power differences in organizations, the authors concluded that

> Gender differences in power reflect differential access to a variety of resources for power. For example, through differential selection, women may be placed in jobs with relatively little power in comparison with those occupied by men, and these positions are maintained over time through tracking. Even when women obtain organizational assets, their value as resources for power appears to be less than that for men holding the same assets. (p. 81)

Power, as noted in Chapter 6, has been split into two types: *power-over*, referring to domination and control of one person or group over another, which is the way many men use power; and *power-to* or *empowerment*, which is primarily the way women exercise power. Jeane Kirkpatrick (1974), former U.S. ambassador to the U.N., contended that implicit in any discussion about women's share of power and their political behavior is the assumption that gender differences in power are relevant to politics.

Female politicians, like women in corporations, face a similar glass ceiling. However, while women are not a power group in American politics, some female politicians are individually quite powerful and influential. Patricia Schroeder, D-Colorado, for example, is one of the U.S's most prominent female politicians and one of the longest-serving women in Congress. Since her election to public office in 1972, Schroeder has established herself as a high-profile champion of liberal and women's causes, as well as a successful fundraiser. The public knows her as a peace activist who pushed her way onto the all-male Armed Services Committee and has come as close as any woman to top committee ranks. When Schroeder made a short-lived presidential run in 1988, which concluded with a tearful withdrawal speech, she was ridiculed for weeping in public. Now Schroeder keeps a "tear file" of male leaders who have also done so.

Madeleine Kunin, the former Democratic Governor of Vermont, whose biography (1994) reads like a real-life version of the American dream, has written a book about the special problems politics pose for women. "We had been the backstairs maids to history," she says in *Living a Political Life,* "catching power on the fly . . . We knew the structure called politics was not our creation. It was built by them for them" (p. 19). Kunin refers here to the fact that men wrote both the Declaration of Independence and the Constitution. Among the problems that plague women are stereotypic ascriptions of personality traits to female (and male) candidates, stereotypes about political ideologies (i.e., all Democrats are liberals), and the persistence of the double standard. Women in politics face two additional problems. Traditionally, women have lacked two basic attributes necessary to running for office which are believed to be linked to gender differences: financial independence to raise funds successfully, and the stature to exercise leadership.

Like women leaders in other contexts, such as sports, female politicians have to walk a tightrope between appearing too feminine or not feminine enough, thus existing in a no-win situation. If they take pains to look attractive, they are called vain. Rhode (1995) quoted one example, in the *New York Times* coverage of a mass rally for equal rights. The headline, "Leading Feminist Puts Hairdo Before Strike," (*New York Times,* 1970, p. 30), referred to Betty Friedan's delayed appearance because of a previous appointment at the beauty shop. On the other hand, as Rhode (1995) pointed out, women who defy cultural standards of femininity are subject to ridicule. "These women are portrayed as the last refuge of homely harpies whose views about men stem from their presumed inability to attract them" (p. 696). Rhode concluded that female candidates in media coverage often need not so much a different image, but a different debate, one which focuses less on personal style and more on political substance.

Women candidates who manage to overcome these problems receive little credit for their achievements in one area, and are criticized in the other. Kathleen Brown, for example, the daughter of one former California governor, Edmund G. "Pat" Brown and sister of another, presidential hopeful Jerry Brown, was considered a front-runner for the 1994 gubertorial nomination. As state treasurer of California, her campaign chest exceeds $5 million, and she had been commended for successfully managing the state's $24 million investment portfolio. In one night, Brown raised $850,000. Thus, Brown had cleared the biggest hurdle of running for office in California and most other states: money. She also did a praiseworthy job cleaning up a backlog of bonds and carried out the largest borrowing program in the country at rates favorable to the state. But she had been criticized for her lack of leadership in failing to take a forceful stand on issues such as immigration, crime, and the state's economic recovery. Her positions, pro-choice and anti-death penalty, seldom became platforms. The harshest criticism of her has, in fact, resulted less from what she has said about her views on political issues, but from what she has *not* said. Governor Wilson's press secretary said: "A leader takes a stand, Kathleen Brown strikes a pose" (Hewitt, 1994, p. 15). Yet, if the amount of money managed by Brown is a criterion, she is one of the most powerful women in the country.

Kathleen Brown also illustrates the public's interest in the personal character-istics and backgrounds of political leaders. Like many other male and female political leaders, she comes from a privileged background. Her pedigree—"Politics is a genetic defect with me," she says—makes her a card-carrying member of a family dynasty with a long-time involvement in local, state, and national politics (Hewitt, 1994). The Browns have been called the Los Angeles version of the Kennedys, with similar political ambitions, but without the obvious dysfunctions and tragedies. Kathleen spent her childhood apprenticing in the art of politics, while her father was serving his two terms as governor. In 1974, she campaigned for her brother Jerry; in 1975, she was elected to the Los Angeles Board of Education. Brown spent a good part of the 1980s in New York, where she earned a law degree from Fordham University and practiced as a corporate attorney, until her return to Los Angeles in 1987.

Brown's case also shows that, especially in law, women and men with certain educational backgrounds, social class, and occupations have a greater-than-aver-age chance of becoming political leaders. Like Brown, Pat Schroeder, Dianne Feinstein, and Barbara Boxer are professional women, trained as lawyers, who have risen to political leadership. According to Blondel (1987) these women and other female politicians demonstrate that access to leadership in politics is limited. Blondel argues that, despite repeated claims to the contrary, it is simply not the case that everyone has the same chance of becoming the president of the United States. In interview after interview, Witt, Paget, and Matthews (1994) found that regardless of a woman candidate's education, demonstrated leadership ability, or charisma, the simple fact that she is biologically different is potentially damag-ing to her political destiny. After all, as Driscoll and Goldberg (1993) stated, the first barrier women experience is a visual one. Women *look* different, making them immediately visible as "something other," not unlike blacks or Asians.

Women candidates who have recently run for highly visible state or national office have waged increasingly combative campaigns. They stressed their tough-ness and aggressiveness, trying to convince voters that women are more than simply caring, nurturant, and compassionate. Ann Richards, for example, por-trayed herself as a tough political opponent in the 1990 Texas gubertorial race by mud-slinging her opponent, Clayton Williams. However, by aggressively attacking her opponent, Richards risked destroying the advantage by "lowering" herself to his level (Morris, 1992). The election of Ann Richards as the first woman governor of Texas was a personality contest, a gender contest, and a contest of perceptions in which Richards was perceived to be more savvy and experienced (*Current Biography Yearbook*, 1991).

Similarly, Dianne Feinstein also took on a "masculine" concern when she supported the death penalty and made it a central issue in her 1990 bid for governor of California. At the same time, Feinstein tried to convince voters that she was a caring person. Her efforts paid off: Feinstein got her highest marks in the race against Republican Pete Wilson from those who put caring first. The last *Los Angeles Times* polls before the election showed that voters ranked Feinstein 29% better than Wilson on the environment, 32% better on health care, and 12% better on education. Wilson, on the other hand, got high marks for doing what voters expect of Republican men. He led Feinstein in the polls by 24% on the economy, 18% on crime, and 18% on taxes. As in the context of sports, women leaders in politics must walk a fine line between reassuring voters of their toughness and not coming across as too aggressive. Cantor and Bearnay (1992) pointed out, this is especially true for Democratic women candidates, because the three stereotypes of being liberal, supporting family and children's issues, and being female reinforce one another. We see this clearly the love–hate relationship the public has with Hillary Rodham Clinton, who, as a Democratic woman with substantial power, perplexes the public and the media.

Prevailing stereotypes of personality traits of male and female candidates and lingering double standards interact with other stereotypes about candidates' political ideologies. Stereotypes suggest that Democrats are more liberal and more competent in handling what Shapiro and Majahan (1986) have labeled the "compassion" issues—poverty, education, abortion, and health care. Democrats have had an advantage on these issues, since they set up many of the current government assistance programs such as Social Security, unemployment benefits, and Medicare. Republicans, on the other hand, are perceived to deal better with big business, the military, and defense issues (Leeper, 1991; Sapiro, 1983). Women politicians are keenly aware of issue stereotyping in issues involving the Equal Rights Amendment, reproductive freedom, and organizational flexibility, including parental leave and child care in the workplace. They also know that issue stereotyping hurts because female elected officials will not achieve full participation in politics as long as it exists. As Klein (1984) noted, contemporary expectations of greater female honesty and compassion had earlier parallels in the "clearinghouse" arguments used to gain women the vote in the 1900s and 1910s. According to this argument, women deserved the right to vote because of the belief that their stronger social conscience and greater moral fortitude would motivate them to "clean up" politics, ushering in a new American era.

In addition to stereotypes about personality characteristics and political beliefs, the double standard is also alive and well across issues and party lines. A female candidate's clothes and hairstyle, her age, or her husband can matter as much as her stand on issues. When Barbara Boxer, for example, during the 1992 Senate race was described as a "youthful and vibrant 51-year-old" (Matthews, 1992), women wondered how old a male candidate running for office would have to be in order to be portrayed in the same manner. Voters intensely scrutinized the husbands of 1984 vice presidential nominee Geraldine Ferraro (John Zaccarro), and of 1990 California gubertorial candidate Dianne Feinstein (Richard Blum), while spouses of male candidates went largely unnoticed. Thus, women candidates find themselves in multiple double-binds. From being judged more harshly to being taken less seriously, women in politics often receive different treatment than their male counterparts, and have to play by different rules. District of Columbia delegate Eleanor Holmes Norton says "Congresswomen have to play two political games: their own looking out for women and women's issues and the House game which keeps them respected members who are seen as political realists, people who understand how this place operates" (Phillips & Edmonds, 1992, 2A).

Currently, the economy and crime issues dominate the political scene, and voters have less confidence in women than men in both matters. National defense is an issue where women clearly have a disadvantage and have difficulty maintaining their credibility against men. Doubts about women's ability to be "tough enough" during national security crises were made clear during the Persian Gulf War, when male candidates capitalized on their advantage on this issue. Operation Desert Storm showed that a military crisis is one of the worst things that could happen to a woman candidate running for office. In 1990, Claudine Schneider, D-Rhode Island, lost her senate race with incumbent Claiborne Peel. Peel, a self-proclaimed foreign policy expert, used pictures of his visits to the troops in Saudi Arabia in campaign advertisements reminding voters of men's accomplishments in times of war and security crises. Similarly, in 1990, Paul Simon, D-Illinois, responded to the Middle East crisis by calling for a preemptive strike against Iraq. This was a move his opponent for the Senate, Lynn Martin, R-Illinois and former Secretary of Labor in the Bush administration, was unable to match.

The 1990 Senate race between Lynn Martin and Paul Simon provides a good example of the interrelationships between gender stereotypes and stereotypes about political belief systems. Throughout the race, voters consistently rated liberal Democrat Paul Simon as less competent to handle family issues than his conservative Republican opponent Lynn Martin, who received her low ratings on defense issues. Differing expectations about the types of issues handled by male and female, Republican and Democrat candidates, have proved the most consistent form of political gender stereotyping. These gender-based ascriptions of different traits, behaviors, or political beliefs to male and female politicians have had more negative consequences for women than for men (Dodson & Carroll, 1991; Welch & Thomas, 1991). On the other hand, in some issues, women have a credibility edge. Voters, for instance, believe that women are more likely to enforce drunken driving laws and start drug prevention programs. The current health care reform may be a turn-around issue for women, since, according to pollsters, women have a significant edge over men here. Although much has been made of the advantage of Democrats over Republicans on health care issues, equally important is the likelihood that a Republican woman can neutralize any advantage for a Democratic man on this issue.

Although women remain marginal in high elected offices and are few in elite positions in politics, they became much more visible in recent years. Women have moved into the national political arena in both party and pressure group politics (Tilly & Gurin, 1990). As a result, women's participation in electoral policies has increased significantly, although some people continue to believe that politics is not a birthright for girls as it is for boys. With this increase in participation came changes in voters attitudes toward female candidates. Overall, the number of voters who believe that men are better suited emotionally for politics than women has declined from 44% to 20% in 1993 (Lake & DiVall, 1993, 15A). Overall, voters indicated that women are more in touch with people, care more about people, are better listeners, and work better at negotiations, all important legislative characteristics. However, voters also thought that women are not as good as men in handling crises, supervising big budgets, and being tough—all important executive characteristics. As Lake and DiVall noted, voters fundamentally doubt that women are tough enough, and when they are, voters are uncomfortable with this image.

The year 1992 became known as the "Year of the Woman." That year, when a record number of Republican and Democratic women candidates sought public office, has often been heralded as a banner year for women in politics. Grunewald (1992) tried to show what the U.S. Senate would look like if its male-female proportions were reversed. The author pictured 98 women and 2 men on the Capitol steps, and began her article with:

> *Old Joke*: If women ran America, there would never be war, just some intense negotiations every 28 days.
> *New Wisdom*: Though men do run America, they have to stop telling this joke, because there has been a year for women candidates. (p. 39)

In 1992, many women entered the political arena for the first time—Lynn Yeakel of Pennsylvania, for example, went from almost zero name recognition in March of 1992 to more than 2.2 million votes in November. A total of 106 women from 35 states received major party nominations for the House, and 11 women from 10 states ran for Senate. Among the more widely publicized races were those of Carol Moseley-Braun, D-Illinois, the first black woman senator, and Patty Murray of Washington who tells of a male legislator sneering she could not be effective because she was "just a mom in tennis shoes" (Hasson, 1992, p. 2A). These women joined political veterans Dianne Feinstein and Barbara Boxer, who were simultaneously elected senators in California. In addition, the Clinton administration filled several positions with women, including Energy

Secretary Hazel O'Leary; Health and Human Services Secretary Donna Shalala; Surgeon General Joycelyn Elders; and Supreme Court Justice Ruth Bader Ginsburg.

Yet, despite these gains, several writers questioned how much change actually occurred in the political representation of women. Faludi (1992), for example, stated that the "Year of the Woman" in politics did not feel very much different, since neither women nor women's issues dominated the political discourse. Moreover, she argued that the media habitually exaggerate the significance of small gains for women. Yet, during the much-fabled "Year of the Woman" in politics, not one representative of a major woman's policy organization appeared on any leading TV talk show (Wolf, 1993). Daughton (1994) called our attention to the irony contained in the label "Year of the Woman." The author argues that the label was indicative of the lack of potential for dramatic change. More specifically, designating *one* year as "the year of the woman, explicitly limits and confines women's achievements and expectations to a 12-month span; in reality, social change takes for longer" (Daughton, 1994, p. 106).

In 1993 the races were more difficult for women. Women ran primarily for executive posts, such as governorships and mayoralties, instead of legislative races in the House and the Senate. Results of those races showed that voters are more cautious in electing women to executive posts than to legislative posts. Women won some of these races. Republican Governor of New Jersey, Christine Whitman, for example, a former Somerset County freeholder, rocketed out of obscurity with her near-win over U.S. Senator Bill Bradley in 1990. Immediately afterwards, she started her run for governor and in 1993 she succeeded. But Mary Sue Terry, D-Virginia and Attorney General with an established track record of being tough on crime, was defeated in Virginia's gubertorial race because she was perceived as a "pseudo-candidate." Overall, women won some races in 1993, but in far fewer numbers and by lower margins. The predictions are that the coming election years at the state and national level will continue to be tough for women candidates.

In 1994, dubbed by the media as the "Year of the Angry White Male," midterm elections revealed the widest gender gap, with women overall voting for Democratic candidates 52 to 47% while men supported Republicans 57 to 41%. Many white women switched their allegiance in 1994, favoring Republicans by 52 to 46% (compared with 1992's pro-Democratic margin of 51 to 49% (Woods, 1995).

While optimists proclaimed 1992 as a watershed year that changed the face of American politics, pessimists remind us although the number of women in the Senate tripled, women in the Senate only account for 6% but represent 52% of the population. The following year, a total of 53 women were members of Congress; they held 6 out of a 100 Senate seats and 47 of the 435 House seats. Even though some called 1992 the "Year of the Woman," candidates, pollsters, and voters alike realize that it will take an entire decade and more to change the complexion of American politics. If history is any indicator, another 75 years may pass before 60 women serve in Congress. Likewise, given the current rate of change, women may not attain numerical equality in government for another 317 years, taking us well into the 24th century.

The record number of women running for political office in 1992 was, in part, a reaction to the Anita Hill/Clarence Thomas hearings in the fall of 1991. The hearings energized women, both individually and collectively, into political action. As discussed in Chapter 5, the televised roll call to confirm Thomas' appointment to the Supreme Court which showed 98 male senators and two female senators present had a shocking and electrifying impact on women. It vividly showed the need for more representation of women in the top of the law-making body of the government. The political turmoil stirred by Thomas's confirmation hearings provided the necessary jolt for more women, Democrats and Republicans, to run for political office.

Clearly, Anita Hill sparked an unprecedented mobilization of women voters since women won the right to vote in 1920 (Witt et al., 1994). The Senate Judiciary Committee, that all-male body that provoked rage and galvanized women into action after the Clarence Thomas confirmation hearings, now has two female members: Senators Dianne Feinstein and Carol Moseley-Braun have joined the panel.

Several other factors converged to create the so-called "Year of the Woman." One was the growth of organizations formed during the 1970s and 1980s to support women candidates. By the 1990s, those groups had come of age. In 1985 Ellen Malcolm started EMILY's (Early Money Is Like Yeast) List, to give pro-choice Democratic women the financial backing to run. EMILY'S, List, for example, gave over $400,000 to Ann Richards. The creation of the GOP WISH (Women in the House and Senate) List followed; this raised $150,000 during its first two months. Other influential organizations include the Women's Campaign Fund and the National Women's Political Caucus. These funding organizations formed to help women raise the necessary money to run successful campaigns, since the belief persists that women candidates have greater difficulties raising campaign funds. They often appeal to women's philanthropy and stress the importance of their financial contributions to the political success of women candidates. These funding organizations became an established part of Washington's pressure group community. In 1992, EMILY's List claimed to be the largest political action committee, raising $6 million for women candidates.

The shift from the Cold War to economic and social issues has also been an important factor, since it shifted voting patterns of men and women. Klein (1984) argued that a key issue for women voters today is their sense of economic vulnerability. Economic concerns supersede earlier issues such as child care, family leave, and sex discrimination, the platforms on which women ran when they first entered politics in visible numbers. The shift to a preoccupation with economics has profoundly affected the nature of political leadership. In the past, political leadership was exercised primarily in foreign affairs and defense, areas in which women traditionally lacked experience. In these political arenas, there are clear-cut criteria by which leaders' successes and failures are evaluated. Victory, heroism, and defeat in wars are easily assessed. However, the situation is much less definitive on the economic front, where successes are often difficult to perceive because short-term benefits are frequently obtained only at the expense of some members of the community. The redistribution of wealth is an example. Therefore, while international relations continue to be a major issue for political leaders, they have ceased to be the main focus of attention (Blondel, 1987), nor are they a primary marker of a leader's success or failure.

CONCLUSIONS

Women leaders in sports and politics continue to challenge these "masculine" worlds. The result is that not only are women slowly changing these contexts, but that the contexts are changing women. If women are going to increase their visibility as sports and political leaders, they have to pursue leadership opportunities in the same way men do. In the meantime, however, much of society still encourages men to dream big and women to dream of big men (Grunewald, 1992).

More than 20 years after the passage of Title IX, women's participation in sports remains strongly tied to gender stereotypes. Even though women have some power in sports as athletic directors and administrators, they are so few in numbers that their overall impact is extremely limited. In politics, even if more women win, victory will not always be sweet. Presently no woman holds a full committee chairpersonship in Congress, a position which is a source of real power. Although many blame this situation on women's lack of seniority in high-level political office, the male, dominant culture of Capitol Hill is also a culprit. Elections in recent years have shown that change is a high priority among voters. Change is the chief ally of female candidates running for political office, since women are more likely than men to challenge the status quo, and especially since the public has become more and more concerned with the improvement of economic and social conditions. Ann Richards, Barbara Boxer, Barbara Mikulski, Madeleine Kunin, Pat Schroeder, and Dianne Feinstein are among the handful of women who are leading a growing parade of female politicians toward the presidency of the United States—the last threshold women must cross (Witt et al., 1994). Daughton is hopeful when she says, "As more and more women enter politics, their public presence may gradually come to seem more familiar and less threatening. Then perhaps the ultimate gender-related problem of presidential campaigns, that the successful ones are limited to males only, will be solved at last" (p. 116).

9   Women Leaders Worldwide: The Global Connection

> The best reason for believing that more
> women will be in charge before long is that
> in a ferociously competitive global economy,
> no company can afford to waste valuable
> brain power simply because it's wearing a
> skirt.
>
> *Anne Fisher, 1992*

INTRODUCTION

In recent years we have seen a proliferation of predictions of new international
realities, globally interdependent systems, and an increasing awareness of the
global dimensions and interconnectedness of today's world as the community of
nations is becoming smaller and smaller. Naisbitt and Aburdene (1990) pointed
out that the more the economies of the world integrate, the less important are
the economies of individual countries, and the more important are the economic
contributions of individuals and individual companies. Global competitive battles
account for many of the changes with which today's leaders have to cope. Conger
(1993b) quoted the U. S. Commerce Department, which estimated that in 1987,
80% of U.S. firms faced significant foreign competition in their domestic markets.
Today, for all intents and purposes, all business transactions are international.
Global competition, according to Waitley (1995) is powered by information
technology, and so is information access. Leaders need to understand how these
forces interact in the global environment. In addition, global competition also
requires that leaders are able to bridge cultural distances to improve their relationships with followers, since cultural differences influence the full range of interactions between leaders and followers (Redding, 1990). Numerous studies (e.g.,
Black & Mendenhall, 1991; Mendenhall & Oddou, 1986; Tung, 1984) have
shown that when a leader adapts her behavior so that it more closely approximates
that of another culture, her relationship with the people of that culture improves.

The trend toward increasing globalization has several consequences for leaders and leadership. First, there is continually mounting competition among organizations active in the global marketplace. Second, multinational corporations (MNCs) have multiplied in response to the trend toward globalization. As we are moving closer to the global economy, the distinctions between domestic and international business have become blurred. American firms send leading executives and support personnel abroad, and foreign companies establish subsidiaries in the United States. Moreover, a growing number of American firms have merged with foreign companies. Another mark of globalization is the move of labor-intensive organizations toward low-wage world regions (Calas & Smircich, 1993). A law firm in England, for example, may have all word processing jobs performed by women in Taiwan and then have the files returned to England via electronic mail. In today's MNCs, leaders have to interact with increasingly diverse constituencies that are often geographically dispersed.

International organizations such as the United Nations, the European Union (EU), the Organization for Economic Corporation and Development, and the International Labor Organization have played a significant role in putting women's issues on the public agenda of member countries (Adler & Izraeli, 1994). However, women are only slowly beginning to participate in the global village. They contribute only a negligible portion of the expatriate managerial population (Adler & Izraeli, 1994) since few U. S. companies utilize women effectively in international assignments. In a survey of 70 corporations, Moran, Stahl & Boyer Inc. (1988) found that only 5% of the 4,774 U.S. expatriates assigned overseas by these firms were women. Similarly, Lee (1995) found that, based on data collected by an international relocation management company, women on overseas assignments made up about 12% of the expatriate population.

Dimensions of Cross-Cultural Differences

The contextual features emphasized in this chapter are cultural characteristics and markers that produce differences in leadership and leadership perceptions among leaders and followers from various cultures. The word "culture" has many meanings. Schein (1991) formally defined culture as

> a pattern of shared basic assumptions that the group learned as it solved its problems of external adaptation and internal integration, that has worked well enough to be considered valid and, therefore, to be taught to new members as the correct way to perceive, think, and feel in relation to these problems. (p. 12)

It is the sum of the social characteristics of a group which developed from the group's history, myths, leadership practices, formal and informal rules, communications system, reward practices and many other determinants—humor, dress code, the organizational grapevine—of culture. According to Schein (1991), culture springs from three sources: 1) the beliefs, values, and assumptions of the founders of organizations; 2) the learning experiences of group members as their organization evolves; and 3) new values, beliefs, and assumptions brought in by new group members and their leaders.

Hofstede's work (1980a) on the relationship between values and organizational practices has had a significant impact in the field of cross-cultural studies. Hofstede set up four criteria by which cultures differ. The first dimension is called *power distance*, which refers to the extent to which a culture accepts that power is unevenly distributed in a given society. More specifically, power distance can be seen as a society's endorsement of inequality, and its inverse as the expectation of relative equality in organizations and institutions (Franke, Hofstede, & Bond, 1991).

The second dimension, *uncertainty avoidance*, indicates the extent to which a society feels threatened by uncertain and ambiguous situations; it taps feelings of discomfort in unstructured and unusual circumstance. People try to avoid these situations by establishing more formal rules, believing in absolute truths, and rejecting deviant ideas and behaviors. *Individualism/collectivism* is the third cultural dimension. Individualism refers to the tendency of individuals primarily to look after themselves and their immediate families. Collectivism, on the other hand, is characterized by a tight social framework in which people expect their groups (families, clans, organizations) to look after them and, in exchange, feel absolute loyalty to their groups. Japan is an example of a collective culture, while in the U.S. individualism is predominant. Finally, the fourth dimension, *masculinity/femininity* refers to the dominant values regarding gender roles that prevail in different cultures. In certain cultures, masculinity connotes aggressiveness and possession of money and power, while femininity represents values such as caring for others and maintaining the quality of life.

Hofstede's (1980a) study at IBM involving 80,000 employees from 67 countries indicated significant differences by country along these four dimensions, particularly in terms of individualism and power distance. These cultural dimensions, in turn, play themselves out in terms of leadership differences between nations because they create differential expectations which govern the interactions between leaders and followers. The author also reported in another study of 40 nations that countries showed extreme positions on the four cultural dimensions. The United States rated high on the individualism scale, while Asian countries expressed a clear preference for collectivism. Finally, Hofstede (1989) suggested that cultures that rate high in masculinity (e.g., Japan, Austria, Venezuela, Italy) look less favorably on women in leadership roles. On the other hand, cultures rated highest in "feminine" values (e.g., Sweden, Norway, and the Netherlands) were not necessarily the ones with the highest number of female leaders. In sum, Hofstede argued that differences in cultural values, rather than in material structural conditions, are ultimate determinants of human behavior (Franke, Hofstede, & Bond, 1991). Rosen (1984) used the term "leadership systems" to describe leadership roles as well as the specific institutional supports and constraints that influence the exercise of leadership in different cultures. The author noted that most contemporary ethnographic data from primitive as well as complex societies show a clear male bias in their leadership systems.

Cultural competence and cultural adaptation are key leadership skills in the global environment because cultural knowledge and appreciation of diversity are keystones of transcultural interactions. Cross-cultural savvy and adaptation are prerequisites for leading effectively in a global environment. Cultural competence includes language and communications, aesthetics, time orientation, social institutions, religion, personal achievement, personal space, and intercultural socialization (Bonvillian & Nowlin, 1994). Cross-cultural competence is important because it allows leaders and followers to bridge the wide cultural gaps that exist between Eastern and Western societies. Thomas and Ravlin (1995) found that the effectiveness of cultural adaptation as a strategy for reducing cultural distance between a foreign leader and the followers depended on the extent to which the leader's behavior matched the expectations of the followers. In addition, the authors reported that cultural adaptation induced perceptions of similarity and resulted in higher perceived effectiveness.

Language skills are important elements of cultural competence and cultural adaptation because language gives critical access to culture, appreciation of cultural diversity and different organizational structures, the ability to forge strategic alliances and partnerships with foreign nations, and a global vision of shared goals. While approximately 95% of the Japanese who conduct business in the United States speak English, only 1% of Americans with business transactions in Japan speak Japanese. Among Europeans, cultural competence translates into the ability to speak several languages and to integrate people across boarders. As a result, European business leaders are better equipped to deal with cultural diversity than their American counterparts (Calori & Dufour, 1995). American MNCs have largely neglected the role of cultural competence and cultural adjustment in their selection and training of expatriate managers, choosing instead to emphasize technical competence (Black, Mendehall, & Oddou, 1991).

Differences in socialization practices in the various nations around the world give rise to different conceptions of leadership (Bass, 1991). These different conceptualizations manifest themselves in the language used. For example, the English word "leader" does not easily translate into French, Spanish, or German; therefore, *le leader*, *el lider*, and *der Leiter* are often used instead of the available French, Spanish, or German words, *le meneur*, *el jefe*, or *der Führer* which capture different conceptualizations of leadership, since these native terms tend to connote leadership that is primarily directive (Graumann, 1986). Thus, culturally based expectations of leader behaviors are reflected in the language spoken by the leader and her followers.

This chapter examines differences among women leaders from a cross-cultural perspective. As Rosen (1984) noted, any survey of world cultures reveals that in all sociocultural systems there are leaders. More specifically, the author states:

> These [the leaders] are persons or groups of persons who can mobilize human, material, and symbolic resources of society toward specific social needs. At the same time, the mere existence of leaders tends to gloss over differences of such magnitude among these persons that any universal, parsimonious definition of leadership appears unlikely. (Rosen, 1984, p. 39)

Prominent national political leaders included Bandaranaike of Sri Lanka who became the world's first woman prime minister in 1960. Since then, Indira Gandhi, Golda Meir, Isabel Perón, Margaret Thatcher, Benazir Bhutto, Corazon Aquino, and Mary Robinson have risen to chief positions in their respective countries, demonstrating that women in many countries have achieved greater representation in political than economic systems. Berthoin Antal and Izraeli (1993), for example, found that women accounted for 38% of the members of Parliament in Sweden, 34% in Norway, 33% in Sweden, and 21% in the Netherlands. However, transferring role models of female leaders from the political to the economic realm apparently is not easy. As one journalist (Bebbington, 1988) remarked:

> Margaret Thatcher and Gro Harlem Brundtland have run countries of 57 million and four million people respectively. So why does the prospect of a woman at the helm of VW or Philips still seems such a long way off? (p. 2)

In fact, a recent survey conducted by Fisher (1992) for *Fortune,* which polled 201 chief executives of America's largest companies, revealed that only 16% of the respondents believed that it is "very likely" or "somewhat likely" that they will be succeeded by a female CEO.

WOMEN LEADERS IN EUROPE

Europe has witnessed sweeping changes in recent years. The reunification of Germany, the collapse of the former Soviet Union, and the emergence of the developing democracies in Eastern Europe have not only redrawn the European map, but created significant leadership challenges. Experts on European politics now predict that as nation-states gradually disappear under the auspices of the European Union as the major integrating force, nationalism and cultural differences among the member states of the EU will slowly decrease, although they are unlikely to disappear completely.

European scholars and practitioners treat leadership very differently from their American counterparts. Approaches favored by most European scholars show a strong managerial bias which pervades European leadership thought (Hosking & Hunt, 1982). Leadership in Europe is typically either defined as a subset of managerial tasks or equated with management. One of the better known leadership theories in Europe is the Harzburg model, which treats leadership as a co-worker relationship based on the principle of delegation. In the Harzburg model, the leadership relationship between superiors and co-workers is based on carefully prescribed delegation of tasks by managers and on the assumption of responsibility by co-workers within their prescribed area of responsibility (Grunwald & Bernthal, 1983, p. 234). Responsibility for decisions is not assigned to a single or a few top managers, but to workers at all levels, thereby democratizing the decisionmaking process.

The founder of the Harzburg model, Reinhold Höhn, claims that this theory represents a major departure from the traditional German patriarchal form of authority built on principles of order and obedience (Höhn, 1962). According to the author, the Harzburg model reflects a new form of leadership based on leader-follower relationships. Hohn argues that leadership as defined by the Harzburg model is achieved through job descriptions and the general leadership directive (Höhn, 1962, 1979). Job descriptions delineate the duties and responsibilities of the co-workers. The general leadership directive, on the other hand, is an official order issued by management to assure a uniform leadership style, the violation of which can lead to dismissal from the organization (Grunwald & Bernthal, 1983). Höhn (1962) suggested that aspects of the general leadership directive include duties of the supervisor and co-workers, staff-line relationships, teamwork, and the leader's responsibilities in co-worker relationships.

Critics of the Harzburg model have argued that rather than democratizing decisionmaking, this process is consolidated by the general leadership directive, thereby reinforcing existing positional power structures and maintaining the status quo in organizations (Reichard, 1973). Similarly, Wunderer and Grunwald (1980) asserted that when compared to various models of participatory and collaborative leadership, the Harzburg model contains only one necessary condition for such leadership, namely that of providing a measure of decentralization of decisionmaking. More specifically, according to the authors:

Even though characterized as "the model of leadership in a co-worker relationship," the Harzburg model is not democratic or cooperative. Rather it is a form of managerial dogma based on normative and moralistic appeals. Entirely management based, it considers the organization's economic goals as legitimate, giving little consideration to goals and needs of individual co-workers. (Wunderer & Grunwald, 1980, p. 80)

In contrast to American leadership theorists, European scholars have little interest in developing models or theories of leadership. In that sense, the Harzburg model is an exception. Moreover, while American leadership theories include a wide set of variables, including leader traits, behaviors, contingency factors, motivational characteristics of leaders and followers, and contextual factors, European approaches to leadership are primarily concerned with the distribution of control and decisionmaking authority in organizations (Hosking & Hunt, 1982).

Considerable cultural differences exist among European countries. These stem from a variety of sources, including differences in language (9 languages are currently spoken in the EU), industrial development, religion, housing costs, child care provisions, and maternity and paternity leave policies that account for the differential percentages of working women in the various nation-states. As Kanter (1994) noted, globalization does not mean homogenization. Thus, Europe is not a single culture, but a collection of diverse countries in which nationalism and national sovereignty continue to be strong and centuries-old cultures are difficult to change. The cultural differences within Europe, therefore, make it difficult for common leadership philosophies and practices to evolve. With respect to Europe's identity, Jean Monet, the architect of the European Community and predecessor of the EU, said if he had known better, he would have started the unification of Europe with culture as a vehicle instead of starting with economics (Guttman, 1995).

In the welfare states of central Europe, the majority of women work in large-scale service bureaucracies. It is these large service bureaucracies that provide most of the leadership opportunities for women. In many European countries, the lack of child-care services and irregular school hours and days make it difficult for women to hold down full-time professional employment. In addition, in many nation-states, occupational sex segregation is prevalent. For example, Sweden has the most sex-segregated work force in the Western world, with 40% of educated women employed in four jobs: secretary, clerk, cleaner, and nurse (Driscoll & Goldberg, 1993).

Typically, women who gain access to managerial and leadership positions do so in organizations that lack power and that therefore are often not attractive to men. For example, Hörburger and Rath-Hörburger (1980) found a considerable number of women in upper-echelon positions of the European Parliament, one of the institutions of the EU. The EU is answerable to Parliament, and Parliament alone guarantees its independence; it keeps a constant watch on the EU's activities, making sure that it faithfully represents the Union's interests. In addition, Parliament plays a part in the Union's legislative procedure. Since the European Parliament is not a lawmaking body, the entry of women into upper-level positions is not perceived as a threat to men vying for leadership positions. Nevertheless, despite the lack of decisionmaking power, women have been able to raise women's issues and influence policy in the European Parliament and other institutions in the EU.

Few comparative studies of women in leadership positions in different European countries exist. But the limited number of empirical investigations that have been conducted cast doubt on the realization of an integrated Europe in the near future. Tollgerdt-Anderson (1993), for example, compared Scandinavian, French, German, and English advertisements to examine differences between these countries about attitudes, values, and demands for leadership. The authors examined advertisements for executives, extracted leadership qualities from these ads, and compared them by country. The findings showed there were significant differences between the European countries in leadership demands, which ranged from the ability to cooperate or taking initiative to high levels of energy, flexibility, and personality attributes. For example, Scandinavian ads gave priority to leaders' ability to cooperate as well as their personal and social attributes. In German, French, and British ads, on the other hand, while these characteristics were considered important as requirements for leadership, this was true to a much lesser extent than in the Scandinavian countries. In these countries, leadership qualities were distributed across the attributes under investigation with no single characteristic being reported more important than another. Thus, the requirements for a good leader varied from culture to culture. Except within Scandinavia (i.e., Norway, Finland, Sweden), the differences between the rest of the European nations were quite substantial.

In a second cross-cultural study, Apfelbaum (1993) analyzed French and Norwegian women in leadership positions. Most of the women leaders in both countries held posts as cabinet or subcabinet ministers. As in the previous study, specificities of the cultural context clearly polarized the two samples. Overall, the Norwegian women viewed their leadership experiences in a very positive way and had a deep sense of the legitimacy of their roles as leaders, a feeling which was alien to the French women. Norwegian women leaders felt in control of the situation and believed that gender was not a constraint. French women leaders, on the other hand, believed that gender hindered women's participation in leadership situations, citing Edith Cresson as an example.

Appointed in May 1991, Cresson briefly served as prime minister under Mitterand, but never had the full support of her party. According to *Current Biography Yearbook* (1991), not since Joan of Arc has a woman attained such a powerful position in France. The appointment of Cresson, a socialist known for her sharp tongue, impatience, belligerence, intelligence, and stubbornness, was controversial from the beginning. Although Cresson had held several prior political appointments, including a seat in the European Parliament, the Ministry of Agriculture, Ministry of Trade and Tourism, and minister of European affairs, at the time of her election women in politics were still a rarity in France. The French press pinned many nicknames on her including "la battante" (the fighter), Mitterand's "Iron Lady" (likening her to Margaret Thatcher), "the perfumed one" (referring to her stylishness and promotion of French designer clothes as part of her efforts to revitalize French industry), and "La Pompadour" (an allusion to the influential mistress of Louis XV). While Cresson held the leadership position of prime minister, rumors spread about a romantic relationship between Cresson and Mitterand, insinuating that she and the French president shared more than a political philosophy. Cresson's response:

> Every time a woman gets nominated or elected somewhere, it is customary to hear that she made it by her physique or by providing favors for some man. Not one woman has ever been selected without the explanation that she slept with so-and-so. Unfortunately, we are still in that stage. (*Current Biography Yearbook*, 1991, p. 166)

Now EU Commissioner in charge of Education, Research and Development, and Human Resources, Cresson is committed to a united Europe as envisioned by Jean Monet and former European Community President Jacques Delors.

A second important gap between the two cultures in the Apfelbaum study concerned the way in which French and Norwegian women leaders saw the private and public domains of their lives. French women reported disruptions in their private lives much more frequently and had much higher divorce rates than their Norwegian counterparts. They saw their private lives as problematic, felt their leadership positions placed their personal lives at risk, and had difficulties balancing private and public lives in interpersonal relationships. According to Apfelbaum:

> With traditional French values about relations between men and women still in place, both women and men alike may find their gendered personal identities threatened by women's entrance into positions of leadership. For the Norwegian women leaders, politics is a more transient activity, one of management rather than power. This construction may explain why these women were from the onset willing to engage in the battle for equality and why simultaneously men were less resistant about sharing their positions with women. But there are also fundamental differences in the traditionally defined roles of Norwegian women and men concerning courtship, intimacy, and relations with family and children. (pp. 424–425)

According to Genovese (1993), Norway provides an unusual context for female leadership, which is highlighted in the study by Apfelbaum. Genovese points out that Norwegian society has always maintained a strong commitment to egalitarian values and social justice and, therefore, provides a context conducive to feminist politics. Similarly, Bystydzienski (1988) suggested that the unusually high representation women in Norway have achieved is a combination of long-term favorable conditions which not only include the public acceptance of values of justice and equality, but also a relatively open, participatory electoral system and specific environmental opportunities (e.g., the debate over whether Norway should enter the European Economic Community). In addition, the women's movement, which brought together coalitions of various feminist groups, was instrumental in getting more women into politics.

The present prime minister of Norway, Gro Harlem Brundtland, is a good example of such a women. Inspired by the Norwegian feminist movement of the 1960s and 1970s, Brundtland became a champion of feminist issues, campaigned for the liberalization of abortion laws, and promoted increased participation of women in politics. In 1986, she earned many accolades for appointing eight women to her 18-member cabinet who, in turn, aggressively worked to advance other women's issues and feminist principles.

PROFILES OF EUROPEAN WOMEN LEADERS

Building on the importance of specificity of cultural context, profiles of two women leaders, Mary Robinson of Ireland and Tansu Ciller of Turkey, two very different European nations, are presented here. The political systems, religion, values, customs, and attitudes toward women in general, and women leaders in particular, are almost antithetical in these two countries.

Mary Robinson of Ireland

Ireland is a nation in constant political and religious upheaval polarized along Catholic and Protestant lines. The separation of Northern Ireland (an autonomous province of England) from the rest of the country has created political and social apartheid that has led to violent terrorist activities since the late 1960s.

Mary Robinson is Ireland's first woman president, who won the presidential election on December 3, 1990. She came to this position of political leadership as one of Ireland's foremost international lawyers and politicians known for her secular sophistication (Duffy, 1992). She is also a radical feminist who often speaks for the liberalization of Ireland's divorce and abortion laws and against laws making homosexuality a punishable offense. Her prospects of winning the election as a woman in a male-dominated country were slim. According to one biographical sketch:

The notion that an ardent feminist could prevail in a presidential election in a country whose government had alternated between two conservative, male-dominated parties for nearly three quarters of a century was inconceivable. Dublin bookmakers listed her as a 1,000-to-one underdog, and conservatives smugly regarded her nomination, according to one observer, as a harmless gesture by the libertarian Left. (*Current Biography Yearbook*, 1991, p. 478)

Robinson was born to parents both of whom were physicians and Roman Catholics. She attended boarding school in Dublin and finishing school in Paris. After obtaining her master's degree from Harvard Law School, an experience that Robinson describes as transformational, she studied law at Trinity College in Dublin. At age 24, Robinson became the youngest professor in the history of her alma mater, where she taught constitutional and criminal law. In 1969 she was elected to the Senate as a candidate for Labour, Ireland's third largest party.

Robinson married a fellow lawyer and Protestant, Nicholas Robinson, whom she considers an excellent role model of a supportive spouse. Duffy (1992) described Mary Robinson as the classic overachiever, with plenty of ambition and the kind of bottomless stamina often possessed by successful politicians. Before her election as president, she had gained a reputation as a champion for liberal causes, and was well known in Irish and European courts for her position on divorce, contraception, and abortion arguing for these rights in a country that is 95% Catholic (Dean, 1991).

Robinson's office is largely ceremonial, since she has no executive power. In fact, constitutionally, she is proscribed from traveling abroad without the permission of Ireland's prime minister, and from conducting public policy. Essentially she has no official duties other than calling a general election on the advice of the prime minister. She does command regular briefings from the government on domestic and international policy (*Current Biography Yearbook*, 1991).

Yet Robinson exercises strong symbolic leadership. Bolman and Deal (1991) use the term "symbolic leadership" to describe a leader's deployment of symbols and stories to disseminate a vision that engenders loyalty among followers. The authors suggest that, symbolically, the task of the leader is to interpret experience. Leaders also use symbols to capture attention and discover and communicate a vision. "Effective symbolic leadership is a two-way street, an accomplishment which is possible only for leaders who understand the deepest values and most pressing concerns of their constituents" (p. 443). Robinson uses a variety of symbols to chart a new social course for her country. In an interview with the *Los Angeles Times*, she said, "I represent a new and more pluralistic Ireland." According to Dean (1991), Robinson was elected on a locally radical platform of reshaping the president's job from idle figurehead to functional personification of a changing nation. Her ultimate political goals, her vision, are a unified Ireland

and an end of the Protestant-Catholic killings in Northern Ireland. She continues to address the role of women in politics, is committed to contribute to the international protection of human rights, and promotes a single European market. Robinson hopes to use her presidency, which expires in 1997, as a catalyst for change and leadership.

Tansu Ciller of Turkey

Countries such as India and Israel have a long history of female leadership. In Turkey, however, the election of a woman as prime minister was both surprising and unorthodox. In Turkey, the West and the Middle East, Christianity and Islam, the Roman and the Byzantine worlds meet. Turkey is the bridge between the Western and Islamic world. The Ottoman Empire was almost a textbook example of a patriarchal state (Ozbudum, 1993). Moreover, Turkey was, and to some extent still is, a class-conscious nation with a rigid dichotomy between the ruling class and the ruled. During the past decades, however, Turkey has undergone rapid economic growth and major social transformation (Pevsner, 1984). The country has changed dramatically because of urban and overseas migration, the spread of education and communications, the growth of industry and an organized labor force, and the increasing commercialization of agricultural production and marketing. Today, Turkey is more democratic than most of its neighbors, but less democratic than the Western European countries it wishes to join.

Turkey is a regionally diverse country in which male authority is evident in all walks of life (Kandiyoti, 1977). In many rural areas, women are still barred from public functions, and their power is restricted to negotiations of marriage unions and alliances within the village. Integration into a market economy, as Abadan (1967) noted, eroded the status of women. The author found that women's political participation in parliament has steadily declined since the foundation of the republic, especially after the transition to a multiparty system. Moreover, women's work does not receive social recognition, regardless of the extent of their economic contributions (Kandiyoti, 1977).

Because of the social status of Turkish women, the election of Tansu Ciller was particularly unusual. A newcomer to politics, Dr. Ciller first served as Turkey's economy minister in 1991, and held that position until she was elected prime minister in June 1993. She succeeded Suleiman Demirel as the leader of the True Path party, apparently because members of her party believed that they could win over their major opposition, the Motherland party. Ciller's other major opponents were representatives of militant Islam. She has the following to say about Islamic fundamentalism:

The cold war is over and the Berlin Wall is down. Fundamentalism is

the challenge for the next decade. But we should not look at fundamentalism as only an Islamic threat because similar extremism can again
emerge in Europe. The thing is not to build new walls. Turkey is the
only democratic, secular country in the Islamic world. It could serve as
a bridge between the two sides. (''Will Turkey be the next Iran? p. 52)

To deal with Turkey's deep economic crisis, which resulted from the devaluation
of the Turkish currency, Ciller proposed austerity measures which include price
increases up to 100% and prospective layoffs of thousands of workers in state
industries. In an interview with *U.S. News and World Report* (Coleman, 1994),
Ciller said:

> Our economic [austerity] package is courageous. It won't be easy to
> implement. I have to get the support of the people. I tell them that if
> we don't do those now, it will be a lot harder later. It's like needing an
> operation. If you don't have it, you will suffer more than if you did.
> (p. 52)

At the time of this writing, it was uncertain whether or not Ciller's austerity
program, which is the key to economic recovery, will pass parliament.

In contrast to Ireland's Mary Robinson, who is very popular at home and
abroad, Ciller has had a rough start and continues to fight economic and political
battles at home. Ciller's position as prime minister is threatened by several
factions and pre-existing conditions: opposing political parties, such as the Motherland party and Islamic fundamentalism; Kurdish guerilla fighting; lack of financial support from the EU (although it is Turkey's largest trading partner); and
the old-guard male establishment. Described as bright, attractive, and plausible,
Ciller's major goals are finding a solution to Turkey's economic crisis and
privatizing state-owned industries and banks. Many of Ciller's fellow Turks see
her, both by her sex and by her American education, as a symbol of Turkey's
insistence on wanting to be part of the West. Turkey has been an associate
member of the European Union for 30 years and is pleading to gain entry into
the European Union.

WOMEN LEADERS IN ASIA

In Asia, as in Europe, there is a considerable amount of variability across countries
in language, history, industrial development, and customs. In all Asian nations,
women make up a sizable portion of the work force. A small number of them
are found in middle- and upper-level management positions, and still fewer
women hold leadership positions. Because of the culturally defined ''domestic
role'' of women in the Far East, both men and women—but especially men—have

strong reservations about working for a female supervisor (Carney & O'Kelly, 1987). In Japan, for example, there are almost no women managers higher than clerical supervisors, especially in large MNCs. In general, Japanese society expects women to work until marriage, quit to raise children, and return, as needed, to low-level, part-time positions after age 40 (Jelinek & Adler, 1988).

According to Steinhoff and Tanaka (1994), Japan has a double-peaked (M-shaped) distribution of female employment by age and marital status. The overwhelming majority of young, unmarried women are in the labor force. Female participation in the work force then drops during the early years of marriage and childbearing, since many companies force their women to resign when they marry and have children, although this policy is gradually changing. Women who resigned during their childbearing years and a growing number of older, married women later return to the labor force. Moreover, the "parlite" (a Japanese abbreviation for "part-time elite") jobs for Japanese women in areas such as consulting, research, or programming are rare. Most employed women with children have full-time manufacturing or service-sector jobs requiring few skills and conferring little prestige (Takenaka, 1992). Although Japan is still one of the most macho cultures in the world, things are changing, albeit slowly. Women have begun to hold a few major positions in the upper ranks of Japanese politics.

Despite changing attitudes in the general population and the increasing number of women entering and re-entering the workforce, Japanese employers have made few efforts to accommodate promotion-track women who wish to alter the gendered balance of work and home responsibilities (Molony, 1995). In addition, many companies have instituted a two-track system for women, a Japanese version of the "mommy track." Although allegedly gender-neutral, promotion to the management (the elite) track is most often chosen by men, while women opt for a less pressured, general employee track (Masuda, 1990). Lack of child care services, the pressures of long commutes, business socializing after hours, and the lack of desire of Japanese men to help with household and childrearing tasks are further disincentives that reinforce gender role divisions in Japan.

Equal opportunity laws did not go into effect in Japan until 1986. The purpose of the law was to "harmonize women's home life and work life while improving women's welfare, defined as respect for motherhood while not meaning sexual discrimination" (Molony, 1995, p. 287). However, this law only asks companies to grant women an opportunity, and does not constitute a guarantee of employment. Thus, this law is weakly defined, since it stipulates only that Japanese firms "make efforts" to avoid discrimination against women in recruitment, selection, position assignments, and promotions, and does not specify any penalties for violations of its provisions (Black, Stephens, & Rosener, 1992). In view of the lack of penalties for noncompliant organizations, equal treatment of women and men in the work place is difficult to enforce in Japan. Although the

Child Care Leave Law was passed in 1992, only a small number of women (and still a smaller number of men) take advantage of the provision of the law in order to keep their careers on track. Finally, sexual harassment is an accepted part of the male working environment, despite a new law prohibiting it (Graven, 1990). Therefore, it is not surprising that a large number of women in the Japanese workforce feel discriminated against.

In India, women are constitutionally equal to men, but are culturally defined as primarily responsible for the children and the home (Jelinek & Adler, 1988). Women in Singapore are better off than women in most other Asian countries, largely due to Singapore's booming economy. China, on the other hand, is a society with mixed feudal, socialist, and autocratic features which, despite its openness to Western ideas, remains a collectivistic culture (Korabik, 1994). Chinese values are important factors in determining and shaping Chinese organizations and leadership practices. In fact, the influence of Chinese cultural values on managerial practice are so significant that it distinguishes Chinese managerial practices from Western practices (Redding, 1982). More specifically, Hicks and Redding (1983) commented that "as there are well over a hundred developing countries, the almost perfect correlation between Chinese heritage and economic success could hardly be due to chance" (p. 22).

Chinese heritage and history have their philosophical roots in Confucianism which embraces the following key principles: 1) "the stability of society is based on unequal relationships between people; 2) the family is the prototype of all social organizations; 3) virtuous behavior toward others consists of treating others as one would like to be treated oneself; and 4) virtue with regard to one's tasks in life consists of trying to acquire skills and education, working hard, not spending more than necessary, being patient, and persevering" (Hofstede & Bond, 1988, p. 8). These Confucian principles and values are summarized by the term *Confucian dynamism* which refers to the acceptance of the legitimacy of hierarchy and valuing the perseverance of thrift. Empirical research (e.g., Hofstede & Bond, 1988) has shown that Confucian dynamism has been positively correlated with national economic growth rates in several Asian countries, including China and Singapore.

Lockett (1988) identified four additional key aspects of Chinese culture to include: 1) respect for age and hierarchical position; 2) group orientation; 3) the concept of "face"; and 4) the importance of relationships. Among these features, the concept of "face" is the only one requiring some brief comment, since the remaining three are commonly understood. According to Tu (1984) the concept of "face" connotes the dignity of the person resulting from interpersonal relationships with his or her superiors, peers, and subordinates. It is a reflection of social acceptance and respectability. Ho (1976a) suggested that "face" is essentially the recognition by others of an individual's standing and position. Therefore, it is very important for Chinese managers to avoid losing face, and Chinese management practices are designed to utilize subtle actions, rather than public reprimands which allows managers and subordinates to keep face in difficult situations.

Chinese cultural values permeating the practice of leadership as well as attitudes toward women include absolute authority of the leader, time orientation, cohesiveness within the organizational hierarchy, compromise in conflict resolution, and the acceptance of ordering relationships (Mun, 1986; Tan, 1989). In international negotiations, for example, the Chinese team enters the meeting room in protocol order, with the highest ranking person coming in first. Unlike Latin Americans or Europeans from the Mediterranean basin, the Chinese always begin meetings on time. As in many other Asian communities, the Chinese avoid open conflict and confrontation. Interpersonal harmony in the organization is maintained in this way, without openly showing any sign of confrontation (Huat, 1990).

Korabik (1994) pointed out that many Chinese women have been socialized to be shy and unassertive, traits which do not prepare women for leadership roles. Mao Zedong once said, ''A man in China is usually subjected to the domination of three systems: 1) the state systems (political authority); 2) the clan systems (clan authority); and 3) the supernatural systems (religious authority).'' As for women, in addition to being dominated by these three systems of authority, they are also dominated by the men (authority of husband) (Tian, 1981). Today, the Chinese government advocates the ''four selves—self reliance, self-confidence, self-respect, and self-strengthening—over the traditional three obediences to one's father, husband, and son (Cox, 1995, p. 2A).

Despite the economic reforms, which lifted the standard of living of the Chinese, women in China work harder and earn less; get fewer chances to own property or start a business; make up 80% of China's illiterate and semi-illiterate population; and live in a society that places a clear premium on male life—just as it did in the days of the emperors (Cox, 1995). Thus, a profound gender gap remains in China despite governmental efforts to promote gender equality.

Hong Kong is returning to mainland China in 1997. Even though Hong Kong has long been a British colony, it is basically a Chinese society; over 95% of the population is Chinese. It is a strange blend of Asian and European cultures, with a totally international demeanor in a high-pressure business environment (Rossman, 1990). Government intervention in business and commerce has been minimal in Hong Kong. Sex discrimination in employment continues to be legal and the number of women among corporate managers is negligble (DeLeon & Ho, 1994). Gender identity of women managers in Hong Kong is based on powerful male/female stereotypes in the Chinese culture. These stereotypical perspectives of women's traits as rendering them inferior for leadership restrict women's access to leadership positions (Ho, 1984).

The reversion from a capitalist to a communist nation, when Hong Kong returns to mainland China, raises many leadership issues. Among them is the problem of managers leaving Hong Kong. In a government survey conducted in 1990, 16% of Hong Kong residents stated that they had plans to migrate (Roberts, 1992). The vacancies created by these largely male departing managers may offer leadership opportunities for women, especially since China has promised to maintain Hong Kong's capitalist system and democratic freedoms. In Hong Kong, along with Taiwan, Thailand, and Singapore, attitudes toward women are more positive than in Japan and China. Companies stress the issue of competence in the workplace, rather than gender.

In Korea, as discussed by Soh (1993), "despite constitutional declarations of equality, the cultural norms and values that guide gender relations in everyday life continue to be based on the Chinese cosmology of yin/yang complementarity (i.e., the harmonious combination of yin and yang—the feminine passive and the masculine active principles, respectively) fortified by the traditional Confucian ideology of male superiority" (pp. 73–74).

Lao Tzu, who wrote the *Tao Te Ching* in the 5th century B.C. described the leader in terms of the complementarily of the yin and yang. Leaders, he noted, are often seen as powerful warriors who rule by force. This is the yang, or masculine, aspect of leadership. But they also must act like healers. This is the yin, the feminine aspect of leadership. Korean women's status and confidence are further undermined by their acceptance of the Confucian adage that it is a virtue if a woman has no ability (Xi, 1985).

In Asia, then, the minority status of women is common in most nation-states. In most Asian countries, people lived under the patriarchal system of gender relations for more than two millennia of their recorded history, although the specifics of the gender hierarchy prevalent at any given time have varied throughout history (Kim, 1979). Moreover, in many of the Asian countries, gender is not the only important variable of social stratification. Age and rank often come before gender in guiding the behavior of men and women in public, formal situations (Soh, 1993). Change in these countries is slow and often insidious. Among the major forces for change is the influence of foreign firms operating in Asian nation-states, particularly in Japan, since foreign firms are more likely than their Asian host countries to offer leadership opportunities to Asian women.

Aung San Suu Kyi: Burmese Dissident Leader

Aung San Suu Kyi is the leader of the prodemocracy movement and co-founder of the National League for Democracy of Burma. The National League for Democracy, the country's most powerful opposition party, rejects the leading military regime that has governed and controlled Burma since 1962. Suu Kyi has been under house arrest for nearly 6 years because of her attempts to introduce democratic reforms into her country. Her efforts violated the government ban on political activity and constituted the sole reason for her arrest (*Current Biography Yearbook*, 1992). In 1991, Suu Kyi was awarded the Nobel Peace Prize for her nonviolent struggle for democracy and human rights in Burma, which her son accepted on her behalf. Her husband, Michael Aris, upon learning that his wife had been awarded the Nobel Peace Prize said, "Many will now know for the first time of her courageous leadership of the nonviolent struggle for the restoration of human rights in her country" (Suu Kyi, 1991, p. xxviii).

The single most significant influence in her life was her father, Aung San, the founder of modern Burma who was assassinated in 1947, when Suu Kyi was 2 years old. During her studies abroad, Suu Kyi became consumed, to the point of obsession, with learning more about her father. She wrote a biographical essay about her father which was published in her book *Freedom from Fear* (Suu Kyi, 1991) in which she stated:

It was only when I grew older and started collecting material on his life and achievements that I began to learn what he had really been like and how much he managed to achieve in his thirty-two years. Not only did I then conceive an admiration for him as a patriot and statesman, but I developed a strong sense of empathy as I discovered many similarities in our attitudes. It is perhaps because of this strong bond that I came to feel such a deep sense of responsibility for the welfare of my country. (p. 24)

The heritage of her father, whose writings, achievements of his 32-year life, and exhortation to his people are part of Burma's history, became an obsession with Suu Kyi which occupied much of her adolescence and adulthood.

Aung San Suu Kyi grew up under privileged circumstances. She was educated in India, England, the United States, and Japan. After 20 years of exile in London, Suu Kyi returned to Burma in 1988 to take care of her dying mother. At the time of her return, the civilian government had crumbled, leaving the defense ministry and the army in charge. Riots between students demonstrating against the government and the police resulted in bloodshed and rising numbers of student deaths. The attempt of the government to suppress the protest marches claimed many more victims than the slaughter in Tienanmen Square a year later. Suu Kyi was quoted saying, "I obviously had to think about it [involvement in politics], but my instinct was that this was not a time when anyone who cared stayed out. As my father's daughter, I felt I had a duty to get involved" (Whitney, 1991, A10).

Suu Kyi is a charismatic leader who took it upon herself to form a democratic system of government in which all the regions and ethnic groups of Burma would be represented. Her long time friend Ann Pasternak Slater, niece of the Russian writer Boris Pasternak, offered the following description of Suu Kyi:

Many, like myself, must have first been drawn to Suu by her beauty. Our perdurable love and admiration are for her pilgrim soul—for her courage, determination and abiding moral strength, gifts already glowing in her Chrysalis period—as a student and young mother. (Suu Kyi, 1991, p. 266)

According to Pasternak, Suu Kyi is a political reformer and true egalitarian. She has "an integrity, a steadfastness of purpose, an unswerving determination and single-minded persistence in attaining a goal, a seriousness going hand in hand with a sense of humor, a dignity and resolve in the face of persecution and adversity" (p. 257) which made her the hope and inspiration of an oppressed people.

From her father, Suu Kyi inherited oratory skills and the ability to manage crowds and keep them under control. She pleaded with leaders around the world to support the Burmese quest for democracy and unity. Her studies in India introduced her to the teachings of India's nationalist leader Mohandas K. Gandhi, which provided the philosophical basis for her nonviolent approach to civil disobedience that marked her campaign for democratic reforms in 1988 and 1989.

While under house arrest, Suu Kyi's party, the National League for Democracy, voted for her in the 1990 election and gave two-thirds of the parliament seats to her party. Despite international pressures, the military regime refuses to release her unless she renounces her political ideology and leaves Burma never to return, which for Suu Kyi is not negotiable. In 1990 Suu Kyi was awarded the 1990 Sakharov Prize for Freedom of Thought during a special session of the European Parliament; she was unable to accept the award, because she was under house arrest in Rangoon. In July 1995, a month prior to the fourth United Nations World Conference on Women in Beijing, Suu Kyi was released. However, she will not leave her Burma, because she fears not being allowed to return to her native country if she does leave.

Suu Kyi is an inspirational leader who identifies with the struggle of her country. The Norwegian Nobel Committee when awarding her the Nobel Peace Prize stated that it wished

to honor this woman for her unflagging efforts and show its support for the many people throughout the world who are striving to attain democracy, human rights and ethnic conciliation by peaceful means. (Suu Kyi, 1991, p. 236)

Suu Kyi is internationally recognized for her courageous quest to reconcile civil and military authorities of Burma; her activism is a symbol of more civil rights and greater political roles for women in Asia.

WOMEN LEADERS IN LATIN AMERICA

I chose Latin America and its women leaders for several reasons. First, Latin America is a region of developing countries predicted to grow significantly in economic influence and rise to a world economy in the years to come. After decades of political unrest, military coups, and misappropriation and embezzling of millions of public funds, everywhere in Latin America national sentiments are giving way to economic realities (Naisbitt & Aburdene, 1990). The growth of local industry and the recent interest in the creation of a hemispheric free zone between Latin America and the U.S. show the importance Latin America will achieve in the future world economy. Like Europe and Asia, Latin America is a culturally diverse region populated by Europeans (Argentina, Costa Rica, Chile, Columbia, Uruguay, and southern Brazil), Indians (Bolivia, Paraguay, Ecuador, and Guatemala), and Caribbeans (Puerto Rico, the Dominican Republic, Panama, Honduras, and parts of Venezuela).

According to Black et al. (1992), one of the most far-reaching and visible, yet the most difficult to overcome, of the barriers to women's leadership is the male machismo ethic. *Machismo* is prevalent in all social strata, but particularly among males at lower levels of the social scale, where prowess is a substitute for power. It is reflected in the tendency of Latin American men to respond to aggression, heroism, and charisma more than to logic, persuasion, and consensus (Rossman, 1990). Latin American cultures, like those of Asia, place significant pressures on women to fulfill their socially prescribed role of the family caretaker. In contrast to Asian women, these cultural attitudes are not only upheld and protected, but cherished by Latin American women. They manifest themselves in the female counterpart of the machismo ethic, known as *marianismo*. Not only is the role of family caretaker accepted by Latin American women, but often it is jealously defended.

Like European women leaders, Latin American women's influence is clearly seen in the political arena. Unlike the developing countries of Asia, where women lead reform movements and a few businesses, Latin American women have attained leadership positions mostly through political appointments; it is in politics where women have the most influence. Corazon Aquino, for example, led the Philippines in a revolution that ended the 20-year reign of Philippine dictator Ferdinand Marcos. Aquino was an unlikely candidate for the presidency of the Philippines, having played the role of dutiful wife and mother while her husband's political career skyrocketed. Despite her lack of political experience, Corazon Aquino created a strong moral alternative to the corruption and repression of the Marcos regime, which won her the election in 1986.

More recently, Violeta Barrios de Chamorro was elected president of Nicaragua in 1990, at a time when the country was devastated by civil war and a deteriorating economy. Like Aquino, she entered the political arena after the assassination of her husband, Pedro Chamorro, in 1978. Pedro Chamorro, owner of the nation's largest newspaper, *La Prensa*, and leader of the Democratic Union for Liberation, was committed to reshaping Nicaraguan politics. Violeta Chamorro took over the newspaper and continued to pursue her husband's political goals, which included rebuilding a collapsed economy, reducing chronic unemployment, ending the censorship which had tightened around *La Prensa* after the assassination of Pedro Chamorro, and decreasing the large foreign deficit. Outraged by the death of their leader, the Democratic Union for Liberation staged a general strike which escalated into civil war waged by the Sandinista, the contras (anti-Sandinista rebels) and other opposition groups. Daniel Ortega's inauguration took place on the sixth anniversary of Pedro Chamorro's assassination.

In 1989, Violeta Chamorro was chosen as the National Opposition Union's candidate to run against Ortega, since she was the only opposition figure in Nicaragua whose stature and prestige rivaled Ortega's own (Edmisten, 1990). She ran on a platform that promised reconstruction of Nicaragua, end of the military draft, amnesty to political prisoners, and the restoration of private property rights and the principles of a free-market economy (Uhlig, 1990). The name Chamorro and the political vision her assassinated husband had articulated, her ownership of *La Prensa*, and her "mother figure" image contributed to her victory in the presidential election.

The two leaders selected as representatives of female leadership in Latin America, Eva Perón and Isabel Perón, share a common bond, namely the same husband, Juan Perón. Above and beyond that, both women illustrate very different types of leadership. Eva exercised nonpositional leadership. Isabel, on the other hand, who became the first female chief of state in the Americas in 1974, practiced positional leadership through the office of the presidency of Argentina. As with the women leaders discussed before, Eva and Isabel Perón's leadership has to be examined in the context of the culture the two women embodied: Peronism of the post-World War II era in Argentina, political instability of the region, and the need for economic development. These factors shaped the political and personal lives of these two women. The Argentina which had chosen Juan Perón as its leader was not only one of the richest countries of South America, it was also one of the richest countries in the world. World War II had left Argentina a creditor nation (Taylor, 1959) due to money lent to other countries during the war.

Eva Perón: Nonpositional Leader of Argentina

More so than any other person, and certainly more than any other woman in the history of Latin America, Eva Perón has been the object of much speculation, controversy, and admiration, as well as hatred. She was Argentina's flamboyant and charismatic first lady, politically known as "Evita." By the time she died on July 26, 1952, she was undoubtedly the second most powerful figure in Argentina, though she held neither an elected post nor an official position in Perón's government. Eulogies of "Eva the Saint" and diatribes of "Eva the Bad" created a cult around her. Argentines worshipped her long after her death, and Eva was the model Isabel Perón tried to emulate during her presidency. Many Argentines described Eva's leadership not as political, but as spiritual, moral, or religious. Yet they also disapproved of the corruption and illegality she encouraged in Perón's government.

Eva Perón's life is a story of rags to riches. She rose from humble beginnings in a pueblo outside of Buenos Aires to international renown as Argentina's first lady. An illegitimate child, Eva left her family at age 15 in 1934 to migrate to Buenos Aires, like thousands of Argentines at the time, in search of a better future. During her first years in the nation's capital, the cultural mecca of Latin America during the 1930s, she supported herself mostly by working on radio programs, since she could not find work as an actress. By 1939 she had become somewhat of a success as an actress, having appeared in 20 plays, 5 movies, and at least 26 soap operas (Fraser & Navarro, 1985).

Juan Perón began to emerge as a controversial figure and first came to power in the summer of 1944, with the support of the working classes. Eva met him at a fundraiser for earthquake victims. Eva had pleaded for the victims over the radio and later attended a rally where she met Perón, a 48-year-old widower twice her age. From then on, her life was swallowed up by his political career. Perón became president of Argentina in 1946 with the help of the working class vote and the military and, after 18 years in exile, again in 1973. He used a combination of personal charisma, collective political ritual, and economic policies that were intended to redistribute income to workers and to forge a social movement. Belief in Perónism was enhanced in considerable part through public devotion to his second wife, "Evita" (Turner & Miguens, 1983).

Until her death in 1952, Eva immersed herself in all aspects of government. Wherever she went, she ensured the audience that she represented Juan Perón and carried his authority. According to Navarro (1977), "Perón's decision to rely on Eva for maintaining his personal contact with labor legitimized the activities she had been carrying out and altered their political value significantly" (p. 237). Eva began to act as an extension of Perón, and her activities in the Ministry of Labor were the basis of the political power she accumulated from 1948 onward.

The nature of her power is best seen in the Fundicacion Eva Perón, the Eva Perón Foundation, which provided assistance for any person in need. Through the Foundation, she gained control over two other governmental departments, the Department of Public Health and Sanitation and the Ministry of Education

(Main, 1980). The primary goal of the Foundation was to complement the social goals of the Perón government, with Eva as a leader of the social reform movement. Her prominence and power in the Perón regime was second only to Perón himself. In fact, by 1951 many Argentines asserted that Eva ruled the country (Frazer & Navarro, 1985). In addition to the Foundation, Eva controlled her own political army of 5 million workers, her *descamisados* ("the shirtless ones"), members of the General Confederation of Labor, or CGT. The term "descamisado" first appeared on October 17, 1947. It was used pejoratively to describe Perón's supporters as they gathered in the Plaza de Mayo, the central square of Buenos Aires, demanding his freedom (Navarro, 1977). In 1951 there were rumors of Eva's candidacy for vice president to run on a Perón-Perón ticket. When the army threatened to withdraw its support of Juan Perón should Eva announce her candidacy, she refused the nomination, even though she wanted it and had allowed the CGT to stage a massive demonstration for her.

Eva Perón died in 1952 at the age of 33 after a 10-month battle with cancer, during which she maintained a grueling schedule of speeches and public appearances, working a demanding dawn-to-dark routine. She broadcasted her last presidential campaign speech in 1951, just before being taken to the hospital to be operated on for cancer. After her death, Juan Perón lost his grip on Argentina, was overthrown by a military coup, and was forced to flee the country.

The story of Eva Perón confronts us with the enigma of power attributed to a woman in a traditionally and formally patriarchal society, a society that devalues women in relation to men. She made politics a legitimate activity for women, but as an extension of women's traditional family responsibilities (Navarro, 1977). The mythology surrounding Eva Perón contains imagery explicitly associated with a feminine ideal, i.e., uncontrolled power, and revolutionary leadership (Taylor, 1979). Her very presence was a flamboyant challenge to the traditional belief in the inferiority of women and the authority of men (Main, 1980).

The leadership of Eva Perón is an excellent example of the unity of leadership and followership to which Hollander (1992a) called attention. Hollander argued that both leadership and followership can represent active roles, and Eva illustrated the complementarity of both roles. She was a textbook example of how followers affect and even constrain a leader's activity. According to Hollander:

> The role of the follower can be seen as holding within it potential for both assessing and taking on leadership functions. In addition to directing activity, these include decision making, goal setting, communicating, adjudicating conflict, and otherwise maintaining the enterprise. (p. 71)

Eva Perón clearly exercised these leadership functions. Yet without Juan Perón, she would have, as she explained in her autobiography, remained "a humble sparrow" while he was "a mighty condor." Juan Perón confirmed her leadership skills and intuition, structured her insight, and offered a channel for her intelligence, sensitivity, and energy (Taylor, 1979).

The follower perspective, according to Hollander (1992a) has proven to be a useful avenue to understanding leadership, and has been increasingly employed. The impact of followers' perceptions and expectations on the leader, and the leader's response to followers, are important aspects of the interdependent processes of leadership and followership. Eva Perón was a classic example of a follower who made significant contributions to leadership, in this case that of Juan Perón. As Hollander (1992b) argued, "given the need for mutual responsiveness, leadership and followership can be considered two reciprocal systems which require synchronization" (p. 46). In Eva and Juan Perón, we see an example of proactive followership and synchronization of the leadership and followership functions.

Isabel Perón: Positional Leader of Argentina

Juan Perón continued to use Eva's image after he returned from exile in Madrid in 1973 to resume the presidency of Argentina for a second time, and built his political message on her popularity. Perónism and the cult of "Evita" remained strong symbols of the past. However, years of bureaucratic authoritarian rule by the military and shifting international markets had weakened the working classes politically, and, consequently, Juan Perón's power base.

Isabel Perón became the first female president in Latin America when she took office after the death of her husband, Juan Perón, on July 1, 1974. Nine months before her election as president, in an well-orchestrated comeback designed to secure Juan Perón the presidency, Isabel ran with her husband on the same ticket as vice president, and was elected to that position. Along with the presidency, however, Isabel inherited problems that even her husband found intractable: a battered economy, a divided Perón movement, and an appalling level of political violence (*Current Biography Yearbook*, 1975).

Like Eva, Isabel, born as Maria Estala Martinez on the wrong side of the tracks, moved from one of the provinces to the capital of Argentina when she was a child. She had little formal education, although reportedly she studied French, ballet, and Spanish dancing. At age 20, Isabel joined a folk music ensemble, which appeared at a nightclub in Buenos Aires. She met Perón, then in exile in Panama, when her dance troupe performed in Panama City in 1956. According to the official version, Isabel maintained she was a ballerina when she was introduced to Juan Perón in 1956. She traveled with him as his secretary and followed him to Spain where he was offered permanent exile.

Isabel Martinez and Juan Perón were married in Madrid in 1961. Unlike her predecessor, Eva, who was charismatic and possessed considerable leadership skills, Isabel had little to offer to the Argentine people. As Main (1980) noted, Isabel too had ambitions, but she was lacking in the drive, the daring, the political opportunism, and the overwhelming belief in her own destiny which had carried Eva forward with such irresistible impetus. She tried to emulate Eva's dress, hairstyle and mannerisms, much to the chagrin of the Argentine people, who resented Isabel's attempts to cast herself in the mold of the idolized ''Evita.'' Unlike her predecessor, who stirred the masses, Isabel was shy and a poor public speaker.

During the days of Isabel, leftist terrorist activities reached their peak. In addition, Argentina was wavering at the brink of yet another economic collapse. The country was in chaos, with inflation having risen to 350% and political assassinations averaging three a day. Continued economic problems, military violence, and political repression, as Hodges (1976) noted, made it virtually impossible for Isabel to lead the country. In 1975, in a carefully planned coup, Isabel was arrested and later put on trial for embezzling public funds, as well as charged with fraud. Under the subterfuge of taking her to her residence, the helicopter carrying her developed ''engine trouble'' and diverted to the airport, where armed soldiers took her into custody and placed her under house arrest.

Although Isabel has not participated in Argentine politics since her ousting as president, and refuses to allow Perónist leaders to visit her in her current home in Spain, she remains the living link to the past, the last surviving Perón. Isabel benefitted from the legacy of ''Evita'' but, at the same time, was limited by this legacy to exercise formal control. Her leadership only existed in the shadows of Juan and Eva Perón, since Isabel was unable to exorcise the ghost of ''Evita.'' Overall, her presidency received poor ratings, partly because of her lack of experience and leadership skills, and partly because of the Latin American ma-chismo ethos, the same force that kept Eva from the vice presidency in 1951.

CONCLUSIONS

Globalization has resulted in a shrinking world in terms of the increasing scope of international business, communications, and transportation. In this chapter, we examined women's leadership in developed and developing countries. The women leaders discussed here included both effective and ineffective leaders. The profiles of the women leaders presented here suggest, as Apfelbaum and Hadley (1986) noted, that it makes little sense to lump together as comparable the leadership of all countries of our Western world on the grounds that they are all democracies. Moreover, most of the women leaders presented here hold or held elective positions, moving up faster in politics than in corporations. This observation led Driscoll and Goldberg (1993) to conclude that despite the prominence of some individual women who have become world leaders through family power, women such as Indira Gandhi, Benazir Bhutto, Corazon Aquino, and Violeta Chamorro, the doors to leadership remain locked for many women across the world. As I point out in Chapter 10, one way of overcoming the underutilization of women in leadership roles is through leadership education and succession planning.

This chapter highlighted the importance of cultural specificity and context in shaping women's (and men's) leadership, both domestically and internationally, which makes it difficult to generalize about female (and male) leaders. However, there are some discernible patterns. In all countries discussed here, it has been easier for women to attain positions of political leadership than those of economic leadership. Most of the individuals described are women who held or hold elective positions as heads of countries. Several women, including Isabel Perón, Aung San Suu Kyi, Corazon Aquino, and Violeta Chamorro inherited their leadership positions from their husbands or fathers, which is another common thread. And finally, none of the women leaders discussed in this chapter, as Genovese (1993) noted, fundamentally challenged the patriarchal structure of her society—an action that would have amounted to political suicide.

10 Leadership Education and Development: Preparing Leaders for the 21st Century

> Those of you who are overly ambitious may attempt to acquire [leadership] qualities over a short period of time. As I, Attila [the Hun] have found in my own life, these qualities . . . simply take time, learning and experience to develop. There are few who will find shortcuts. There are simply rare opportunities to accelerate competence, and without paying the price, no matter how great or small, none will become prepared to lead others.
>
> *Wess Roberts*

INTRODUCTION

The above quote from Roberts's *Leadership Secrets of Attila the Hun* (1987) captures many issues that leadership educators have to grapple with. Trying to teach leadership may be a lot like trying to teach sex. If you really need lessons, well . . . (Huey, 1994a). The author of the above quote refers to the old view of leadership, that is, "leaders are born"; or the "you-have-the-right-stuff-or-you-don't" approach to leadership. The once widely held belief that leaders are born and not made is less commonly accepted today. To those who assume that leaders are born, discussions of leadership education and development appear superfluous, since they believe that leadership abilities are determined by an inborn set of traits and characteristics (see Chapter 3). These traits presumably are not modifiable through training and education. From that position, leadership is unteachable, because it is assumed that it involves a set of qualities inherent in leaders. On the other hand, those who subscribe to the "leadership-is-learned-school" keep a watchful eye on existing and developing leadership education programs, since we believe that leadership develops over time through a variety of learning experiences. One recent application of this approach is found in the work of McCall, Lombardo, and Morrison (1988), who studied highly effective executives to determine the factors which accounted for their success. The researchers concluded:

> People who emerge as candidates for executive jobs come with a lot of givens, but what happens to them on the job matters. Knowledge of how the business works and ability to work with senior executives, learning to manage government, handling tense political situations, firing people—these and many others are lessons of experience. They are taught on the firing line by demanding assignments, by good and bad bosses, and by mistakes, setbacks, and misfortunes. Many executives are blessed with characteristics that give them an edge in learning these things, but learn them they must. (p. 5)

Similarly, Conger (1992) maintained that many elements of leadership can be taught, and that training plays a vital role in the development of leaders. He points out that to be successful, training must be designed to 1) develop and refine certain teachable skills; 2) improve the conceptual abilities of leaders; 3) tap individuals' personal needs, interests, and self-esteem; and 4) help leaders see and move beyond their interpersonal blocks (Conger, 1992, p. 34).

There has been a growing recognition of the need for more leaders. Gardner (1961) stated that every society needs a continuous flow of leaders who will comfort the afflicted and afflict the comfortable. As a result, leadership education has become big business, with hundreds of programs promising to produce better leaders. It is one of the hottest training topics, following total quality management (TQM), organizational excellence, and business reengineering. Leadership training programs are targeted for all levels, from young children to senior executives. Young people today are educated for leadership and encouraged to become CEOs through activities ranging from joining Boy and Girl Scouts to delivering newspapers. At the other end of the age spectrum, we find senior executives flocking to workshops and seminars to learn about the latest panaceas for the widely perceived leadership crisis.

Many companies today offer leadership courses for their employees. Stephan, Mills, Pace, and Ralphs (1988), in a survey of Fortune 500 companies, asked business leaders, "If you could put the top 10% of all executives into a seminar, what would be the topic?" Most of the respondents' answers revolved around leadership. Similarly, Fulmer (1988), in a survey of universities with executive education programs, reported that the only topic mentioned more than once was leadership, specifically transformational and visionary leadership. Today more than 60% of the largest American companies offer some type of leadership training. Southwest Airlines, for example, offers leadership classes for all employees. The approach of Southwest Airlines and other companies such as GE is consistent with Lee's (1989) argument that "leadership is no longer the exclusive domain of the inhabitants of Executive Row. The nurturing of "corporate Gandhis," as one consultant terms it, has given way to a focus on developing leadership abilities among employees at all levels of our organization" (Lee, 1988, p. 19). Executives as well as managers, supervisors, and hourly employees can learn to develop a vision, take risks, and build consensus and trust among subordinates and peers. In addition to the private sector, government agencies and military academies offer leadership education for senior-level personnel, or send their senior managers to independent institutes that provide leadership education. The Center for Creative Leadership (CCL), for example, is one of the best known independent organizations specializing in leadership training.

Institutions of higher education have also responded to the call for more effective leadership. An estimated 600 university and colleges now offer formal leadership and leadership related courses as part of their undergraduate and graduate programs. Executive leadership programs have been developed at graduate business schools including those at Harvard, Wharton, Stanford, and Kellogg. Leadership education at the college and university level spans a wide range of programs, ranging from workshops and week-long, executive-style leadership seminars built into MBA programs, to comprehensive programs, offering academic degrees in leadership studies.

Academic courses in leadership, according to Spitzberg (1987), may be divided into two categories: those that are based on the social sciences and management literature, and those that place leadership training in the context of liberal arts education. In search for alternative training models, Sayles (1993) recently suggested that the principles of medical education may be applied to leadership education. The author argued that if leaders were trained like doctors, they would learn the painstaking skills of diagnosis and careful examination, test their hypotheses and carry around in their heads the maps of their worlds that provide them with causalities and explanations. Despite the proliferation of leadership programs, Cleveland (1985) found that leadership education is lagging far behind the demand curve for leaders. He suggested that a healthy, democratic society needs hundreds of thousands of leaders who can "get it all together." Likewise Burns (1978) pointed out that we need women and men who help us lead ourselves and grow, who enable us to remove the obstacles to effective functioning; we need leaders who see and pursue shared purposes. Cleveland contended that if complexity and change in contemporary society are growing faster than anything else, then the education of women and men to manage complexity and change should be the fastest growing function of American higher education. The author concluded that equipping minds for leadership ought to be what is "higher" about higher education.

In addition to the programs mentioned above, there are special leadership training programs and seminars for women. Austin (1992) commented on these programs by noting that the message seminar designers are sending is that women somehow need to fix themselves—to correct their career-derailing tendencies—

before they can become leaders. The Center for Creative Leadership, for example, offers a "Women's Leadership" program designed to provide women with the opportunity to develop greater self-awareness and understanding as female leaders and to examine the impact of organizational context on their personal and professional choices. The program is filled with assessment exercises, private staff feedback sessions, and discussions of current research findings about women and leadership (Austin, 1992).

Not only has leadership education become a growth industry, but at least one author, a self-proclaimed foe of leadership studies (DeMott, 1993), believes it has become a cult embraced by both private and public entities: governmental bureaucracies, nonsectarian youth agencies, academic institutions, and the corporate complex. According to DeMott, "leadership education is a racket created by academics to cheat American taxpayers and the federal government" (DeMott, 1983, p. 61). In fact, DeMott is obviously disturbed with the leadership studies "racket," since he labeled it "choice academic pork." The author claims that the leadership studies cult is a specimen of "late 20th century academic avarice and a precise gauge of some recent professional descents into pap, cant and jargon." Skepticism of leadership studies as an academic discipline, and the gimmicky treatment of leadership in both the scholarly and popular literature, is healthy. However, among the realities of the last decade of this millennium is the fact that our personal, professional, and organizational lives have become increasingly complex so that individuals of all ages potentially profit from leadership—and including self-leadership—training.

In addition to formal leadership education programs, leaders need to spend more time educating themselves and others. As Starratt (1993) states:

> This means raising questions, challenging assumptions, asking for opinions, looking beyond tomorrow's solutions to the larger challenge. The leader must become something of a Socratic gadfly, bothering people enough until they begin to think more thoroughly, discuss them together, take time to appreciate the significance of what they are doing. The leader must encourage others to fashion a collective vision of where they should be going. (p. 148)

CONTEMPORARY APPROACHES TO LEARNING TO LEAD

Leadership education, training, and development have been around since the time of Socrates, who made it his business to prepare Athenian youths for leadership roles and paid with his life for these efforts. In *The Republic*, Plato pondered over how a society should carry out the education of its leaders. He advocated a common education of future leaders and everyone else to provide a foundation of common values and collective identities. Only later would future leaders be separated from other youth and receive specialized education, particularly through the study of philosophy.

Similarly, as noted in Chapter 9, Confucius, who taught his lessons in practical ethics around 500 B.C., derived a set of key principles from Chinese history that offer guidance for self- and leadership development. Since Plato's and Confucius' time, many leadership training programs have been implemented, some in the context of the military academies, others in the context of formal religions, and still others in the context of educational institutions. In fact, leadership training may be found anywhere. Gardner (1990) suggested that leaders are selected and educated by their culture, workplace, network, or the system; in short, in whatever setting they find themselves. Burnside (1990), called for new wine-skins in leadership education because the particular challenges of our time do not tolerate any rigidly applied approach or the application of a perspective formed long ago. Conger (1993a) agreed that much of what we learn about leadership today is based on requirements of previous decades, not on the challenges of the 21st century.

Requirements for 21st-Century Leadership

Before reviewing existing approaches to leadership education, we therefore need to ask ourselves what the requirements for 21st century leadership are, and examine to what extent current leadership programs meet these requirements. Gardner (1990) indicated that for leaders to function effectively in the complex world of today and tomorrow, "they need critically important skills that involve agreement-building, networking, the exercise of nonjurisdictional power, and institution-building" (p. 119). These are some of the skills that presumably come easier to women than men. Astin and Leland (1991) suggested that effective leadership demands the ability to assess a situation, to engage others in collective efforts, and to bring about needed change. Conger (1993a) emphasized that future leaders at all levels will have to become: 1) strategic opportunists; 2) globally aware; and 3) capable of managing highly decentralized organizations.

I believe that critical requirements for 21st century leaders include the ability to think metaphorically, globally, and futuristically. As discussed in Chapter 1, metaphors are powerful tools which empower new vision, new language, and cognitive schemata that allow us to think differently about leadership. Metaphors are instrumental in that they help us to tie various aspects of leadership together into a meaningful whole. Metaphors, therefore, give leadership new meaning because they are pervasive not just in language but in thought an action (Lackoff & Johnson, 1980). The need for leaders to think globally and develop cross-cultural competencies was highlighted in the last chapter. Finally, thinking futuristically challenges leaders to envision newer forms of leadership. It also steers leadership educators away from yesterday's leadership skills. However, despite the search for new leadership skills which fit the demands of the 21st century, it is recognized that tomorrow's leaders will continue to require many of the attributes that have always distinguished the best leaders—intelligence, commitment, energy, courage of conviction, and integrity (Huey, 1994b).

Many leadership experts agree that successful leaders must possess a special gift for forecasting change and anticipating reality. Organizational scholars (e.g., Beneviste, 1994) asserted that companies of the future are likely to be more fluid and less structured than the traditional hierarchical organization. Klenke (1994), among others, called attention to technological transformations that challenge the nature, purpose, and structure of contemporary organizations as organizational pyramids are being flattened and hierarchical structures dismantled. Old (bureaucratic) organizational designs are disappearing, a result of the trend of the quality revolution, information technology, consumerism, and globalization intersecting in the 1990s (Vroman, 1994). Organizational structures of tomorrow call for flexible, adaptive, even boundaryless forms that facilitate change and renewal. This means that leaders must be able to build cultures that are congruent with rapid technological and organizational change. Current research on emerging organizational forms suggests that women's leadership skills are well suited to such circumstances (e.g., Eagly, Makhijani, & Klonsky, 1992; Jurma & Wright, 1990).

A common theme present in most discussions of leadership for the 21st century is the leader's ability to create, articulate, and communicate not only a vision, but, more importantly, a global vision. Bennis (1990) talks about leaders managing the dream when he discussed the leader's capacity to create a compelling vision, one that takes people to a new place:

> While leaders come in every size, shape, and disposition—short, tall, neat, sloppy, young, old, male, and female—every leader I talked with shared at least one characteristic: a concern with a guiding purpose, an overarching vision. (p. 44)

The "vision thing" has indeed become an overarching concept when thinking about leadership requirements for the next century. Organizations whose leaders have no vision are doomed to work under the burden of mere tradition; they cannot prosper and grow, because they are reduced to keeping things the way they have always been (Snyder & Graves, 1994). The "vision thing" has been an important rhetoric in the last presidential elections and came to be known as the "V word." As Wendt and Fairhurst (1994) reminded us, "Bush's labeling of the "vision thing" became a campaign issue and produced candidates who tried to pass themselves off as leaders with a vision" (p. 181). Similarly, Clinton highlighted the vision process when he introduced the "New Covenant."

Yet "vision" is difficult to define. A leader's vision is different from the mission of the organization and its strategic plan. Haas (1992) captured these differences when he said that "vision is what we can be, mission is what we want to be, and the strategic plan is how we get there" (p. 138). Thus, a leader's vision implies an understanding of the present and the past. More important, as Quigley (1994) noted, "it offers a road map to the future—how people are to act and interact to attain what they regard as desirable" (p. 37). Likewise Hitt (1988) suggested that "leaders inhabit the future (compared to managers who live in the present); they perceive their accountability to be defined in terms of future change, progress, or results. They eat, drink, and sleep the future while seeing the present as simply a transition point from past to future" (p. 250). In addition to the future orientation, for most leaders, the vision includes the organization's most fundamental values, aspirations, and goals.

Korn/Ferry International recently conducted a survey of 1,500 senior business leaders from 20 different countries asking them to describe key traits or talents desirable for CEOs today and important for CEOs in the year 2000. The majority of the respondents indicated that the ability to imagine, articulate, and communicate a "strong sense of vision" was the most important attribute of a CEO, both now and in the future. In fact, 98% of the business leaders identified it as the single most important ability of CEOs for the year 2000 (Korn, 1989).

For many leadership theorists and practitioners, vision has become a requisite of leadership. Conger, Kanungo and Associates (1988) believe that visioning skills can be enhanced in several ways. The authors recommend courses in creative thinking to stimulate a person's capacity of contemplating change. One program, the LEADER LAB at the Center of Creative Leadership, uses visualization to expand participants' ability to capture the leadership dilemmas they are facing and to envision change. The program helps participants to identify, articulate, and carry out their visions and translate them into reality and action. However, despite widespread interest in it and its intuitive appeal, vision remains a hypothetical, intangible construct connoting meaning more than denoting it (Kriger, 1990). Nevertheless, few would disagree with Reagan who believed that to grasp and hold a vision is the very essence of successful leadership everywhere.

Preparations for Leadership

Because leadership is multidimensional, its development can be approached from a number of perspectives (Burnside & Guthrie, 1992). Preparing women and men for leadership roles may be accomplished through training, education, development, and experience. Although interrelated, leadership training, education, and development represent different approaches to preparing tomorrow's leader. According to Calás and Smircich (1993) the difference between training and education is the difference between being a doer and being a thinker, between technical competence and knowledge.

Conger (1992) suggested that leadership training today falls into one of four categories: 1) skill building programs, which include training in decisionmaking, communication, conflict resolution, and visioning skills; 2) conceptual approaches, designed around theoretical concepts, such as the distinction between leaders and managers; 3) outdoor ventures, designed to build teamwork and experiment with risk-taking; and 4) feedback programs, which provide participants with information on how they rank on a set of leadership dimensions. These approaches are described in greater detail in the following section.

Leadership training is geared to the development of discrete skills that contribute to leadership effectiveness. Conger and Kanungo (1988) suggest that all forms of leadership training serve two basic functions:

> First, they provide an individual with an awareness of the nature and dynamics of leadership and with the various behaviors involved in it. Furthermore, through training the individual discovers his or her own standing with respect to these behaviors and thereby his or her potential for developing leadership qualities. This is the information function of training. The second basic function of training is to build the requisite skills for fulfilling leadership roles. In order to achieve this skill-building function, training must provide opportunities to develop new modes of behavior and attitudes and to practice matching them to a predetermined standard. (pp. 312–313)

In general, leadership training is relatively narrow in scope, focusing on task-specific applications and skills. Leadership skills as currently taught in training programs are simplistic, one-dimensional descriptions of behavior, such as how to listen more effectively or delegate more often (Burnside & Guthrie, 1992). Compared to leadership education and leadership development, which require a longer time horizon, training is usually short-term in nature. Most leadership training programs are offered by commercial vendors in the form of workshops and seminars.

Leadership education, as used here, refers to formal academic programs in leadership. These programs are typically designed to develop the learner's capacity to think critically about complex leadership issues and situations. In contrast to leadership training, which emphasizes skill development, leadership education programs stress cognitive processes. In the past, leadership courses and programs at colleges and universities focused on leadership theories and group dynamics; now they cover a variety of leadership related issues, such as community leadership, motivation, multiculturalism, and leadership internship courses.

Many of the women and men who will be our leaders in the year 2005 have now completed college and are working in their first jobs. Individuals who are preparing themselves today for future leadership roles need assignments that provide them with opportunities to apply theory to practice and test the utility of leadership theories learned in school. They need organizations willing to serve as leadership incubators, so that aspiring leaders can experiment with new approaches to leadership developed by a generation that has less investment in established theories. Aristotle believed that young people have exalted notions because they have not been humbled by life or learned its necessary limitations. The young women and men who will be tomorrow's leaders need years of experience to fine-tune and perfect their leadership skills. They need the lessons of experience to fulfill their leadership potential. They are also the young people who have to make their contributions to the study of leadership to ensure that we do not teach tomorrow's leaders leadership theories and principles of yesterday. And some of them have to accept the daunting task of educating leaders of the generation that follows them.

Leadership development presupposes that leadership development is a lifelong endeavor which unfolds over a person's lifespan. According to Burnside & Guthrie (1992) leadership development can be seen as a process of gaining increased self-awareness, planning and carrying out more effective actions, and seeking ways of sustaining development over time. Alternately, leadership development may also be viewed as a series of paradigm shifts, from dependence to independence to interdependence (Covey, 1989). Most of us start the developmental process of becoming a leader in a dependent state; we are relying on previous approaches to leadership, which are based on value and belief systems inherited from our family and society at large. As we mature toward independence, we become more self-reliant because we learn from our leadership successes and failures, and grow increasingly more confident in our leadership abilities and competencies. According to Covey, interdependence is a choice that only independent women and men can make.

Developing oneself as a leader takes time. If we take leadership development seriously, it occupies much of our life space across the entire lifespan. As the lifespan has stretched so, too, have our leadership resources (Astin & Leland, 1991). Several developmental models with a long-term horizon are found in the literature that have specific implications for leadership development. Morrison (1992), for example, introduced a three-component model of leadership development. The three elements of the model are challenge, recognition, and support. The author describes these three elements as follows: 1) the *challenge* of new situations and difficult goals prompts leaders to learn the lessons that will help them perform at higher levels; 2) *recognition* includes acknowledgement of achievements and rewards for accomplishments, along with resources to continue high performance; while 3) *support* entails acceptance and understanding, along with the benefits that help a leader incorporate her leadership role into a full and fulfilling life. Morrison's model assumes that to sustain development, all three elements must be present in the same relative proportion over time.

Levinson's (1986) lifespan model of adult development emphasizes the importance of transitions between major periods of the life cycle. For example, the author discusses the dynamics of the early adult transition as the developmental period from 17 to 22, during which preadulthood draws to a close and the era of early adulthood gets under way. Likewise, the midlife transition, from roughly age 40 to 45, brings about the termination of early adulthood and the start of middle adulthood. Each transition period is marked by a specific developmental task. The central task of midlife transition, for example, is a new step in individuation. To the extent that this occurs, Levinson argues, we become more compassionate, more reflective and judicious, attributes which not only apply to human development but are also relevant to leadership. The author also uses the metaphor of seasons when discussing phases of the lifespan, and their corresponding transitions, which raises the question whether there are seasons in leadership development as there are seasons in love, war, politics, and artistic creation.

Developing leaders also experience transitional periods in which new leadership may replace the old. New top business leaders, for example, are expected to adjust their leadership quickly to produce bottom-line results, model a clear and compelling vision, and establish credibility and trust and adjust their leadership style to a new context. What was once a new CEO's honeymoon has been recast as a period of early vulnerability for top executives (Frederickson, Hambrick, & Baumrin, 1988). Levinson's work suggests that leadership development programs should be keyed to stages and transition points in a person's development. Thus, a mapping of leadership processes on Levinson's conception of human development may result in innovative approaches to leadership development that are consistent with a lifespan development perspective.

Finally, none of the approaches just described can afford to overlook the importance of *experience*. Leaders at all levels need practice, practice, and more practice to yield new knowledge from their experiences, which can be applied to the future leadership situations in which they find themselves. They also need opportunities to test concepts and theories in a variety of leadership situations and in different contexts. We can teach aspiring leaders a lot, including how to be more imaginative, to communicate better, and to think critically, and to be more self-aware. But leadership education, training, and development must be enhanced by lessons learned from experience, which according to one author make up 80% of a leader's growth, the remaining 20% are shaped by training and study (Main, 1987).

Experience is gathered through job assignments or rotations, startup ventures, willingness to confront and deal with failure, mentorships and other significant relationships, high stakes, and challenging the barriers to leadership opportunities faced by women and people of color. Adair (1993) summarized the role of experience and practice in developing leaders as follows:

All the academic study of leadership does is to teach one about leadership, not how to lead. It is certainly useful for people to clarify their concepts of leadership, either as a prelude or as an interlude in the practical work of leading others. But leadership is learned primarily through doing, and nothing can replace the necessary cycle of experiment, trail-and-error, success and failure, followed by reflection and reading. (p. 371)

Job experiences are receiving increasing recognition as a potent form of leadership development (Heisler & Benham, 1992; Ohlott, Ruderman, & McCauley, 1994). Key job assignments can place high potential women in positions of visibility and serve as developmental experiences for future leadership opportunities. They also may be instrumental in changing the ways in which women solve problems, handle decisions, and approach risk-taking.

LEADERSHIP TRAINING, EDUCATION, AND DEVELOPMENT PROGRAMS

Conger (1992) participated in several leadership programs which he described in a book entitled *Learning to Lead*. He classified the different approaches as: 1) leadership training through personal growth; 2) leadership development through conceptual understanding; 3) leadership development through feedback; and 4) leadership development through skill-building. In this section, these four approaches are reviewed. Subsequently, we will take a look at leadership programs specifically designed for women.

Personal Growth Programs

Programs in this class build on personal growth groups; examples are the National Training Laboratory (NLT) in Bethel, Maine; Outward Bound; and EST (Ehrhard Training Seminar), which were particularly popular in the 1980s. Central to EST is a 60-hour marathon experience, spread over two weekends, that combined elements of a conventional encounter group with the rigors of a Marine Corps boot camp (Conger, 1993b). NLT puts participants in touch with their feelings, while Outward Bound programs are designed to foster personal growth through wilderness adventures. According to Conger (1993b) wilderness programs are marketed to the corporate world as a means of building teams and encouraging greater leadership and risk-taking in the office. The basic premise of these programs is if managers could successfully repel cliffs and raft whitewater rapids, they could exhibit greater boldness, risk-taking, and teamwork back on the job. Haldeman (1995) notes that there was a time when ''corporate types drew inspiration from sales sermons and pep rallies; today it's high wires and zig lines''

(p. 60). According to the author, more than 100 organizations nationwide now offer risk-filled adventures to employers and employees seeking to boost morale and promote leadership.

Conger (1992) attended one Outward Bound program, the Pecos Learning Center in Santa Fe, New Mexico, which he described as an adventure-based, outdoor experience designed to push participants past their personal safety boundaries. The program consists of three parts, the first of which provides an introduction to individual and organizational change. The second part involves outdoor activities such as rock-climbing, a blind trust walk, cliff jump (used as a metaphor for risk-taking in life), and crossing a river over a rope bridge. The third part is intended to help participants achieve greater personal intimacy and a personal vision. Many personal growth programs rest on the premise that self-awareness is a catalyst for change.

Main (1987) quoted one business leader who participated in an Outward Bound program:

When people walk across a beam 25 feet above the ground (with a safety line attached), the apprehension that showed at their faces at the beginning and the triumph at the end—all of it captured on videotape for replay later in the day—brought out the feelings that they all have when they undertake a new project and complete it. And the encouragement and cheers of other executives showed how much support can mean at the office, even for the most senior people. (p. 100)

Outdoor training is an unconventional approach to developing leaders, which promotes both individual initiative and effective team-building. According to Carlton (1993) experiential learning in the form of outdoor experience invites the heart, the head, and the body to engage with the experience. The author argued that:

Whatever way the outdoor is managed for leadership development, the human response will add yet another huge set of variables to the overall larder of experience. The intellectual, emotional, and physical response of an individual will change and change again in relation to other individuals' changing responses, or as groups interact with other groups. The permutations of the learning experience are as endless as they are powerful in outdoor programs. (p. 457)

The major question raised by leadership training programs through outdoor ventures deals with the transfer of learning, since the context of outdoor adventures and the leader's daily environment are very different from one another. Drawing links between a whitewater rafting trip and organizational leadership may be easy for poets and actors, but is less clear to leaders facing global challenges in uncertain environments. Therefore, there may be little point in sending a person to an outdoor leadership program unless the learning acquired in the program is pertinent to the leader's daily setting. Finally, many of the "rocks and ropes" programs are designed with male leaders in mind; little is known about how many women participate in these programs and whether or not their experiences differ from those of men. In his evaluation of personal growth training as a means of developing leaders, Conger (1993b) concluded that it is clear that these programs offer opportunities to experience teamwork, risk-taking, self-acceptance, and reflection. However, the question of whether they are related to leading others at work cannot be affirmatively answered.

Conceptual Approaches

According to Huey (1994b), programs in this group are built on the idea that if you grasp the context, you can act on it. These leadership education programs, whether offered as executive leadership programs through universities, such as Harvard, Wharton, and Kellogg, or independent consultant firms, such as the Tom Peters Group, have a strong cognitive and intellectual component. The distinguishing feature of the programs in this category is that they are designed around leadership concepts and theories which are supplemented by exercises, assessments, cases, and simulations. In these programs, learning is largely cognitive.

On the academic side, the education of leaders at colleges and universities has led to the widespread observation in many countries that leaders emerged from certain elite institutions, such as the Ivy League schools in the U.S., Tokyo University, Oxford, and the military academies. The University of Tokyo, for example, more than any of the country's other elite institutions, educates Japan's future leaders for global competition. Proficiency in foreign languages is stressed because it makes a difference to future leaders in the areas of mutual understanding, international diplomacy, and establishing global alliances and networks. American and British universities, on the other hand, have less stringent requirements about language proficiency, relying on the ubiquitous use of the English language.

In several countries, including France and Japan, future leaders and managers are directly recruited from graduates of a small number of elite universities offering the Master of Business Administration (MBA) degree, the goal of which is to prepare students for positions of business leadership. These schools, until very recently, have been male-dominated. INSEAD, the leading business school in France, reported that the past few classes have been averaging 12% women among the new students. Similarly, IESE, the major business school in Barcelona, Spain, counts 17% of women among its MBA students (Bebbington, 1988).

However, as this author reported, when we look at programs beyond the MBA degree, the number of women enrolled in executive development programs is considerably smaller. According to Bebbington, only once over the past 3 years has the proportion of women in INSEAD's development courses for executives approached 4%. At the London School of Economics, where the percentage of women in MBA and executive development programs has been the highest, the proportion of women enrolled in executive development programs is still disappointing but not negligible, hovering around 6%. The low representation of women in these programs results from a combination of factors, including admission policies which favor previous executive experience, and societal stereo- types regarding fast-tracking female executives that prevent women from seeking admission. By not gaining access to elite schools, women are excluded from one critical path of gaining access to business leadership.

The realities of the educational systems in some countries result in early exclusion of women from leadership opportunities. In Japan, for example, as Steinhoff and Tanaka (1994) observed, college men are recruited for managerial careers, while women are selected for clerical jobs. Similarly, the apprenticeship system in Germany, which absorbs 60% of high school graduates and represents the main bridge from school to work, routes young girls into non-managerial paths. In both cases, once excluded, it is almost impossible for women to pursue the management route in later years (Berthoin Antal & Izraeli, 1993).

Some programs in this category of conceptual approaches to leadership education are derived from specific leadership theories. Learning about leadership is based on discussions of concepts and applications of theoretical concepts to real-life leadership problems. Klenke (1993) discussed some of the prescriptions and descriptions for leadership education embedded in leadership theories (see Chapter 3) from which leadership education programs have been developed. Theoretical perspectives such as the behavioral, situational, and social exchange approaches assume that women and men become leaders by learning leader behaviors or leadership styles, participating in leadership situations, or seeking leadership development opportunities, rather than because of innate personality traits.

Theoretically grounded leadership education programs have been derived from Fiedler's (1967) contingency theory, Graen's (Graen & Cashman, 1975) social exchange theory, and Bass's (1985) transformational theory of leadership. For example, LEADER MATCH (Fiedler, Chemers, & Mahar, 1976) is a training program modeled after Fiedler's contingency theory of leadership. LEADER MATCH assumes that since appropriate personal characteristics of the leader are not amenable to change, training must focus on changing the situations leaders find themselves in. The training program is designed to allow leaders to identify their leadership style (task- or relationship-oriented, for example), which, ac- cording to Fiedler, is a function of the leader's personality and several situational variables, including task structure, group morale, and leader position power. Leaders can then modify the leadership situation to produce the best outcome for themselves, given their leadership style. Thus, LEADER MATCH intends to improve the skill of leaders and increase their effectiveness in understanding and managing situational contingencies.

Graen's social exchange theory, also known as vertical dyad linkage (VDL), departs from the premise that leaders establish a special exchange relationship with a small number of trusted followers (the "in group"). On the other hand, the exchange relationship established with the remaining followers (the "out group"), is substantially different. Graen developed a leader training program based on VDL concepts, which is designed to enhance leaders' goal-setting and negotiation skills; Graen et al. reported that VDL based training for leaders resulted in real group productivity improvements (Graen, Novak, & Sommerkamp, 1992). The training program accomplished these improvements through an activity called "dyadic contracting." This means that the leader is trained to assess her or his power to produce results valued by in-group followers and negotiate the exchange of these outcomes for desired follower behaviors and performance levels (McElroy & Stark, 1992, p. 245).

Still another conceptually based program, the Transformational Leadership Development program, was introduced by Bass (1985). This program employs instrument developed by Bass known as the Multifactor Leadership Questionnaire (MLQ), discussed in Chapter 3, which classifies leaders as either transactional or transformational. Based on their scores on this assessment, which is completed before training, leaders who wish to become transformational participate in a program that includes training in such skills as communication, analytical problemsolving, team-building, role-modeling, and the development of a personal leadership plan based on feedback of participants' leader behaviors. In addition to workshops, this program includes a 3-month interval during which participants diagnose key areas for improving transformational leadership and develop a broader understanding of its associated behaviors. Leadership training that employs the transformational theme, despite its skill component, is nevertheless basically a conceptual approach (McElroy & Stark, 1992).

On the commercial side, "The Leadership Challenge" was developed by Kouzes and Posner (1987) and is offered through Tom Peters's management consulting firm (Peters is the author of *In Search of Excellence*). The Leadership Challenge uses a five-step model of leadership which promises participants extraordinary results in their organizations. The five-step model includes the following parts:

1) leaders challenge the process; this means that they are pioneers willing to step out into the unknown, take risks, and experiment with novel solutions;

2) leaders inspire a shared vision and get others to buy into their dreams;
3) leaders enable others to act; that is, they do not achieve success by themselves, but enlist the support of others in the form of teamwork and collaboration;
4) leaders model the way or lead by example; and finally
5) leaders encourage the heart, which they accomplish by celebrating milestones, recognizing accomplishments, and individual contributions.

According to Kouzes and Posner, these practices are not the private properties of leaders, but are available to anyone who wants to accept the leadership challenge (1987).

Feedback Programs

Feedback is an important training technique that has been used to change many leadership behaviors, including women's and men's self-evaluations as leaders, achievement ratings, and performance feedback. Observation has shown that leadership skills increase after feedback. Likewise, research reveals that feedback influences leaders' self-ratings and followers' ratings, and that women and men respond differently to feedback. Women are often socialized to be more sensitive and react more strongly to negative feedback, or disapproval than men. This was shown by Roberts and Nolen-Hoeksma (1989) who found that women's self-evaluations were affected differently by positive and negative feedback, while men's were not. The authors found that women were more willing to modify their own evaluations in line with what they heard from others, while men treated others' evaluations with skepticism and maintained a positive outlook about their abilities.

This third category of Conger's (1992) classification of leadership programs employs feedback after the assessment of an individual's leadership style. A good example of a feedback-oriented program is the Leadership Development Program, offered by the Center of Creative Leadership, a nonprofit educational institution specializing in leadership training for managers and executives. This 6-day program employs a combination of tests, surveys, assessment exercises, and individual goal-setting. It is based on the philosophy that effective leadership development begins with assessment of self and others and constructive feedback from several sources, such as Center staff, peers, and via instrumentation.

Skill Building Programs

The term "skill," according to Yukl (1994), refers to a person's ability to perform various types of cognitive and behavioral activities in an effective manner. Skills can be aligned on a continuum ranging from the general, such as the interpersonal or administrative type, to the specific, such as listening, conflict resolution, or decisionmaking skills. One of the most commonly used classifications of leadership and management skills divides them into three groups: 1) *technical* skills, which involve methods, processes, and procedures pertinent to task performance; 2) *interpersonal* skills, which include empathy, diplomacy, and persuasiveness; and 3) *conceptual* skills, such as problemsolving ability, convergent and divergent thinking, concept formation, and idea generation (Katz, 1955). As Mann (1965) pointed out, technical skills are primarily concerned with things, interpersonal skills deal primarily with people, and conceptual skills deal with ideas and concepts.

Many leadership skills programs are offered by consulting firms or sold by commercial vendors. These programs rely on skills that are teachable, provide participants with concrete experiences, and target tangible leadership skills that, at least in theory, are applicable to the realities of organizational life. Since skills are behavioral, skill-building assumes that the potential for improving leadership effectiveness through skill practice exists. Therefore, skill-building programs usually involve a heavy dose of practical applications.

These four categories of leadership training, education, and development programs may not be all-inclusive, but Conger's (1992) taxonomy provides a useful overview of the kinds of leadership programs available for practicing, aspiring, and potential leaders at all levels. Life-long learning is increasingly stressed not only for individuals but some of the responsibility for such learning has been shifted to the organization. Peter Senge (1990a, 1990b) coined the term the "learning organization," an organizational system characterized by its capacity to adapt to rapid environmental changes. The "learning organization" promotes systems thinking, creativity and shared vision, personal efficacy, team learning, and challenging mental models. In "learning organizations," the leaders of these organizations are charged with leadership development; they are "responsible for building organizations where people are continually expanding their capabilities to shape their future—that is, leaders are responsible for learning" (Senge, 1990b, p. 442).

LEADERSHIP TRAINING, EDUCATION, AND DEVELOPMENT: FOR WOMEN ONLY

Leadership educators, practitioners, and consultants have grappled with the question of whether women require special consideration to become effective leaders, and, if so, what kind of training is needed. Initially, special leadership programs were developed because of the commonly held assumption that the way to place women in leadership positions was to provide them with additional training.

These programs depart from the assumption that if barriers to women's leadership are identified and removed, women do not need special consideration. Programs in this category are designed to help women to "catch up" with their male colleagues by substituting training for experience in the workplace, which women are presumed to lack.

Despite women's achievements in education, industry, government, and non-traditional occupations, the belief persists that they are not tough enough to handle difficult leadership situations. As a result, universities, commercial vendors, and women's professional associations have designed programs specifically for women. Like the rest of the programs promising the consumer to develop the leader within, "leadership-for-women-only-programs" are a profitable business. Bennis (1988) assessed the proliferation of these programs as follows:

> What we see today are all kinds of workshops and seminars where women undergo metaphorical sex change, where they acquire a tough-talking, no nonsense, sink or swim philosophy. Ironically, men are simultaneously asked to shed the same masculine character traits that women are encouraged to imitate through their own form of non-assert-iveness and sensitivity training programs. So it's ok, even better than ok for old Charlie to cry in his office. How marvelous! How liberating! Women impersonate the macho male stereotype and men impersonate the counter-macho stereotype of the women. (p. 44)

While the above quote is now somewhat dated, since most women have learned that emulating men does not guarantee success, promotion, or access to leadership, it still carries a message. The message is, as Shavlik and Touchton (1988) contend, that if women had not been so busy emulating men, they would have contributed their own ideas derived from personal experiences at work and at home. Instead, most women have been concerned with trying to change themselves, rather than their places of work. It is only recently that organizations realized that they need to make places of work more hospitable for women.

Many of the for-women-only leadership training programs are targeted at first-line supervisors and entry-level managerial women. The majority offer one or two-day workshops or seminars. Women's participation in high-ticket items, such as the one-week "Women Leadership" program offered by the Center of Creative Leadership, or the executive development programs at Ivy League universities, is more limited.

Women not only have limited access to leadership opportunities, but to educational opportunities that enhance their development of leadership skills and competencies. Many women remember encountering differential learning opportunities as early as their elementary and secondary school years. Research has shown that both male and female teachers foster the intellectual and profes-sional development of males and often overlook the contributions of female students. These patterns, established in elementary and secondary school, continue in higher education, despite legal mandates such as the passage of Title IX in 1972. This legislation outlawed sex discrimination in education programs receiving federal funds. As a result of this law, fields traditionally reserved for males, such as engineering and medicine, have enrolled increasing numbers of females. However, women continue to run into barriers in their quest for leadership by being treated differently in classroom situations.

Thus, public policy and education do not fundamentally change the prevailing perception that women who wish to be leaders have to be extremely well qualified, possess a proven record of accomplishments, and be overprepared for their positions (Shavlik & Touchton, 1988). Thus stereotypes persist and women are often required to go the extra mile (i.e., exceptional performance is expected of them). Coupled with stereotypes and additional performance requirements are women's own negative attitudes against women in leadership roles. Instead of developing differential training programs, organizations and institutions of higher learning need to foster a gender-positive environment (Leong, Snodgrass, & Gardner, 1992). This is defined as a setting in which gender does not work as a negative factor in evaluating a person's individual worth and leadership potential. A gender-positive environment is one "in which the dominant value set luxuriates in diversity and innovation" (Leong et al., 1992, p. 217). If we add to this gender-positive environment a leadership driven milieu in which the organization or community breaks with current traditions, stereotypes, and past approaches to leadership and makes leadership development a priority, not only women and men but society will benefit.

LEADERSHIP DEVELOPMENT AS SELF-DEVELOPMENT

Preparation for leadership roles, whether through education, development, or training, begins as a process of self-development and self-leadership. Many leaders are self-taught and gain their leadership skills through trial and error. Philosophers from the ancient Greeks to Confucius have taught us that only by knowing ourselves can we know others and lead them. Thus, one of the main tasks of the leader is to assume responsibility for her own development. Centuries ago, Lao-Tze said:

> A leader is best when people barely know he exists. Not so good when people obey and acclaim him. Worse when they despise him. If you fail to honor people, they fail to honor you. But of a good leader, who talks little, when his work is done, his aim fulfilled, they will say "we did it ourselves." (quoted in Adair, 1989, p. 45)

Burnside and Guthrie (1992) believe there are two major aspects to self-development of leaders: learning to learn and clarifying one's sense of purpose. We discussed the importance of learning from experience earlier in this chapter. While most leaders acknowledge the importance of their formal education, significant learning experiences are gathered after they receive their formal education. Kolb (1983) argued that experiential learning methods are best suited to the developmental needs of adults. They include analyses of leadership situations, reflection on action, introspection, or maintenance of personal journals. Learning to learn is not limited to experiential learning. Leaders need:

> To learn to help others to learn how to learn; to share their knowledge without letting their intentions become orders; to work with groups as equals as well as leaders; to be open to influence from those who question the most basic truths; to encourage creative thinking; and to inspire others to make the same commitments to organizational success they did when others entrusted them to make important decisions. (Fry & Pasmore, 1983, p. 296)

When discussing sense of purpose, Burnside and Guthrie (1992) noted that identifying one's own sense of purpose, that is, the ideals towards which leaders are striving, is necessary before these leaders can build a shared sense of purpose which followers are willing to commit to. Closely related to self-development is self-leadership, a term which Manz (1983) introduced as a leadership alternative designed to involve people in the development of their own leadership. The author starts with the assumption that to understand our own self-leadership practices, we must know the importance of who we are and how we view the world (Manz, 1991). Self-leadership also requires that we exercise control over ourselves through strategies such as self-observation (i.e., determining when, why, and under what conditions we engage in certain behaviors), self-goal setting to include both short-term and long-term objectives, and the use of self-reward and self-punishment. In addition to these behavioral strategies, the mental aspect of self-leadership, labeled "inner leadership," focuses on individuals' leading themselves by employing cognitive strategies such as self-talk and mental imagery (Manz & Neck, 1991). Self-leadership can be practiced in many contexts, from families to large-scale organizations.

Finally, self-help books have added yet another dimension to leadership development. These how-to books generally focus on a limited set of leadership concepts or skills to help the reader improve her leadership skills. Examples in this category are Tom Peters's *The One Minute Manager* and Stephen Covey's *The 7 Habits of Highly Effective People*. Leadership competencies covered in these self-help books typically include motivation, decisionmaking, and communications.

CONCLUSIONS

Conger (1993a) argued that our approaches to developing leaders will have to change, which means putting aside our current models. One way of changing how we develop leaders is through systematic integration of education, training, and experience, all of which enhance self-development and self-leadership. Such programs must acknowledge that leadership is multidimensional and dynamic and requires a strong motivation to lead along with a complex set of leadership skills. Development of single-sex leadership training programs raises many questions about how women's leadership is defined and whether or not women have particular training needs. While some of them may be well-intentioned, since they represent action to increase women's access to leadership opportunities, they do not address the basic issue, namely challenging the dominant cultures in our organizations and institutions. Corporations, educational institutions, government agencies, and community organizations must be responsive to the developmental needs, including leadership development, of both women and men, and incorporate diversity into training programs. They must make a commitment to identify, encourage, and develop individuals with the desire and motivation to lead, and promote new and different thinking about leadership so that women and men can discover pathways to lead themselves and others effectively.

11 Conclusions

> A mind once stretched to a new idea never goes back to its original dimension.
>
> *Oliver Wendell Holmes*

In this book, we examined women's access to leadership and women in leadership roles, and how these roles are embedded in the context in which both women and men exercise leadership. Women's roles as leaders in diverse contexts, such as politics, history, religion, sports, and technology, to name only a few, were discussed to reinforce the fundamental premise of this book, namely that leadership is always dependent on context. Moreover, in addition to this contextual perspective, I have argued that the relationship between gender and leadership is primarily, although not only, cultural. To bring some coherence to the complex interactions between gender, leadership, and culture, I offered the prism metaphor as a series of interconnected lenses as a contextual framework to study women and leadership.

If there is one word that captures the essence of contemporary organizations, societies, nations, and cultures, it is the word "change." The changes we are facing in today's and tomorrow's world demand a new breed of leaders and the creation of a new leadership agenda. Women leaders are very much part of the widespread change processes, which are both revolutionary and evolutionary.

The days when women leaders were viewed as deficit males are a relic of the past. However much admired women, such as Rosie the Riveter (the epitome of the female workforce during World War II), Queen Victoria (the monarch), Madame Pompadour (mistress of Louis XV), and Oprah Winfrey (the talkfest mogul), the days when they were treated as special cases who inhabit the furthest reaches of ordinary existence also belong to yesterday's world. Instead of treating women leaders as exceptions or anomalies who are categorized as "women leaders," and not just "leaders," we have to acknowledge that the number of women leaders will eventually reach a critical mass. As Kuhn (1970) noted, when the number of anomalies to a paradigm grows to a critical mass, we are forced to reconcile that paradigm.

The exigencies of global competition, deregulation of many industries, and accelerating technological innovations dictate change. Contemporary organizations, from families to nations, respond to this "brave new world" by restructuring, reengineering, and reinventing themselves. Flexible networks are replacing hierarchical organizations. These new organizational forms, delayered, downsized, and operating through a network of market-sensitive business units are changing the global business terrain (Snow, Miles, & Coleman, 1992). Global thinking is taking the place of national perspectives. Globalization today, according to Snow et al. (1992), is a "compelling reality, with at least 70–85% of the economy of the United States feeling the impact of foreign competition" (p. 5). Burnside and Guthrie (1992) believe that the changes and challenges of the next century are so serious that they could virtually paralyze leaders.

Demographic shifts are adding yet another dimension to the changes taking place globally as increasingly so-called minorities, including women and Hispanics, are becoming large majorities. With the increases of women and minorities in the workplace and the shrinking numbers of white males, women and minorities can no longer be denied access to leadership.

It is against this rapidly changing landscape that we need to reframe our leadership theories and practices. In Chapter 1, I raised the question of how to define leadership so that contemporary definitions do not exclude half of our population, that is, women. Yet the dynamics of our times make it virtually impossible to come forward with an all-encompassing definition of leadership that can fully account for the range of theories and applications to which we are exposed. As a result, from a definitional perspective, leadership remains a "dance of ambivalence" (Leland, 1994, personal communication).

The scientific quest for a generic model of leadership has given way to multidisciplinary approaches which have replaced single-paradigm models drawn, for example, from specific disciplines, such as social psychology or political science. The roots of leadership have been sought in traits, behaviors, and situational contingencies. Deciphering the roots of leadership is as much a challenge today as it was when the formal study of leadership began around the turn of the century. One of the roots identified by early leadership scholars is the extensive use of personality traits. Among the traits that have been discerned regularly among effective leaders are dependability, an achievement orientation, dominance, extroversion, self-confidence, intelligence, energy, emotional stability, and openness to experience (Kets de Vries, 1994). The scope of approaches discussed here ranged from trait theory to deconstructionism and cross-cultural studies. Until the current generation of leadership theories, including transactional, transformational, visionary, and charismatic leadership, came on the scene, most models focused on attributes of the leader, such as traits and behaviors, rather than on the interaction between leaders and followers. Today, leadership studies is a field made up of many interpretive perspectives, and representing different scholarly approaches and cultural practices. One specific interpretive community is created by female leadership scholars and women practicing leadership in many different contexts.

Consistent with the contextual perspective adopted here, instead of asking the question, "Do female and male leaders act similarly?", we need to ask, "In what contexts and under what conditions do female and male leaders act similarly?" Attempts to generalize about the leadership qualities or abilities that women possess upon closer examination seem to collapse like a house of cards (Adair, 1989). As pointed out in Chapter 6, gender-based discrimination, and biological and socialization differences between women and men either individually and collectively fail to account for the magnitude of the differences between female and male leaders. Even in recent studies (e.g., Atwater & Roush, 1994) conducted in settings such as the military academies, which actively recruit women for leadership positions, the number of women leaders is relatively small (around 10%).

Because of our inability to account for the small number of women leaders and because of the fact that research on women leaders is hampered by the small number of women found in leadership roles, current discussions have shifted to a gender-holistic, humanitarian perspective (e.g., Eisler, 1991). This perspective gives equal value to female and male leaders. Epstein (1991) stated:

> It is up to leaders of business and other institutions to affirm the humanitarian values that women are associated with but that men also can (and do) express if they are not made to feel embarrassed about showing them. And those qualities of toughness and drive that many men are made feel comfortable with should be prized in women who wish to express them when they are appropriate. The category is "people," not men and women. (p. 151)

Similarly, Driscoll and Goldberg (1993) suggested that organizations that seek the talent of both genders must reexamine their own cultures from top to bottom, to determine if gender differences affect what women strive for and achieve as leaders. The authors believe that the glass ceiling may just turn out to be nothing more than a misfit between a male-created corporate culture and the psychological development and life experiences of women who work there.

Effective leadership depends on a complex pattern of interactions among leaders, followers, and situations. The way individual elements of this interaction pattern combine is determined by the contexts in which female and male leaders are found. Today's generation of leaders, whether female or male, is characterized by being more open to consensus-building, participation in decisionmaking, and empowerment of followers. An earlier preoccupation with leadership tasks has been replaced by the mutuality and reciprocity of leader-follower relations. Today's leaders formulate and communicate a shared vision of the future that creates a common ground among people of differing views and responds creatively to the dynamic changes. According to Burnside (1990):

> This is the kind of leading that has the will to build a new future out of the materials of the present. This kind of leading thinks globally, seeks to embrace all of humanity socially, and acts to create a future out of the particular situation in which it finds itself. (p. 3)

This book, by design, does not provide the reader with ready-made answers or quick-fix solutions to leadership problems and challenges. Instead, it offers a conceptual framework for women and men to analyze leadership issues in the context in which leader-follower relationships are observed or experienced. The one certainty that does exist is that in today's and tomorrow's environments, women and men need to learn the strengths of each other's leadership styles and practices. They need to support each other's ways of leading, as opposed to treating one approach as necessarily better than the other. Both female and male leaders and followers share the concern about the future because that is where they are spending their lives. For women, as newcomers to the art, science, and practice of leadership,

> there is a tide in the affairs of women which, taken
> at the flood, leads God knows where.
>
> *Lord Byron*

REFERENCES

Abadan, N. (1967). Turkey. In R. Patai (Ed.), *Women in the modern world* (pp. 82–105). New York: Free Press.

Abrams, M. (1981). The woman's world of Jesse Barnard. *Graduate Woman, 75*, 4, 24–29.

Abramson, P., Goldberg, P., Greenberg, H., and Abramson, L. (1977). The Talking Platypus Phenomenon: Competency ratings as a function of sex and professional status. *Psychology of Women Quarterly, 2*, 114–124.

Aburdene, P., & Naisbitt, J. (1992). *Megatrends for women*. New York: Villard.

Acker, J. (1990). Hierarchies, jobs, and bodies. *Gender and Society, 4*, 139–158.

Adair, J. (1989). *Great leaders*. Surrey, England: The Talbot Adair Press.

Adair, J. (1993). Leadership skills. In M. Syrett & C. Hogg (Eds.), *Frontiers of leadership* (pp. 371–372). Cambridge, MA: Blackwell.

Adler, N., & Izraeli, D. (1994). *Competitive frontiers: Women managers in a global economy*. Cambridge, MA: Blackwell.

Albrecht, S., Werns, G., & Williams, T. (1995). *Fraud: Bringing light to the dark side of business*. Burr Ridge, IL: Irwin.

Apfelbaum, E. (1993). Norwegian and French women in high leadership positions. *Psychology of Women Quarterly, 17*, 409–429.

Apfelbaum, E., & Hadley, M. (1986). Leadership Ms. - qualified: II. Reflections and initial case study investigation of contemporary women leaders. In C. Graumann & S. Moscovici (Eds.), *Changing conceptions of leadership* (pp. 199–221). New York: Springer Verlag.

Alexander, D. (1979). The effect level in the hierarchy and functional area have on the extant Mintzberg's roles are required by managerial jobs. *Academy of Management Proceedings*, 186–189.

Anon, (1992, June 8). Corporate women. *Business Week*, 74–83.

Aries, C. (1976). Interaction patterns and themes of male, female, and mixed groups. *Small Group Behavior, 7,* 7–18.

Arinder, K. (1993, Fall). A separate female morality? The developmental accounts of Gilligan and Kohlberg. *IBIS: Journal of Inquiry and Discourse,* 5–8.

Ash, M. K. (1981). *Mary Kay Ash.* New York: Harper & Row.

Ash, M. K. (1984). *Mary Kay on people management.* New York: Warner.

Astin, H., & Leland, C. (1991). *Women of influence, women of vision.* San Francisco: Jossey-Bass.

Atwater, L., & Roush, P. (1994). An investigation of gender on followers' ratings of leaders, leaders' self-ratings, and reactions to feedback. *Journal of Leadership Studies, 1,* 37–52.

Auerbach, J. (1988). *In the business of child care.* New York: Praeger.

Austin, N. (1992, January). Leadership seminars: The good, bad and the baloney. *Working Women,* 22–24.

Avolio, B., Waldman, D., & Yammarino, F. (1991). Leading in the 1990s: The four I's of transformational leadership. *European Industrial Training, 15,* 9–16.

Barnard, C. (1939). *The functions of the executive.* Cambridge, MA: Harvard University Press.

Bartol, K. (1974). Male vs. female leaders: The effect of leader need for dominance and follower satisfaction. *Academy of Management Journal, 17,* 225–232.

Bartol, K., & Butterfield, D. (1976). Sex effects in evaluating leaders. *Journal of Applied Psychology, 67,* 446–454.

Bartol, K., & Wortman, M. (1979). Sex of leader and subordinate role stress: A field study. *Sex Roles, 5,* 513–518.

Bass, B. (1956). Leadership opinion as forecasts of supervisory success. *Journal of Applied Psychology, 40,* 345–346.

Bass, B. (1959). Great men or great times? *Adult Leadership, 8,* 7–10.

Bass, B. (1985). *Performance beyond expectations.* New York: The Free Press.

Bass, B. (1991). *Bass & Stogdill's handbook of leadership* (3rd ed.). New York: The Free Press.

Bass, B., & Avolio, B. (1990). The implications of transactional and transformational leadership for individual, team, and organizational development. In R. Woodman & R. Pasmore (Eds.), *Research in organizational change and development* (pp. 231–272). Greenwich, CT: JAI Press.

Beard, M. (1946). *Women as force in history: A study in transitions and realities.* New York: Macmillan.

Bebbington, C. (1988). Ladies don't climb ladders. *Eurobusiness, 1,* 12–17.

Becker, D. (1994, January, 25). Coaches' pay sees gender gap. *USA Today,* 1C.

Belenchy, M., Clinchy, B., Goldberger, N., & Tarule, J. (1986). *Women's way of knowing: Redevelopment of self, voice.* New York: Basic Books.

Beneviste, G. (1994). *The twenty-first century organization*. San Francisco: Jossey-Bass.

Bennis, W. (1959). Leadership theory and administrative behavior: The problem of authority. *Administrative Science Quarterly, 4*, 259–301.

Bennis, W. (1988). *Why leaders can't lead: The conspiracy continues*. San Francisco: Jossey-Bass.

Bennis, W. (1990). Managing the dream: Leadership in the 21st century. *Training: The Magazine of Human Resource Development, 27*, 43–48.

Bennis, W. (1993). Managing the dream: Leadership in the 21st century. In W. Rosenbach & R. Taylor (Eds.), *Contemporary issues in leadership* (pp. 213–218). Boulder, CO: Westview.

Bennis, W., & Nanus, B. (1985). *Leaders: Strategies of taking charge*. New York: Harper & Row.

Bensman, J., & Givant, M. (1975). Charisma and modernity: The use and abuse of a concept. *Social Research, 42*, 4, 570–614.

Berthoin Antal, A., & Izraeli, D. (1993). A global comparison of women in management: Women managers in their homelands and as expatriates. In E. Fagenson (Ed.), *Women in management* (pp. 52–96). Newbury Park, CA: Sage.

Billings, C. (1989). *Grace Hopper, Navy admiral and computer pioneer*. Hillsdale, NJ: Enslow Publishers.

Birrell, S. (1988). Discourses on the gender/sport relationship: From women in sport to gender relations. *Exercise and Sport Science Review, 16*, 459–502.

Birrell, S., & Cole, C. (1990). Double fault: Renee Richards and the construction and naturalization of difference. *Sociology of Sport Journal, 7*, 1–21.

Black, J., & Mendenhall, M. (1990). Cross-cultural training effectiveness: A review and theoretical framework for future research. *Academy of Management Review*, 15, 113–136.

Black, J., Mendenhall, M., & Oddou, G. (1991). Toward a comprehensive moldel of international adjustment. *Academy of Management Review, 16*, 291–317.

Black, M. (1962). *Models and metaphors*. Ithaca, NY: Cornell University Press.

Black, S., Stephens, G., & Rosener, J. (1992). Women in management around the world: Some glimpses. In U. Sekaran & F. Leong (Eds.), *Womanpower* (pp. 223–251). Newbury Park, CA: Sage.

Blau, P. (1983). Critical remarks on Weber's theory of authority. *American Political Science Review, 57*, 305–315.

Blauvelt, H. (1995, January 9). Title IX levels playing field for women. *USA Today*, 9, p. 2A.

Blinde, E., Taub, D., & Han, L. (1993). Sport participation and women's personal empowerment: Experience of the college athlete. *Journal of Sport and Social Issues, 17*, 47–60.

Blondel, J. (1987). *Political leadership*. Newbury Park, CA: Sage.

Blum, T., Fields, D., & Goodman, J. (1994). Organization-level determinants of women in management. *Academy of Management Journal, 37*, 241–268.

Blumenfeld, L. (1994, May). Ultimate feminist: Hillary Rodham Clinton. *Cosmopolitan*, 214–216.

Boal, K., & Bryson, J. (1987). Charismatic leadership: A structural and phenomenological approach. In J. Hunt, B. Baliga, P. Dachler, & C. Schriesheim (Eds.), *Emerging leadership vistas*. Lexington, MA: D.C. Heath.

Bobko, P. (1985). Removing assumptions about bipolarity: Toward variation and circularity. *Academy of Management Review, 10*, 99–108.

Bogardus, E. (1934). *Leaders and leadership*. New York: Appleton Century.

Bohan, J. (1993). Regarding gender: Essentialism, constructionism and feminist psychology. *Psychology of Women Quarterly, 17*, 5–21.

Bolman, L., & Deal, T. (1991). *Reframing organizations: Artistry, choice, and leadership*. San Francisco: Jossey-Bass.

Bolman, L., & Deal, T. (1995). *Leading with soul*. San Francisco: Jossey-Bass.

Bonvillian, G., & Nowlin, W. (1994, November/December). Cultural awareness: An essential element in doing business. *Business Horizons, 37*, 44–50.

Borman, E. (1990). *Small group communication: Theory and practice*. New York: Harper & Row.

Boulding, E. (1992). *The underside of history: A view of women through time*. Newbury Park, CA: Sage.

Boutlier, M., & San Giovanni, L. (1983). *The sporting woman*. Champaign, IL: Human Kinetics.

Bradford, S. (1897). *Harriet Tubman: The Moses of her people*. New York: Corinth.

Brass, D. (1985). Men's and women's networks: A study of interaction patterns and influence in organization. *Academy of Management Journal, 28*, 327–343.

Bray, D., Campbell, R., & Grant, D. (1974). *Formative years in business: A long-term AT&T study of managerial lives*. New York: Wiley-Interscience.

Brenner, O., Tomkiewicz, J., & Schein, V. (1989). The relationship between sex role stereotypes and requisite management characteristics revisited. *Academy of Management Journal, 32*, 662–669.

Breshko-Breshkovskaya, K. (1931). *The hidden springs of the Russian Revolution*. Stanford: University of California Press.

Bretl, D., & Cantor, J. (1988). The portrayal of men and women in U.S. television commercials: A recent content analysis and trends over 15 years. *Sex Roles, 18*, 595–609.

Brock, P. (1993, May 10). Anita Roddick. *People, 39*, 101–106.

Brockner, J., & Adsit, L. (1986). The moderating impact of sex on the equity-satisfaction relationship. *Journal of Applied Psychology, 71*, 585–590.

Brown, L. (1979). Women and business management. *Signs: Journal of Women in Culture and Society*, *5*, 266–288.

Brown, R. (1976). Social theory as metaphor. *Theory and Society*, *3*, 169–197.

Brown, V., & Geis, F. (1994). Turning lead to gold: Evaluations of men and women leaders and the alchemy of social consensus. *Journal of Applied Psychology*, *46*, 4, 811–824.

Bryman, A. (1992). *Charisma and leadership in organizations*. London: Sage.

Bryman, A. (1993). Charismatic leadership in business organizations: Some neglected issues. *Leadership Quarterly*, *4*, 3/4, 289–304.

Bunch, C., & Fisher, B. (1976). What future for leadership? *Quest*, *2*, 3–13.

Burke, R., & Greenglass, E. (1987). *Work and family*. Chichester, England: Wiley.

Burns, J. (1978). *Leadership*. New York: Harper & Row.

Burnside, R. (1990, August 22–24). *Leading creatively into the 21st century*. Paper presented at the International Conference on Creativity and Leadership, Lappeenranta, Finland.

Burnside, R., & Guthrie, V. (1992). *Training for action: A new approach to executive development*. Greensboro, NC: Center for Creative Leadership.

Butler, P. (1976). *Self-assertion for women: A guide to becoming androgynous*. Reading, MA: Addison-Wesley.

Butterfield, D., & Powell, G. (1981). Effect of group performance, leader sex, and rater sex on ratings of leader behavior. *Organizational Behavior and Human Performance*, *28*, 129–141.

Bystydzienski, J. (1988). Women in politics in Norway. *Women & Politics*, *8*, 73–95.

Calas, M., & Smircich, L. (1993). Dangerous liasons: The "feminine-in-management" meets "globalization." *Business Horizons*, *36*, 71–81.

Calori, R., & Dufour, B. (1995). Management European style. *Academy of Management Executive*, *9*, 3, 61–73.

Campbell, R., & Ritchie, R. (1993, April 30-May 2). *The persistence of women managers in long-term careers in a single organization*. Paper presented at the 8th Annual Conference of the Society for for Industrial and Organizational Psychology, San Francisco, CA.

Cantor, D., & Bearnay, T. (1992). *Women in power*. New York: Houghton Mifflin.

Cantorella, E. (1987). *Pandora's daughters* (translated by M. Fant). Baltimore, MD: John Hopkins University Press.

Carey, A., & Bryant, B. (1995, March 26). Women-owned business growth. *USA Today*, p. B1.

Carlson, M. (1994, January). Born to run. *Working Woman*, 44–47.

Carlton, D. (1993). Developing leaders using the outdoors (pp. 454–461). In M. Syrett & C. Hogg (Eds.), *Frontiers of leadership*. Cambridge, MA: Blackwell.

Carlyle, T. (1813). *On heroes, hero-worship, and the heroic in history*. Boston: Heath.

Carlyle, T. (1841). *On heroes and hero-worship*. Boston, MA: Adam.

Carmody, J. (1993, June 16). Minorities still shut out, survey reports. *Washington Post*, p. B12.

Carney, L., & O'Kelly, C. (1987). Barriers and constraints to the recruitment and mobility of female managers in the Japanese labor force. *Human Resource Management, 26,* 193–216.

Carroll, G., Clift, E., & Finenman, H. (1992, March 30). Will Hillary hurt or help? *Newsweek, 119,* p. 31.

Carroll, S. (1984). Feminist scholarship on political leadership. In B. Kellerman (Ed.), *Leadership: A multidisciplinary perspective* (pp. 139–156). Englewood Cliffs, NJ: Prentice-Hall.

Castle, C. (1913, August). A statistical study of eminent women. *Archives of Psychology, 7.*

Catalyst (1992). Women in engineering. Catalyst: New York.

CBS Television Network (1986a, March 30). NCAA Women's Division I Basketball Championship, UCS-Texas, Lexington, KY.

CBS Television Network (1986b, March 31). NCAA Men's Division I Basketball Championship, Duke-Louisville, Dallas, TX.

Chen, C., & Meindl, J. (1991). The construction of leadership images in the popular press: The case of Donald Burr and People Express. *Administrative Science Quarterly, 36,* 521–551.

Clark, A., & Clark, J. (1982). Highlights and action replays: Ideology, sport, and the media. In J. Hargraves (Ed.), *Sport, culture and ideology* (pp. 62–87). London: Routledge & Kegan Paul.

Cleveland, H. (1985). *The knowledge executive: Leadership in an information society*. New York: Truman Talley.

Clover, W. (1989). Transformational leaders: Team performance, leadership ratings, and first hand impressions. In K. Clark & M. Clark (Eds.), *Measures of leadership*. West Orange, NJ: Library of America.

Coakley, J. (1986). *Sport in society: Issues and controversies*. St. Louis, MO: Times/Mirror/Mosby.

Cohen, G. (1993). *Women in sport*. Newbury Park, CA: Sage.

Cohen, D., & Bradford, L. (1989). Influence without authority: The use of alliances, reciprocity, and exchange to accomplish work. *Organizational Dynamics, 17,* 5–17.

Colby, A., & Damon, W. (1983). Listening to a different voice: A review of Gilligan's "In a Different Voice." *Merrill-Palmer Quarterly, 29,* 473–481.

Coleman, F. (1994, June 6). Will Turkey be the next Iran? *U.S. News and World Report*, 51–52.

Collins, S. (1995). *Our children are watching: Ten skills for leading the next generation to success.* Barrytown, NY: Barrytown.

Conger, J. (1989). *The charismatic leader.* San Francisco: Jossey-Bass.

Conger, J. (1990). The dark side of leadership. *Organizational Dynamics, 19,* 44–55.

Conger, J. (1992). *Learning to lead.* San Francisco: Jossey-Bass.

Conger, J. (1993a). The brave new world of leadership training. *Organizational Dynamics, 22,* 46–58.

Conger, J. (1993b). Personal growth training: Snake oil or pathway to leadership. *Organizational Dynamics, 22,* 19–30.

Conger, J., & Kanungo, R. (1987). Toward a behavioral theory of charismatic leadership in organizational settings. *Academy of Management Review, 12,* 637–647.

Conger, J., Kanungo, R., & Associates (1988a). *Charismatic leadership.* San Francisco: Jossey-Bass.

Conger, J., & Kanungo, R. (1988b). Training charismatic leadership: A risky and critical task (pp. 309–323). In J. Conger, R. Kanungo & Associates (Eds.), *Charismatic leadership.* San Francisco: Jossey-Bass.

Conlin, J. (1994, February). Survival of the fittest. *Working Woman,* pp. 29–31; 68–72.

Connell, R. (1987). *Gender and power: Society, the person, and sexual politics.* Stanford, CA: Stanford University Press.

Conrad, E. (1943). *Harriet Tubman.* Washington, DC: Associated Publishers.

Cooper, G., & Kingsley, P. (1985). *The change makers: Their influence on British business and industry.* London: Harper & Row.

Corner, J. (1991). Meaning, genre and context: The problematics of "Public Knowledge" in the new audience studies. In J. Curran & M. Gurevitch (Eds.), *Mass media and society* (pp. 267–306). London: Edward Arnold.

Cosell, H. (1985). *Woman on a seesaw: The ups and downs of making it.* NY: Putnam.

Costa, P. (1991, May 17). A conversation with Rosabeth Moss Kanter. *Harvard Gazette,* p. 5.

Covey, S. (1989). *The 7 habits of highly effective people.* New York: Simon & Schuster.

Cowan, A. (1989, August 21). Women's gains on the job: Not without heavy tolls. *New York Times,* pp. A1, A14.

Creedon, P. (1989) (Ed.). *Women in mass communication.* Newbury Park, CA: Sage.

Creedon, P. (1994). *Women, media, and sport.* Thousand Oaks, CA: Sage.

Crocker, J., & McGraw, K. (1984). What is good for the goose is not good for the gander. *American Behavioral Scientist, 27,* 357–369.

Crosby, F. (1987). *Spouse, parent, worker: Gender and multiple roles.* New Haven, CT: Yale University Press.

Culler, J. (1982). *On deconstruction: Theory and criticism after structuralism.* Ithaca, NY: Cornell University Press.

Current biography yearbook. (1975). New York: H. W. Wilson.

Current biography yearbook. (1991). New York: H. W. Wilson.

Current biography yearbook. (1992). New York: H. W. Wilson.

Current biography yearbook. (1993). New York: H. W. Wilson.

Dark, S. (1969). *Twelve more ladies.* Freeport, NY: Books for Libraries Press.

Daughton, S. (1994). Women's issues, women's place: Gender related problems in presidential campaigns. *Communication Quarterly, 42,* 2, 106–119.

Davis, D. (1990). Portrayals of women in prime-time network television: Some demographic characteristics. *Sex Roles, 23,* 325–332.

Davis, F. (1991). *Moving the mountain: The women's movement in America since the 1960s.* New York: Simon & Schuster.

Dean, P. (1991, October 21). Walking taller. *Los Angeles Times,* p. E2.

Deaux, K. (1984). From individual differences to social categories: Analysis of a decade of research on gender. *American Psychologist, 39,* 105–116.

Deaux, K. (1985). Sex and gender. *Annual Review of Psychology, 36,* 49–81.

Del Greco Wood, A. (1995, February). Instructional technology in the business environment. *Multimedia Today, 3,* 18.

DeLeon, C., & Ho, S. (1994). The third identity of modern Chinese women: Women managers in Hong Kong. In N. Adler & D. Izraeli (Eds.), *Competitive frontiers* (pp. 43–56). Cambridge, MA: Blackwell Publishers.

Del Rey, P. (1978). The apologetic and women in sport. In C. Oglesby (Ed.), *Women and sport: From myth to reality* (pp. 107–112). Philadelphia, PA: Lea & Febiger.

DeMott, B. (1993). Choice academic pork: Inside the leadership studies rackett. *Harper's Magazine, 287,* 61–77.

DePree, M. (1992). *Leadership jazz.* New York: Dell.

Dervin, B. (1981). Mass communication and changing conceptions of the audience. In R. Rice & W. Paisley (Eds.), *Public communication campaigns* (pp. 71–87). Beverly Hills, CA: Sage.

De Swarte Gifford, C. (1981) Women in social reform movements. In R. Ruether & R. Keller, *Women and religion in America* (pp. 294–340). New York: Harper & Row.

De Tocqueville, A. (1947). *Democracy in America.* New York: Oxford University Press.

DiMarco, N., & Whitsitt, S. (1975). A comparison of female supervisors in business and government organizations. *Journal of Vocational Behavior, 6,* 189–196.

Dobbins, G. (1985). Effects of gender on leader's responses to poor performers:

An attributional interpretation. *Academy of Management Journal, 28,* 587–598.

Dobbins, G. (1986). Equity vs. equality: Sex differences in leadership. *Sex Roles, 15,* 513–525.

Dobbins, G., & Platz, S. (1986). Sex differences in leadership: How real are they? *Academy of Management Review, 11,* 118–127.

Dodson, D., & Carroll, S. (1991). *Reshaping the agenda: Women in state legislatures.* Brunswick, NY: Center for the American Woman in Politics.

Domain, B. (1989, July 3). What the leaders of tomorrow see. *Fortune, 120,* 48–62.

Dominguez, C. (1992). The glass ceiling: Paradox and promises. *Human Resource Management, 31,* 385–392.

Donnell, S., & Hall, J. (1980). Men and women as managers: A significant case of no significant differences. *Organizational Dynamics, 9,* 60–77.

Douglas, S. (1994). *Where the girls are: Growing up female with the mass media.* New York: Random House.

Dreher, P., & Ash, R. (1990). A comparative study of mentoring among men and women in managerial, professional, and technical positions. *Journal of Applied Psychology, 75,* 539–546.

Driscoll, D., & Goldberg, C. (1993). *Members of the club: The coming of age of executive women.* New York: The Free Press.

Drucker, P. (1988, January 6). Leadership: More than doing dash. *Wall Street Journal,* p. 16.

Drucker, P. (1990). *Managing the non-profit organization.* New York: HarperCollins Publishers.

Dubek, P. (1979). Sexism in recruiting management personnel for a manufacturing firm. In R. Alvarez (Ed.), *Discrimination in organizations* (pp. 88–99). London: Jossey-Bass.

Dubin, R. (1986). Leadership metaphors. In J. Adams (Ed.), *Transforming leadership.* Alexandria, VA: Miles River Press.

Duby, G. (1991). *France in the Middle Ages, 987–1460.* Cambridge, MA: Blackwell.

Duffy, M. (1992, July 6). Symbol of new Ireland. *Time,* pp. 50–52.

Duncan, M. (1990). Sports photographs and sexual difference: Images of women and men in the 1984 and 1988 Olympic Games. *Sociology of Sport Journal, 7,* 22–43.

Duncan, M., & Hasbrook, C. (1988). Denial of power in televised women's sports. *Sociology of Sports Journal, 5,* 1–21.

Dunning, E. (1986). Sport as a male preserve: Notes on the social sources of masculine identity and its transformation. *Theory, Culture & Society, 3,* 79–90.

Durka, E. (1990, November 11). Women and Hollywood: It's still a lousy relationship. *Los Angeles Times*, p. 8.

Dukess, K. (1995, June). Comrades in cosmetics. *Working Woman*, pp. 11–12.

Eagan, M. (1992, March 8). America is not ready for a his and hers presidency from the Clintons. *Boston Herald*, p. A8.

Eagly, A., & Johnson, B. (1990). Gender and leadershyp style: A meta-analysis. *Psychological Bulletin, 108*, 233–256.

Eagly, A., & Karau, S. (1991). Gender and the emergence of leaders: A meta-analysis. *Journal of Personality and Social Psychology, 60*, 685–710.

Eagly, A., Makhijani, M., & Klonsky, B. (1992). Gender and the evaluation of leaders. *Psychological Bulletin, 111*, 1–22.

Eagly, A., & Steffan, V. (1986). Gender and aggressive behavior: A meta-analytical review of the social psychological literature. *Psychological Bulletin, 100*, 309–330.

Eddy, M. (1894). *Yes and no*. Boston: E. J. Foster.

Eddy, M. (1906). *Manual for the mother church*. Article XII: Relation of members to Pastor Emeritus. Boston: J. Armstrong.

Edlund, C. (1993). Humanistic model of leadership. Quoted in Baker, T. Practice Network. *The Industrial/Organizational Psychologist, 31*, 2, 62–62.

Edmisten, P. (1990). *Nicaragua divided: La Prensa and the Chamorro legacy*. Pensacola, FL: University of West Florida Press.

Edwards, P. (1990). The Army and the microworld: Computers and the politics of gender identity. *Signs: Journal of Women in Culture and Society, 16*, 102–127.

Ehrlich, E. (1989, March 20). The mommy track. *Business Week*, 126–131.

Eichler, M. (1980). *The double standard*. London: Croom Helm.

Eisler, R. (1987). *The chalice and the blade*. New York: HarperCollins Publishers.

Eisler, R. (1991, January/February). Women, men, and management: Redesigning our future. *Futures, 23*, 3–18.

Epstein, C. (1991, January/February). Ways men and women lead. *Harvard Business Review, 69*, 150–151.

Equal writes. (1992, April 16). *USA Today*, p. 1A.

Eskilon, A., & Wiley, M. (1976). Sex composition and leadership in small groups. *Sociometry, 39*, 183–194.

Etzioni, A. (1961). *A comparative analysis of complex organizations*. New York: The Free Press.

Evans, E. (1923, September). Women in the Washington scene. *Century Magazine*, 507–517.

Evans, R. (1977). *The feminists*. New York: Barnes & Noble Books.

Fairhurst, G., & Snavely, K. (1983). Majority and token minority group relationships: Power acquisition and communication. *Academy of Management Review, 8*, 2, 292–300.

Faludi, S. (1991). *Backlash: The undeclared war against American women.* New York: Doubleday.

Farrell, A. (1995). Feminism and the media: Introduction. *Signs: Journal of Women in Culture and Society, 20,* 642–644.

Fayol, H. (1906). *Administration industrielle et generale.* Paris: Dunod.

Feagin, J. (1992). Not taking gendered racism seriously: The failure of the mass media and the social sciences. *Journal of Applied Behaviorial Science, 28,* 400–406.

Felsenthal, C. (1993). *Power, privilege, and the* Post. New York: Putnam & Sons.

Felshin, J. (1974a). Triple option for women in sport. *Quest, 21,* 12.

Felshin, J. (1974b). The dialectic of women and sport. In E. Gerber (Ed.), *The American woman in sport* (pp. 179–210). Reading, MA: Addison-Wesley.

Ferrante, K. (1994). Baseball and the social construction of gender. In P. Creedon (Ed.), *Women, Media, and Sport* (pp. 238–256). Thousand Oaks, CA: Sage.

Ferraro, G. (1985). *Ferraro: My story.* New York: Bantam Books.

Fiedler, F. (1964). A contingency model of leadership effectiveness. In L. Berkowitz (Ed.), *Advances in experimental social psychology* (Vol. 1). New York: Academic Press.

Fiedler, F. (1967). *A theory of leadership effectiveness.* New York: McGraw-Hill.

Fiedler, F., & Chemers, M. (1974). *Leadership and effective management.* Glenview, IL: Scott, Foresman.

Fiedler, F., Chemers, M., & Mahar, L. (1976). *Improving leadership effectiveness: The LEADER MATCH concept.* New York: Wiley.

Fiedler, F., & Garcia, J. (1987). *New approaches to effective leadership: Cognitive resources and organizational performance.* New York: Wiley.

Fields, D. (1987). *One smart cookie.* New York: Simon & Schuster.

Fisher, A. (1992, September 21). When will women get to the top? *Fortune, 117,* 44–56.

Fiske, J. (1987). *Television culture.* Padstow, England: Methuen.

Fitt, L., & Newton, D. (1981). When the mentor is a man and the protege is a woman. *Harvard Business Review, 59,* 3–4.

Fleishman, E. (1953). Leadership climate, human relations training and supervisory behavior. *Personnel Psychology, 4,* 205–22.

Flinders, C. (1993). *Enduring grace.* New York: HarperCollins Publishers.

Forfreedom, A. (Ed.) (1972). *Women out of history: A herstory anthology.* Los Angeles, CA: Roc-Pacific Typographics.

Franke, R., Hofstede, G., & Bond, M. (1991). Cultural roots of economic performance: A research note. *Strategic Management Journal, 12,* 165–173.

Fraser, N., & Navarro, M. (1981). *Eva Perón.* New York: W. W. Norton.

Frazier, A. (1989). *Warrior queens.* New York: Alfred Knopf.

Frederickson, J., Hambrick, D., & Baumrin, S. (1988). A model of CEO dismissal. *Academy of Management Review, 13,* 255–270.

French, J., & Raven, B. (1959). The bases of social power. In D. Cartwright (Ed.), *Studies in social power* (pp. 150–167). Ann Arbor: University of Michigan Press.

Friedan, B. (1975). *The feminine mystique.* New York: Dell.

Friedman, W., Robinson, A., & Friedman, B. (1987). Sex differences in moral judgment? A test of Gilligan's theory. *Psychology of Women Quarterly, 11,* 37–46.

Fry, R., & Pasmore (1983). Strengthening management education (pp. 269–296). In S. Srivista & Associates (Eds.), *The executive mind.* San Francisco: Jossey-Bass.

Fulmer, R. (1988). Corporate management and education: The state of the art. *Journal of Management Development, 7,* 57–68.

Furnham, A., & Bitar, N. (1993). The stereotyped portrayal of men and women in British television advertisements. *Sex Roles, 23,* 3/4, 297–310.

Gable, D. (1993, August 30). Series shortchange working class and minority Americans. *USA Today,* p. 4D.

Gaines, J. (1993). "You don't necessarily have to be charismatic . . .:" An interview with Anita Roddick and reflections on charismatic processes in the Body Shop International. *Leadership Quarterly, 4,* 347–359.

Gardner, J. (1961). *Excellence.* New York: Harper & Row.

Gardner, J. (1987). Leaders and followers. *Liberal Education, 73,* 4–8.

Gardner, J. (1990). *On leadership.* New York: The Free Press.

Gartner, M. (1994, February 17). Female athletes make the grade. *USA Today,* p. 11A.

Gauteraux, G. (1990, Spring). Admiral Cobol: An interview with Grace Hopper. *Micrcomputer Buying Guide,* 4–7.

Geertz, C. (1966). Religion as a cultural system. In M. Banton (Ed.), *Anthropological approaches to the study of religion.* London: Tavistock.

Geis, F., Brown, V., Jennings, J., & Corrado-Taylor, D. (1984). Sex vs. status in sex-associated stereotypes. *Sex Roles, 11,* 771–785.

Genovese, M. (1993). *Women as national leaders.* Newbury Park, CA: Sage.

George, C. (1975). *Women in American history.*

Gerbner, G., & Gross, L. (1974). Cultural indicators: The social reality of television drama. Unpublished manuscript.

Gherardi, S. (1994). The gender we think, the gender we do in our everyday organizational lives. *Human Relations, 47,* 591–610.

Gibb, C. (1968). Leadership: Psychological aspects. In D. Sills (Ed.), *International Encyclopedia of the Social Sciences* (pp. 91–113). New York: Macmillan.

Gibbons, E. (1955). *The history and decline of the Roman Empire.* Chicago: Encyclopedia Britannica.

Gies, F. (1981). *Joan of Arc: The legend and the reality.* New York: Harper & Row.

Gilligan, C. (1982). *In a different voice: Psychological theory and women's development*. Cambridge, MA: Harvard University Press.

Gray, J. (1992). *Men are from Mars, women are from Venus*. New York: HarperCollins.

Gitlin, T. (1980). *The whole world is watching: Mass media and the unmaking of the new left*. Berkeley: University of California Press.

Goodstein, J. (1994). Institutional pressures and strategic responsiveness: Employer involvement in work-family issues. *Academy of Management Journal, 37*, 350–382.

Graen, G., Alvares, K., Orris, J., & Martella, J. (1970). A contingency model of leadership effectiveness: Antecedents and inevitable results. *Psychological Bulletin, 74*, 275–286.

Graen, G., & Cashman, J. (1975). A role-making model of leadership in formal organizations: A developmental approach (pp. 143–165). In J. Hunt & L. Larson (Eds.), *Leadership frontiers*. Kent, OH: Kent State University Press.

Graen, G., Novak, M., & Sommerkamp, P. (1992). The effects of leader-member exchange and job design on productivity. *Organizational Behavior and Human Performance, 30*, 109–131.

Graumann, C. (1986). Changing conceptions of leadership. In C. Graumann & S. Moscovici (Eds.), *Changing conceptions of leadership*. New York: Springer.

Graven, K. (1990, March 21). Sexual harassment at the office stirs up in Japan. *Wall Street Journal*, p. B1.

Greendorfer, S. (1993). Gender role stereotypes and early childhood socialization. In G. Cohen (Ed.), *Women in sports* (pp. 3–14). Newbury Park, CA: Sage Publications.

Greene, C. (1979). Questions of causation in the path-goal theory of leadership. *Academy of Management Journal, 22*, 22–41.

Greenhaus, J., & Beutell, N. (1985). Sources of conflict between work and family roles. *Academy of Management Review, 10*, 76–88.

Greenhaus, J., & Parasuraman, S. (1987). A work-non-work interactive perspective of stress and its consequences. *Journal of Organizational Behavior Management, 8*, 37–60.

Greenlaw, P., & Kohl, J. (1982). Age discrimination and employment guidelines. *Personnel Journal, 57*, 23–28.

Grunewald, L. (1992, June). If women ran America . . . *Life*, 38–47.

Grunwald, W., & Lilge, H. (1980). *Partizipative Führung*. Stuttgart, Germany: Haupt.

Grunwald, W., & Bernthal, W. (1983). Controversy in German management: The Harzburg model experience. *Academy of Management Review, 8*, 233–241.

Guillemin, H. (1970). *Joan, Maid of Orleans*. New York: Saturday Review Press.

Guralik, D. (1976). *Webster's New World dictionary of the American language.* New York: The World Publishing Company.

Guttman, R. (1995, February). EU Commissioner Edith Cresson. *Europe,* 10–12.

Haas, H. (1992). *The leader within.* New York: HarperCollins.

Hagberg, J. (1984). *Real power.* Minneapolis, MN: Winston Press.

Haigh, C. (1988). *Elizabeth I.* New York: Longman.

Haldeman, R. (1995, January). Urban man conquers his nature. *Travel & Leisure,* 60–63, 102–107.

Halpin, A., & Winer, B. (1957). A factorial study of leader behavior descriptions. In R. Stogdill & A. Coons (Eds.), *Leader behavior: Its description and measurement.* Columbus, OH: Ohio State University, Bureau of Business Research.

Hammer, S. (1978). When women have power over women. *Ms., 7,* 49.

Hammerschmidt, P. (1992, September). An extra $11,724 for the guys. *Working Woman,* p. 21.

Hansen, C., & Hansen, R. (1988). How rock music videos change what is seen when boy meets girl: Primary stereotypic appraisal of social interactions. *Sex Roles, 19,* 287–316.

Hare-Mustin, R., & Maracek, J. (1990a). The meaning of difference: Gender theory, postmodernisms, and psychology. *American Psychologist, 43,* 455–465.

Hare-Mustin, R., & Maracek, J. (Eds.) (1990b). *Making a difference: Psychology and the construction of gender.* New Haven: Yale University Press.

Hart, S., & Quinn, R. (1993). Roles executives play: CEOs, behaviorial complexity, and firm performance. *Human Relations, 46,* 5, 543–558.

Hasbrook, C., Hart, B., Mathes, S., & True, S. (1990). Sex bias and the validity of believed differences between male and female interscholastic athletic coaches. *Research Quarterly for Exercise and Sport, 63,* 259–267.

Hasson, J. (1992, September 17). Women are poised to make history. *USA Today,* p. 2A.

Heilbrunn, J. (1994). Can leadership be studied? *Wilson Quarterly, 18,* 2, 65–72.

Heilman, M., Black, C., Martell, R., & Simon, M. (1989). Has anything changed? Current characterization of men, women, and managers. *Journal of Applied Psychology, 74,* 935–942.

Heilman, M., Block, C., Martell, R., & Simon, M. (1989). Has anything changed? Current characterizations of men, women, and managers. *Journal of Applied Psychology, 74,* 6, 935–942.

Heisler, W., & Benham, P. (1992). The challenge of management development in North America in the 1990s. *Journal of Management Development, 11,* 16–31.

Helgesen, S. (1990). *The female advantage: Women's way of leadership.* New York: Doubleday/Currency.

Hellwig, B. (1992, September/October). Executive female's breakthrough. *Executive Female*, 43–46.

Helmich, D. (1974). Male and female presidents: Some implications of leadership style. *Human Resource Management, 13*, 25–36.

Henning, M., & Jardim, A. (1977). *The managerial woman.* Garden City, NY: Anchor.

Hewitt, B. (1994, June 6). The browning of California. *People*, pp. 15–17.

Hewlitt, S. (1991). *When the bough breaks: The cost of neglecting our children.* New York: Basic Books.

Hickman, C. (1990). *Mind of a manager, soul of a leader.* New York: Wiley.

Hicks, B. (1975, December). Babe Didrikson Zaharias: "Where I go, the galleries go. Let the rest starve." *WomenSports*, 18–25.

Hicks, G., & Redding, S. (1983). The story of East Asian economic miracle. Part I: Economic theory be damned. *Euro-Asia Business Review, 2*, 24–32.

Highlen, P. (1994). Reawakening to the co-essence model of sport. In P. Creedon (ed.), *Women, media, and sport* (pp. 314–338). Thousand Oaks, CA: Sage.

Hill, M. (1993, January 8). All about Hillary in a quarterly. *USA Today*, p. 2A.

Hillard, D. (1984). Media images of male and female professional athletes: An interpretive analysis of magazine articles. *Sociology of Sport Journal, 1*, 251–262.

Hitt, W. (1988). *The leader-manager.* Columbus, OH: Batelle.

Ho, D. (1976). On the concept of face. *American Journal of Sociology, 81*, 867–884.

Ho, S. (1976). Women into management—in Hong Kong? *New Asia College Academic Annual, 18*, 273–283. Hong Kong: The Chinese University of Hong Kong.

Ho, S. (1984). Women managers in Hong Kong: Traditional barriers and emerging trends. *Equal Opportunities International, 3*, 7–29.

Hoch, P. (1972). *Rip off the big game.* New York: Anchor.

Hodges, D. (1976). *Argentina, 1943–1976: The national revolution and resistance.* Albuquerque, NM: University of New Mexico Press.

Hoffman, C., & Hurst, N. (1990). Gender stereotypes: Perception or rationalization? *Journal of Personality and Social Psychology, 58*, 197–208.

Hofstede, G. (1980a) *Culture's consequences: International differences in work-related values.* Beverly Hills, CA: Sage.

Hofstede, G. (1980b). Motivation leadership, and organization: Do American theories apply abroad? *Organizational Dynamics, 8*, 42–65.

Hofstede, G., & Bond, M. (1988). The Confucian connection. *Organizational Dynamics, 16*, 5–21.

Höhn, R. (1962). *Menschenführung im Handel.* Bad Harzburg, Germany: Verlag WWT Bad Harzburg.

Hohn, R. (1979). *Stellenbeschreibung und Führungsanweisung*. Bad Harzburg, Germany: Verlag WWT.

Hollander, E. (1978). *Leadership dynamics: A practical guide to effective relationships*. New York: Free Press.

Hollander, E. (1992a). The essential interdependence of leadership and followership. *Current Directions in Psychological Science, 1,* 71–78.

Hollander, E. (1992b). Leadership, followership, self, and others. *Leadership Quarterly, 3,* 43–54.

Hoover, D. (1968). *Understanding Negro history*. Chicago: Quadrangle.

Hörburger, H. & Rath-Hörburger, F. (1980). *Europa's Frauen Gleichberechtigt? Die Politik der EG Länder: Gleichberechtigung der Frau im Arbeitsleben*. Hamburg, Germany: Verlag Otto Heinvetter.

Horner, M., Nadelson, C., & Nortman, M. (1983). *The challenge of change*. New York: Plenum.

Hosking, D., & Hunt, J. (1982). Leadership research and the European connection: An epilogue. In J. Hunt, U. Sekaran, & C. Schriesheim (Eds.), *Beyond establishment views*. Carbondale, IL: University of Illinois Press.

House, R. (1971). A path-goal theory of leader effectiveness. *Administrative Science Quarterly, 16,* 321–338.

House, R. (1977). A 1976 theory of charismatic leadership. In J. Hunt & L. Larson (Eds.), *Leadership: The cutting edge*. Carbondale, IL: Southern Illinois University Press.

House, R., & Baetz, M. (1979). Leadership: Some empirical generalizations and new research directions. In B. Staw & L. Cummings (Eds.), *Research in organizational behavior* (pp. 341–423). Greenwich, CT: JAI.

House, R., & Baetz, M. (1990). Leadership: Some empirical generalizations and new research directions. In L. Cummings & B. Staw (Eds.), *Leadership, participation, and group behavior*. Greenwich, CT: JAI.

House, R., & Dessler, G. (1974). The path-goal theory of leadership: Some post hoc and a priori tests. In J. Hunt & L. Larson (Eds.), *Contingency approaches to leadership*. Carbondale, IL: Southern Illinois University Press.

House, R., & Howell, J. (1992). Personality and charismatic leadership. *Leadership Quarterly, 3,* 81–108.

Howell, S. (1990). *Reflections of ourselves*. New York: Peter Lang.

Howell, J., & Avolio, B. (1992). The ethics of charismatic leadership: Submission or liberation? *Academy of Management Executive, 6,* 2, 43–54.

Howell, J., & Frost, P. (1989). A laboratory study of charismatic leadership. *Organizational Behavior and Human Decision Processes, 43,* 243–269.

Huat, T. (1990). Management concepts and Chinese culture. *Advances in Chinese International Studies, 1,* 277–288.

Huey, J. (1994a, February 21). The new post-heroic leadership. *Fortune,* 42–50.

Huey, J. (1994b, February 21). The leadership industry. *Fortune,* 54–56.

Hutch, R.(1991). *Religious leadership.* New York: Peter Lang.

Hyde, J., & Linn, M. (Eds.), (1986). *The psychology of gender: Advances through meta-analysis.* Baltimore: John Hopkins University Press.

Ibarra, H. (1993). Personal neworks of women and minorities in management: A conceptional framework. *Academy of Management Review, 18,* 56–87.

Immegart, G. (1992). Leadership and leader behavior. In N. Boyan (Ed.), *Educational administration.* New York: Congman.

Institute for Women's Policy Research (1993). *Trends in women's labor force participation: Fact sheet.* Washington, DC: Institute for Women's Policy Research.

Irwin, I. (1921). *The story of the Woman's Party.* New York: Harcourt, Brace.

Irwin, I. (1964). *Up hill with banners flying.* Penobscot, ME: Travesty.

Jago, A., & Vroom, V. (1982). Sex differnces in the incidence and evaluation of participative leader behavior. *Journal of Applied Psychology, 67,* 776–783.

James, W. (1880). Great men, great thoughts, and their environment. *Atlantic Monthly, 46,* 441–459.

James, W. (1985). *Varieties of Religious Experience.* Cambridge, MA: Harvard University Press. (Original work published 1902.)

Janda, K. (1960). Toward the explication of the concept of leadership in terms of the concept of power. *Human Relations, 13,* 345–363.

Janis, I. (1980). The influence of TV on personal decision-making. In S. Whitney & R. Abeles (Eds.), *Television and human behavior: Beyond violence and children* (pp. 161–190). Hillsdale, NJ: Lawrence Erlbaum.

Jansen, S., & Sabo, D. (1994). The sport/war metaphor: Hegemonic masculinity, the Persian Gulf War, and the New World Order. *Sociology of Sport Journal, 11,* 1–17.

Jaques, E., & Clement, S. (1991). *Executive leadership.* Cambridge, MA: Basil Blackwell.

Jarratt, E. (1990). Feminist issues in sport. *Women's Studies International Forum, 13,* 491–499.

Jelinek, M., & Adler, N. (1988). Women: World-class managers for global competition. *Academy of Management Executive, 2,* 11–19.

Jennings, E. (1960). *The anatomy of leadership.* New York: Harper & Row.

Jones, B. (1989). *Leadership and politics.* Lawrence, KS: University of Kansas Press.

Jurma, W., & Wright, B. (1990). Follower reactions to male and female leaders who maintain or lose reward power. *Small Group Research, 21,* 97–112.

Kahn, A., & Jean, P. (1983). Integration and elimination or separation and redefinition: The future of the psychology of women. *Signs: Journal of Women in Culture and Society, 8,* 659–670.

Kandiyoti, D. (1977). Sex roles and social change: A comparative appraisal of Turkey's women. *Signs: Journal of Women in Culture and Society,* *3,* 57–73.

Kane, M. (1987). The "new" female athlete: Socially sanctioned image or modern role for women. *Medicine and Sport Science, 24,* 101–111.

Kane, M., & Parks, J. (1992). The social construction of gender difference and hierarchy in sport journalism - Few new twists on very old themes. *Women in Sport and Physical Activity Journal, 1,* 1, 49–83.

Kane, M., & Snyder, E. (1989). Sport typing: The social "containment" of women in sport. *Arena Review, 13,* 77–96.

Kanter, R. M. (1977). *Men and women of the corporation.* New York: Basic Books.

Kanter, R. M. (1989). *When giants learn to dance.* New York: Simon & Schuster.

Kanter, R. M. (1994). Change in the global economy: An interview with Rosabeth Moss Kanter. *European Management Journal, 12,* 1–9.

Katz, D. (1960). Leadership practices in relation to productivity. In D. Cartwright & A. Zander (Eds.), *Group dynamics* (pp. 612–628). Evanston, IL: Row Peterson.

Katz, D. (1973). Patterns of leadership. In J. Knutson (Ed.), *Handbook of political psychology* (pp. 203–223). San Francisco: Jossey-Bass.

Katz, D., & Kahn, R. (1978). *The social psychology of organizations.* New York: Wiley.

Katz, R. (1955). Skills of an effective administrator. *Harvard Business Review, 33,* 33–42.

Kaye, E. (1993, October). The face of power. *Working Woman,* 50–53.

Keele, R., & DelaMare-Schaeffer, M. (1984). So what do you do now that you don't have a mentor? *Journal of NAWDAC, 47,* 36–40.

Keith, S. (1987). A strategy for the female math student in battle. In H. Nelson and M. Rengel (Eds.), *Gender and curriculum: Theory and practice* (pp. 87–95). St. Joseph/Collegeville, MN: College of St. Benedict/St. John's University.

Keller, A. (1989, March 20). The mommy track: Juggling kids and careers in corporate America takes a controversial turn. *Newsweek,* 126–131.

Kellerman, B. (1986). *Political leadership: A source book.* Pittsburgh, PA: University of Pittsburgh Press.

Kelly, J. (1984). *Women, history, and theory.* Chicago: Chicago University Press.

Kelly, R. (1983). Sex and becoming eminent as a political organizational leader. *Sex Roles, 9,* 1073–1090.

Kennan, N., & Hadley, M. (1986). The creation of political leaders in the context of American politics in the 1970s and 1980s. In C. Grauman & S. Moscovici (Eds.), *Changing conceptions of leadership* (pp. 145–169). New York: Springer Verlag.

Kenny, D., & Zacarro, S. (1983). An estimate of variance due to traits in leadership. *Journal of Applied Psychology, 68,* 678–685.

Keto, C. (1989). *The Africa centered history perspective.* Blackwood, NJ: KA Publications.

Kets de Vries, M. (1994). The leadership mystique. *Academy of Management Executive, 8,* 73–92.

Kim, J. (1993, August). Women at work: The crying game. *Working Woman, 9.*

Kirkpatrick, J. (1974). *The political women.* New York: Basic Books.

Kirkpatrick, S., & Locke, E. (1991). Do traits really matter? *Academy of Management Executive, 5,* 48–60.

Klein, E. (1984). *Gender politics: From consciousness to mass politics.* Cambridge, MA: Harvard University Press.

Klenke, K. (1991). New human resources infrastructures: Computer-mediated performance appraisals. *Proceedings of the 1991 Association of Computer Machinery/SIGCPR Conference,* 80–93.

Klenke, K. (1993). Leadership education at the great divide: Crossing into the 21st century. *Journal of Leadership Studies, 1,* 111–128.

Klenke, K. (1993/4). Meta-analytic studies of leadership: Added insights or added paradoxes. *Current Psychology, 12,* 326–343.

Klenke, K. (1994). Information technologies as drivers of new organizational forms. In R. Baskerville, S. Smithson, O. Ngwenyama, & J. DeGross (Eds.), *Transforming organizations with technology* (pp. 323–342). Amsterstam: North-Holland.

Knepper gets no backup: Houston teammate says "male ego" was talking (1988, March 16). *Austin American Statesman,* p. C2.

Knoppers, A. (1989). Coaching: An equal opportunity occupation? *Journal of Physical Education, Recreation and Dance, 60,* 38–43.

Kolb, D. (1983). *Experiential learning: Experience as the source of learning and development.* Englewood Cliffs, NJ: Prentice-Hall.

Kolbe, R. (1991). Gender roles in children's television advertising: A longitudinal content analysis. *Current Issues and Research in Advertising, 13,* 197–206.

Kohlberg, L. (1981). *The philosophy of moral development: Essays in moral development* (Vol. 1). New York: Harper & Row.

Korabik, K. (1994). Managerial women in the People's Republic of China: The long march continues. In N. Adler & D. Izraeli (Eds.), *Competitive frontiers* (pp. 114–126). Cambridge, MA: Blackwell.

Korn, L. (1989, May 22). How the next CEO will be different. *Fortune,* 157.

Kotter, J. (1987). *The leadership factor.* New York: The Free Press.

Kotter, J. (1990a). *A force for change.* New York: The Free Press.

Kotter, J. (1990b, May/June). What leaders really do. *Harvard Business Review,* 103–111.

Kotter, J. (1992). *Learning to lead.* San Francisco: Jossey-Bass.

Kouzes, J., & Posner, B. (1987). *The leadership challenge*. San Francisco: Jossey-Bass.

Kram, K. (1985). *Mentoring at work*. Glenview, IL: Scott, Foresman.

Kriger, M. (1990, August). *Towards a theory of organizational vision*. Paper presented at the Annual Meeting of the Academy of Management, San Francisco.

Kroeger, B. (1994, July). The road less rewarded. *Working Woman*, 50–56.

Kruse, L., & Wintermantel, M. (1986). Leadership MS. Qualified I.: The gender bias in everyday thinking. In C. Graumann & S. Moscovisci (Eds.), *Changing conceptions of leadership*. New York: Springer.

Kuhn, A., & Beam, R. (1982). *The logic of organizations*. San Francisco: Jossey-Bass.

Kuhn, T. (1970). *The structure of scientific revolutions*. Chicago: University of Chicago Press.

Kuhnert, K., & Lewis, P. Transactional and transformational leadership: A constructive/developmental analysis. *Academy of Management Review, 12*, 648–657.

Kunesh, M., Hasbrook, C., & Lewwaithe, R. (1992). Physical activity socialization: Peer interactions and affective responses among a sample of sixth grade girls. *Sociology of Sport Journal, 9*, 385–396.

Kunin, M. (1994). *Living a political life*. New York: Albert Knopf.

Kurtzig, S. (1991). *CEO: Building a $400 million company from the ground up*. New York: W.W. Norton.

Kushell, E., & Newton, R. (1986). Gender, leadership style, and subordinate satisfaction: An experiment. *Sex Roles, 14*, 203–209.

Lackoff, G., & Johnson, M. (1980). *Metaphors we live by*. Chicago: University of Chicago Press.

Lake, C., & DiVall, L. (1993, November 18). Voter cynicism is a boom for women. *USA Today*, p. 15A.

Lansing, R., & Ready, K. (1988). Hiring women managers in Japan: An alternative for foreign employers. *California Management Review, 30*, 3, 112–127.

Lao-tsu (1993). *Tao te Ching*. New York: Ballentine.

Larson, L., Hunt, J., & Osborn, R. (1976). The great "hi-hi" leader behavior myth: A lesson from Occam's Razor. *Academy of Management Review, 19*, 628–641.

Larwood, L., Szwajkowski, E., & Rose, S. (1988). Sex and race discrimination resulting from manager-client relationships: Applying the rational bias theory of managerial discrimination. *Sex Roles, 18*, 9–29.

Laws, J. (1975). The psychology of tokenism: An analysis. *Sex Roles, 1*, 51–67.

Lazarsfeld, P., & Merton, K. (1948). Mass communication, popular taste and organized social action. In L. Bryson (Ed.), *Communication of ideas* (pp. 95–118). New York: Harper.

Lee, C. (1989, July 20). Can leadership be taught? *Training*, pp. 19–26.

Lee, J., & Wah, S. (1994). Chinese values and organizational practices: A study in Singapore. *International Journal of Management, 11*, 946–953.

Leeper, M. (1991). The impact of prejudice on female candidates: An experimental look at voter inference. *American Politics Quarterly, 19*, 248–262.

Lefkowitz-Horowitz, H. (1986, April). *Before Title IX.* Paper presented at Stanford Humanities Center Sport and Culture Meeting.

Leland, C. (1994, July 7-10). *Leadership and gender.* Plenary session presented at the Annual Leadership Education Conference, University of Richmond, Richmond, VA.

Leong, F., Snodgrass, C., & Gardner, W. (1992). Management education: Creating a gender positive environment. In U. Sekara & F. Leong (Eds.), *Womanpower* (pp. 192–220). Newbury Park, CA: Sage.

Lerner, G. (1986). *The creation of patriarchy.* New York: Oxford University Press.

Levinson, D. (1978). *Seasons of a man's life.* New York: Ballentine.

Levinson, D. (1986). A conception of adult development. *American Psychologist, 41*, 3–13.

Lewin, K. (1951). *Field theory in social science.* New York: Harper & Row.

Lewis, J. (1992). Women's history, gender history, and feminist politics. In C. Kamarae & D. Spender (Eds.), *The knowledge explosion: Generations of feminist scholarship* (pp. 154–160). New York: Teacher's College.

Lewis, L. (1990). *Gender politics and MTV: Voicing the difference.* Philadelphia: Temple University Press.

Lewis, R. (1975). *Margaret Thatcher: A personal and political biography.* London: Routledge & Kegan Paul.

Likert, R. (1961). *New patterns of management.* New York: McGraw-Hill.

Likert, R. (1967). *Human organization.* New York: McGraw-Hill.

Lockett, M. (1988). Culture and problems in Chinese management. *Organization Studies, 9*, 475–496.

Loden, M. (1985). *Feminine leadership: Or how to succeed in business without being one of the boys.* New York: Times.

Lord, R., & Maher, K. (1991). *Leadership and information processing.* Boston: Unwin Hyman.

Lox, J. (1995, August 25). China's women make small strides. *USA Today*, p. 2A.

Lubiano, W. (1992). Black ladies, welfare queeens, and state minstrels: Ideological war by narrative means. In Morrison, T. (Ed.), *Race-ing justice, engendering power.* New York: Pantheon.

Lumpkin, A. (1982). The contributions of women to the history of competitive tennis in the twentieth century. In Reed, H. (Ed.), *Her story in sport: A historical analogy of women in sport* (pp. 509–526). West Point, NY: Leisure Press.

Lumpkin, A., & Williams, L. (1991). An Analysis of *Sports Illustrated* feature articles, 1954–1987. *Sociology of Sport Journal, 8,* 16–32.

Lunardini, C. (1986). *From equal suffrage to equal rights.* New York: New York University Press.

Maccoby, E., & Jacklin, C. (1974). *The psychology of sex differences.* Palo Alto, CA: Stanford University Press.

MacKinnon, C. (1987). *Feminism unmodified: Discourses on life and law.* Cambridge, MA: Harvard University Press.

Macklin, M., & Kolbe, R. (1984). Sex role stereotyping in children's advertising: Current and past trends. *Sex Roles, 13,* 34–42.

Main, J. (1987, September 28). Wanted: Leaders who can make a difference. *Fortune,* 92–102.

Main, M. (1980). *Evita: The woman with the whip.* New York: Dodd, Mead.

Mann, F. (1965). Toward an understanding of the leadership role in formal organization. In R. Dubin (Ed.), *Leadership and productivity.* San Francisco: Chandler.

Mann, R. (1959). A review of the relationship between personality and performance in small groups. *Psychological Bulletin, 56,* 241–270.

Manstead, A., & McCulloch, D. (1981). Sex role stereotyping in British television advertisements. *British Journal of Social Psychology, 46,* 171–192.

Mant, A. (1983). *Leaders we deserve.* Oxford: Martin Robertson.

Manuel, F. (1968). Newton as the autocrat of science. *Daedalus, 97,* 969–1001.

Manz, C. (1983). *The art of self-leadership.* Englewood Cliffs, NJ: Prentice-Hall.

Manz, C. (1991). *Mastering self-leadership.* Englewood Cliffs, NJ: Prentice-Hall.

Manz, C., & Neck, C. (1991). Inner leadership: Creating productive thought patterns. *Academy of Management Executive, 5,* 87–95.

Marlow, J. (1979). *The great women.* New York: A & W Publishers, Inc.

Martin, P. (1990). Rethinking feminist organization. *Gender and Society, 4,* 182–206.

Maslow, A. (1954). *Motivation and personality.* Nework: Harper & Row.

Masuda, R. (1990, September). Nice try, but . . . *Look Japan,* 4–7.

Matthews, C. (1992, September 31). Crashing the men's senate club. *San Francisco Examiner,* p. A13.

McCall, M., & Lombardo, M. (Eds.) (1978). *Leadership: Where else can we go?* Durham, NC: Duke University Press.

McCall, M., Lombardo, M., & Morrison, A. (1988). *The lessons of experience.* Lexington, MA: Lexington Press.

McCormick, J. (1995, January). Changing gears. *Working Woman,* 45–47, 74–76.

McDermott, P. (1995). On cultural authority: Women's studies, feminist politics, and the popular press. *Signs: Journal of Women in Culture and Society, 20,* 668–683.

McElroy, J., & Stark, E. (1992). A thematic approach to leadership training. *Journal of Management Issues, 4,* 241–253.

McGhee, P., & Frueh, T. (1980). Television viewing and the learning of sex role stereotypes. *Sex Roles, 6,* 179–188.

McMurran, K. (1985, July 29). Mary Kay Ash. *People Weekly,* pp. 57–60.

Media Report to Women (1992, Spring). *Scoring the news media: Underrepresentation of women continues.* 2–3.

Media Report to Women (1993, Fall). *U.S. first ladies and the media: Why is it always open season?* 13.

Media Report to Women (1994a, Winter). *Where are the women in radio? Inside Media finds dearth of women on air, behind scenes.* 4–5.

Media Report to Women (1994b, Spring). *The faces of the news.* p. 6.

Meindl, J. (1990). On leadership: An alternative to conventional wisdom. In B. Staw & L. Cummings (Eds.), *Research in organizational behavior* (pp. 159–203). Greenwich, CT: JAI.

Meindl, J., Ehrlich, S., & Dukerich, J. (1988). The romance of leadership. *Administrative Science Quarterly, 30,* 78–102.

Mellaart, J. (1965). *Earliest civilizations of the Near East.* New York: McGraw-Hill.

Mendenhall, M., & Oddou, G. (1986). Acculturation profiles of expatriate managers: Implications for cross-cultural training programs. *Columbia Journal of World Business, 21,* 73–79.

Messner, M. (1988). Sports and male domination: The female athlete as contested ideological terrain. *Sociology of Sport Journal, 5,* 197–211.

Messner, M., & Sabo, D. (Eds.) (1990). *Sport, men, and the gender.* Champaign, IL: Human Kinetics Books.

Metheney, E. (1965). *Connotations of movement in sport and dance.* Dubuque, IA: W. C. Brown.

Miller, C., & Cummings, G. (1992). An examination of women's perspectives on power. *Psychology of Women Quarterly, 16,* 415–428.

Miller, L. (1995, April 13). Women trail men in med school tenure. *USA Today,* p. 8D.

Miller, S. (1975). The content of news photos: Women's and men's roles. *Journalism Quarterly, 52,* 70–75.

Millet, K. (1970). *Sexual politics.* New York: Avon Books.

Milmine, G. (1971). *The life of Mary Baker G. Eddy and the history of Christian Science.* Grand Rapids, MI: Mary Baker House.

Mintzberg, H. (1973). *The nature of managerial work.* New York: Harper & Row.

Mintzberg, H. (1980). *The nature of managerial work.* Englewood Cliffs, NJ: Prentice-Hall.

Molony, B. (1995). Japan's 1986 equal opportunity law and the changing discourse on gender. *Signs, 20,* 8–30.

Moran, Stahl, & Boyer, Inc. (1988). *Status of American female expatriate employ-ees: Survey results.* Boulder, CO: Moan, Stahl & Boyer, Inc., International Division.

Morgan, G. (1980). Paradigms, metaphors, and puzzle solving in organization theory. *Administrative Science Quarterly, 25,* 605–622.

Morgan, G. (1986). *Images of organization.* Beverly Hills, CA: Sage.

Morgan, M. (1982). Television and adolescents' sex role stereotypes: A longitudi-nal study. *Journal of Personality and Social Psychology, 43,* 947–955.

Morgan, M. (1987). TV sex role attitudes and sex role behavior. *Journal of Early Adolescence, 7,* 269–282.

Morris, C. (1992). *Storming the statehouse: Running for governor with Ann Richards and Dianne Feinstein.* New York: Charles Scribner's Sons.

Morrison, A. (1992). *The new leaders: Guidelines on leadership diversity in America.* San Francisco: Jossey-Bass.

Morrison, A., White, R., Van Velsor, E., & The Center of Creative Leadership (1987). *Breaking the glass ceiling: Can women reach the top of America?* Reading, MA: Addison-Wesley.

Moscovici, S. (1986). Epilogue. In C. Graumann & S. Moscovici (Eds.), *Changing conceptions of leadership.* New York: Springer Verlag.

Mun, K. (1986). Characteristics of the Chinese management: An exploratory study. In R. Clegg, D. Dunphy, & G. Redding (Eds.), *The enterprise and management in East Asia.* Hong Kong: University of Hong Kong, Centre of Asian Studies.

Murray, M. (1994, May). How fair are work-family program? *Working Woman,* p. 13.

Murray, M. (1991). *Beyond the myths and magic of mentoring.* San Francisco: Jossey-Bass.

Murray, M. (1908). Priesthoods of women in Egypt. *International Congress of History and Religions, 1,* 2–224.

Naisbitt, J., & Aburdene, P. (1990). *Megatrends 2000.* New York: William Morrow.

Naison, M. (1972, July/August). Sports and the American empire. *Radical America, 55,* 107–110.

Nanus, B. (1992). *Visionary leadership.* San Francisco: Jossey-Bass.

Navarro, M. (1977). The case of Evita Perón. *Signs: Journal of Women in Culture and Society, 3,* 229–240.

Nehamas, A. (1987, October 5). Truth and consequences: How to understand Jacques Derrida. *The New Republic,* 31–36.

Nelson, M. (1991). *Are we winning yet? How women are changing sports and sports are changing women.* New York: Random House.

Nelton, S. (1991, May). Men, women and leadership. *Fortune,* 16–22.

Leading feminist puts hairdo before strike. (1970, August 27). *New York Times*, p. 30.

Nies, J. (1977). *Seven women: Portraits from the radical tradition.* New York: The Viking Press.

Nieva, V., & Gutek, B. (1981). *Women and work.* New York: Praeger.

Noe, R. (1988). An investigaion of the determinants of successful assigned mentoring relationships. *Personnel Psychology, 41,* 457–479.

Noumair, D., Fenichel, A., & Fleming, J. (1992). Clarence Thomas, Anita Hill, and us: A group relations perspective. *Journal of Applied Behaviorial Science, 28,* 377–387.

O'Brain, P. (1994, June). Reality bites. *Working Woman,* 40–43.

Oglesby, C., & Shelton, C. (1992). Exercise and sport studies. In C. Kamarae & D. Spender (Eds.), *The knowledge explosion: Generations of feminine scholarship* (pp. 181–190). New York: Teachers College Press.

Ohlott, P., Ruderman, M., & McCauley, C. (1994). Gender differences in managers' developmental job experiences. *Academy of Management Journal, 37,* 46–67.

O'Leary, V., & Hansen, D. (1982). Trying hurts women, helps men: The meaning of effort. In H. J. Bernadin (Ed.), *Women in the work force* (pp. 100–123). New York: Praeger.

O'Leary, V., & Ickovics, J. (1992). Cracking the glass ceiling: Overcoming isolation and alienation. In U. Sekaran & F. Leong (Eds.), *Womanpower* (pp. 7–30). Newbury Park, CA: Sage.

Osborn, R., & Vicars, W. (1976). Sex stereotypes: An artifact of leader behavior and subordinate satisfaction. *Academy of Management Journal, 19,* 439–449.

Ozbudum, E. (1993). State elites and democratic political cultures in Turkey (pp. 247–268). In L. Diamond (Ed.), *Political culture and democracy in developing countries.* Boulder, CO: Lynne Rienner.

Pagels, E. (1979). *The gnostic gospels.* New York: Random House.

Paglia, C. (1990). *Sexual persona.* New Haven, CT: Yale University.

Paisley, W. (1981). Public communication campaigns: The American experience. In R. Rice & W. Paisley (Eds.), *Public communication campaigns* (pp. 15–40). Beverly Hills, CA: Sage.

Parker, V., & Kram, K. (1993, March/April). Women mentoring women: Creating conditions for corrections. *Business Horizons, 36,* 42–51.

Patterson, R. (1975). Women in management: An experimental study of the effects of sex and marital status on job performance ratings, promotability ratings, and promotion decisions. *Dissertation Abstracts International, 36,* 3108–3109 B.

Pavett, C., & Lau, L. (1983). Managerial work: The influence of hierarchical level and functional specialty. *Academy of Management Journal, 26,* 170–177.

Peel, R. (1966). *Mary Baker Eddy: The years of discovery.* Boston, MA: The Christian Science Publishing Society.

Peel, R. (1971). *Mary Baker Eddy: The years of trial.* New York: Holt, Rinehart & Winston.

Peters, T. (1990, September). The best managers will listen, motivate, support: Isn't that just like a woman? *Working Woman,* 216–217.

Peters, T., & Austin, N. (1986). *A passion for excellence.* New York: Random House.

Petry, A. (1955). *Harriet Tubman: Conductor on the underground railroad.* New York: Crowell.

Pettigrew, A. (1985). Contextualist research: A natural way to link theory and practice. In E. Lawler, A. Mohrman, S. Mohrman, G. Ledford, T. Cummings, & Associates (Eds.), *Doing research that is useful for theory and practice* (pp. 222–228). San Francisco: Jossey-Bass.

Petty, M., & Bruning, N. (1980). A comparison of the relationships between subordinates' perceptions of supervisory behavior and measures of subordinates' job satisfaction for male and female leaders. *Academy of Management Journal, 23,* 717–725.

Petty, M., & Lee, G. (1975). Moderating effects of sex of supervisor and subordinate on relationships between supervisory behavior and subordinate satisfaction. *Journal of Personality and Social Psychology, 60,* 624–628.

Pevsner, L. (1984). *Turkey's political crisis.* New York: Praeger.

Pfeffer, J., & Salancik, G. (1978). Determinants of supervisory behavior: A role set analysis. *Human Relations, 28,* 139–153.

Phillips, L., & Edmonds, P. (1992). Getting a voice heard, a daily balancing act. *USA Today,* p. 12A.

Polster, M. (1992). *Eve's daughters: The forbidden heroism of women.* San Francisco: Jossey-Bass.

Pomeroy, S. (1975). *Goddesses, whores, wives, and slaves.* New York: Schocken Books.

Pondy, L., Frost, P., Morgan, G., & Dandridge, T. (Eds.) (1983). *Organizational symbolism.* Greenwich, CT: JAI.

Popper, K. (1989). The critical approach versus the mystique of leadership. *Human Systems Management, 8,* 259–265.

Porter, L., & Lawler, E. (1968). *Managerial attitudes and performance.* Homewood, IL: Irwin.

Postema, P., & Wojciechowski, G. (1992). *You've got to have balls to make it in this league: My life as an umpire.* New York: Simon & Schuster.

Povich, L. (1994, November). Culture shock. *Working Woman,* p. 6.

Powell, G. (1988). *Women and men in management* (1st ed.). Beverly Hills, CA: Sage.

Powell, G. (1993). *Women and men in management* (2nd ed.). Newbury Park, CA: Sage.

Powell, G., & Butterfield, A. (1984). If good managers are masculine, what are bad managers? *Sex Roles, 7/8,* 477–484.

Powell, G., & Butterfield, A. (1994). Investigating the "glass ceiling" phenomenon: An empirical study of actual promotions to management. *Academy of Management Journal, 37,* 1, 68–86.

Quigley, J. (1994). Vision: How leaders develop it, share it, and sustain it. *Business Horizons, 37,* 37–41.

Ragins, B. (1991). Gender effects in subordinate evaluations of leaders: Real or artifact? *Journal of Organizational Behavior, 12,* 259–268.

Ragins, B., & Sundstrom, E. (1989). Gender and power in organizations: An empirical investigation. *Psychological Bulletin, 105,* 51–88.

Rak, D., & McMullen, L. (1987). Sex role stereotyping in television commercials: A verbal response mode and content analysis. *Canada Journal of Behavioral Science, 19,* 25–9.

Redding, S. (1990). Cognition as an aspect of culture and its relation to management processes: An exploratory view of the Chinese case. *Journal of Management Studies, 17,* 127–148.

Reichard, C. (1973). *Managementkonzeption der Öffentlichen Verwaltung.* Berlin: de Gruyter, 1973.

Rest, J. (1979). *Development in moral issues.* Minneapolis, MN: University of Minnesota Press.

Reynolds, B. (1994, June 3). If women are lucky, in 300 years they may be priests. *USA Today,* 13A.

Rhode, D. (1995). Media images, feminist issues. *Signs: Journal of Women in Culture and Society, 20,* 685–709.

Rice, R., Instone, D., & Adams, J. (1984). Leader sex, leader success, and leadership process: Two field studies. *Journal of Applied Psychology, 69,* 12–32.

Rich, A. (1976). *Of woman born.* New York: W.W. Norton.

Riley, S., & Wrench, D. (1985). Mentoring among women lawyers. *Journal of Applied Social Psychology, 15,* 374–386.

Roberts, D. (Ed.) (1992). *Hong Kong 1992: A Review of 1991.* Hong Kong: Government Information Services.

Roberts, T., & Nolen-Hoeksema, S. (1989). Sex differences in reactions to evaluative feedback. *Sex Roles, 21,* 725–747.

Roberts, W. (1987). *Leadership secrets of Attila the Hun.* New York: Warner Books.

Roche, G. (1979). Much ado about mentors. *Harvard Business Review, 57,* 14–24.

Roddick, A. (1991). *Body and soul.* New York: Crown.

Rosen, D. (1984). Leadership systems in world cultures. In B. Kellerman (Ed.),

Leadership: Multidisciplinary perspectives. Englewood Cliffs, NJ: Prentice-Hall.

Rosener, J. (1990, November/December). Ways women lead. *Harvard Business Review, 68,* 119–125.

Rosenberg, R. (1986). Offer of proof concerning the testimony of Dr. Rosalind Rosenberg [EEOC v. Sears]. *Signs: Journal of Women in Culture and Society, 11,* 757–760.

Rosenkrantz, P., Vogel, S., Bee, H., Broverman, J., & Broverman, D. (1968). Sex role stereotypes and self-concepts in college students. *Journal of Consulting and Clinical Psychology, 32,* 287–295.

Rossman, M. (1990). *The international business woman.* New York: Praeger.

Rost, J. (1991). *Leadership for the 21st century.* New York: Praeger.

Rost, J. (1993). Leadership development in the new millennium. *Journal of Leadership Studies, 1,* 91–110.

Rothschild, J. (1976, September 2-5). *Female power: A Marxist perspective.* Paper presented at the Annual Meeting of the American Political Science Association, Chicago.

Ruether, R., & Keller, R. (1981). *Women and religion in America.* New York: Harper & Row.

Ruether, R., & McLaughlin, E. (Eds.) (1979). *Women of spirit.* New York: Simon & Schuster.

Sabo, D. (1987). *The football coach as officiant in patriarchal society: Conformity and resistance in the social reproduction of masculinity.* Paper presented at the meeting of the North American Society for the Sociology of Sport, Edmonton, Alberta, Canada.

Sabo, D., & Messner, M. (1993). Whose body is this? Women's sports and sexual politics. In G. Cohen (Ed.), *Women in sport* (pp. 15–26). Newbury Park, CA: Sage.

Sabo, D., & Runfola, R. (1980). *Jock: Sports and male identity.* Englewood Cliffs, NJ: Prentice-Hall.

Sanders, M. (1993). Television: The face of network news is male. In P. Creedon (Ed.), *Women in mass communication* (2nd ed.). Newbury Park, CA: Sage Publications.

Sapiro, V. (1983). *The political integration of women: Roles, socialization, and politics.* Urbana: University of Illinois Press.

Sashkin, M., & Rosenbach, W. (1993). A new leadership paradigm. In W. Rosenbach & R. Taylor (Eds.), *Contemporary issues in leadership* (pp. 201–217). Boulder, CO: Westview.

Saxonhouse, A. (1985). *Women in the history of political thought.* New York: Praeger.

Sayles, L. (1993). *The working leader.* New York: The Free Press.

Schein, V. (1973). The relationship between sex role stereotypes and requisite management characteristics. *Journal of Applied Psychology, 57,* 95–100.

Schein, E. (1991). *Organizational culture and leadership.* San Francisco: Jossey-Bass.

Schickel, R. (1991, October 14). Hollywood's new directors. *Time,* 75–78.

Schopenhauer, A. (1994). *Philosophical writings.* New York: Continuum.

Schriesheim, C., & Kerr, S. (1977). LPC: A response to Fiedler. In J. Hunt & L. Larson (Eds.), *Leadership: The cutting edge.* Carbondale, IL: Southern Illinois University Press.

Schriesheim, J., & Schriesheim, C. (1980). A test of path-goal theory of leadership: Some suggested directions for future research. *Personnel Psychology, 33,* 349–370.

Schwartz, F. (1989). Management and the new facts of life. *Harvard Business Review, 67,* 65–76.

Scott, J. (1986). Gender: A useful category of historical analysis. *American Historical Review, 91,* 1053–1075.

Scruggs, O. (1975). The meaning of Harriet Tubman. In C. George (Ed.), *Women in American history.* New York: Syracuse University Press.

Seidman, S. (1992). An investigation of sex role stereotyping in music videos. *Journal of Broadcasting and Electronic Media, 36,* 209–216.

Seltzer, J., & Bass, B. (1987). Leadership is more than initiation and consideration. Paper presented at the annual conference of the American Psychological Association, New York.

Senge, P. (1990a). *The fifth discipline: The art and practice of the learning organization.* New York: Doubleday/Currency.

Senge, P. (1990b). The leader's new work: Building learning organizations. *Sloan Management Review, 32,* 440–463.

Shapiro, R., & Mahajan, M. (1986). Gender differences in policy preferences: A summary of trends from the 1960s to the 1980s. *Public Opinion Quarterly, 50,* 42–61.

Shavlik, D., & Touchton, J. (1988). Women as leaders. In M. Green (Ed.), *Leaders for a new era.* New York: Collier Macmillan.

Shields, S. (1987). Women, men and the dilemma of emotion. In P. Shaver & C. Hendrick (Eds.), *Sex and gender* (pp. 229–250). Newbury Park, CA: Sage.

Sigelman, L., Sigelman, C., & Walkosz, R. (1992). The public and the paradox of leadership: An experimental analysis. *American Journal of Political Science, 36,* 11–31.

Signorielli, N. (1989). Television and conceptions about sex roles: Maintaining conventionality and the status quo. *Sex Roles, 21,* 341–360.

Smith, A. (1980). *The politics of information.* London: MacMillan Press LTD.

Smith, C. (1989). Women's movement media and cultural politics. In P. Creedon

(Ed.), *Women in mass communications: Challenging gender values* (pp. 278–296). Newbury Park, CA: Sage.

Smith, P., & Peterson, M. (1988). *Leadership, organizations, and culture*. Beverly Hills, CA: Sage.

Smith, P., & Smits, S. (1994, February). The feminization of leadership. *Training & Development*, 43–46.

Snow, C., Miles, R., & Coleman, H. (1992). Managing 21st century network organizations. *Organizational Dynamics, 20,* 5–20.

Snyder, N., & Graves, M. (1994). Leadership and vision. *Business Horizons, 37,* 1–7.

Sochen, J. (1974). *Herstory: A woman's view of American history*. New York: Alfred.

Soh, C. (1993). Sexual equality, male superiority, and Korean women in politics: Changing gender relations in a "patriarchal democracy." *Sex Roles, 28,* 73–90.

Spitzberg, I. (1987). Paths of inquiry into leadership. *Liberal Education, 71,* 24–28.

Stangl, J., & Kane, M. (1991). Structural variables that offer explanatory power for the underrepresentation of women coaches since Title IX: The case of homologous reproduction. *Sociology of Sport Journal, 8,* 47–60.

Starratt, R. (1993). *The drama of leadership*. Washington, DC: The Falmer Press.

Statham, A. (1987). The gender model revisited: Differences in management styles in men and women. *Sex Roles, 16,* 409–429.

Staurowsky, E. (1990). Women coaching male athletes. In M. Messner & D. Sabo (Eds.), *Sport, men, and the gender order*. Champaign, IL: Human Kinetics Books.

Steinhoff, P., & Tanaka, K. (1994). Women managers in Japan. In N. Adler & D. Izraeli (Eds.), *Competitive frontiers: Women managers in a global economy* (pp. 79–100). Cambridge, MA: Blackwell.

Stephan, E., Mills, W., Pace, W., & Ralphs, I. (1988). HRD in the Fortune 500: A survey. *Training and Development Journal, 42,* 26–42.

Steson, A. (1913). *Reminiscences, sermons, and correspondence*. New York: Putnam & Sons.

Stevens, D. (1920). *Jailed for freedom*. New York: Boni & Liveright.

Stogdill, R. (1948). Personal factors associated with leadership: A survey of the literature. *Journal of Psychology, 25,* 35–71.

Stogdill, R. (1963). *Manual for the Leader Behavior Description Questionnaire: Form II: An experimental revision*. Columbus, OH: Bureau of Business Research, University of Ohio.

Stogdill, R. (1974). *Handbook of leadership*. New York: Free Press.

Stogdill, R., & Startle L. (1948). Methods for determining patterns of leadership behavior in relation to organization structure and objectives. *Journal of Applied Psychology, 32,* 286–291.

Stone, A., & Lee, J. (1995, March 17). "Glass Ceiling" report adds fuel to debate. *USA Today,* p. 4A.

Stone Blackwell, A. (1917). *The little grandmother of the Russian Revolution.* Boston: Little, Brown.

Stroh, L., & Brett, J. (1993, April 30–May 2). How do female managers who leave the organization differ from male managers. Paper presented at the 8th Annual Conference of the Society of Industrial and Organizational Psychology, San Francisco.

Suu Kyi, A. S. (1991). *Freedom from fear.* New York: Penguin Books.

Swanson, D. (1981). A constructivist approach. In D. Nimmo & K. Sanders (Eds.), *Handbook of political communication* (pp. 169–191). Beverly Hills, CA: Sage.

Swim, J., Borgida, E., Maruyana, G., & Myers, D. (1989). Joan McKay versus John McKay: Do gender stereotypes bias evaluations? *Psychological Bulletin, 105,* 409–429.

Takenaka, E. (1992). The restructuring of the female labor force in Japan in the 1990s. *U.S.–Japan Women's Journal* (English Supplement), *2,* 3–15.

Tan, H. (1989). *Business organization and management: A comparison between Japanese and Chinese firms.* Singapore: National University of Singapore, Department of Japanese Studies.

Tannen, D. (1990). *You just don't understand: Women and men in conversation.* New York: William Morrow.

Tashjian, V. (1990). *Don't blame the baby: Why women leave corporations.* Wilmington, DE: Wick & Co.

Taylor, F. (1911). *The principle of scientific management.* New York: Harper.

Taylor, J. (1979). *Eva Perón: The myth of a woman.* Chicago: University of Chicago Press.

Taylor, S. (1981). A categorization approach to stereotyping. In D. Hamilton (Ed.), *Cognitive processes in stereotyping and intergroup behavior.* Hillsdale, NJ: Erlbaum.

Terborg, J. (1977). Women in management: A research review. *Journal of Applied Psychology, 62,* 647–664.

Theberge, N. (1985b). Toward a feminist alternative to sport as a male preserve. *Quest, 10,* 193–202.

Theberge, N. (1985a). Sport and women's empowerement. *Women's Studies International Forum, 10,* 387–393.

Thomas, H., & Thomas, D. (1942). *Living biographies of famous women.* Garden City, NY: Garden City Publishing Co.

Thomas, D., & Ravlin, E. (1995). Responses of employees to cultural adaptation by a foreign manager. *Journal of Applied Psychology, 80,* 133–146.

Thomas, H., & Thomas, D. (1942). *Living biographies of women.* Garden City, NJ: Garden City Publishing Co.

Thompson, C., Thomas, C., & Maier, M. (1992). Work-family conflict: Reassessing corporate policies and initiatives. In U. Sekaran & F. Leong (Eds.), *Womanpower* (pp. 59–84). Newbury Park, CA: Sage.

Thompson, J., & Thompson, W. (1994). *Margaret Thatcher: Prime minister indomitable.* Boulder, CO: Westview Press.

Tian, J. (1981, July). Women in the early stages of Chinese feudal society. *Women of China*, 35–36.

Tichy, N., & Devana, M. (1986). *The transformational leader.* New York: Wiley.

Tilly, L., & Gurin, P. (Eds.) (1990). *Women, politics, and change.* New York: Russell Sage.

Time. (1970a, June 15). Liberating women. p. 93.

Time. (1970b, August 31). Who's come a long way, baby? p. 16.

Tollgerdt-Anderson, I. (1993). Attitudes, values and demands on leadership: A cultural comparison. *Management Education and Development, 24*, 48–57.

Tosi, H. (1985). When leadership isn't enough. In J. Hunt & J. Blair (Eds.), *Leadership on the future battlefield* (pp. 119–132). Washington, DC: Pergamon- Brassey.

Tosi, H. (1991). The organization as context for leadership theory: A multi-level approach. *Leadership Quarterly, 2*, 205–228.

Trempe, J., Rigny, A., & Haccoun, R. (1985). Subordinate satisfaction with male and female managers: Role of perceived supervisory influence. *Journal of Applied Psychology, 70*, 44–47.

Tu, W. (1984). *Confucian ethics today: The Singapore challenge.* Singapore: Federal Publications.

Tuchman, G., Daniels, A., & Benet, J. (1978). *Hearth and home: Images of women in the mass media.* New York: Oxford Press.

Tucker, R. (1981). *Politics as leadership.* Columbia, MO: University of Missouri Press.

Tucker, R., & Liefeld, W. (1987). *Daughters of the church.* Grand Rapids, MI: Academie Books.

Tung, R. (1984). *Business negotiations with the Japanese.* Lexington, MA: Lexington Books.

Tung, R. (1988). Career issues in international management. *Academy of Management Executive, 2*, 3, 241–244.

Turner, F., & Miguens, J. (1983). *Juan Perón and the reshaping of Argentina.* Pittsburgh, PA: University of Pittsburgh Press.

Uhlig, M. (1990, February 11). Opposing Ortega. *New York Times Magazine, 35*, 62–65, 72.

Unger, R. (1979). Toward a redefinition of sex and gender. *American Psychologist, 34*, 1085–1094.

Unger, R. (1981). Sex as a social reality: Field and laboratory research. *Psychology of Women Quarterly, 5,* 645–653.

Unger, R., & Crawford, M. (1992). *Women and gender: A feminist psychology.* New York: McGraw Hill.

United States Department of Labor (1987). *Workforce 2000.* Washington, DC: U.S. Government Printing Office.

United States Department of Labor (1991). *A report on the glass ceiling initiative.* Washington, DC: Department of Labor.

United States Office of Personnel Management (1989, March 31). *Report on minority groups and sex by pay and appointing authority* (EPMD Report No. 40). Washington, DC: U.S. Office of Personnel Management.

United States Small Business Administration (1993). *Women business owners.* Washington, DC: United States Printing Office.

U. S. News and World Report (1994, June 6). Will Turkey be the next Iran? p. 52.

Vandeberg, L., & Streckfuss, D. (1992). Prime-time television's portrayal of women and the world of work. *Journal of Broadcasting and Electronic Media, 36,* 195–208.

Van Fleet, D., & Saurage, J. (1984). Recent research on women in management. *Akron Business and Economic Review, 15,* 15–24.

Van Nostrand, C. (1993). *Gender responsible readership.* Newbury Park, CA: Sage.

Van Velsor, E., & Hughes, M. (1990). *Gender differences in the development of managers: How women managers learn from experience.* Greensboro, NC: Center for Creative Leadership.

Van Zoonen, L. (1994). *Feminist media studies.* Thousand Oaks, CA: Sage.

Vincent, R., Davis, D., & Bornszkowski, L. (1987). Sexism on MTV: The portrayal of women in rock videos. *Journalism Quarterly, 64,* 750–750.

Vroman, W. (1994). Workplace by design: Mapping the high performance workscape. *Academy of Management Executive, 8,* 83–86.

Waitley, D. (1995). *Empires of the mind.* New York: William Morrow.

Waldman, D., Bass, B., & Einstein, W. (1987). Leadership and outcomes of the performance appraisal process. *Journal of Occupational Psychology, 60,* 177–186.

Walker, L. (1984). Sex differences in the development of moral reasoning: A critical review. *Child Development, 55,* 677–691.

Wallis, C. (1989, December 4). Onward, women. *Time,* p. 80.

Wallston, B., & Grady, K. (1985). Integrating the feminist critique and the crisis in social psychology: Another look at research methods. In R. Unger & B. Wallston (Eds.), *Women, gender, and social psychology* (pp. 7–33). Hillsdale, NJ: Erlbaum.

Walsh, K. (1993, January 26). How Hillary Clinton plans a bold recasting of the job description for a President's spouse. *U.S. News and World Report,* p. 46.

Watson, C. (1988). When a woman is the boss. *Group and Organization Studies, 13*, 163–181.

Weber, M. (1947). *The theory of social and economic organizations* (Trans. R. A. Henderson & T. Parson). New York: The Free Press.

Weber, M. (1956). *Wirtschaft und Gesellschaft (Economy and Society)* (4th ed.). Tübingen: Mohr.

Weber, M. (1965). *The sociology of religion*. London: Methuen.

Weed, F. (1990). The victim-activist role in anti-drunk driving movement. *The Sociological Quarterly, 31*, 459–473.

Weed, F. (1993). The MADD queen: Charisma and the founder of Mothers Against Drunk Driving. *Leadership Quarterly, 4*, 329–346.

Welch, S., & Thomas, S. (1991). Do women in public office make a difference? In D. Dodson (Ed.), *Gender and policymaking: Studies of women in office*. New Brunswick, NJ: Center for the American Woman in Politics.

Wendt, R., & Fairhurst, G. (1994). Looking for the "vision thing": The rethoric of leadership in the 1992 presidential election. *Communication Quarterly, 42*, 2, 180–195.

Wheeler, C. (1994, September/October). How much ink do women get. *Executive Female*, p. 51.

White, R., & Lippitt, R. (1960). *Autocracy and democracy: An experimental inquiry*. New York: Harper.

Whitney, C. (1991, October 15). Burmese opposition leader wins the Nobel Peace Prize. *New York Times*, p. A10.

Whitson, D. (1990). Sport and the social construction of masculinity. In M. Messner & D. Sabo (Eds.), *Sport, men, and gender* (pp. 19–29). Champaign, IL: Human Kinetics Books.

Wildavsky, A. (1984). *The nursing father: Moses as a political leader*. University of Alabama Press.

Wildavsky, A. (1989). A cultural theory of leadership. In B. Jones (Ed.), *Leadership and politics*. Lawrence, KS: University Press of Kansas.

Willner, A. (1984). *The spellbinders: Charismatic political leadership*. New Haven, CT: Yale University Press.

Wills, G. (1994). *Certain trumpets*. New York: Simon & Schuster.

Wilson, F. (1992). Language, technology, gender, and power. *Human Relations, 45*, 883–904.

Wintermantel, M., & Christman, U. (1983). Person description: Some empirical findings concerning the production and reproduction of a specific text type. In G. Rickheit & M. Bock (Eds.), *Psycholinguistic studies in language processing*. Berlin: de Gruyter.

Witt, L., Paget, K., & Mathews, G. (1994) *Running as a woman: Gender and power in American politics*. New York: The Free Press.

Wolf, N. (1990). *The beauty myth*. New York: William Morrow.

Wolf, N. (1993). *Fire with fire.* New York: Random House.

Woods, H. (1995, May). Women may decide the preidency in '96: Here's why. *Working Woman,* 26.

Woolger, J., & Woolger, R. (1989). *The goddess within: A guide to eternal myths that shape women's lives.* New York: Fawcett Columbine.

Woodward, H. (1953). *The bold woman.* New York: Farrar, Straus.

Wunderer, R., & Grunwald, W. (1980). *Fuhrungslehre.* New York: de Gruyter.

Xi, L. (1985, January). Are women intellectually inferior to men? *Women of China,* 37.

Young, H. (1989). *The iron lady: Biography of Margaret Thatcher.* New York: Farrar Straus-Giroux.

Yukl, G. (1981). *Leadership in organizations.* Englewood Cliffs, NJ: Prentice-Hall.

Yukl, G. (1989). Managerial leadership: A review of theory and research. *Journal of Management, 15,* 251–289.

Yukl, G. (1994). *Leadership in organizations.* Englewood Cliffs, NJ: Prentice-Hall.

Zacarro, S., Foti, R., & Kenny, D. (1991). Self-monitoring and trait-based variance in leadership: An investigation of leader flexibility across multiple group situations. *Journal of Applied Psychology, 76,* 308–315.

Zaleznik, A. (1977). Managers and leaders: Are they different? *Harvard Business Review, 55,* 67–80.

Zaleznik, A. (1990). *The managerial mystique: Restoring leadership in business.* New York: Harper & Row.

Zedek, S., & Mosier, K. (1990). Work in the family and employing organization. *American Psychologist, 45,* 240–257.

Zey, M. (1984). *The mentor connection.* Homewood, IL: Irwin.

Zey, M. (1988). A mentor for all reasons. *Personnel Journal, 67,* 46–51.

Index

𝕊 *Springer Publishing Company*

WOMEN AND SUICIDAL BEHAVIOR

Silvia Sara Canetto, PhD, and **David Lester,** PhD, Editors

A comprehensive and definitive work on women and suicide is long overdue, especially because women in most countries are more likely than men to exhibit suicidal behavior. This book fills a major gap in the suicide literature and contrasts with previous works that have tended to address suicidal behavior on women from a male perspective. This volume considers the social and cultural factors involved and also provides useful intervention strategies.

Partial Contents:

I: INTRODUCTION. Women and Suicidal Behavior: Issues and Dilemmas, *S. S. Canetto & D. Lester*

II: EPIDEMIOLOGY. Women and suicidal behavior: Epidemiology, Gender, and Lethality in Historical Perspective, *H. I. Kushner* • The Epidemiology of Women's Suicidal Behavior, *S. S. Canetto & D. Lester*

III: THEORIES. Gender Socialization and Women's Suicidal Behaviors, *A. Kay Clifton & D. E. Lee* • Through a Glass Darkly: Women and Attitudes Toward Suicidal Behavior, *J. M. Stillion* • The Pseudosuicidal Female: A Cautionary Tale, *B. Joyce Stephens*

IV: DIVERSE EXPERIENCES OF SUICIDAL WOMEN. Suicidal Behavior and Employment, *B. Yang & D. Lester* • Suicidal Adolescent Latinas: Culture, Female Development, and Restoring the Mother-Daughter Relationship, *J. K. Zimmerman & L. H. Zayas* • Suicidal Behavior in African-American women, *M. H. Alston & S. Eylar Anderson* • Suicidal Behavior in Asian-American Women, *F. A. Ibrahim* • American Indian Female Adolescent Suicide, *T. LaFromboise & B. Howard-Pitney* • Elderly Women and Suicidal Behavior, *S. S. Canetto*

V: INTERVENTION. Suicidal Women: Intervention and Prevention Strategies, *S. S. Canetto* • Women as Survivors of Suicide: An Experience of Integration, *L. Sapsford*

Springer Series : Focus on Women

1994   296pp   0-8261-8630-0   hardcover

536 Broadway, New York, NY 10012-3955 • (212) 431-4370 • Fax (212) 941-7842

Springer Publishing Company

COUNSELING ADULTS IN TRANSITION, 2nd edition
Linking Practice with Theory

Nancy K. Schlossberg, EdD
Elinor B. Waters, EdD, and
Jane Goodman, PhD

In this updated edition of a highly successful text, the authors expand on their transition model, which offers effective adult counseling through the integration of empirical knowledge and theory with practice. The authors combine an understanding of adult development with practical strategies for counseling clients in personal and professional transition. A framework is provided for individual, group, and work settings. The final chapter goes beyond intervention to discuss issues such as consulting and advocacy.

Contents:

Contributions of Adult Development Theories to the Transition Framework • The Transition Framework • A Framework for Helping: Factors that Influence Negotiating the Transition • What Counselors Hear About Individual Transitions • What Counselors Hear About Relationship Transitions • What Counselors Hear About Work Transitions • What Can Counselors Do to Help Individuals in Transition? • What Can Counselors Do in Groups to Help Adults in Transition? • Group Counseling Practice

1995   320pp   0-8261-4231-1   hardcover

536 Broadway, New York, NY 10012-3955 • (212) 431-4370 • Fax (212) 941-7842

SP *Springer Publishing Company*

SELF-ESTEEM
Research, Theory, and Practice

Chris Mruk, PhD

Low self-esteem is frequently an underlying factor in a range of psychological disorders, including depression, suicide, and certain personality disorders. The recent explosion of research and literature on self-esteem only emphasizes the need for a comprehensive examination of what we know and do not know about

this complicated issue. Dr. Mruk provides a thorough analysis of the vast literature, from which he derives the most practical and effective methods available for the enhancement of self-esteem. His recommendations are based on both qualitative and quantitative findings, and take into account both individual and societal factors.

Contents:

- The Meaning and Structure of Self-Esteem
- Self-Esteem Research Problems and Issues
- Self-Esteem Research Findings — A Consensus
- Major Self-Esteem Theories and Programs
- A Phenomenological Theory of Self-Esteem
- Enhancing Self-Esteem Phenomenologically
- Appendix

Behavioral Science Book Service Selection
1994   240pp   0-8261-8750-1   hard

536 Broadway, New York, NY 10012-3955 • (212) 431-4370 • Fax (212) 941-7842

Springer Publishing Company

SUCCESSFUL GRANT WRITING
Strategies for Health and Human Service Professionals

Laura N. Gitlin, PhD and **Kevin J. Lyons,** PhD

This book guides the reader through the language and basic components of grantmanship. It illustrates how to develop ideas for funding, write the sections of a proposal, organize different types of project structures, and finally, how to understand the review process.

Each chapter describes a specific aspect of grantmanship and suggests innovative strategies to implement the information that is presented. The appendices contain helpful materials, such as a list of key acronyms, examples of timelines and sample budget sheets. The strategies in this volume are beneficial to individuals and departments in academic, clinical, or community-based settings.

> SUCCESSFUL
> GRANT
> WRITING
> *Strategies for Health and Human Service Professionals*
>
> LAURA N. GITLIN, PHD
> KEVIN J. LYONS, PHD
>
> Springer Publishing Company

Partial Contents:
- Becoming Familiar with Funding Sources
- Developing Your Ideas for Funding
- Learning about your Institution
- Common Sections of Proposals
- Preparing a Budget
- Technical Considerations
- Strategies for Effective Writing
- Understanding the Process of Collaboration
- Understanding the Review Process

1996   235pp   hardcover   0-8261-9260-2

536 Broadway, New York, NY 10012-3955 • (212) 431-4370 • Fax (212) 941-7842